THE KENYAN TJRC

Between 1963 and 2008, Kenya experienced systematic atrocities, economic crimes, ethnic violence, and the illegal taking of land. To come to terms with these historical injustices and gross violations of human rights, the Kenyan Truth, Justice and Reconciliation Commission (TJRC) was established. From the perspective of an insider and academic expert, *The Kenyan TJRC: An Outsider's View from the Inside* reveals for the first time the debates and decisions made within the Commission, including how the Kenyan Commission became the first such commission to recommend that its chair be prosecuted for gross violations of human rights. This book is one of the few insider accounts of a truth commission and one of the few that reflects on the limitations and opportunities of such a commission. *The Kenyan TJRC* provides lessons and recommendations to those interested in addressing historical injustices through a truth commission process.

Ronald C. Slye is a professor of law at Seattle University, School of Law. He was one of three international commissioners on the Kenyan TJRC, and in addition to his teaching and writing in the area, he was a consultant to the South African Truth and Reconciliation Commission. He was corecipient of the Trial Lawyers of the Year Award for human rights litigation in the USA in 1995 and is coauthor of *International Criminal Law and Its Enforcement* (2015), one of the leading casebooks on international criminal law in the US market.

The Kenyan TJRC

AN OUTSIDER'S VIEW FROM THE INSIDE

RONALD C. SLYE

Seattle University

With a Foreword by Archbishop Desmond Tutu

CAMBRIDGE
UNIVERSITY PRESS

CAMBRIDGE
UNIVERSITY PRESS

University Printing House, Cambridge CB2 8BS, United Kingdom

One Liberty Plaza, 20th Floor, New York, NY 10006, USA

477 Williamstown Road, Port Melbourne, VIC 3207, Australia

314–321, 3rd Floor, Plot 3, Splendor Forum, Jasola District Centre, New Delhi – 110025, India

79 Anson Road, #06–04/06, Singapore 079906

Cambridge University Press is part of the University of Cambridge.

It furthers the University's mission by disseminating knowledge in the pursuit of education, learning, and research at the highest international levels of excellence.

www.cambridge.org
Information on this title: www.cambridge.org/9781108422031
DOI: 10.1017/9781108380010

First published 2018

Printed in the United States of America by Sheridan Books, Inc.

A catalogue record for this publication is available from the British Library.

Library of Congress Cataloging-in-Publication Data
NAMES: Slye, Ronald, author. | Tutu, Desmond, writer of foreword.
TITLE: The Kenyan TJRC : an outsider's view from the inside / Ronald C. Slye; with a foreword by Archbishop Desmond Tutu.
DESCRIPTION: New York, NY : Cambridge University Press, 2018. | Includes index.
IDENTIFIERS: LCCN 2018001772 | ISBN 9781108422031 (hardback) | ISBN 9781108434508 (pbk.)
SUBJECTS: LCSH: Kenya. Truth, Justice and Reconciliation Commission. | Kenya. Truth, Justice and Reconciliation Act, 2008. | Truth commissions–Kenya–History. | Transitional justice–Kenya. | Human rights–Kenya. | Reconciliation–Political aspects–Kenya. | Kenya–Politics and government–2002-
CLASSIFICATION: LCC KSK2095 .S59 2018 | DDC 323.49096762–dc23
LC record available at https://lccn.loc.gov/2018001772

ISBN 978-1-108-42203-1 Hardback

To JS and CQSS

Contents

Figures

Maps

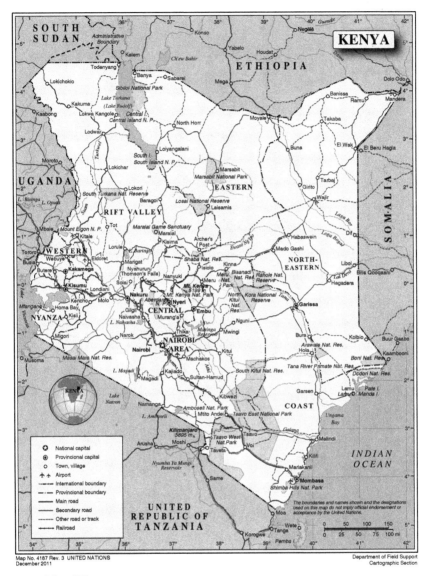

Map No. 4187 Rev. 3 UNITED NATIONS
December 2011

Department of Field Support
Cartographic Section

MAP 1 Map of Kenya
(Map No. 4187 Rev.3, December 2011, United Nations, reproduced with permission)

Foreword

How does one move beyond ... beyond a genocide, crimes against humanity, apartheid? The latter was the question that faced my country with the election of Nelson Mandela in 1994. How were we to move beyond apartheid? How could we create a new South Africa that was different from, better than, but still acknowledge, our tragic past?

To answer that question, we looked to other countries that had undergone similar transitions, particularly Argentina and Chile. In the end, we settled on the creation of the Truth and Reconciliation Commission (TRC), which I was blessed to chair. We realized that in order to create a united South Africa, we would require a measure of forgiveness – forgiveness that would not only enable the healing of a nation, but would, for those who embraced it, begin the healing of individuals who had perpetrated crimes, or who had suffered, under apartheid. National unity and reconciliation are dependent upon some amount of tolerance and forgiveness. That said, they are equally dependent on truth and justice.

☛ Forgive me for being a bit biased in my assessment that the South African TRC accomplished a good deal. New information was revealed, and there were remarkable instances of forgiveness and apology. As with any human endeavor, however, this endeavor also suffered from its limitations and flaws. Some of those were self-imposed, and some were beyond our control. The delay in providing reparations and the failure to prosecute those who did not apply for, or were denied, amnesty were outside of our control. It is unrealistic to expect any one process to shoulder the full weight and responsibility of addressing a long history of injustices. Addressing such divided pasts in a meaningful way is a complex challenge that requires multiple actors and a long-term commitment. One need only look at South Africa today to realize that as a country we have a long way to go to address the demons of our past. Notwithstanding these limitations, and perhaps because of our successes, the

South African TRC is still a model that other societies adopt and adapt to address their own tragic histories. Just as we looked to the efforts of other countries in designing our own truth commission, so too do many other countries today look to the South African commission for inspiration and guidance.

Kenya is one of the more recent examples of an effort to improve upon what we did in South Africa. After the near-genocidal violence that accompanied the 2007 presidential election in Kenya, the Kenyan people embraced a series of initiatives to strengthen national unity and prevent a reprise of the violence. One of those initiatives was the creation of the Kenyan Truth, Justice and Reconciliation Commission (TJRC). The Kenyan Commission turned out to be far more controversial than the South African one. Some have condemned it as a failure; others have praised its successes. In fact, today, prominent politicians in Kenya increasingly call for the full implementation of the recommendations provided in the TJRC's final report. How then can we evaluate the Kenyan Commission?

In this volume, Ron Slye has provided us with a detailed and rich account of the TJRC's accomplishments and failures that can be used to evaluate the Kenyan effort. Ron was introduced to the practical side of truth commissions when he became a consultant to the South African Commission. He went on to spend much of his academic life studying, researching, writing about, and reflecting on how best to address mass atrocities and legacies of injustice, including the proper role of truth commissions. Small wonder that he was then chosen to be one of three international commissioners (and the only non-African) on the Kenyan TJRC. He thus came to the Kenyan Commission with a good deal of knowledge and thoughtfulness about what such a process could and could not accomplish.

The Kenyan Commission was designed to be an improvement on the South African Commission. Most importantly, the Kenyan Commission was required to look at violations of socioeconomic rights (such as the right to access to housing, water, food, education, health care, etc.) in addition to the more traditional types of violence: killings, torture, sexual violence, and disappearances. The South African Commission has in fact been criticized for not including such structural violations as part of the core of its mandate. The Kenyan Commission also implemented innovative practices to solicit testimony concerning the violation of socioeconomic rights and put in place practices and procedures that resulted in the largest participation by women in a truth commission process to date. There were also notable failures in terms of fulfilling all of the terms of its broad mandate, but also concerning the Commission's acquiescence in the president's demand to remove references to his father's land dealings. Finally, the Kenyan Commission was hampered by the fact that its chair was linked to three types of human rights violations the commission was charged with investigating. As Ron so ably recounts, this became a major challenge for the Commission, both internally and externally, as they tried to agree to a process to evaluate those conflicts of interest. It is a sobering story that reminds us that even the best-designed institutions are dependent on the character and integrity of those chosen to serve them.

I am sometimes asked if truth commissions are useful at all. Aren't they just a soft form of justice, or even a vehicle to prevent justice? Absolutely not. If done well, they increase public knowledge about what happened and, in some cases, why it happened and who is responsible. To appreciate the power of the truth, one only needs to read Ron's description of the enormous lengths to which the president of Kenya went in order to remove the reference to his father's land transactions. The paragraphs that were altered merely recounted the testimony of a witness; they were not part of the findings of the Commission. In other words, the Kenyan Commission did not conclude that the president's father had engaged in illegal land dealings. They merely reproduced in their report testimony of a witness to that effect – testimony that was given in public and under oath. Nevertheless, the president and his advisors resorted to threats and bribes to have that testimony removed. It is a sobering reminder of the power of the truth.

More than revealing truth, truth commissions provide a safe space for individuals of all walks of life to tell their stories, to recount their experience of the gross violations of human rights that are the focus of such commissions. The Kenyan Commission received over 40,000 statements from individual Kenyans detailing their experience with a wide range of human rights violations. This is the largest number of individual statements ever collected by a truth commission – it is almost twice as much as we received in South Africa. The fact that so many Kenyans engaged with the Commission – including the more than 1,000 who testified in their public hearings and the hundreds of groups who submitted written memoranda – is a testimony to the need for such a process. Regardless of whether one views the Kenyan Commission as a success or a failure, there is no question that the people of Kenya, like most people throughout the world who have suffered from such violations, desire an opportunity to tell their stories and to learn the truth about the individuals and institutions who are responsible for the violations that they and their loved ones suffered. While the TJRC's final report includes some of those stories, the Kenyan government has refused to produce more than a handful of copies of the report, and has removed it from the internet. I am pleased that Ron's university has made it available online for all of those who want to read it, including the brief, twenty-two-page executive summary and the dissent that he wrote with the other three international commissioners. It is, therefore, fitting that Ron has included an entire chapter recounting some of those stories. It is, in the end, those individuals, and those stories, that are at the heart of why Ron and so many like him do the work that they do.

Archbishop Desmond Tutu

Acknowledgments

I have many people to thank who provided invaluable support during my work in Kenya and supported me in the writing of this book. Seattle University (SU) did not hesitate to provide me with a three-year leave of absence so that I could live and work in Kenya. Three successive deans supported me during this period: Kellye Testy, Mark Niles, and Annette Clark. I also received sage advice from my SU faculty colleagues Maggie Chon and Natasha Martin, and with my frequent coauthor and coworker, Beth van Schaack. Earl Sullivan, Annie Omata, and Alison Pastor provided fantastic research assistance, and the students in my transitional justice seminar in the fall of 2015 provided useful suggestions on an earlier draft of this manuscript. I also received useful feedback from the human rights seminar run by Jim Silk at Yale Law School, and the summer scholarship workshop at Seattle University School of Law. Nora Santos and Junsen Ohno provided enormous support to me before, during, and after I was in Kenya. Barbara Swart, Bob Menanteaux, and Tina Ching provided much needed library and web-related assistance.

While I was in Kenya, Stephen Maroa provided invaluable support to me and my family. Stephen was far more than a driver. He gave me insights into Kenya that I could not receive anywhere else. I developed positive relationships with all of the commissioners at one time or another, though as recounted in this book some of those relationships became strained at times, or even broken. While I benefited and learned a good deal from each of the other commissioners, I will always have the fondest memories of my work with Berhanu Dinka. He and his wife, Almaz, were generous hosts, providing some of the best Ethiopian food I have ever eaten. Berhanu was always a calm and soothing presence. I confided in him; asked, and often followed, his advice; and, through his example and counsel, learned how to adapt my more Western-trained assumptions and instincts to an African context.

Berhanu passed away in June of 2013, shortly after we had finished our work. I had hoped to consult with him in the writing of this book, and I know that it is less complete because of his absence. I felt his presence, and heard his voice, as I wrote and rewrote this manuscript. His influence can be felt throughout the book.

The staff of the TJRC did a tremendous job under often trying circumstances. There were so many dedicated individuals that worked for the Commission, and who worked enormous hours to uncover new information about past injustices; to provide a voice to the many Kenyans who engaged with us; and who made sure, as the saying goes, "that the trains ran on time." Japhet Biegon, our director of research during most of our life, deserves special mention. He brought an unusual level of integrity, sophistication, organization, and calm to his work and the Commission. Without him, not only would our final report be far less than what it is, but it would probably not exist. His dedication to Kenya, human rights, and social justice provides me with optimism about the future of Kenya.

I also learned and received wise counsel from numerous leaders from Kenyan civil society. In particular Binaifer Nowrogee and Muthoni Wanyeki were always available with wise advice and counsel. They are some of the most sophisticated civil society leaders I have come across anywhere, and Kenya is lucky to claim them. My optimism about the future of Kenya, which is sometimes difficult to muster, is sustained by these two and other similar leaders, including George Kegoro, Mugambi Kiai, Maina Kiai, and many others.

As I was learning how to adapt to a highly political environment and how to navigate the numerous challenges we faced, I relied upon two sets of people outside of Kenya. Norman and Constance Rice have become good friends over the years. I benefited enormously from their wise counsel, which is informed by decades of experience in public life. When I was feeling distraught and pessimistic, I knew if I reached out to either of them I would receive a perspective and wisdom that would help me get over the latest hurdle and move on with the important work we were doing. Anu and Zak Yacoob played a similar role. They, too, collectively have decades of experience in public life. During my time in Kenya, I would often escape to South Africa to recharge, and Anu and Zak were always generous with their time and wisdom. Priscilla Hayner and Yasmin Sooka were also useful sounding boards and sources of wisdom. Yasmin is one of the few people to have served on two truth commissions, and I benefited, and continue to benefit, from her wisdom and experience.

The staff of the Panel of Eminent African Personalities provided important support to the three international commissioners as we transitioned to Kenya.

Ambassador Nana Effah-Apenteng always provided wise counsel and was the source of many fascinating stories concerning Kenyan and African politics, often recounted over late night dinners. Gerry Bennet, and then Justin Jepson, provided counsel and support during some of the most challenging parts of our operations. Last, but by no means last, Neha Sanghrajka was an invaluable supporter to both me and the Commission. It was Neha who first identified me as a potential commissioner – so I have her to both thank and blame! Neha worked harder than anyone else I ever came across in Kenya. My optimism for Kenya's future is also based upon Neha's commitment to her country and its future.

I would be remiss if I did not thank the numerous members of the diplomatic community who provided support, and sometimes provided much-needed criticisms and advice. As I cannot mention all of them, I thank them here collectively. While the United Nations played a mixed role with the Commission, two officials in particular played important positive roles in our work. The UN resident coordinator in Nairobi, Aeneas Chuma, often provided wise and calm counsel. Ozonnia Ojielo was a strong anchor in an often rocky sea, whether it was navigating Kenyan civil society, the United Nations, or the Kenyan government. Ozonnia brought a level of sophistication and insight that was invaluable to both me and the Commission.

As I began to write the book and to seek a publisher, Michaela Wrong generously agreed to meet me and provide advice. I have enjoyed and learned much from her numerous books. One of the books I always recommend to my students, and which I read as I made my move to Kenya, is her book about Kenya, *It's Our Turn to Eat*. I tried to write this book so it would be as easy to read, as accessible, and as informative, as Michaela's books. I am grateful for her example and wise counsel.

Dave Danielson, who has been a friend and a fellow traveler in the worlds of accountability and transitional justice, was an invaluable reader and editor of an earlier version of this manuscript. Dave provided the sort of service that I always crave, and that we all need, but so rarely get: brutal, honest, and constructive criticism. Dave warned me that he was a brutally honest reviewer, and he did not let me down. This book is much better as a result of his input, and I am forever grateful for his suggestions and advice.

John Berger at Cambridge University Press has been a joy to work with. Ever patient with my missing deadlines, John identified a number of peer reviewers who provided numerous useful suggestions for the manuscript, some of which I adapted and which have made the book stronger. I want to thank those anonymous reviewers for taking the time not only to read the manuscript, but also to provide useful suggestions and feedback. The team at

Cambridge was also first class, including Emma Collison, Mathavan Ishwarya, and Elizabeth Kelly, who made the production side of publication a breeze.

David Krut generously allowed me to reprint the artwork by Diane Victor that graces the cover. My thanks to both him and Diane Victor for their support.

Archbishop Desmond Tutu has been a guiding presence in my life since we first briefly met in the 1990s when I worked with the South African Truth and Reconciliation Commission. As you will see in the following pages, he played a small but important role during our early efforts to address the conflicts of our chair. He is one of the few moral voices in the world today and continues to have the courage to speak truth to power in all parts of the world. At a time when he had retired and was no longer taking on new projects (he claimed this time to have *really* retired), he generously agreed to write a foreword for this book. I am humbled by his work, both big and small, every day.

Finally, I could not have done any of this without the constant support of Jen. She joined me for two of the three years that I lived in Kenya and provided a haven of sanity, comfort, and love in what was often a turbulent sea of politics, intrigue, and seemingly insurmountable challenges. Without her support, I could not have done the work that I did, or written the book that is before you. She has also now given me Charlie, whose smile and glee make it so much easier to have confidence and optimism about the future of our world.

Timeline

Introduction

In April 2009, I received a call from someone working for the African Union's Panel of Eminent African Personalities informing me that I was on a short list of candidates to serve as one of three international commissioners with the Kenyan Truth, Justice and Reconciliation Commission (TJRC). When I asked how short the list was, he said he could not tell me. A week later, I received a second call from the same person informing me that I was now on a "very short" list and wanting to know if I would take the position if offered it. I asked how short the "very short" list was, and he again replied that he could not tell me. I had been approached for positions earlier in my professional life where a similar question had been posed to me: if offered, would I accept? In my early professional life, I was less thoughtful about such questions and invariably responded yes. In this case, I asked for twenty-four hours to think about the question, which I was given. At the time, I did not know much about Kenya. At this point, I had spent a few days in Nairobi for reasons related to some of my academic work. While I had studied Kenya over the years, and even worked as a law student for PEN International concerning the detention of Professor Maina wa Kinyatti, I did not consider myself particularly knowledgeable about Kenya and its history.

As I was contemplating whether to say yes to the possible offer to join the Kenyan TJRC, I did not know who the other international commissioners would be – or even who they might be. The six Kenyan commissioners that were to join the three international commissioners had not been chosen yet. There were a lot of unknowns. The possibility of being out in the real world again, engaging firsthand with the many issues to which I had devoted my academic life, was in the end too tempting for me to pass up. I asked myself: if the other commissioners proved to be problematic, or if other information came to me that made me question the wisdom of serving on such a commission, would I be willing to resign? After giving it some thought, I concluded that I would be willing to take that risk and resign if necessary. Little did I know at the time how prescient my thought process would be, as less than a year later I would be revisiting the question of whether I should resign. I informed the Panel of Eminent African Personalities that I would accept the position if it were offered to me. Twenty-four hours later, it was offered to me, and I accepted.

In 2009, I was a tenured professor of law at Seattle University. I taught my classes well and had published a number of articles and books in the areas of international human rights law, international criminal law, and transitional justice. While my career had been mostly academic up until that point, I had some practical legal experience in the areas of human rights and transitional justice. My academic career began with a strong link to practice. Upon graduating from law school, I was a clinical law professor at Yale, where I taught, among other things, an interdisciplinary transactional clinical class that focused on homelessness, housing, and economic development. After teaching for two years, I moved to Manhattan to work for a small boutique law firm that specialized in environmental law as well as real estate, housing, and a small amount of international human rights law. My time as a full-time attorney was short-lived. While I learned a good deal during my two years at the law firm, I longed to return to an environment where I had more control over what I did rather than being subordinate to partners or clients. I thus returned to Yale to help run the human rights center based at the law school. For three years, I engaged in a wide variety of activities related to international human rights law, from organizing conferences and speaker series, to teaching courses on human rights and assisting with an international human rights clinic, to working with students on a variety of human rights–related projects. Three years later, I had an opportunity to move to South Africa. This was 1996, two years after the election of Nelson Mandela and the formal end of apartheid. I was a fellow at the Community Law Centre of the University of the Western Cape. While I worked on issues of housing and poverty at the Community Law Centre, I ended up spending most of my year in South Africa working with that country's Truth and Reconciliation Commission. I became a consultant with the Commission's research department, providing assistance on how to interpret the Commission's mandate and researching and drafting small parts of what ended up being the Commission's final report. I attended a number of the public hearings of the Commission and engaged in numerous debates with both commissioners and staff on a wide variety of issues.

In 1997, I was offered a visiting professorship at Seattle University School of Law, which then became a permanent appointment two years later. My previous experience, particularly in South Africa, provided inspiration for much of my subsequent teaching and writing. I continued to return to South Africa while the TRC was still operating and for many years after it finished its work. I was the inaugural holder of the Bram Fisher Visiting Professorship in Human Rights at the University of the Witwatersrand (also known as "Wits") in Johannesburg, South Africa. I became an honorary professor at Wits and established a five-week program that brought together law students from the USA and Africa to study topics ranging from legal writing to international criminal law at that university.

In January 2009, Barack Obama became president of the United States promising to make torture illegal and to close the US-run prison in Guantanamo Bay, Cuba. During those early days of the first Obama administration, many proposals were floated concerning the closing of Guantanamo and making a clean break from the discredited policies of the newly departed administration of George W. Bush. One of the issues being debated was whether US officials who engaged in torture and other cruel, inhuman, or degrading treatment should be prosecuted for their crimes. Senator Patrick Leahy proposed that the US establish what he called a "South African–style" truth and reconciliation commission. He argued that we should take a page from Nelson Mandela and South Africa and embrace reconciliation, and that we thus consider amnesty for those responsible for wrongdoing rather than prosecution in order to encourage confessions about what had been done and why. While I did not oppose such an approach, I was concerned that the understanding of what South Africa did and why it worked (to the extent that it did), was not well understood by Senator Leahy and others, at least as reflected in how they publicly spoke about the choices available. I thus wrote a newspaper article that made two points. First, I pointed out that if we were serious about reconciliation along the South African model, we would facilitate engagement between individuals detained in Guantanamo and other US facilities with those US officials who had tortured and abused them. It was not clear to me that that was what Senator Leahy and others were proposing. Second, amnesty did not mean no prosecution. In South Africa, prosecutions occurred alongside the amnesty process. In fact, providing the carrot of amnesty in return for the confession of perpetrators was only possible if there was a credible threat of prosecution. If the proposal was to provide amnesty and foreclose prosecution, it was difficult to imagine why anyone would come forward to confess. Within twenty-four hours of the publication of this opinion piece, I was contacted by the Nairobi office of the Panel of Eminent African Personalities asking if I would consider applying for a position with the Kenyan TJRC. I provide in these pages my experience over the next four years serving as one of nine commissioners on the Kenyan TJRC.

The purpose of this book is to clarify the history and legacy of the Kenyan TJRC. We as a Commission did a mediocre job of engaging with the public about our purposes and operations. There is a good deal of misinformation, most particularly outside of Kenya, concerning the Commission's history and its work. I meet colleagues at conferences who still believe that I resigned from the Commission (which I did not) and that the Commission either fell apart without completing its work or that it is still ongoing (neither of which is true). Some are under the impression that the Commission focused on the 2007 election–related violence. While the violations committed after the 2007 election were a part of our mandate, the mandate entrusted to us was far broader. Even within Kenya, there is very little understanding of what the truth commission did, in part because of the government's decision to block publication of the report and refusal to engage with, much less follow, our numerous findings and recommendations.

This book then highlights some of our accomplishments. While we were by no means perfect, we did accomplish a good deal – far more than most people are aware. Yet I also acknowledge the mistakes we made and the challenges we faced. While many are aware of the challenges – the conflicts of interest of our chair, the interference by the president in the content of our report – here, too, there is much misinformation. Some of the failures were caused by forces outside of the Commission's control – and some of those forces have not been adequately revealed or discussed. I hope to remedy that state of affairs with this book. Some of the failures were due to our own limitations and failings. The purpose here is not to point fingers – though I do identify important actors and the mistakes they made and take some responsibility myself – but to lay bare who did what and, to the extent I can, why. I do, of course, have my own, sometimes strongly held, opinions about what we should have done. I express those opinions here, but I hope that I do so in a way that acknowledges other views and judgments about what we did.

Chapters 1, 3, and 5 provide the most detail concerning the two major challenges we faced: the conflicts of interest of our chair and the interference by the president in our final report. In those chapters, I endeavor to convey what it was like to experience the development of these issues firsthand. I hope to lay bare the issues around our chair and the various efforts we made to address them in a way that clarifies rather than obfuscates the issues presented. I also reveal the events leading up to the intervention of the president's office to the best of my ability (I was out of the country during some of the events that led to that intervention). Some of the information in both of these sections will be made public here for the first time, and part of my purpose is to enrich the historical record about these events. Beyond documenting what happened, I also believe that both of these challenges provide important lessons to future truth commissions, and to future attempts to increase accountability and the rule of law in Kenya.

Chapter 2 provides the history of how and why the TJRC was created and critically discusses the broad mandate that we were given. Chapter 4 provides a window into some of the most important work we undertook through our public engagement with victims and survivors. The full extent of that engagement and the important contribution many Kenyans made to our work can be found throughout our 2,100-page report.

Chapter 6 discusses the relationship between the ICC and the TJRC. That relationship was mostly one of avoidance by both institutions. In this chapter, I also discuss the efforts by the Kenyan government to oppose the work of the International Criminal Court (ICC). Those efforts are similar to, and in some cases directly related to, the efforts by the government to control, slow down, and stop some of the work of the TJRC. The last chapter provides some concluding remarks and lessons that I have taken from the experience of my work in Kenya during my four years as a commissioner.

I have established a website that provides access to many of the documents on which I relied on writing this book: https://digitalcommons.law.seattleu.edu/tjrc/. Most importantly, a full copy of the final report, including the dissent that I and the other two international commissioners submitted, can be found at the website. This is particularly significant, as the government has removed the official TJRC website, and it is thus extremely difficult to find a copy of our final report. I have also included in the website transcripts of our public hearings, a resource that, as far as I am aware, has not been made available to the public. References to the hearings are in the form of RTJRC [date] [place], and can be found accordingly on the website. While I do refer in the book to some of the testimony we heard in our *in camera* hearings, I do not include those transcripts here, as the testimony provided at such hearings is and must remain confidential. The website also has a list of the html addresses referred to in the book for ease of access.

1

The Endgame

The inclusion of foreigners in processes in Kenya has always been controversial. Adding foreigners to the TJRC and other institutions created in response to the near-genocidal violence after the 2007 election was viewed by some as problematic. Some prominent politicians, however, felt that the inclusion of foreigners would be a minor nuisance. As John Michuki said in Parliament, "Of course [foreigners] will be there. They will be our employees and we will control them!"[1]

During the early afternoon of May 21, 2013, I was sitting in a coffee shop in the Yaya Shopping Centre in Nairobi. Yaya, as it was colloquially known, was one of the many fancy shopping malls that had sprouted up in Nairobi to serve the growing moneyed class of Kenyans and the steady stream of expats who worked at the United Nations or one of the many sizeable embassies that served Western interests in the East African region. By 2013, its appeal to the wealthy in Nairobi had been overtaken by the even more upmarket Westgate Shopping Mall. Exactly four months later, the Westgate Shopping Mall would be the site of a brutal attack that left close to seventy people dead, including young children who were competing in a cooking competition sponsored by a local radio station, and close to two hundred wounded. Al-Shaabab, an al-Qaida affiliated group, claimed responsibility for what it described as retaliation for the actions of the Kenyan military in Somalia. Yaya was owned by Nicholas Biwott,[2] a flamboyant politician and businessman, former right-hand man of President Daniel arap Moi, and who has variously been called the "Total Man" and the "Prince of Darkness." Biwott was rumored to be involved

---

[1] John Michuki, who was then Minister for the Environment, was speaking about the advantages of a Kenyan special tribunal to prosecute those suspected of responsibility for the 2007–2008 post-election violence, which would have foreign participation. Hansard, Kenya National Assembly, February 4, 2009, page 37.

[2] Nicholas Biwott died on July 11, 2017.

6

in numerous corruption scandals, and we would later investigate him for his alleged involvement in a high-profile political assassination that would also indirectly involve our chair.

My work with the Kenyan Truth, Justice and Reconciliation Commission (TJRC) was finished, and I was spending a few hours with various members of Kenyan civil society, the diplomatic community, and local journalists reflecting on the failures, challenges, and accomplishments of the Commission. I was conscious of the fact that I was at the end of a very long, and at times tortuous, process. During that time we had been written off as a complete failure by prominent Kenyan stakeholders; we had sued and been sued by our chairman over his links to human rights violations we were to investigate; one of our most accomplished Kenyan colleagues had resigned in protest; I had threatened to resign; we had been publicly called incompetent and embezzlers by the minister of justice whose ministry at the time controlled all of our finances; and on numerous occasions, civil society, the media, the government, and members of Parliament had called for our disbandment.

Despite these and other challenges, I had persevered in the belief that while we were not perfect, we were able to accomplish, and, in fact, had accomplished, some significant progress in addressing some of the atrocities and injustices that make up Kenya's post-independence history. At the same time, I had to acknowledge that our successes were limited. This was difficult for me, as perhaps it is difficult for all who are intensely immersed in a highly public process onto which critics and supporters projected their own agendas, beliefs, and limitations. Part of me refused to conclude that the previous four years of my life had been for naught. Yet part of me also had to acknowledge that our process had been flawed, even from the beginning. This was in part because of the peculiar circumstances of our own Commission, but also in part because of the limitations of the much-touted tools that we now deploy to address past atrocities and injustices. Some of our failures were peculiar to the Kenyan situation, but some were inevitable given the limitations of the processes that the international community has adopted to deal with these moments of "transitional justice." It was during those early conversations at the Yaya Shopping Centre that I began to engage with the tension I felt between the promise of these mechanisms and their inherent limitations, between our failures and the clear accomplishments we had achieved over a four-year period.

***

Four years earlier, on July 22, 2009, I was formally appointed by the President of Kenya to serve as one of three international Commissioners on the nine-person Kenyan Truth, Justice and Reconciliation Commission (TJRC).

I was the only non-African. During the intervening four years one of the Kenyan commissioners had resigned leaving us with only eight commissioners; our chair had "stepped aside" for fourteen months because of his connection to three human rights violations we were to investigate; we had received over 40,000 statements concerning gross violations of human rights, the largest of any truth commission to date; we had spent a year holding public and private hearings in every corner of the country; we had developed innovative mechanisms for including women in our process and for soliciting information concerning violations of socioeconomic rights; we had unearthed previously undisclosed documents about some of the worst violations in Kenya's history; we had completed a final report of over 2,100 pages that, among other things, recommended that our chair be investigated and, if the evidence warranted, prosecuted for his involvement in the worst massacre in the history of Kenya; and most recently, the president demanded that we remove allegations concerning his father's illegal and irregular land dealings. There was a lot to discuss.

The agreement to create the Kenyan TJRC was part of a package of reforms negotiated by, among others, the former UN Secretary General Kofi Annan after the near-genocidal violence arising from the disputed 2007 presidential election. Those negotiations resulted in the creation of a coalition government incorporating representatives from the two major parties that had vied for the presidency, the Orange Democratic Movement (ODM) and the Party of National Unity (PNU). The incumbent, Mwai Kibaki of the PNU, remained as president, and the leader of the ODM, Raila Odinga, occupied the newly created position of prime minister. The parties agreed to establish a truth commission in order to better understand how a disputed presidential election could bring the country to the brink of genocide. Modeled on the successful truth commission established by Nelson Mandela in South Africa, the Kenyan TJRC was tasked with investigating a wide range of human rights violations from December 12, 1963, (the date Kenya achieved independence from Britain) to February 28, 2008 (the date at which the agreement brokered by Kofi Annan was signed). We were also directed to examine the antecedents to such violations, thus empowering us to examine violations during the pre-independence period under British colonialism. In addition, we were empowered to investigate or make recommendations "concerning any other matter with a view to promoting or achieving justice, national unity, or reconciliation ..."[3] A very broad mandate indeed.

[3]   The Truth, Justice and Reconciliation Act, No. 6 of 2008 (Kenya), as amended [TJRC Act], Art. 5(2).

On July 22, 2009, the nine Commissioners (six Kenyans and three internationals) were appointed by President Kibaki. The other two non-Kenyans were a diplomat from Ethiopia who had worked extensively with the United Nations (Ambassador Berhanu Dinka), and a judge from Zambia who had chaired a significant commission on torture in her country (Judge Gertrude Chawatama). The Kenyan Commissioners were a pretty diverse lot. As I was later to learn, ethnic representation in Kenyan institutions (particularly government institutions) was almost as important (and for some people far more important) than skills and expertise. While there are forty-two ethnicities in Kenya (and even that is open to debate – some argue that the number is much larger), the six Kenyan Commissioners represented most of the major ethnic groups in the country: Kalenjin, Kikuyu, Luo, Luhya, and Somali. They included a career diplomat who had played an important role in peace and conflict resolution both in Kenya and in other parts of Africa (Ambassador Bethuel Kiplagat, who would be our chair); a prominent human rights activist who had been directly involved in human rights work during some of the worst periods in Kenyan history and who, beside me, was the only commissioner to have ever worked for a truth commission (Kaari "Betty" Murungi); a former Naval officer (Ahmed Farah); an expert in conflict resolution who had the most grassroots experience of any of us, having worked with local peace groups in various parts of Kenya (Tecla Namachanja Wanjala); a prominent attorney who had extensive experience working with refugees, both in Kenya and in the region (Margaret Wambui Ngugi Shava); and an attorney and law professor who had been the president of the Law Society of Kenya (Professor Tom Ojienda).

The chief justice, who would later play a controversial role with respect to our Commission, administered the formal oath of office to us on the morning of August 3, 2009. I joined the other commissioners in pledging "faithfully and fully, impartially and to the best of my ability, [to] discharge the trust and perform the functions and exercise the powers devolving upon me by virtue of this appointment without fear, favour, bias, affection, ill-will or prejudice."[4] At the end of our terms as commissioners, I and the other two international commissioners would release a public statement decrying that some of our colleagues had acted contrary to that oath of office.

***

In August 2012, I had returned to Seattle University to resume teaching at the law school. I had returned to Seattle under the impression that we had

---

[4] TJRC Act, *supra* note 3, Second Schedule.

mostly finished our work. Our final report was close to completion; all that
was left was for us to secure an appointment with the president so we could
formally hand over our report to him. I was mistaken. Unbeknownst to me, we
had succumbed to pressure from the Kenyan government to delay the release
of our report until after the March 2013 elections. I later learned that some of
my fellow commissioners had actively lobbied in support of this additional
year to delay the release of our report.

Less than two months before I found myself in the coffee shop at Yaya,
Uhuru Kenyatta and William Ruto had been elected as president and deputy
president. Prior to their election, both had been indicted by the International
Criminal Court (ICC) for their alleged involvement in the post-election
violence that had given rise to the creation of the TJRC. Our report still had
not been released, and thus the information it contained was unknown to
the voters as they went to the polls. Ironically, the report included very little
new information about Kenyatta and Ruto, though it did contain damning
information about a number of their political allies – as well as damning
information about some of their political opponents. I had returned to Kenya
in the beginning of May 2013. During the three weeks I was to spend in Nairobi
that month, we would face one of our biggest challenges as a Commission:
Would we agree to remove references to allegations of land grabbing by Jomo
Kenyatta, the first president of Kenya and father of the current president?
Although the law required us to deliver the report directly to him,[5] President
Kenyatta had refused to meet with us while some of his closest advisors threatened and bribed us to have references to his father's land dealings removed
from our report. This blatant interference in our work divided us along lines
of nationality – the five remaining Kenyan commissioners supporting the
removal, and the three international commissioners opposed. Our legislation forbade us from being "subject to the control or direction of any person
or authority" and required us to act "independently of any political party,
Government, or other organizational interests."[6] These events tested our fide-
lity to the oath we had taken to uphold this independence four years earlier.

The president's interference was not the only serious challenge we faced
as a Commission. We had survived numerous challenges, both internal and
external, many of which had divided us. None of those challenges had resulted

---

[5]   Our legislation, unlike that of all previous Kenyan commissions of inquiry, required not
     only that we hand our report over to the president, but also that we make the report public.
     This requirement was inserted to avoid the unfortunately common practice of such reports
     being handed over to the president only to never be released to the public. To this day,
     numerous such reports have never been made public.
[6]   TJRC Act, *supra* note 3, at Art. 21.

in us being divided by our nationality, by ethnicity, or by other personal characteristic. The last test we faced – the one presented by the intervention of the Office of the President – broke this trend and divided us based upon our nationality. What is surprising is not that we were so divided based upon nationality at the end of our process. It was instead surprising that our previous divisions were not so easily explained by such superficial characteristics. We started off as nine individuals, all immensely qualified and accomplished in our respective fields. We spent four years working with each other and with a staff of close to one hundred other professionals. We fought, argued, reconciled, celebrated, and accomplished an enormous amount during those four years. We finished with only eight of us, and in the last year, we were mostly united until the intervention by the Office of the President. This book provides my best assessment of how we reached this last and biggest challenge. It is a candid appraisal of our successes and our failures. It is a story that involves the misdeeds of some of the most powerful people in Kenya's history, beginning with the founding president, Jomo Kenyatta, and ending with his son, Uhuru Kenyatta. It is a story that touches upon the role of Western and other foreign powers in Kenya, both positive and negative. It is a story that provides a window into the dynamics of Kenyan civil society, highlighting both its courage and strength and also its strategic limitations and political missteps. Finally, it is an insider's account of the most important effort to date by Kenya to grapple with a legacy of historical injustices, including assassinations, massacres, the use of rape by the military and the police to control and oppress local communities, and numerous other gross violations of human rights. It is an insider's story as experienced by an outsider.

This chapter introduces the events that we came to refer to as "the endgame" – the political maneuverings at the end of our operational period that threatened to derail all that we had accomplished in the last four years. It provides a day-by-day insider's account of the political pressure exerted by the president and his administration to protect the reputation of his father, and the efforts by commissioners to either support or oppose this threat to our integrity and political independence.

THE SEED IS PLANTED

On January 23, 2011, Salim Ali Toza testified before us in a public hearing: "In 2005 I was attacked by sixteen policemen in my home. I escaped and went to live outside Kenya for two and a half months. I left my child, who had been hurt, behind. I did not have even a single cent. I later decided to come back home and die."

Toza testified during the Commission's public hearings in Kwale, a small town near the Indian Ocean, just south of Mombasa. The focus of most of Toza's testimony, however, was not how he had been brutally attacked by the Kenyan police. He devoted the vast majority of his testimony to how he and many others had lost their land to powerful government officials.

Toza's story is an all-too-familiar one in Kenya. His family had lived in the region for generations, working and living on the fertile land. He was born into the Digo ethnic group, which is one of nine ethnic groups that make up the Mijikenda tribe. It is believed that the Mijikenda migrated to the Kenyan coastal area approximately three hundred years ago from northern Africa. The Mijikenda consider parts of the region's forests to be sacred. As a result of this belief, some forests in the region have not been touched for hundreds of years, thus providing a rich, and rare, source of biodiversity on the planet.

Ownership and control of land has been a contentious issue in Kenya since the time of British colonial rule. As in many other parts of their empire, the British grabbed the most fertile and lucrative land in Kenya, particularly in the Rift Valley, part of which came to be known as "Happy Valley" after the decadent parties and related scandals among the white colonial elite. (The peculiar lifestyle of the residents of Happy Valley is the subject of a film, *White Mischief*[7], which is based upon the true story of a scandalous love triangle that resulted in murder.)

Kenya achieved independence from Britain in 1963. The newly elected president of the Republic of Kenya, Jomo Kenyatta (the father of the current president, Uhuru Kenyatta) quickly began to acquire much of the valuable land in Kenya for himself, his family, and his close friends and allies. According to Toza's testimony, President Kenyatta unlawfully took 250 acres of prime beach land that had been entrusted to members of the local community during British colonial rule in the 1930s. The owners of the land, including Toza's father, were offered the equivalent of US $84 per acre of land, far below the then-market value. Toza's father refused the payment and, with other dispossessed residents, unsuccessfully fought to keep the land in the hands of the local community. Toza testified that an acre of this land today would sell for around US $180,000. This is a sizeable amount of money for a Kenyan; Kenya's gross domestic product per capita in 2014 was a little over US $1,000.

Toza was not the only person who testified before the Commission concerning land forcefully taken by powerful government officials. His testimony, however, enjoys the dubious distinction of being removed at the direction of

---

7   *White Mischief* (Directed by Michael Radford, 1987).

senior officials in the president's office from our final report. The government of Jomo Kenyatta's son, Uhuru, used its powers to cajole, bribe, and threaten commissioners and senior staff of the TJRC to have this and other references to his father's land grabbing removed from the report, including references to the testimony of Toza. I know, as I was offered a bribe to do just that, and refused.

THE BEGINNING OF THE ENDGAME

When I left Kenya in August 2012, we had been planning to submit our report in the next few months. I returned to my university assuming that our work was mostly finished except for minor edits and polishing of the report, to which I could contribute electronically from the United States. My leaving was also precipitated by a decision made by the United Nations and the African Union to cease their support of the three international commissioners. To ensure the security and confidentiality of drafts of the final report and related communications, I had developed with our director of research, Japhet Biegon, a set of passwords to protect documents sent electronically to me in the United States.

When I returned to Seattle, I continued to reach out to my fellow commissioners to get updates on the status of the final report, including when we would be handing it over to the president and releasing it to the public. From July to October 2012, I received minimal information from my colleagues in Kenya. I sent numerous emails, text messages, and voicemail messages. I made clear that my university had arranged to allow me to return to Kenya for short periods of time if needed and that I would always be available to participate in any Commission meetings by phone. These messages were met with silence.

I was reduced to reading about us in the Kenyan newspapers, which reported in September 2012 that the Commission was lobbying for an additional six- to twelve-month extension in order to keep working on the report. This was of particular concern to me, given that the presidential elections were now scheduled to take place in March 2013. When I had left Kenya, all commissioners agreed that we should issue our report before the elections – in part so that the information provided in the report could be used by the Kenyan people in evaluating various candidates, including their involvement in past violations and their proposals for addressing the recommendations we would make in our report. We also agreed that we should release the report a number of months before the election for two reasons. First, releasing the report shortly before the election would not give people time to digest, and debate, our findings and recommendations. Second, releasing the report shortly before the election increased the risk that the report and its contents would be politicized by the political elite as they and their allies vied for public office. As we were finishing the report in August 2012, the elections were still seven months away, more than enough time for our report to be distributed and debated if it was released as originally planned, in the next two months.

In October, I received a phone call from Commissioner Shava requesting that I return to Nairobi to help the Commission lobby Parliament for an additional extension. Margaret Shava comes from a well-connected family in the Kikuyu elite and is related to the Kenyatta family. While she comes from a privileged and elite background, she had rebelled in her own way, devoting much of her professional life as a lawyer to working on refugee policy and advocacy in the Sudan, the DRC, and other parts of Africa. She had also married outside of her ethnic group, which was a rare occurrence within her community and frowned upon by some of her relatives and the Kikuyu establishment. Despite these acts of rebellion, she continued to mingle among Kenya's elite. An active board member and supporter of the major horse-racing venue in Nairobi, she often invited us on Sundays to enjoy the races from her VIP box, where we were often joined by some of the political and economic elite of Kenya.

I had seen reports in the Kenyan press that we were seeking an additional extension, but I discounted them as mere speculation, as no one had consulted with me concerning such an extension. This was the first time I had been informed by someone within the Commission that we were, in fact, seeking an extension. I asked Commissioner Shava how long of an extension we were requesting from Parliament. She responded that we were requesting an additional year – which would mean handing over our report in May 2013. When I asked why we were requesting such a large extension – did we really need that much more time?; had any work been done on the final report since I had left? – she told me that we were not the ones who wanted us to have an additional year. It was the government, she informed me, who wanted us to have until May 2013 (presumably so that our report would come out after the upcoming elections). Why, I then asked, are *we* lobbying Parliament for something that the government wants but which, I believed at the time, we as a Commission did not want? Her reply: It would be unfair to have the government do all of the lobbying for the extension. Well, of course this did not make much sense. If the extension was something that we did not want, but was something the government wanted, then why not let the government succeed or fail on its own? What I quickly realized was that the Commission

FIGURE 1.1 Gado – We Need More Time
Image courtesy of Gado (gadocartoons.com).

(presumably all or a majority of the other commissioners) also wanted an extension so that our report would be released after the election.

I asked Commissioner Shava whether any work had been done on the final report since I had left in August. She told me that some work had been done in August, but nothing since then because they had been so busy lobbying for an extension. (There were also more understandable reasons for the lack of progress on the report, including the recent and serous illness of the Commissioner who was overseeing the writing of the final report, Ambassador Berhanu Dinka.) My immediate (unspoken) reaction was that if we had spent just one or two more months working on the report itself rather than spending that time lobbying for an extension, we would have been done with the matter, and there would have been no need for us to lobby for additional time. But such a course of action would have been contrary to the political forces that were being pressed upon the Commission – both externally and, I was soon to learn, internally – to make sure the report was released after the election.

I was reluctant to return to Kenya to lobby for legislation that I did not understand, for which I had had no part in developing, and that seemed to unnecessarily delay the completion of all of the hard work we had put in over the last few years. It was also clear that we were requesting the delay not because we needed the time to complete our work, but because the government did not want our report to come out before the upcoming elections. My decision not to return to assist in our lobbying efforts was sealed when I was also informed that the Commission would not cover my expenses to return to Kenya from Seattle – presumably either I or my university were meant to cover those expenses.

Shortly after being informed of the decision to lobby Parliament for more time, I began to hear from my fellow commissioners and senior staff about the current work of the Commission. As part of our lobbying efforts, a number of commissioners and senior staff met with the Parliamentary Committee on Justice and Legal Affairs (the committee that was our primary link to Parliament) at the end of October. The Committee was skeptical about supporting an extension, given all the additional time we had already requested and received (we were already over a year late in finishing our work). They wanted assurances from us that we were making progress on finishing our work and, in particular, that we had made substantial progress in writing our final report. Our senior staff had been instructed by some of the commissioners to bring drafts of the final report to the meeting with the Parliamentary Committee.

During the meeting, one of the Kenyan commissioners instructed the staff to share the draft of the report to the Committee, which was then done. Some of the commissioners present at the Committee meeting were not informed of the decision to share copies of the report with the MPs and expressed their disproval. I was told that one copy of the draft report was passed among the Committee members during the meeting and that the draft was then returned immediately to the Commission. The meeting only lasted an hour or two at the most. It was, therefore, unlikely that any one MP was able to see or retain much of what was in the draft. Nevertheless, a dangerous precedent had been set: we had indicated our willingness to share drafts of the report to people outside of the Commission prior to its release to the public. This was clearly contrary to our oath of office, the legislation creating the Commission, and the internal rules we had adopted as a Commission concerning the confidentiality of the content of the final report prior to its release. Shortly after this meeting, Parliament granted us an extension to May 3, 2013.

Almost immediately after a draft of the report had been shared with members of Parliament, officials in the Ministry of Justice advised us to be careful and conservative about our findings and recommendations. I do not know if these words of caution were a direct response to feedback the Ministry had received from the Parliamentary Committee or whether we had also by this time shared a draft of our report with the Ministry.

Meanwhile, key donor and civil society organizations with whom we had worked in the past began to express concern that we had finished the final report but were deliberately withholding it for political reasons. I knew that their suspicions were in part mistaken, as the final report was, in fact, not finished; we continued to edit and draft new sections given the additional time. The concerns were not, however, unreasonable, given that many of my colleagues had repeatedly stated publicly that the report was done or near done months ago, and we had now apparently agreed to postpone releasing the report until after the elections (though, as far as I am aware, we never stated so publicly). To make matters worse, we never responded to these concerns raised by our erstwhile partners, thus further fueling suspicion about our motives and intentions.

The following months continued with little communication from my fellow commissioners. Senior staff and I continued to communicate and work together on drafts of the final report, and I would occasionally hear from senior staff about the activities of some of the other commissioners, including efforts to alter the content of the report without consulting with other commissioners and efforts to keep political leaders informed about the content of the report.

THE PRESIDENTIAL ELECTION: A MISSED OPPORTUNITY

The Kenyan elections of March 4, 2013, were preceded by a number of televised debates among the major presidential candidates. Watching the debates live on my computer in Seattle made it even clearer to me how useful our report would have been if released before the election. The debates included discussions on land, corruption, and historical injustices, along with other issues that were within our mandate and that we discussed in our report. In particular, the report included the voices of the *wananchi*[8] on many of these issues, including their firsthand experience with such injustices. If our report had been released in a timely manner before the debates, it would have provided an opportunity for the voices of the thousands of Kenyans we had heard throughout the country to be included in this important national discussion. Instead, the conversation was held without the benefit of the voices of the many Kenyans who had shared their stories with us and without the benefit of our findings and recommendations. The Commission was rarely mentioned,

---

[8]   Swahili for "ordinary people," or "the public."

if at all, during the debate. It was another example of our missing an opportunity to facilitate and contribute to a national debate about the issues central
to our mandate.

Despite fears of a repeat of the violence associated with the 2007 election,
the 2013 election was mostly peaceful, with few incidents of reported violence.
Like the previous presidential election in 2007, concerns were immediately
raised about the fairness of the balloting. Unlike in 2007, however, disputes
over the validity of the election were adjudicated by the newly created Supreme
Court. In 2007, one of the contestants, Mwai Kibaki, had unilaterally declared
victory and had been sworn in surreptitiously during a midnight ceremony,
leading to violence that claimed the lives of over a thousand people, displaced
hundreds of thousands, and ultimately resulted in the intervention of the
ICC and the creation of the TJRC. In 2013, despite serious concerns raised
domestically and internationally about the fairness of the election – including
reported irregularities with the election and even with the court proceedings
themselves – the unanimous decision of the Supreme Court affirming the
victory of Uhuru Kenyatta and William Ruto was generally accepted by the
Kenyan people.

Shortly after the elections, and after months of negotiations over who would
cover my expenses, the Commission agreed to fly me back to Kenya for three
weeks in March 2013 to work on the final stages of our final report. I hoped
that being present for a few weeks would provide me with a better sense of
where we were in terms of the report and related matters.

I arrived in Nairobi on Monday evening, March 11th – one week after the
election and three weeks before the Supreme Court decision deciding its
legality. I immediately proceeded to Naivasha, where we had all agreed the
commissioners and senior staff would meet to continue work on the report.
Given that I would only be in the country for three weeks, I was prepared to
be completely available to the rest of the team in Naivasha. I thus awoke on
Tuesday morning, ready to work, only to find that I was the only commissioner
on site.

Over the next two days commissioners and staff began to trickle in. As
I began to have face-to-face conversations with commissioners and staff,
I quickly learned that one of the reasons I had not been receiving regular
updates was that Ambassador Kiplagat had ordered the staff not to send any
documents or other information to me. I also learned that during the same
period, Ambassador Kiplagat had also been maneuvering to have me removed
from the Commission, arguing, among other things, that I had effectively
resigned by not being present at the Commission. This was particularly ironic,
given that Ambassador Kiplagat had left the Commission for fourteen months

stating that he was "stepping aside" while he continued to receive his full salary and did no Commission-related work. In fact, he spent some of his "stepping aside" time working to undermine the credibility of the Commission as he fought any public accounting of his conflicts of interest.[9]

While progress had been made on the report during my absence, I quickly learned that there was still much work to be done. I spent most of my time working with our director of research and other staff on drafting and editing text. While I had been away, tensions had developed between the commissioners and the staff working on the report. In a number of private conversations I had with fellow commissioners, they asked me to try to facilitate relations with the staff so that we could get the report done. Many of the Kenyan commissioners came and went during this period as they juggled the work we were doing with their other activities, both personal and professional. One commissioner was rarely on site yet had insisted that we pay for his room the entire time in case he decided to show up at some point.[10]

I returned to the USA at the end of March to finish teaching. During my absence, a number of significant events occurred that would influence the endgame surrounding the production of our final report.

"NOT A SINGLE COMMA SHALL BE CHANGED!"

The election of Uhuru Kenyatta and William Ruto in March 2013 heralded a subtle though important shift in political power and alignment in Kenya. Kenyatta and Ruto had been on opposite sides of the political contest in 2007, Kenyatta being aligned with Kibaki's PNU and Ruto with Odinga's ODM. In addition, Ruto's Kalenjin ethnic group had been historically hostile to Kenyatta's Kikuyu ethnic group. Much of the ethnic violence associated

---

[9] For more on the issues raised by Ambassador Kiplagat and the effect they had on the Commission, *see* Chapters 3 and 5 in this book. *See also* Truth, Justice and Reconciliation Commission (Kenya), REPORT OF THE TRUTH JUSTICE AND RECONCILIATION COMMISSION [TJRC FINAL REPORT], Vol. I, Ch. 4.

[10] Commissioner Ojienda continued with two other jobs while he was a commissioner. He continued to teach his university courses, and he continued his private law practice. While he was always vague about whether he was engaging in such activities outside of the Commission, he was quoted in the press in February 2016 as insisting that he had engaged in the practice of law on behalf of the Mumia's sugar company starting in 2011, while he was still a commissioner. This is doubly troubling, as we had received testimony critical of the employment and environmental practices of the Mumia's sugar company. Commissioner Ojienda made this public statement to defend himself against allegations of corruption arising from large payments he had received from Mumia's during that time. *See* Susan Muhindi, "Court Stops Ojienda Probe over Legal Fees," *The Star*, February 6, 2016.

with elections was committed by Kalenjins and Kikuyus against each other. The alliance between Ruto and Kenyatta was thus viewed with some surprise by longtime observers of Kenyan politics. It was an alliance explained not by historical ethnic relations but by a strong common interest against the ICC and accountability for the 2007 post-election violence.[11] Political opponents of the pair referred to their combined ticket as an "Alliance of the Accused." The election of Kenyatta and Ruto on a platform that included vilifying the ICC was thus reasonably viewed as a shift away from accountability and a further entrenchment of impunity in Kenyan politics. This shift had a direct effect on the final days of the Commission.

Coinciding with these broader political shifts at the national level, disputes arose within the Commission concerning the land chapter. Commissioner Shava had expressed concerns about portions of the land chapter and had submitted suggested changes to the research department in the third week of April. At the end of April (and thus a matter of days before May 3, the day by which we were legally obligated to make the report public and hand it over to the president), she inquired about the status of her changes with the research department, who directed her to call the commissioners working on the report at Elementaita, a resort on the shores of Lake Elementaita, about ninety minutes outside of Nairobi. She called Commissioner Farah, who was chairing a meeting of the three other commissioners who were still working on the report. Commissioner Farah responded that, given the late stage of the process, no changes would be made to the land chapter. He did inform Commissioner Shava that she could, if she so desired, write a dissenting opinion to the land chapter. In her recounting of the conversation, Commissioner Shava reported that "Commissioner Farah stated categorically and emphatically that as a Kenyan, he was fully satisfied with the second draft [of the Land Chapter] and that if I was not, then I could write a dissenting opinion, and that this was the position of all Commissioners present in the room with him." A colleague told me that Commissioner Farah emphatically stated to the others in the room that "not a single comma shall be changed" in the land chapter. Given the later turn of events, this dispute between commissioners Shava and Farah over the content of the land chapter was to prove ironic.

Commissioner Farah's overly heated response to Commissioner Shava was typical of the way he approached the work of the Commission. A heavyset

---

[11] For a thoughtful analysis of the political appeal of the alliance, *see* Gabrielle Lynch, "Electing the 'Alliance of the Accused': The Success of the Jubilee Alliance in Kenya's Rift Valley," 8 *Journal of East African Studies*, 93–114 (2014).

Somali with political ambitions, Commissioner Farah adopted very strong (and often loudly expressed) views on an issue. Notwithstanding the volume by which he voiced the certainty of his position, Commissioner Farah was known to alter his view according to various political interests both inside and outside the Commission. His strong personality resulted in very serious clashes with his fellow commissioners. One resulted in a physical altercation with a fellow commissioner; another risked becoming a criminal matter until two of us on the inside mediated a settlement. Despite his bluff and bluster, Commissioner Farah also displayed periodic acts of generosity, having, for example, presented me with a full Muslim outfit (complete with sandals), which I wore when we held hearings in the predominantly Somali northeastern region of the country. He was most committed to issues concerning the Somali population, including our investigation into the Wagalla massacre.

Commissioner Shava circulated to all commissioners on April 30 a statement setting forth her conversation with Commissioner Farah, asserting that she had only at that moment been made aware that her position was a minority one; that her input to the land chapter had been ignored; and that the fact that she was only now told that the other commissioners disagreed with her comments, combined with the general silence from other commissioners concerning this matter up until this point, implied that she had "been deliberately deprived of the right to dissent."

Dissenting opinions in a truth commission report are not unprecedented. The final reports of the truth commissions in South Africa and Liberia, for example, include dissenting opinions. We had carefully considered the process by which a commissioner could dissent during the first year of our existence as we struggled to address Ambassador Kiplagat's conflicts of interest. Many of us, myself included, assumed that Ambassador Kiplagat would dissent from part of our report given his personal interest in a number of the issues we would examine. During the last year of our existence, as we became more concerned that Ambassador Kiplagat would use the right to dissent to delay the release of our report, we drafted a set of internal rules that not only reaffirmed the right of each commissioner to dissent but also set forth the procedures a commissioner must follow in order to have the dissent included as part of the final report. These procedures included two important provisions concerning the right of any commissioner to dissent from all or part of the report. The first was that a commissioner who exercised the right to submit a dissenting opinion was bound to sign the report. The corollary to this is that a commissioner who did not exercise his or her right to dissent was not bound to sign the report. Second, a commissioner who indicated his intention to dissent needed to provide the dissent within forty-eight hours. This last rule was designed to prevent a commissioner from using the right to dissent to delay the release of the report.

I immediately responded to Commissioner Shava's concerns (while I was at the Amsterdam airport on my way back to Kenya). I noted that I had not seen the final version of the land chapter, nor had I seen her comments, and thus I could not at the moment comment on the quality or wisdom of either of them. I made clear that, as far as I was concerned, she had a right to file a dissent if she wanted and that, given the delayed notice to her and the lateness of the hour, I indicated I was willing to be flexible about our forty-eight-hour rule for filing a dissent. I also suggested that her dissent be placed immediately online with the online version of the report, printed for distribution, and that we make clear online and in the printed version that her dissent was legally part of the report. I was the only commissioner who responded to Commissioner Shava to address her concerns. Neither Commissioner Shava nor any other commissioner responded concerning my proposal that she be given more than the required forty-eight hours to file her dissent. Commissioner Shava never raised the issue with us again, and she did not submit a dissent for the land chapter. It is not clear if she knew at this point that her dissent would be unnecessary, given the subsequent course of events.

When I landed back in Nairobi on May 2, I found everyone visibly exhausted and tense. Some commissioners were barely speaking with each other. Officially, we were waiting to get an appointment with the president to hand over the report. I learned that we had been approached by the Ministry of Justice a few weeks earlier, requesting that we provide them with an advance copy of the report. The Ministry explained that they wanted to see the report prior to the handing over so they could brief the president on its contents. I was told we resisted that request, but either shortly before or just after I returned, we apparently did hand over copies of the report to the permanent secretary in the Office of the President, Francis Kimemia, and the Attorney General, Githu Mugai. The advance copies of the report we handed over were not complete. I am told that they did not include the important chapter containing our findings and recommendations, which was probably correct, as I knew those sections had not yet been finalized. We handed over these advance copies trusting that this would result in a quick appointment with the president – this would turn out to be quite naïve of us.

Within days of my return I became aware of political pressure being exerted on us to change parts of the report – specifically sections of the land chapter, but also other sections of the report. Commissioner Shava had raised a concern about a table in the land chapter that listed prominent individuals who, according to various sources (including investigations undertaken by the government, the media, and civil society), had acquired land under suspicious circumstances during the first Kenyan government of President Jomo Kenyatta. Commissioner Shava's concern was that the list was a very selective one, listing only twenty-four people. She argued that if we were to include such a list, we should make it as comprehensive as possible. In addition to not being a complete list of those who benefited during the first Kenyatta administration, we had not included a similar list of those who had similarly benefited under the Moi and Kibaki administrations. We were unfortunately so late in our process that it was not possible to construct a more comprehensive list of those who received land irregularly or illegally under all three administrations. I was concerned about the appearance of singling out one period of history over another, thus creating the perception that we were treating one community less fairly than others, and I agreed that we should remove the table. The fact that the table was publicly available (it had recently been published in one of the major national newspapers) meant that not including it in our report did not mean it would be withheld from the public.

At the time that I was asked to weigh in on the decision about the table in the land chapter I was under the impression that the discussions relating to the content of our report were all internal to the Commission. I was quickly to learn that this was not the case. This became clear to me as other commissioners and staff recounted to me events over the past two months and as I began to interact with government officials over the content of the report.

PRESIDENTIAL INTERVENTION

On May 7, four days after we were legally required to hand over our final report, I was sitting in an office at our printers with two other commissioners and our director of research, when my phone rang with an unknown number. When I answered, a soft voice asked, "Is this Slye?" When I responded yes, the caller said his name was Kimemia and wanted to know if I was in a meeting. I replied that I was, and he then asked if he could call me later, to which I said yes. I hung up and looked at my colleagues.

"I think that was Francis Kimemia."

Francis Kimemia, at the time, was one of the most powerful people in the Kenyan government. He was secretary to the cabinet, and the permanent secretary in the Office of the President. He had succeeded Francis Muthaura who had resigned from the position after he had been indicted by the ICC for his alleged role in the violence arising from the 2007 election. (In March 2013, the Prosecutor of the ICC dropped the charges against Muthaura after a key prosecution witness was discredited.) I was told that Kimemia was a loyal hatchet man for Kenyatta. The ICC Prosecutor's pre-trial brief in the Kenyatta case alleged that Kimemia played a key role on behalf of Kenyatta in organizing some of the violence after the 2007 election. He was in close contact with the president, and the assumption was that when he spoke he was speaking directly on behalf of the president.

I was surprised that Kimemia was calling me. Over the last few days, I had learned that he had had a number of conversations with some of the Kenyan Commissioners. This was the first and, as far as I am aware, only time that he had reached out to one of the international commissioners.

Sometime in April, I was told, Commissioner Shava had leaked a draft of the land chapter to a lawyer who was close to the Kenyatta family.[12] It was this leak that initiated a series of events that led to Kimemia calling me, and that eventually led me and the two other international commissioners to write a dissent to the land chapter.

Shortly after Commissioner Farah had insisted to Commissioner Shava in late April that "not a single comma" in the land chapter was to be changed, he apparently received a phone call from Kimemia. Immediately after that phone call, Commissioner Farah returned to the report-writing meeting and immediately started to demand changes to the land chapter. It was never made clear to me what Kimemia said or promised in his conversation with Commissioner Farah that led to such an abrupt reversal in his position.

Sometime after the land chapter had been leaked and Commissioner Farah had reversed himself on whether it should be changed, but before I had returned to Kenya on May 2, we gave an advance (though incomplete) copy of the report to Kimemia. In addition to changes to the land chapter, Kimemia had apparently communicated with some commissioners and staff about other changes he wanted made to the report, including removing references to Jomo Kenyatta in connection with the assassination of J. M. Kariuki, removing other references to members of the Kenyatta family, and removing all references to William Ruto. While these "proposals" were sometimes vetted with other commissioners, often they were conveyed directly to the staff with instructions that the changes should be made immediately.

My first indication that something was seriously amiss occurred on May 6, when I happened to visit our printer's office to check on the status of the production of the report. When I arrived, I found commissioners Shava and Farah standing over our staff and directing which parts of the report to remove concerning the Kenyatta family. When I asked them under what authority

---

[12] A few months after the incidents related here, that same lawyer was appointed to a senior legal position in the government.

they were changing the content of the report, they replied that we had to remove references to Kenyatta, as the matters involving him were *sub judice*.[13] It was not clear to me what matters were considered to be *sub judice* and before which court. I noted that if we were going to remain silent on matters currently before various courts, we should remove all of our discussion of the Wagalla massacre, police brutality, the Mau Mau period, etc. Neither commissioner argued further at that point, and they left without the changes being made. This incident indicated that far more was happening behind the scenes than I had realized, so I made a point to be at the printer's office as much as I could and started to try to keep better track of my fellow commissioners and senior staff.

The next day, May 7, was when I received the call from Kimemia. Given the confrontation I had had with commissioners Shava and Farah the day before about removing references to the Kenyatta family, I was curious, and a bit concerned, about the purpose of the call. The call came while I was meeting with some of the other commissioners and senior staff. They were equally surprised and concerned that Kimemia had called me directly and asked if I wanted them to leave the room when I called him back. I immediately responded no; I wanted them present so that I would have witnesses to at least my half of the conversation.

I dialed the number and Kimemia immediately picked up. He first thanked me for agreeing to take out the table in the land chapter that listed the Kenyatta family, among others, as having obtained land illegally or irregularly. While I still felt there was merit in removing the table, I was very uneasy with the perception that I had assisted in changing our report at the behest of the government – a state of affairs about which I was only now being made aware. I later learned that Commissioner Farah had told Kimemia how cooperative I had been and that Commissioner Farah had also suggested that Kimemia call me to push for further changes.

After thanking me for my help, Kimemia then asked if I would take a look at paragraph 257 of the land chapter as, according to him, it posed similar problems to the now-removed table. I told him that I would take a look at it, being careful not to commit to more than looking at the paragraph. He then observed that while we all wanted the TJRC report and its recommendations to be implemented, it would be difficult for the president to implement a report that reflected badly on his family. He also, at least three times during

---

[13] Literally meaning "before the court." The phrase is generally used to indicate that because a particular matter is pending before a court of law, it should not be discussed elsewhere until the court reaches its final decision.

the conversation, said that I should stop by his office in State House and say *Jambo*. This last was particularly curious. *Jambo* is an informal Swahili form of hello and mostly associated with tourists. Kenyans tend to use the more formal *Habari* instead. I was later to learn from my Kenyan colleagues that being invited to "come by and say *Jambo*" was code for being offered a bribe. I was told by Kenyan friends that in my case, given that I was foreign, I would probably be given a large amount of dollars or euros, rather than Kenyan shillings. I never stopped by Kimemia's office, so I never found out how much he was willing to give me nor whether he in fact intended to pay me at all in return for making changes to the report.

When I hung up I immediately asked to see paragraph 257 of the land chapter. Paragraph 257 recounted Toza's testimony before the Commission at our public hearing in Kwale. While the paragraph did not include direct quotations from Toza's testimony, three of the seven sentences in the paragraph ended in a footnote referencing Toza's testimony. As the information provided in the paragraph was provided to us under oath in a public hearing, and as we had made express reference to that testimony to indicate the source of information in that paragraph, I immediately made it clear to the commissioners and senior staff present that I did not support any changes to the paragraph and that it should stand as we had originally approved it.

To muddy matters even further, Kimemia called our CEO (who was then Tom Chavangi Aziz) on the evening of the next day (May 8) and stated that I had agreed to change paragraph 257. The following morning (May 9), Chavangi and Commissioner Farah went to the printers to try to change or remove paragraph 257, claiming that I had agreed to the change. Luckily, I had kept my colleagues in the room during my phone conversation; all were able to verify that I had only agreed to look at the paragraph, which I had done, and that I had made clear in their presence that I was opposed to any changes. I immediately called the printers and made clear that I had not agreed to any changes to the report. Once it was made clear that I had not approved the change, the paragraph was left untouched. Now that it had been made clear to me that the request for changes was coming from outside the Commission, I strongly felt that unless a clear untruth was brought to our attention we should not, to paraphrase Commissioner Farah, change even a single comma of the report.

During all of this back and forth on the land chapter, Ambassador Dinka was in a Nairobi hospital undergoing medical tests. A career UN diplomat from Ethiopia, Berhanu Dinka had worked closely with Kofi Annan on a number of diplomatic missions in Africa and other parts of the world. He began his career in the Ethiopian diplomatic corps, but under the military dictatorship of Mengistu Haile Mariam, he was arrested and imprisoned for close to four years – in fact, he was the only one among us who had spent time in detention. He never learned why he had been detained. Berhanu was full of amazing stories from his rich and varied life, including how he survived his years in detention without being executed, the year and a half he spent working closely with Nelson Mandela to bring peace to Burundi, and his time as governor of Kampong Cham province in Cambodia leading up to that country's first democratic elections in 1993.

In August 2012, shortly after I had left Kenya, a small growth was discovered on Ambassador Dinka's lung during a routine medical examination. The biopsy indicated it was malignant, so he had traveled to New York to undergo a series of treatments. The treatments were reported to be successful, in part because of the early stage at which he had caught the cancer.

In April 2013, Ambassador Dinka had returned to Kenya. He was tired and run down because of the cancer treatment. He was frequently absent from the office, and at one point, he checked himself into a local hospital for additional tests.

Judge Chawatama and I had been very careful not to involve Ambassador Dinka unnecessarily in all of the last-minute wrangles around the land chapter. Unbeknownst to us, however, Commissioner Farah had approached Ambassador Dinka and, as it was later reported to us, secured his approval for those changes to the land chapter demanded by the Office of the President. Armed with this apparent approval, Commissioner Farah and our CEO spent much of May 12th and 13th at the printers demanding that the changes be made as, according to them, they had been approved by a majority of commissioners. Judge Chawatama and I learned about this turn of events and immediately proceeded to the printers. Once there, we were given a copy of the pages reflecting the latest changes and were told that Commissioner Farah had now taken a copy to show Kimemia and secure his approval.

Judge Chawatama and I were shocked at this turn of events, not only because of the merits of the decision but also because of the procedure – there was no formal meeting of the Commission to discuss these changes nor even a request for approval of such changes by email or telephone as our internal rules allowed. We immediately decided that if these changes were allowed into the final version of the report without following our agreed upon procedures, we would refuse to sign the volume of the report containing the censored land chapter. We also made clear to our fellow commissioners through email and text messages that it was our view that the land chapter as we had earlier and formally approved it was the final version. Only if a commissioner presented proposed changes to all commissioners and a majority of us approved those changes, as provided for in our internal rules of procedure, could the content be changed.

Commissioners Wanjala and Ojienda called me in response to these recent messages and made clear that they, too, agreed with us that the land chapter should stand as we had originally approved it. That meant that at least four out of the eight of us did not approve of these recent changes.

Reluctantly, Judge Chawatama and I decided that we had to discuss all of this with Ambassador Dinka. I called Berhanu to ask if he could meet with us to discuss the recent turn in events. He agreed, and we arranged to meet with him at his home the next day, May 14.

I was a bit shocked when I saw Ambassador Dinka that day. He was quite thin and appeared frail, yet as always, he was a gracious and generous host as we gathered in his living room to discuss the current state of affairs. He told us that Commissioner Farah had called him about the changes to the land chapter and that Commissioner Farah had assured him that all of the other commissioners had approved the changes. We both assured Ambassador Dinka that neither one of us had been informed about the proposed changes, much less that we had approved them, and that it was our understanding that the same was true for some of our other commissioner colleagues, given the comments we had received from commissioners Ojienda and Wanjala. Ambassador Dinka made clear that, given this new information, he was no longer in support of the changes demanded by Commissioner Farah.

As we were meeting with Ambassador Dinka, we received a call indicating that Commissioner Farah was back at the printers demanding – as we were told, "yelling" – that the changes be made and that the printer run new copies of the report with the changes for final binding. The aggressive and manipulative turn of events led me, for the first time, to be concerned about my own personal safety. The history of Kenya (as we on the Commission who studied the history so closely were all too well aware) is littered with the mysterious deaths or disappearances of individuals who had challenged powerful officials. I was less concerned (perhaps naïvely) that there would be an intentional attack against me or one of the other international commissioners and was more concerned that an effort to scare us (through, for example, a car accident) might unintentionally lead to serious injury. It was at this point that I contacted someone at the US Embassy to make them aware of my situation and asked for any advice they might have concerning my personal security. The Embassy provided me with a phone number of a political officer who I could contact twenty-four hours a day if I felt I was in danger or that I needed assistance. I ended up not having to use the number but was in contact with embassy officials from time to time over the next few days as I and others received both implicit and explicit threats.

While we were at Ambassador Dinka's home, Commissioner Wanjala called to inform me that she was currently in hiding. She had received numerous calls, some threatening, from government officials to fall into line with the other Kenyan Commissioners and approve changes to the land chapter. She opposed the changes but was concerned about her own safety and the safety of her family. She arranged for me to meet her at her hiding place, and I proceeded to update her on the most recent events. Commissioner Wanjala was clearly concerned about the safety of her family, including her youngest child, who had been born shortly before she joined the Commission in 2009. I told her that I would support her no matter what she eventually decided to do and that I could understand how she might choose the safety of her family over crossing the president. At this point, it was clear to me that there were few, if any, limits to what the president would do to have references to his father removed from the land chapter.

On the same day that we were bringing Ambassador Dinka up to speed on recent events (May 14), our CEO sent a message proposing a Commission meeting given the conflicting information he and other staff had been receiving from commissioners concerning changes to the report. He attached to his message the following message he had received earlier that day from our director of research:

> Yesterday, Commissioner Ahmed Farah informed me that five commissioners had approved amendments to certain paragraphs of the chapter. Under his direct supervision, I made those changes. Later, Commissioner Ron Slye and Commissioner Judge Gertrude Chawatama informed me that they had not been consulted in regard to the proposed amendments. Earlier in the morning, Commissioner Tecla [Wanjala] had informed me that she was not in favour of any more changes. Commissioner Ron and Judge Gertrude also say that Ambassador Dinka says that the changes I effected under the supervision of Commissioner Ahmed Farah [were] far broader than what he approved. Today, I received a letter (attached) from the chairperson, Ambassador Kiplagat, indicating that five commissioners did in fact approve the changes...I have had a telephone conversation with Prof Ojienda who also says he did not approve of any changes to the chapter. As such, it appears to me that five commissioners are not in favour of the changes but Ambassador Kiplagat's letter refers to a decision of five commissioners. Thus, it is not clear to me what is the position of the Commission on the proposed amendments and what version of the chapter stands as the Commission's chapter on land and conflict. Please advise on the way forward.

Attached to the email was a signed letter from Ambassador Kiplagat, also dated May 14, stating that five commissioners supported the amendments to six different paragraphs in the land chapter, and that such changes should thus be made. The letter did not indicate which five commissioners had approved the changes, when or how these approvals had been secured, or any other information about the content of the changes that had been approved. As indicated in the email above – and consistent with my own conversations with my colleagues – there were, at most, three commissioners who had at this point approved the changes to the land chapter (commissioners Shava, Farah, and Kiplagat; as discussed below, Ambassador Kiplagat was not eligible to vote on these changes). It is not clear on what basis Ambassador Kiplagat asserted that five commissioners supported the changes. He had not communicated with me at all to ask whether I supported the changes, nor had he or any other commissioner called for a vote on the matter.

Within minutes of this email from the CEO asking for clarification about the changes, Commissioner Ojienda sent a message to all of the commissioners making clear that he opposed any changes to the report. Within short succession, commissioners Wanjala, Chawatama, Dinka, and I also responded that we opposed any changes to the report. Commissioner Shava made clear that she supported the changes but also noted that, since five of us had now stated our opposition to the changes, she acknowledged that the decision of the Commission was to not make the changes and said she would abide by that decision. Commissioner Farah also weighed in and said that earlier he had secured five votes for the changes, and now that seems to have changed because, he wrote, "some have not been making honest decisions or have been changing without seeing the suggestions." He thus requested that we meet as a Commission to discuss the issue and vote again.

At this point, almost two weeks after we were legally obligated to make the report public, commissioners were unilaterally making changes to the report; we were misrepresenting to each other, both orally and in writing, who had been consulted and who approved such changes; staff were being bullied to make changes to the report and to not inform other commissioners; we still did not have an appointment with the president; the president's office was cajoling, threatening, and offering bribes to commissioners and perhaps staff; and all of this was being done to sanitize the report's discussion of the manner in which the Kenyatta family had come to be the largest landholder in Kenya. At this point, five of the eight commissioners opposed any changes to the report.

Judge Chawatama and I agreed to meet again with Ambassador Dinka on May 15. Commissioner Wanjala came out of hiding to meet with us as well.

Ambassador Dinka was a consummate diplomat, always looking for compromises and ways forward – sometimes, in my view, at the expense of important principles. I think if he were to have spoken candidly, he would have characterized me as a bit idealistic or unrealistic, perhaps even a bit impulsive, and willing to fail based on principle rather than succeed with compromise. In spite of, or perhaps because of, these differences, we worked quite well together. There was even a period in our work at the Commission when he and I switched places, and I was pushing for compromise while he was pushing a more hard-lined and principled position.

As we gathered at Ambassador Dinka's apartment, I was starting to think that there was little we could do to salvage the situation. The government seemed intent on forcing the changes, significant individuals within the Commission were supporting those changes, and those in the middle were being placed under enormous pressure to conform. Given the fluidity of the situation, Ambassador Dinka proposed that we compromise and make some changes to the land chapter. At first I strongly opposed this suggestion. There was an important principle at stake – we were contemplating changes to the final report not because we felt such changes had merit, but because of political pressure from the Office of the President. I had earlier agreed to remove the table in the land chapter because I agreed that it was incomplete and selective. Had I known that the impetus for the change was coming from the government, I would not have agreed to that change.

As we discussed the issue further, my colleagues persuaded me that we should not "throw the baby out with the bathwater." We had worked too hard and for too many years to have the process disintegrate in this way at the end. Over forty thousand Kenyans had submitted statements to us, hundreds of communities had submitted memoranda, and over a thousand had testified at our public hearings, often at great personal risk to themselves. We thus agreed to propose a compromise. For those paragraphs that implicated the Kenyatta family based upon testimony presented to us at our public hearings, we would make clear that the Commission was merely repeating the testimony as part of our narrative truth process. We would thus add language similar to the following to the body of the text: "A witness testified before the Commission that . . ." This would make clear that we were not necessarily asserting that the facts reported to us were true but that we were only recounting what others had testified to us under oath. We also agreed that we would add a sentence at the end of those paragraphs to the effect that the Commission could neither confirm nor deny these allegations. I was less comfortable with this last proposed addition, as such a sentence could be added to most of the paragraphs in the narrative part of the report. Part of the purpose of the narrative in our report was to present the truth of what happened in the past as articulated by those who witnessed these past atrocities. While much of the narrative is undoubtedly factually true, it is in the findings section at the end of the report where we state whether we have enough evidence to assert that a particular fact or allegation is true or not. Like all previous truth commissions, our findings are based upon a "balance of the probabilities." For our findings, we required more than one source of evidence – thus, the mere allegation by one individual would not be sufficient for us to find, on a balance of the probabilities, that the allegation was in fact true. Ironically, we had not made any significant findings with respect to land at all, much less about the Kenyatta family and land, for which we could and should be criticized.

My concern was that if we stated that we could not verify the contents of a particular paragraph, we would be suggesting that other paragraphs without such a sentence were in fact verified, or that for some reason the singled-out paragraph was somehow weaker or less verifiable than the others. In the end, however, I agreed to the proposed changes as, on the merits, I did not believe that they would take away from the substance of the report. The original allegations would remain, and we would make clear through express language what was already accepted by us, that we could not and had not verified forensically every statement in the body of the report.

Commissioner Wanjala agreed with these changes, but she was hesitant to communicate her support for the compromise if she would be the only Kenyan commissioner to do so. I called Commissioner Shava and explained to her the changes we were proposing, and she expressed over the phone her agreement to our proposed changes. I also spoke with Commissioner Ojienda, who did not make clear over the phone whether he supported the compromise language or not. At that moment, I assumed he did not want to compromise at all, given his email from the previous day making clear that he opposed any changes to the report.

While we were at Commissioner Dinka's apartment crafting this compromise, a reporter from The Standard (one of the three major Nairobi-based newspapers) called me and asked what was happening with the report. I gave our standard public response: the report was ready and we were just waiting for an appointment with the president. What I didn't tell the reporter was that I was hoping our compromise would be accepted so we could quickly hand over the report and devote our energies to ensuring that our recommendations, including the provisions recommending reparations to victims, would be implemented. When the reporter asked why there had been such a delay in handing over the report, I suggested he speak to the Office of the President. He then asked me about a reported split among the commissioners – clearly others were talking to the press, and this reporter had received some information about our internal deliberations. I replied that I was not aware of a split among the commissioners. Somewhat exasperated at my unwillingness to confirm what he had heard from others, he then "accused" me of being the only commissioner defending the process. As the day ended on May 15, it appeared we had five commissioners who opposed any changes to the report, with at least four of us proposing a compromise that would allow us to stand united behind the final report.

The next morning (May 16), the dynamic began to shift. First, Commissioner Ojienda sent an email to all of us saying that he had reconsidered his position, and he now supported making the changes to the land chapter demanded by the Office of the President. I am told, but could not verify, that Kimemia or someone else from the Office of the President had called him earlier in the day, thus prompting his abrupt reversal on this issue in less than twenty-four hours. Within minutes, Commissioner Shava sent an email to all of us asking for Commissioner Wanjala to state her position. With Commissioner Ojienda's about-face, Commissioner Wanjala was now the only Kenyan commissioner who had expressed opposition to the changes.

In another remarkable development, Ambassador Kiplagat then weighed in for the first time to say that he supported the changes. This was remarkable for two reasons. First, our legislation makes clear that the chair only votes to break a tie, which at the moment we did not have.[14] Second, and far more importantly, all commissioners, including Ambassador Kiplagat, had agreed that he would have no influence over the content of the three chapters of the report for which he had a conflict of interest, viz. massacres, assassinations, and land. Up until the recent controversy over the land chapter, all of the commissioners had been adamant that Ambassador Kiplagat was not to influence any of these chapters, though we all agreed that he had a right to append a dissent to any or all of these chapters if he desired. (Ambassador Kiplagat had requested that a memo he wrote be appended to the challenges chapter as his dissent, which was done.) Commissioners Farah and Shava, for example, had been quite adamant in the past about enforcing this limitation on Ambassador Kiplagat. This time they were noticeably silent at Kiplagat's active involvement in determining the content of the land chapter.

With the vote tally shifting almost hourly, I joined the two other international commissioners in trying to secure acceptance from the other commissioners of the compromise language we had developed the day before.

---

[14] This is not uncommon with respect to boards of directors. For our legislation, *see* TJRC Act, *supra* note 3, at Third Schedule, Art. 5.

In addition to vote shifting, there was also a lack of clarity about what specific changes were being proposed or approved, as a number of versions had been circulated and references were being made to Commissioner Ojienda's changes, to Commissioner Farah's changes, and later to Commissioner Shava's changes.

With the changed position of Commissioner Ojienda, and the apparent change in our policy with respect to Ambassador Kiplagat's conflict of interest, the prospect of securing approval for our compromise had diminished dramatically. On the same morning of May 16, Commissioner Farah made clear in a phone conversation that he would not accept anything less than removing the paragraphs at issue because, as he said, they were based on only one witness, and they "besmirch" the reputation of the Kenyatta family.[15] On Friday morning (May 17), Commissioner Dinka called Commissioner Farah and secured an oral agreement from him to support our compromise. Commissioner Shava, who had been in favor of the compromise language the day before, was no longer communicating with us. I sent her a number of texts trying to elicit her views on the compromise language. Three hours later, she tried to call me and I missed the call. I immediately tried to call back four times in the span of a minute, but she did not pick up and did not communicate with me again until the following week.

In an effort to keep our compromise on the table, we requested that all commissioners be given a copy of the different versions of the proposed changes. With references to changes proposed by Commissioner Farah, Commissioner Ojienda, and Ambassador Dinka (i.e., our compromise) it was not clear whether we had all seen the specific language of each of the different proposals. Without seeing the actual language, we argued, it was difficult to determine whether to support the changes or not. As we were debating this, Commissioner Wanjala weighed in at 2 p.m. that same Friday and indicated that she now supported the proposed changes to the report demanded by the President's Office. With Commissioner Wanjala's agreement, Commissioner Farah immediately reversed himself on the compromise language (as now all five Kenyan commissioners had agreed to the changes) and Commissioner Shava continued to be silent.

With the stated agreement of five commissioners to the proposed changes demanded by the President's Office, all talk of compromise was now dead.

---

[15] The concern that the paragraph is based upon the testimony of only one witness could, of course, be raised with respect to many paragraphs in the report, including some of those involving the Wagalla massacre and the assassination of J. M. Kariuki, two issues that were particularly important to some of the commissioners now pushing for changes in the land chapter.

Meanwhile, our CEO emailed us the text of the proposed changes, which included new changes to remove references to the Mombasa Republican Council,[16] which I suspect was driven by Commissioner Farah and his political ambitions on the coast rather than by the President's Office. The most radical, and disingenuous, change was the evisceration of Toza's testimony.[17] Most of the paragraph was now removed, and what remained said only that a "private individual" unlawfully grabbed land in 1972. Surprisingly, we retained the reference to Toza's public testimony in support of this statement, which was now improper as he never testified that a private individual had engaged in such activity; he had clearly testified that it was the then-president, Jomo Kenyatta.

THE DISSENT

As I began to reflect that Friday evening about the latest turn of events, there was a part of me that was relieved that the compromise was dead. While I had convinced myself that I could defend the changes (as they were adding language of clarification, rather than removing language of substance), I had been uneasy about making such changes knowing they were in reaction to overt political pressure. With this recent turn of events, I quickly shifted my attention from trying to get agreement on our compromise language to crafting a dissent that would have the support of the other two international commissioners. Given our rules governing dissents, and the fact that we received the final version of the changes demanded by the President's Office in an email at 3:00 p.m. on Friday, May 17, we had until Sunday, May 19, at 3:00 pm to exercise our right to dissent.

On Saturday, May 18, we awoke to front-page stories about the Commission in two of the three major national newspapers. *The Star*, in a front-page story, surprisingly reported that there was a split among the commissioners on the land chapter and that the international commissioners were considering submitting a dissent. This was particularly surprising as we had not yet agreed among ourselves at this point whether we would write a dissent or not. I was not certain that all three of us would agree to submit a dissent, much less agree

---

[16] The Mombasa Republican Council was formed in 1999 to address political and economic grievances of residents in the Coast Province. The MRC advocated for the Coast Province to secede from Kenya. The call for secession, among other allegations concerning their activities, led the Kenyan government to ban the MRC in 2010.

[17] TJRC Final Report, *supra* note 8, at Vol. IIB, para. 257. See the original paragraph and the revised paragraph, which can be compared by viewing the two versions of the final report available on the book's website: http://digitalcommons.law.seattleu.edu/tjrc/.

on its content. *The Standard* reported that I had written the chapter on political assassinations (which was only partially true) and that a Kenyan commissioner had come to my office "and banged on his [i.e., my] door insisting that he has to cooperate. He was told this is Kenya and things have to be done the Kenyan style." This anecdote was partially true. A week or more earlier Commissioner Farah had come to my office and in his usual bombastic style had insisted that I fall into line. The story was written by the reporter who had called me at Ambassador Dinka's apartment while we were working on our compromise proposal; he correctly noted in the story that I had been contacted and had denied the allegations that there was a split in the Commission.

The media reports made it clear that our attempts to keep our internal deliberations and differences private and within the Commission until after the report was made public were becoming increasingly futile. It was not clear whether commissioners or staff were leaking information to the press or if the sources included people outside of the Commission who had become privy to some of our internal deliberations. Regardless of the source, it was clear that we were beginning to lose control over the narrative of the final days of our report writing.

Judge Chawatama, Ambassador Dinka, and I immediately discussed the import of the news in that morning's papers and quickly agreed that we would write a dissent. At three o'clock that Saturday afternoon, with the consent of the other two international commissioners, I sent an email to all commissioners indicating that the three of us were giving notice of our intention to exercise our right to dissent. I had already ascertained that the final version of the land chapter had not yet been printed and bound and thus wanted to notify our senior staff in charge of the report's production that they would be receiving a dissent from the international commissioners so they could plan to have it included in the final version of the report. I thus immediately notified our CEO and director of research that the text of the dissent would be sent to them the next day, Sunday, May 19, to be included in the final report.

As I sat down to write the dissent, I wanted to accomplish three things. First, I wanted to make transparent the political interference of the Office of the President in our work. Second, I wanted to make the content of the changes made under political pressure transparent. Third, I wanted to make clear that we stood behind the integrity of the entire report except for the altered paragraphs. Regarding the first intention, I did not want to name names, as I thought that might distract from the broader messages we were trying to convey. For the second, I wanted to include the original language of the altered paragraphs so that a reader could compare those paragraphs to the ones in the final, revised version and see what alterations had been made. Frankly, I was concerned that the other two international commissioners, particularly Ambassador Dinka, might view the inclusion of the original paragraphs as going too far or as unnecessarily confrontational. I was quickly proven wrong, as both Judge Chawatama and Ambassador Dinka immediately supported the idea of including the text of the original paragraphs.

I spent all of Saturday working on the dissent and chatting with the other two international commissioners. That evening, I decided to go out to dinner with some friends who had nothing to do with the commission. We had a lovely dinner, and I spent three blissful hours not looking at my phone, trying to forget the events of the last few weeks. At the end of the evening, I noticed a number of missed calls from Judge Chawatama. I immediately called her back. She was in a panic because she had not heard from me after she had repeatedly called and was worried that something had happened to me. It was a sobering reminder of the increased risks associated with our current situation, and I promised her I would be more attentive to my phone from now on.

As I worked on the dissent that weekend, I received information indicating that there was movement afoot to have the dissent rejected, though it was not clear on what basis. Shortly after I had sent the notification to the other commissioners of our intention to exercise our right to submit a dissenting view, a series of emotional, fraught, and, at times, incoherent emails ensued. Commissioner Ojienda took the lead on this part of the fight, with supporting views expressed by Commissioner Farah. The other commissioners remained silent. The arguments ranged from issues with our right to submit a dissent to allegations that we were leaking confidential information to the press and to other attacks on our motives and integrity. Commissioner Ojienda's arguments included: (1) "a dissenting chapter must be a new write up on all the issues under consideration with the possibility of new evidence and investigation"; (2) a dissenting opinion would require an actual meeting among commissioners; (3) that Ambassador Kiplagat had suggested changes to chapters with which he had a conflict of interest, those changes were rejected, and he accepted that rejection "with his head held high"; (4) Ambassador Kiplagat signed the "contentious offending chapters"; (5) no one opted to submit a minority position on these "offending" chapters; (6) Commissioner Shava's concerns about the land chapter had been ignored, and yet she agreed to sign the report and "held her beautiful head high and ate humble pie"; (7) we never suggested any amendments to the land chapter but instead our "proposals were reactionary and were merely made to defeat the ones suggested by [Commissioner Farah]"; (8) though we lost by majority vote, we were now getting "personal" on the amendments "as though this chapter had been authored by one of the internationals!"; (9) we were "trying to shift the goal posts," and the rules should not be changed when international commissioners object; and (10) the international commissioners were harassing the other commissioners.

Commissioner Farah also weighed in, accusing me of "leading the international commissioners on a war path to oppose the majority of Kenyan commissioners on ... simple editorials ... raised by Commissioner Margaret Shava" back in April. This was particularly ironic given Commissioner Farah's out-of-hand dismissal of the concerns raised by Commissioner Shava about the land chapter in April and given the fact that I was the only commissioner at the time to indicate that Commissioner Shava had a right to voice her concerns and to write a dissenting opinion expressing her views. Commissioner Farah also curiously argued that our rules of procedure for the report writing (including the procedures for dissenting) had expired on May 3 (the day we were obligated by law to hand over our Report). Finally, he accused me of leaking the story to *The Star* about our planned dissent.[18]

These emails led me to suspect that some of the commissioners were not going to allow us to submit a dissenting opinion to the land chapter. I responded to Commissioner Ojienda, noting, among other things, that our rules were clear concerning the right of a commissioner to dissent and the procedures by which such dissent should be submitted; there was nothing in our procedures setting out any restrictions on the content of a dissent; and that, contrary to what Commissioner Ojienda claimed, Ambassador Kiplagat had dissented from a part of the report, and his minority view was included in the report in the manner he had requested. I asked Commissioner Ojienda and others that might agree with him to please cite to the provisions of our legislation, rules, or procedures to support his various assertions, and to please explain how our interpretation concerning our right to dissent was not supported by the text. There was no response to this request for textual support by Commissioner Ojienda or any other commissioner.

Commissioner Ojienda did, however, respond with new allegations, stating that he had ascertained from *The Star* itself that I was the source for their front-page story about the dissent; that Ambassador Kiplagat's dissent was not

---

[18] While in Kenya, I had made it a practice not to leak stories to the press, though I was often more open in speaking to the press than some of my other colleagues. In this case, a reporter from *The Star* who I respected had contacted me earlier in the week to find out what was happening. To his growing frustration, I continued to insist that everything was fine within the Commission and we were just waiting for the president to give us an appointment for the handing over. To this day, I do not know who his source was for the story claiming that the international commissioners would write a dissent.

appended to the relevant chapter; and that the issue was now settled. In responding to me, however, Commissioner Ojienda made a temporary tactical mistake. He argued that the issue was now settled because the rules to which I was referring (concerning the procedure for a Commissioner dissenting), in his words,

> were relevant before the 3rd of [M]ay. The term of the Commission ended on that day and sufficient copies of the report made available for submission to the head of State... Our mandate period has expired. We have not secured an extension. Under the law, we cannot engage in any report writing business beyond the 3rd [M]ay. No dissents or replies can be written after that date. We only exist for winding up.

I immediately began to draft a response agreeing with Commissioner Ojienda's view that no changes to the report could be made after May 3, which would then invalidate the recent changes to the land chapter, as they were made after May 3. Within minutes of Commissioner Ojienda sending this email, and before I could finish drafting my response, Ambassador Dinka called me and excitedly said we should immediately express our agreement with Commissioner Ojienda's position. I also spoke with Judge Chawatama, who agreed that we should express our agreement with Commissioner Ojienda. I thus sent a message stating that the three of us agreed with Commissioner Ojienda that under the law our report could not be changed after May 3. I noted that we now had four Commissioners expressing that view,[19] meaning that there was no longer a majority approving the changes to the land chapter, and, therefore, the printer should be instructed not to make any of the proposed changes.

To make sure that we were all on the same page, I sent an email to all commissioners asking that each of us vote yes or no on whether we agreed with the following statement: "The official Final Report of the Truth Justice and Reconciliation Commission is the report as it stood on 3 May 2013. Any changes, whether with approval of a majority of Commissioners or otherwise, are not a part of the Official Final Report." I then indicated that I, Judge Chawatama, and Ambassador Dinka agreed with the statement and that, based on recent emails, it appeared that commissioners Farah and Ojienda also agreed with the statement but that they should correct me if we misunderstood their recent communications.

---

[19] At the time, it might have been even five commissioners; as noted above, Commissioner Farah seemed to express the same view that we could do nothing with respect to the report after May 3rd.

While we were now pursuing the admittedly slim possibility that all would agree that the report as it existed on May 3 was the final report, I went to meet Ambassador Dinka in the hospital to get his final approval for the text of our dissent. Normally I enjoyed going over drafts with Ambassador Dinka – while we sometimes took different positions on important issues, we were both good writers and complemented each other's work quite well – but I was a bit uncomfortable having to disturb him while he was in the hospital. As I was leaving to go to the hospital, I received information that our CEO had given strict instructions to the printer to expedite the printing and binding of the land chapter so that it would be done before our dissent arrived. This was one of a number of incidents where the CEO had acted at the instructions of a few commissioners without consulting with the rest of us, much less letting us weigh in on the proper way forward.

As I walked out of my hotel to head to the hospital to meet Ambassador Dinka, I heard someone calling my name. It was Ambassador Amina Moham-med. Ambassador Mohamed had been the permanent secretary in the Ministry of Justice during much of our operational life. She recently had been appointed as the minister of foreign affairs in the new Kenyatta government. Ambassador Mohamed and I often disagreed on various issues. She had even, in a very diplomatic way, called me into her office to slap my wrist (figuratively) for having announced that I was going to resign without first consulting with the president. Despite our differences, I had always been impressed by Ambassador Mohammed's professionalism and had a sense that she was more politically astute and savvy than many of her colleagues.

We chatted briefly, and she asked how things were going at the Commis-sion. I quickly gave her a brief summary of the proposed changes to the land chapter, our efforts at forging a compromise, the rejection of the compromise, and the prospect of the three international commissioners writing a dissent. She appeared to be surprised at this turn of events, though I found it hard to believe that she was completely ignorant about what had been happening at the Commission. She told me that the most important thing was for us to remain intellectually honest. I pointed out to her that if the TJRC were to blow up at this late stage, it would make it more difficult to argue politically that the ICC and the international community should defer to Kenya in addressing the violence arising out of the 2007 election. If it came out that the government was interfering in such a heavy-handed way with a process with so little teeth, then the argument that it would be more hands-off and independent with a local judicial process concerning some of the same indi-viduals would be harder to make. She immediately understood the implica-tions of what I was saying, and as she left me, she clearly looked concerned.

I learned that she had raised my concerns later the same day with the president and some of his closest advisors, but, as far as I could tell, this had no impact on the pressure being brought to bear on the Commission.

My conversation with Ambassador Mohamed that morning, while unplanned, was one of a number of back-channel efforts we made to try to moderate the pressure being exerted on us by the president's office. Judge Chawatama and I, with the knowledge and encouragement of Ambassador Dinka, met twice with Michael Gichangi, the then head of the Kenyan intelligence services. Michael Gichangi was a polished, urbane, and soft-spoken individual. Whenever we met, he would be wearing expensive tailor-made suits. He was good friends with Commissioner Shava, in part because Gichangi had trained in the air force with Commissioner Shava's husband (as well as with the then US Ambassador, Scott Gration). While I viewed Gichangi as a person who could be influenced by reasonable arguments if they coincided with the interests of government elites, I was repeatedly warned by friends in the US government to be extremely careful about him as he was a dangerous man. Our efforts to convince Gichangi that the heavy-handed tactics of the president's office risked backfiring had no discernible impact on the course of events. Gichangi professed to agree with our concerns, but it quickly became clear to us that his main purpose was to distract and delay us. While our efforts to negotiate through this back channel failed, Gichangi did indicate a few times that the president was being informed of developments related to the Commission.

I arrived at the hospital to find Ambassador Dinka in a bed hooked up to numerous medical devices. There was perpetual beeping (which appeared to be coming from a device that was electronically monitoring his blood pressure) in the background. His wife, Almas, finally removed the blood pressure device to stop the beeping so we could concentrate on reviewing and editing the text of the dissent. Berhanu sat up in the hospital bed and slowly read through the dissent, making minor changes with a red pen, which we then went over together. His changes were all relatively minor, and I agreed to all of them. As I sat there by his side at the hospital bed, he looked tired and frail. I was angry that he had to be devoting so much time and energy to these last-minute Commission-related intrigues when he should have been resting and focusing on his health. I was painfully unaware at the time that a few months later, he would succumb to his illness and pass away in New York. Government officials, commissioners, and some of our senior staff were conspiring to change our report and silence our dissent, and here I was in a hospital room making sure that Ambassador Dinka had input into and approved the content of our proposed dissent while he was struggling with a fatal illness.

I finalized the dissent and received the express approval on the final language from Judge Chawatama and Ambassador Dinka, and at three in the afternoon on Sunday, May 19, emailed it to our CEO and our director of research, requesting that they print out copies to be shared with the other commissioners and that they prepare the text for inclusion in the report. I contacted Chavangi, our CEO, and asked that he bring the dissent over to the printer so they could format it and prepare it for inclusion in the relevant volume of the report. Chavangi hesitated, saying that we should send the dissent to the other commissioners and get their comments before we started the process of including it in the report. I was conscious of how tight our deadline was and said that I saw no reason to delay preparing the dissent for inclusion as we knew it was now in its final form. Any response by the other commissioners should also be included, but I did not want the dissent to be held hostage to any delay caused by whether or how the other commissioners would respond to the dissent. As I pushed our CEO on this point, he became more and more resistant. He stated that he was tired of going back and forth to the printers and stated emphatically that he did not want to have to go there yet again. We left it that I would email the dissent directly to the printer, which I then promptly did, copying the other international commissioners, our CEO, and our director of research. It was Sunday evening, May 19.

On Monday, I learned that, notwithstanding his stated reluctance the day before, Chavangi had, in fact, visited the printers first thing that morning to pick up five copies of the final report that had been bound without the dissent. I was furious. I called him and asked what he was planning to do with those five copies. He said that he had secured them for safekeeping. I asked why we even needed them when we knew they were incomplete without the dissent. He replied that he was concerned that the five printed copies might be misused, though he did not indicate who he thought might misuse them or to what effect. I told him that the five copies should be destroyed, as they were not the official version of the report. In response to my demand that the copies be destroyed, he replied that all previous copies should also be destroyed, to which I quickly agreed. He presumably did not want to destroy the copies, as, upon my agreement, he quickly dropped that suggestion and said that he was just following the will of the majority. He was following the majority in rejecting the dissent? No, he said, he was following the majority by including changes to the land chapter. I replied that we all accepted that there were to be changes to the land chapter – we voted, and the majority decided to include the changes. At issue now, I said, was the dissent. He didn't budge an inch. Furious, I hung up the phone.

Later that morning of May 20, Chavangi sent an email to all of the com-missioners indicating that they could pick up a copy of the dissent at the Commission's office and that their responses, if any, would be needed by the printer within forty-eight hours. The next day, Tuesday, May 21, Chavangi sent an email to all commissioners, recounting the conversation between the two of us, whereby I had stated that the version of the report without our dissent was not the official version. In that email, he revealed that he had instructed the printer to print the five copies without the dissent, which he had then picked up "for safe custody." He asked for the commissioners to make clear whether the version he had was the official version or not. The question as he presented it was whether the changes in the land chapter (which he now attributed to Commissioner Shava) were official or not. We had already agreed that the changes to the land chapter were official (so long as we assumed that we could make changes after May 3). The issue was whether the dissent should be included; the answer was clearly yes, which Chavangi and the majority of commissioners were now moving to deny.

THE RELEASE OF THE REPORT

This was the state of affairs as I sat in the coffee shop at Yaya on Tuesday, May 21, reflecting on the past four years. I had still not received a clear answer to the question of whether our dissent would be included as part of the bound version of the final report. At 1:30 p.m., as I was discussing the current state of affairs with friends and colleagues, our CEO sent an email to all of the commissioners with the subject line, "Handing Over Report at State House." Attached to the email was a letter from Francis Kimemia to Ambassador Kiplagat, dated the day before (May 20) and marked urgent and confidential, informing the Ambassador that we should be prepared to be at the president's office at 4:30 the next afternoon (May 21) to hand over the final report. It was not clear why we were only now being informed of this development.

Upon receiving this email, I immediately tried to ascertain what version of the final report was to be handed over – the version with or without our dissent. I called our CEO and asked him which version of the report was being handed over. He replied that he did not know but that he would find out and call me back. After not hearing from him for over half an hour, I called again, only to be told that the version being handed over did not include our dissent. Based upon this information, both Judge Chawatama and I asked that our signatures be removed from the volume of the report that included the land chapter. While forty-eight hours was claimed to be not enough time to include our dissent, the volume of the report including the land chapter was run again and bound without our signatures in a matter of hours before the final handover. When I was finally able to speak to Commissioner Shava, she informed me that she had not read the flurry of emails over the weekend because some of them were vitriolic (she was presumably referring to some of the emails sent by Commissioner Ojienda), and that she did not see how our dissent could be physically included in the report at such a late stage of the process. This logistical barrier appeared to be a red herring, as it had already been demonstrated that the report could be printed and bound within a matter of hours.

It was now less than two hours before we were to assemble to meet with the president. I later learned that some of the staff had been informed about the handover earlier that day but had been expressly ordered by other commissioners not to inform me. Even Commissioner Shava conceded that she had been informed sometime in the "late morning" about the possibility of a handover that afternoon.

I did not attend the handover, primarily because the version of the report being handed over was not, in my view, the official and legal version of the report without our dissent. Even if I had wanted to attend, it would have been difficult for me to have returned home, changed into my suit, and then met everyone at State House given the late notice and the notoriously bad Nairobi traffic. Judge Chawatama did attend the handover but, like me, removed her signature from the volume of the report including the land chapter. Ambassador Dinka elected not to have his signature removed but also did not attend the handover. His absence, however, was due to the fact that he was still in the hospital and not necessarily in protest at the recent turn of events.

That evening, I was driving to meet some friends for dinner who had nothing to do with the Commission. I was staring vacantly out the window at a beautiful sunset when Judge Chawatama called me. Her voice was heavy. They had just left State House after handing over the report. She said she had kept her head low and mostly avoided making eye contact. She was very sad, as was I, that after all of our struggles it had to end this way.

Once the report was handed over to the President, we immediately made it available to the public through our website, www.tjrckenya.org.[20] We also arranged to have an abridged version, which ran a little over twenty pages,

---

[20] Sometime in 2014 or 2015, the TJRC website (which was operated by the Kenyan government) was taken down. A full copy of the final report, including the dissent and other related documents, can be found on the book's website: http://digitalcommons.law.seattleu .edu/tjrc/.

published in the major Kenyan newspapers. The report and its contents dominated the news for the next week. Our findings with respect to assassinations and massacres, as well as the list of over two hundred names that we had submitted for further investigation and possible prosecution, were discussed extensively in the media. The fact that we had recommended that our chair, Ambassador Kiplagat, also be investigated and prosecuted (the only time a truth commission has recommended that one of its own be further investigated, much less its chair) was widely discussed.[21]

The report is over 2,100 pages. In the first few days after it was issued, there were many comments in the media, both pro and con, from people who obviously had not read much, if any, of it. Politicians in particular began to support or oppose the report based upon their assumption of what we had said, rather than based on the actual content of the report. This was abundantly clear when, shortly after the release of the report, a member of Parliament from the opposition ODM party stated emphatically in Parliament that every recommendation in our report should be implemented and that every individual recommended for further investigation and possible prosecution should be investigated immediately. Our director of research sent me a text shortly after this speech, noting that that particular member of Parliament was on our list of those to be investigated. While some may have thought or hoped that our recommendations would be politically skewed against the ruling party and in favor of those in opposition, we had been scrupulous in not favoring one side of the political spectrum over another. If we received or discovered evidence suggesting an individual had been involved in a violation within our mandate, we included that information and appropriate recommendations within our report, regardless of the political affiliation of the individual.

We had also recommended that the president, on behalf of the country, apologize to the numerous victims of historical injustice. This recommendation in particular was criticized extensively shortly after the release of the report. The criticism was twofold. Some criticized the recommendation as weak and ineffective; others took great offense that the president should have to apologize for things for which he was not responsible. Regarding the first, many (though by no means all) of the victims with whom we spoke had, among other things, asked for an official acknowledgment and apology for the harms they had suffered. This was consistent with the wishes of many survivors of gross violations of human rights the world over. Regarding the second, we were asking the president not to apologize for anything he might have done;

---

[21] On why we recommended that our chair be investigated and potentially prosecuted, *see infra* Chapters 3 and 5.

rather, we were asking that as the president, representing the government and the nation, he apologize on behalf of all of those who, in the name of the state, had violated the fundamental rights of the thousands of victims of gross violations of human rights and historical injustices.

Ironically, and significantly, in March 2015, the president used his annual state of the nation address to, in fact, make the apology we had recommended. While we had originally recommended that such an apology be made within six months of the release of our report, the fact that it came almost two years after our recommendation is a relatively small delay in what is a significant, if symbolic, event.[22] In the same address in which he apologized on behalf of the nation, the president announced that he was establishing a ten-billion-shilling fund (approximately US $100 million) for "restorative justice." While it was not clear what he meant by stating that the funds would be used for "restorative justice," his announcement was combined with the revelation that he had received a report from the national prosecuting authority indicating that there would be no further prosecutions for those responsible for the violence arising out of the 2007 elections. It thus appears that the ten-billion-shilling program was to compensate for, and perhaps distract from, this decision not to engage in further investigations or prosecutions related to the election-related violence.

THE DISSENT MADE PUBLIC

With all of the media attention on the various findings and recommendations we had made with respect to a wide range of violations, Judge Chawatama, Ambassador Dinka, and I decided not to make public our decision to dissent from the land chapter. We feared that such an announcement and a public release of the dissent would dominate the news coverage at the expense of the extensive coverage that was being devoted to the rest of the report, including our findings and recommendations. We were also still concerned about our personal safety and wanted to wait until we were all three safely out of the country before going public with our dissent. There had already been some coverage of the fact that Judge Chawatama and I had removed our signatures from the volume of the report that contained the land chapter. We had declined to comment on why we had removed our signatures, indicating that we would be releasing a statement later, explaining our decision.

---

[22] We had also recommended that numerous government agencies, including the police and military, apologize for their institution's involvement with historical injustices. *See* TJRC FINAL REPORT, *supra* note 9, at Vol. IV.

Consequently, a few weeks after all three of us left the country, we issued a press release announcing that we had dissented from the land chapter. We also released a copy of our dissenting opinion, which identified those paragraphs of the report that had been censored and which included the original text of those paragraphs. As we had predicted, our dissent was on the front page of the major newspapers and was one of the top stories on the nightly television news. While we made clear in our dissent that we stood behind the integrity of all of the final report except for the altered paragraphs in the land chapter, some of the media coverage raised questions about the integrity of the entire report. Some even went so far as to misrepresent our dissent, claiming incorrectly that we had disavowed the content of the entire report.

The revelation that our dissent had been suppressed by the Commission led some civil society groups to contemplate going to court to have the dissent declared a part of the report. The dissent had been produced in compliance with our internal procedures, not to mention the right to dissent inherent in the rule of law, and thus there were strong legal arguments that it should form part of the final report. While I thought these were strong legal arguments, I counseled against mounting a legal challenge to have the dissent declared a part of the report. First, the main value of the dissent was its content, which was now part of the public record. The media had done a far more extensive job in making the dissent and its content known than it had with any other aspect of our operations. Second, there was a risk that the lawsuit might fail, which would perversely lessen the legitimacy of the dissent. While I could not imagine a judge in good faith ruling against such a suit, my experience with the Kenyan judiciary had led me to weigh more seriously the risk of losing in evaluating potential litigation. Third, it was not clear what would be gained by winning such a lawsuit, given that the content of the dissent was already public. Fourth, and finally, even in the best of circumstances, lawsuits are expensive and time consuming. It was not clear to me that such a lawsuit was worth spending precious time and resources, given other challenges facing Kenyan society. In the end, the organizations contemplating such a suit decided not to pursue it further.

Over five years since the release of our final report, the only recommendation that has been implemented has been the president's apology. Our extensive recommendations with respect to individuals who should be investigated and prosecuted have been ignored. Our elaborate recommendations for providing reparations to those who suffered from past historical injustices have also been ignored. The ten-billion-shilling "restorative justice" fund announced by the president in March 2015 has the potential to facilitate the implementation of many of the recommendations we made with respect to individual and collective reparations (including the creation of memorials, schools, medical clinics, etc.). As of this writing, however, no new information has been made public concerning this fund, leading many Kenyan observers to conclude that it is yet another in a long list of government promises that have been designed to conceal rather than address historical injustices. I hope those observers will be proven wrong, but all indications to date are that their cynical assessment will be vindicated.

2

The Most Expansive Mandate

FIGURE 2.1 TJRC Commissioners and Kofi Annan/Noor Khamis
(reproduced with permission)

Truth commissions have been around for at least forty years.[1] Argentina's
Comisión Nacional sobre la Desaparición de Personas (the National Commission on the Disappearance of Persons), established in 1983 to identify
disappeared individuals and acknowledge that they were victims of the military government, was the first major truth commission to receive significant
international attention. While early truth commissions were limited in their

---

[1] In her authoritative treatment of truth commissions, Priscilla Hayner lists the Commission of
Inquiry into the Disappearances of People in Uganda since 25 January 1971, which was formed
in 1974, as the first truth commission. *See* Priscilla Hayner, UNSPEAKABLE TRUTHS:
TRANSITIONAL JUSTICE AND THE CHALLENGE OF TRUTH COMMISSIONS (New York: Routledge,
2011), Appendix 1, Chart 1.

scope and weak in their powers, they opened the door for more robust investigations and eventually, in some cases, prosecutions. During their early period of development they were viewed as novel and innovative. While they provided no individual accountability, they did provide victims with a space in which they could share their stories, thus contributing to a national narrative about a divisive past. In addition, and perhaps even more importantly, they provided official acknowledgment to such victims that what had occurred to them was a violation of their fundamental rights.

While truth commissions vary enormously (by the number of years they cover, the types of violations within their mandate, their powers, and how much international involvement and legitimacy they enjoy), they are primarily designed to allow individuals to "tell their truths" about past injustices. Truth commissions are premised on the idea that public dialogue about the past that embraces diverse experiences and viewpoints will further truth through the creation of a national narrative; further justice through providing truth, acknowledgment of the past, and the promise of reparations; further guarantees of non-repetition by recommending systemic and institutional reforms; and further reconciliation and national unity through its contributions to truth and justice. Truth commissions are better designed than courts and other more formal legal processes to examine the systemic, institutional, and root causes of gross violations of human rights, and thus to make recommendations that, if implemented, will minimize the risk of such violations in the future.

The most innovative truth commission, and the one with which many are familiar, was the Truth and Reconciliation Commission in South Africa, chaired by Archbishop Desmond Tutu. The South African commission developed a number of innovative practices of truth commissions. First, the South African commission was one of the first commissions to hold public hearings in all regions of the country. Second, the South African commission held a number of thematic hearings covering, among other issues, prisons, the medical profession, the judiciary, the business community, and women. Third, the South African commission had an innovative, and controversial, amnesty process by which individuals could apply for and, if certain criteria were met, receive legal protection from both civil and criminal liability. Though it was, and still is, viewed with skepticism by many, this innovative amnesty process provided important contributions to truth, acknowledgment, and accountability. It has, however, not been adopted by any other country undergoing a similar transition, and it seems unlikely that it will.[2]

---

[2]   The criticism of the South African amnesty is based in part on the assertion that any amnesty for an international crime is contrary to existing or emerging principles of international law. While it is perhaps the case that amnesties are prohibited under international law for those

Truth commissions have become a popular institution for countries to use in addressing a legacy of gross violations of human rights. In good part because of the perceived success of the South African commission, many countries today reflexively turn to the creation of a truth commission in response to domestic and international pressure to do something about a past of atrocities and injustices. There is no question that truth commissions make a useful contribution as part of a broader effort to address the past, but too often countries and prominent international organizations turn to them as a ready-made solution to a complex situation. Establishing a truth commission is often embraced uncritically as a panacea to address a range of challenges faced by countries with very different histories and very different political, economic, social, and cultural realities. Many countries cynically "check the box" of forming a truth commission in order to signal that they are serious about addressing their troubled pasts, and that signal is often accepted both domestically and internationally as a serious step forward that will ultimately lead to a more just, democratic, and reconciled society.

I do not think all truth commissions are misplaced or that those who advocate for their creation are mistaken in their belief that such a commission can contribute to furthering such lofty goals as truth, justice, and reconciliation in a particular society. I do believe, however, that the international community has become complacent in the range of solutions it considers and often fails to think creatively and comprehensively about how best to address a legacy of gross violations of human rights. Part of the failure of the Kenyan truth commission can be traced to this failure of imagination in considering what institutions and processes would best further Kenya's stated desire to move beyond its history of ethnic conflict, violence, human rights violations, and other injustices.

To oversimplify, there was a sense in Kenya that because a truth commission had been established in South Africa and South Africa was perceived to have dealt thoroughly with its own violative past, such a mechanism would achieve the same result in Kenya. There are two problems with this assumption. First, while the South African truth commission certainly deserves some of the praise it continues to receive internationally, it was by no means a perfect institution, and it operated in a political environment very different than that of Kenya when our commission was created. The South African

most responsible for the worst international crimes, many of us who have studied the matter have concluded that there is far more flexibility with respect to the use of amnesties in addressing a legacy of atrocities, and that such flexibility is normatively positive. *See* THE BELFAST GUIDELINES ON AMNESTY AND ACCOUNTABILITY (Transitional Justice Institute, University of Ulster, 2013).

commission was created after a major political shift from the National Party government of apartheid to the parties of liberation that fought apartheid, most especially the African National Congress. While the National Party and its supporters still wielded significant power in newly democratic South Africa, they were declining and would continue to decline in power and influence. There was no such clear political shift in Kenya. As we set forth in our final report, each successive government in Kenya earned its fair share of blame for historical injustices. In 2002, many Kenyans thought they had finally broken this cycle of violations and impunity with the election of Mwai Kibaki. Kenyans greeted the election of Kibaki with enormous optimism, only to have their hopes dashed as it became clear that the new government elected on a promise of reform quickly fell back to the old, corrupt form of government and systemic injustices that characterized its predecessors. At best, one might argue that Kenya was in the midst of such a political shift, from a legacy of government abuse in all its forms (i.e., corruption, political assassinations, massacres, extra-judicial killings, etc.) to one that at least rhetorically was committed to ending such practices. The South African commission was also created at a time of immense optimism and hope brought about by the end of apartheid, the election of the African National Congress, and – perhaps more importantly – the election, and leadership, of Nelson Mandela. The Kenyan commission was created after a near genocide that took much of Kenyan society and the international community by surprise. There was no Nelson Mandela to provide direction and cohesion to an effort to create a new Kenyan society; rather what was created was a coalition government that was premised on political compromise, and that had the effect of institutionalizing some of the conflicts that facilitated some of those gross violations of human rights that the commission was meant to address.

Second, notwithstanding the more positive environment in which the South African truth commission was created and operated, there are serious doubts about how effective it was in furthering justice and reconciliation. A critical analysis of the South African truth commission is beyond the scope of this book, but some of my South African friends and colleagues increasingly argue that some of the fundamental problems facing South African society today (including increased corruption and political intolerance) may be explained in part by the failure of South Africa to address adequately the effect and legacy of apartheid during those first years of optimism under the presidency of Nelson Mandela. Almost twenty years after the South African truth commission finished its work, victims continue to pursue accountability for apartheid-era atrocities in the courts. In other words, it is not clear that the use of a truth commission in South Africa was as successful or useful as some argue, further raising the question of whether or how such an institution could play a constructive role in Kenya. Those who created the Kenyan commission tried to learn from some of the critiques of the South African commission, while at the same time cutting and pasting parts of the legislation creating the South African commission into Kenyan law with little thought or reflection concerning its applicability to Kenya.

THE ORIGINS OF A KENYAN TRUTH COMMISSION

Efforts to establish a truth commission in Kenya began as early as 1997.[3] That year, Kenya held its second multi-party election, which, like the earlier elections in 1992, was marred by violence. In response, Parliament passed a resolution to set up a truth commission to examine the election-related violence in 1992 and 1997. President Moi instead established a much weaker judicial commission of inquiry into the election violence. The judicial commission's report was not made public, and its recommendations were never acted upon.[4]

In April 2003, President Mwai Kibaki established the Task Force on the Establishment of a Truth, Justice and Reconciliation Commission. Mwai Kibaki had been elected in 2002, during the first multiparty election in Kenya's history. It was also the first election that was not dominated by politically motivated ethnic violence. During the campaign, Kibaki had promised far-reaching reforms. His election was greeted with great anticipation by Kenyans long tired of corruption; ethnic strife; state-sponsored torture, assassinations, and massacres; and impunity. It was a period of seemingly boundless optimism about the future of Kenya. Shortly after Kibaki's election, Gallup found Kenyans to be the most optimistic people in the world. The Kibaki government immediately moved to implement a number of reforms, including investigations into corruption, assassinations, and land. As Michela Wrong sets out in her excellent book, *It's Our Turn to Eat*,[5] the commitment of the Kibaki government to root out corruption at the highest levels of government was at best halfhearted and at worst a cynical ploy to provide a distraction from what was in reality a business-as-usual approach.

---

[3] *See* Godfrey Musila, "Options for Transitional Justice in Kenya: Autonomy and the Challenge of External Prescriptions," 3:3 *The International Journal of Transitional Justice*, 445–464 (2009).

[4] *Id.* at 449.

[5] Michela Wrong, It's Our Turn to Eat: The Story of a Kenyan Whistle-Blower (London: Fourth Estate, 2009).

In addition to exploring the establishment of a truth commission, the newly elected Kibaki administration created other investigative bodies to address past injustices. Parliament established a select committee to investigate the 1990 assassination of Foreign Minister Robert Ouko. The assassination of Ouko and the subsequent investigations would later present a substantial challenge for the TJRC, as we were to learn that our chair was accused of not cooperating fully with either this or any other investigations into Ouko's death.[6] This select committee investigation was the fourth such investigation into the Ouko assassination. Like the earlier investigations, and conforming to most previous government-sponsored investigations into past violations, its results were never made public and thus did little to shed light on the motives behind the killing or the identities of those responsible. Even worse, the suppression of the select committee's conclusions and other controversies surrounding its work fed into the numerous conspiracy theories that continue to surround the assassination and its cover-up.

The Kibaki administration also established a Commission on Land, known as the Ndung'u Commission after its chairman, Paul Ndiritu Ndung'u. The report of this commission also implicated our chair by claiming that he had benefited from either illegal or irregular allocations of land while serving in the Moi government. While its report was uncharacteristically made public, the Ndung'u Commission was also controversial as it appeared to only focus on individuals from certain ethnic groups, and it named individuals, including our chair, without providing them with an opportunity to respond to the allegations in the report.[7]

In addition to these piecemeal efforts to examine historical injustices, the Kibaki administration established a task force to determine whether it should establish a broader truth commission and, if so, what the mandate and powers of such a commission should be. The task force was chaired by Professor Makau Mutua, a prominent Kenyan human rights activist and scholar on the faculty of the law school of the State University of New York at Buffalo. The task force conducted hearings throughout Kenya to ascertain the level of support nationwide for a Kenyan truth commission. They also sponsored a national two-day conference in Nairobi and, a month later, they held another

---

6   Our chair, Ambassador Kiplagat, had been permanent secretary in the Ministry of Foreign Affairs under Robert Ouko. While I am not aware of any allegations that Ambassador Kiplagat was involved in any way in the assassination, some have speculated that he witnessed certain crucial events leading up to the assassination and had not been forthcoming with respect to his knowledge of the actions and motives of some of the prime suspects.

7   Our chair was later to acknowledge that the information in the Ndung'u report concerning his ownership of certain plots of land was accurate, though he was to dispute the allegation that receiving preferential access to land as a government official was improper, irregular, or illegal.

major conference in Nairobi with prominent international experts on truth commissions and human rights. Not surprisingly, both conferences concluded that Kenya should establish a truth, justice, and reconciliation commission.

Synthesizing the information it gathered from its provincial hearings, national conferences, written submissions, and commissioned research papers on truth commissions, the task force issued its report on August 26, 2003, recommending that no later than June 2004, the president should establish a truth, justice, and reconciliation commission with broad powers to address historical injustices committed between 1963 and 2002.[8] The report indicated that the "overwhelming majority of Kenyans" supported an effective truth commission, though it clarified that the basis for this assertion was that 90 percent of those who submitted their views to the task force had expressed such support.

As they traveled the country exploring the nation's interest in a TJRC, members of the task force frequently heard a common set of criticisms. Like many of the previous government commissions in Kenya (over forty since the country's independence), the task force members were criticized as highly paid elites who talked a lot but never achieved anything specific or concrete in the area of promised reforms, accountability, and justice.[9] When we as the TJRC began our public education campaign in January 2010, we would face similar criticisms. In another echo of the tensions that commonly arose with respect to such Kenyan commissions, the final report of the task force was not supported by three of its members, who argued that "it was selective and appeared to target certain leaders."[10]

In addition to the common criticisms leveled at government commissions, the task force was the subject of more specific criticisms arising from its own work, including suggestions that it had artificially inflated the broad support for a truth commission. As one anonymous civil society activist observed:

> I was alarmed when I looked at the [task force] report. Look at the number of people they interviewed, or met, and then came back and told us that an overwhelming number of Kenyans would want a TJRC. I think that across the country they did not meet more than 1,000 people.[11]

---

[8] REPORT OF THE TASK FORCE ON THE ESTABLISHMENT OF A TRUTH, JUSTICE AND RECONCILIATION COMMISSION (Nairobi: Government Printer) (August 26, 2003) [the "TASK FORCE REPORT"].

[9] *See* Lydiah Kemunto Bosire and Gabrielle Lynch, "Kenya's Search for Truth and Justice: The Role of Civil Society," 8:2 *The International Journal of Transitional Justice* 256, 264, at note 33 (2014).

[10] *Id.* at 261, note 20, *citing to* Nixon Ng'ang'a "Truth Body Formed to Probe Rights Abuses" *East African Standard*, October 16, 2003.

[11] *Id.* at 262, note 26.

Two scholars who have studied the issue extensively observed:

[W]hile the majority of people the [task force] met were supportive of a truth commission, the idea that over 90 per cent of Kenyans supported the process seems to have been a figure picked almost at random. More important, the actual conceptualization and articulation of what a Kenyan truth commission should look like was highly personalized around a small group of civil society activists.[12]

This analysis suggests that the creation of a Kenyan TJRC was driven less by broad grassroots national support and more by a top-heavy process dominated by a relatively small, though influential, section of Kenyan civil society. Even if accurate, this conclusion does not, in and of itself, mean that the creation of a TJRC was a bad idea; but it does explain the at times precarious public support the TJRC received, particularly when we lost the support of many of the same elite civil society actors who had pushed for our creation.

Kenya has one of the most active and educated civil societies in Africa. Yet, as I was to learn during my years working with the Commission, Kenyan civil society (particularly the major human rights–oriented organizations based in Nairobi) live in a small but highly contentious and self-referential world – not unlike the "Beltway" environment of Washington, DC. Professor Mutua, himself a prominent member of this Nairobi-based community, has observed that "the high public visibility of a few vocal NGOs deceptively gives the impression of a well-established, ubiquitous and formidable human rights movement. Nothing could be further from the truth."[13]

The Commission's relationship with these Nairobi-based organizations would prove to be an unnecessarily complicated (and ultimately, I am afraid, mostly unproductive) one, informed in part by the history of the task force, the failure of the government to establish a TJRC in 2004 as recommended, and the top-down ownership of the idea of a TJRC by some of the same "few vocal NGOs" identified by Professor Mutua. In contrast, the Commission's relationships with prominent victims' groups (including survivors of the Nyayo House torture chamber, victims of the failed 1982 coup, and families of victims of assassination), while not perfect, were far more supportive and productive.

While there were people both within and outside of the Kibaki administration who would feel threatened by a robust truth commission, the narrow, top-down approach to the creation of a TJRC adopted by the task force failed

---

[12] *Id.* at 262.
[13] *Id.* at 262, note 24, citing to Makau Mutua, KENYA'S QUEST FOR DEMOCRACY: TAMING LEVIATHAN (Kampala: Fountain Publishers, 2008), at 28.

to create a sufficiently broad political movement for its creation. Not surprisingly, therefore, the Kibaki administration did not follow the task force's recommendation in 2004 and refused to establish a TJRC. Notwithstanding this failure, some important reforms were implemented, including the creation of a national human rights organization that, under the initial chairmanship of Maina Kiai, proved to be a surprisingly effective and independent voice furthering the cause of human rights within the country. As time passed and attention shifted to other pressing issues, including ongoing corruption and police brutality, calls for the creation of a TJRC diminished.

Given the lack of political support for a TRJC after the task force report, a significant shift in the political environment would be required to create political pressure for the creation of such a commission. That political shift came primarily from two major challenges to Kenya's stability and legitimacy. First, the response to the near-genocidal violence after the December 2007 elections (commonly referred to in Kenya as the post-election violence or PEV) created political support for a truth commission. As part of the reform agenda arising out of that crisis and facilitated by, among others, the former UN Secretary General Kofi Annan, the members of the newly formed coalition government agreed to establish a TJRC to examine the root causes of that most recent crisis.[14] Second, the threatened involvement of the ICC in providing accountability for those most responsible for the PEV contributed to the political environment that led to the creation of the TJRC.

The origins of the idea of a TJRC as part of the reform agenda are unclear. The mediation sponsored by the Panel of Eminent African Personalities and spearheaded by its chair, Kofi Annan,[15] was conducted under the banner of the National Dialogue and Reconciliation process ("National Dialogue"). The National Dialogue was multifaceted, focusing on an immediate end to the violence; addressing the immediate needs of those injured and displaced as a result of the violence; solving the political crisis created by a disputed election; and agreeing to a number of institutional reforms that, it was hoped, would prevent future political disputes from so quickly devolving into near-genocidal violence.[16] Most of the agreements were negotiated and signed by a team of four individuals from each of the two political parties that had

---

[14] *See* Kenya National Dialogue and Reconciliation, "Truth Justice and Reconciliation Commission" (March 4, 2008); *see also* Kenya National Dialogue and Reconciliation, "Agenda Item Three: How to Resolve the Political Crisis," (February 14, 2008).

[15] The other two members of the panel were Graça Machel and Benjamin Mkapa.

[16] These goals were laid in a four-point agenda: Immediate Action to Stop Violence and Restore Fundamental Rights and Liberties (Agenda 1); Immediate Measures to Address the Humanitarian Crisis, Promote Reconciliation, Healing and Restoration (Agenda 2); How to

contested the election. For Mwai Kibaki's Party of National Unity (PNU), Martha Karua, Sam Ongeri, Mutula Kilonzo, and Moses Wetang'ula were the negotiators and signatories. For Raila Odinga's Orange Democratic Movement (ODM), Musalia Mudavadi, William Ruto, Sally Kosgei, and James Orengo were the negotiators and signatories. Kofi Annan brokered the central power-sharing agreement between the parties on behalf of the Panel of Eminent African Personalities. The agreement laying out the terms of reference for a TJRC, however, was achieved after Annan had departed the talks.[17]

The parties agreed on March 4, 2008, to establish the TJRC within the next four weeks. Perhaps not surprisingly, given previous efforts at similar reforms, it would be over a year before the Commission was created, and its creation was triggered by the second external event, the initiation of an investigation by the ICC into the PEV.[18] I was selected by the Panel of Eminent African Personalities in late April 2009. The Panel indicated to me that the Commission would be created within a matter of weeks and that I should thus prepare my affairs for moving to Kenya. Over the next few weeks, I periodically inquired into the status of the Commission's creation, only to be told that it would be created soon. On July 9th, Kofi Annan handed evidence to the prosecutor of the ICC. It was this act by Mr. Annan that eventually led the prosecutor to seek and obtain approval from a three-judge panel of the ICC to open an investigation into allegations of international crimes committed during the PEV. The involvement of the ICC appeared to have lit a fire under the Kenya government, as less than two weeks later President Kibaki formally appointed me and the other eight nominees to the TJRC.

TJRC LEGISLATION AND MANDATE

Between the March 2008 agreement and the eventual appointment of the TJRC commissioners over a year later, members of Parliament, domestic and international members of civil society, key players in the Ministry of Justice, and other stakeholders participated in the drafting of the Commission's enabling legislation.

Overcome the Current Political Crisis (Agenda 3); Long-Term Issues and Solutions (Agenda 4). *Annotated Agenda for the Kenya Dialogue and Reconciliation* (February 1, 2008).

[17]   While Annan fully supported the creation of the TJRC, the discussion that led to the final agreement on its creation was overseen by Oluyemi Adeniji, the former foreign minister of Nigeria, who replaced Annan as the facilitator of the talks in the final stages. *See* Serena K. Sharma, THE RESPONSIBILITY TO PROTECT AND THE INTERNATIONAL CRIMINAL COURT: PROTECTION AND PROSECUTION IN KENYA (New York: Routledge, 2016), 61.

[18]   For more on the ICC involvement and its effect on the TJRC, *see infra* Chapter 6.

The Kenyan Parliament passed the Truth, Justice and Reconciliation Act[19] on November 28, 2008, which was then amended in July 2009.[20] The act provided for nine commissioners – three international commissioners and six Kenyan commissioners. The Kenyan commissioners were chosen through a fairly robust public process that included formal input from civil society and the newly elected Parliament.[21] The three international commissioners were chosen by the Panel of Eminent African Personalities, consisting of Kofi Annan, Graça Machel, and Benjamin Mkapa. The proportion of one-third foreign and two-thirds Kenyan was an appropriate mix, and it is a structural model that might work well in other post-conflict contexts. The inclusion of foreign commissioners provides an opportunity to choose individual members more for their expertise than for the constituencies they may represent. The Kenyan commissioners – and this is not peculiar to Kenya – were, rightly so, representative of various stakeholders within the country. Thus the Kenyan commissioners came from different ethnic communities, which was particularly important in a country as ethnically divided as Kenya.[22] As I was later to learn firsthand, ethnicity plays an important, if often distracting and even destructive, role in Kenyan politics. The Kenyan commissioners also represented different political constituencies, as well as different sectors of Kenyan society. The Kenyan commissioners thus provided legitimacy and entrée within many important domestic communities. The international commissioners provided legitimacy and entrée in some domestic communities (such as the residents of North Eastern and the Coast who were generally suspicious of the Kenyan commissioners) and some of the international community, as well as providing international legitimacy and objectivity.

While our enabling legislation required international membership among the commissioners, all commissioners enjoyed equal terms of service and powers.

---

[19] TJRC Act, *supra* Chapter 1, note 3.

[20] The Statute Law (Miscellaneous Amendment) Act, 2009, *Kenya Gazette Supplement*, July 23, 2009, 547–548. The amendment most significantly increased the number of Commissioners from seven to nine, and made clear that the Commission could not recommend amnesty for any international crime or gross violation of human rights.

[21] There was, however, concern raised about the process of choosing the Kenyan Commissioners by, among others, Amnesty International. *See* Amnesty International, "Kenya: Concerns about the Truth, Justice and Reconciliation Commission Bill," AFR 32/009/2008 (May 2008) [AI Report], at 7 (criticizing the civil society selection panel as not being sufficiently representative).

[22] This sensitivity to ethnicity or race is not unique to Kenya. When the original names for commissioners for the South African Truth and Reconciliation Commission were presented to President Nelson Mandela, he immediately asked why there were no representatives of the "colored" population. As a result, two individuals from that community were included as members of the Commission.

This equality was tested in the first few months of the Commission when the government proposed to pay the Kenyan commissioners almost half what the international commissioners were being paid. In this first of many conflicts we were to have with the government, we quickly united and demanded that commissioners should be paid the same salary regardless of country of origin, and that the salary provided should be the amount agreed to with the international commissioners. It took us two months to resolve this issue with the government and another two months before we finally began to be paid.

There was no supermajority requirement for reaching a decision by the Commission. Consequently, the three international commissioners could (appropriately, in our view) be outvoted by the Kenyan commissioners.[23] It was only at the end of our process when the president's office directly intervened to change our report that a division developed between international and Kenyan commissioners. All other divisions within the Commission, including some that threatened our very existence, did not cleave along international-domestic lines.

While the international commissioners could be outvoted, the act also provided that at least one international commissioner had to be present at a Commission meeting to constitute a quorum. In other words, while the Kenyan commissioners could outvote the international commissioners, they could not act without the knowledge of at least one of the international commissioners. (The fact that there were only three international commissioners obviously made it impossible for the international commissioners to reach a decision of the Commission without the knowledge, and the vote, of at least two Kenyan commissioners.) This concession to transparency struck an appropriate balance between Kenya and the interests of the international community in what was fundamentally and appropriately a Kenyan process.

Two significant features distinguished the Kenyan commission from truth commissions established in other countries, and they were added to address common criticisms leveled at such earlier commissions. First, we were one of the few truth commissions to include "Justice" in its title.[24] The South African

---

[23] Compare this to the relationship between the international and Cambodian members of the Extraordinary Chambers in the Courts of Cambodia (ECCC), the hybrid tribunal established to prosecute members of the Khmer Rouge. In the ECCC, for example, a decision of the court requires the concurrence of at least one international judge, effectively providing the international judges with a veto power.

[24] The only previous examples appear to be the Haitian Commission Nationale de Vérité et de Justice, which operated from April 1995 to February 1996, and the Mauritius Truth and Justice Commission, which operated from 2009 to 2011. The Sierra Leone truth commission was originally proposed as a Truth Justice and Reconciliation Commission, but it was ultimately called a Truth and Reconciliation Commission. *See* Rosalind Shaw, "Rethinking

truth commission, for example, had been criticized for its lack of reference to justice, spawning cartoons depicting Justice off to the side while Truth and Reconciliation took center stage.[25] There is some evidence that those who negotiated the agreements that led to the creation of the TJRC placed particular emphasis on the importance of justice as a guiding principle of the commission. The two sets of negotiating parties signed a statement of principles regarding long-term issues and solutions that referred to the TJRC under the heading of "Transparency, Accountability, and Impunity," and not under the heading of "Consolidation of National Cohesion and Unity."[26] How much emphasis to give to justice and how much to national unity and reconciliation was to be a recurring, and at times contentious, discussion within the Commission. While one may question the symbolic significance of including (or not) Justice in the title of the Commission, its presence in the title provided support to those of us on the inside who argued for a more justice-oriented approach to parts of our mandate.

Second, in response to perceived deficiencies in the breadth of violations examined by previous commissions, we were given the broadest mandate of any such commission before or since. Previous truth commissions had primarily focused on violations of bodily integrity rights – killings, massacres, sexual violence, torture, disappearances. This limited focus on bodily integrity violations was viewed by some as a mistake, and the failure to include other violations as a missed opportunity. While truth commissions were originally limited to the investigation of state-sponsored violations, particularly disappearances, they were increasingly being asked (at least in the activist and academic communities) to take on a much more sophisticated and comprehensive role of analyzing the structural, systemic, and institutional roots of gross violations of human rights. One of the more trenchant criticisms of the South African commission was its failure to examine apartheid itself as a crime; instead the South African TRC primarily limited itself to acts that

Truth and Reconciliation Commissions: Lessons from Sierra Leone," *USIP Special Report* 130, at 4 (February 2015).

[25] *See, e.g.*, Ronald C. Slye, "Amnesty," in Wilhelm Verwoerd and M. Mabizela, TRUTHS DRAWN IN JEST (Cape Town: David Philip Publishers, 2000), 77–102.

[26] Kenya National Dialogue and Reconciliation, "Statement of Principles on Long-Term Issues and Solutions" (May 23, 2008). Somewhat confusingly, the same document includes a table of implementation mechanisms which does include the TJRC under Consolidating National Unity and Reconciliation and not under Transparency, Accountability and Impunity. Even more confusing, the attached matrix that is expressly referred to in the May 23, 2008, signed agreement is itself dated over two months later, on July 30, 2008.

were illegal even under apartheid law: killings, torture, disappearances, and severe ill-treatment.[27]

Some have argued that the Kenyan mandate was too broad.[28] The breadth of the mandate is best measured not by the length of the time period we were to investigate (forty-five years, from December 12, 1963, when Kenya attained independence, to February 28, 2008, which was the date of the formal signing of the National Accord)[29], but by the breadth of the substantive violations we were obligated to address. The law required us to investigate the following violations of human rights: abductions, disappearances, detentions, torture, sexual violations, murder, extrajudicial killings, ill-treatment, expropriation of property, massacres, economic crimes, violations of socioeconomic rights (health, education, housing, etc.), grand corruption, exploitation of natural resources, irregular and illegal acquisition of public land, economic marginalization, perceived economic marginalization, misuse of public institutions for political objectives, cruel or degrading treatment committed by the state for political objectives, and ethnic tensions.[30] The motivation for such a broad mandate was to make sure that we looked holistically at a broad range of violations, thus ensuring that we would be in a better position to explain and address past violations and develop recommendations to prevent their recurrence.

In the best of circumstances, we (or anyone else, for that matter) would not be able to do justice in a two-year period to all of the specific types of violations that we were required to investigate, much less provide an "accurate, complete and historical record" of all such violations,[31] and "identify and specify the victims of the violations and abuses and make appropriate

---

[27] Though the South African Truth and Reconciliation Commission did conclude that apartheid qualified as a crime against humanity. TRUTH AND RECONCILIATION COMMISSION OF SOUTH AFRICA REPORT (Palgrave Macmillan, 2001) [the "SA TRC REPORT"], Vol. 1, 94–102.

[28] See AI Report, supra note 21, at 10 (criticizing the breadth of the mandate). One astute Kenyan observer of the process noted that "[w]hile the need for a comprehensive inquiry is recognized, the attempt to amalgamate into one process every ill that has afflicted the country is problematic." Musila, supra note 3, at 453.

[29] The act also made clear that we should look at the antecedents to the violations committed during this period (which was a clear reference to the colonial period), and we were also empowered to investigate or make recommendations concerning "any other matter with a view to promoting or achieving justice, national unity, or reconciliation within the context of the Act." TJRC Act, supra Chapter 1, note 3, at Art. 5(2). We thus did look at events prior to independence and a few events after February 28, 2008 that we felt were relevant to understanding issues within our core mandate.

[30] TJRC Act, supra Chapter 1, note 3, at Art. 6.

[31] Id. at Arts. 5(a) – (b).

recommendations,"[32] *and* identify those responsible who should be prosecuted,[33] *and* make recommendations for preventing such abuses in the future.[34] Even this list of objectives does not fully capture all that the act required of us with respect to the substantive areas of our mandate.[35] We were quickly to learn that we were not operating in the best of circumstances.

CHALLENGES OF TIME AND MONEY

We were originally given a two-year operational period to achieve all of the goals set out in our enabling legislation. Given that we were a newly created *ad hoc* Commission, Kenya adopted the best practices of other truth commissions and provided us with a three-month establishment period, during which we were meant to hire the majority of our staff, develop internal policies and procedures, and finalize our work plan. After the three-month setting-up period, we were given two years to focus on our core mandate-related activities. At the end of the two-year operational period, we were obliged to hand over our final report to the president and release it to the public. After the handing over of our report, we would have another three months to wind down the Commission, including organizing and securing our archives. Our legislation also provided that Parliament could grant us an additional six-month period of operations after we submitted such a request and a progress report on our work justifying the request. Under this timeline, we were to begin our operations in November 2009, hand over our report in November 2011, and finish our work by February 2012. If Parliament granted us a six-month extension, we would be obliged to release our report in May 2012, and finish our work by August 2012. In the end, we requested and received additional extensions such that our report was not released until a year later, in May 2013. Some of those extensions were due to conditions outside of our control – the lack of political and financial support we received from the government and other important stakeholders, including affirmative acts by the government to delay (and, as some said, to sabotage) our progress – and some were supported, and perhaps even initiated, by us – the decision to request an additional year so that our report would be released after the March 2013 presidential election.

---

[32] *Id.* at Art. 6(c).
[33] *Id.* at Art. 6(f).
[34] *Id.* at Art. 6(l).
[35] See Articles 5–6 in particular. Article 6 has 20 subsections setting out specific areas of focus and activity.

It is difficult to believe that any of those involved in the drafting of the Commission's mandate genuinely thought that an *ad hoc* Commission with limited resources would be able to address adequately all aspects of this expansive mandate in two years. This is particularly so given that Parliament failed to ensure that we would have immediate and adequate funding upon our creation, forcing us to spend a significant part of our first year lobbying for funding, including our own salaries, and thus little time on the substantive investigations and other activities with which we were entrusted. It was not until January 2011 that we would be given sufficient funds to undertake our major mandate-related activities. This meant that we effectively lost over one year of our original two-year operational period. It was clear that Parliament did not want to make some of the hard choices about what we should cover given the broad history of injustices; instead, Parliament left to us the task of prioritizing among the vast array of violations specified in our mandate but failed to provide us with adequate resources to perform this important task.[36]

CHANNELING SOUTH AFRICA: OUR MISGUIDED AMNESTY

One of the more controversial parts of our mandate concerned amnesty. Unlike the South African TRC, we did not have the power to grant, but only the power to recommend, amnesty. In part as a result of the input of domestic and international human rights organizations,[37] our enabling legislation was amended before we were established to limit our power even to recommend amnesty, making clear that we could not do so for acts that qualified as either an international law crime (i.e., torture, genocide, crimes against humanity, and war crimes) or as a gross violation of human rights. Prior to the amendment, the legislation had already provided that we could not recommend amnesty for extrajudicial execution, enforced disappearance, sexual assault, rape, and torture. In other words, the universe of acts for which we could recommend

---

36 Though if Parliament really wanted to leave it to our discretion, it would have listed all of these areas of activity as examples of what we *could* investigate and analyze to further the goals of truth, justice, and reconciliation. Instead, the act required us to address all of the violations listed without expressly giving us discretion to pick and choose among them.

37 *See, e.g.,* AI Report, *supra* note 21; Multi-Sectoral Task Force on Truth, Justice and Reconciliation Commission, "Analysis and Concerns on the Truth Justice Reconciliation Commission (TJRC) Bill 2008 Adopted by the National Assembly on 23 October 2008 and Assented into Law by President Yesterday" (November 2008). The Office of the High Commissioner for Human Rights (OHCHR) made clear in an early report that if the TJRC were empowered to either grant or recommend amnesty for gross violations of human rights, it would not be able to provide support to the Commission. OHCHR, "Report from OHCHR Fact-Finding Mission to Kenya, 6–28 February 2008," at 17.

amnesty was very limited. Since most of the acts we were supposed to investigate qualified as gross violations of human rights or an international crime, there was little overlap between the core of our mandate and our amnesty powers.

Despite this very limited power with respect to amnesty the act included a very detailed and confusing section on amnesty – in fact, eight of the fifty-three articles in the act were devoted to amnesty. Some of the amnesty provisions in the Kenyan act appear to have been taken verbatim from the South African legislation with little attention to their relevance to the Kenyan situation. They included detailed provisions with respect to the procedures for determining whether to recommend amnesty that are similar to the South African procedures. They also included a set of criteria to which we were to refer in determining whether to recommend amnesty. These criteria repeat almost to the word what was provided in the South African legislation.[38] Those criteria directed us to look at the political motive of the applicant in committing the act for which he was seeking amnesty. The political motive requirement made sense in the South African TRC, which expressly limited itself to human rights violations directly related to the political conflict between the apartheid state and the liberation movements. It made little sense in the case of the Kenyan TJRC, which, except for the amnesty provisions, did not distinguish between acts committed with a political motive and those committed for some other reason. The fact that our mandate was not limited to expressly political activities allowed us to look at a much wider range of violations than our South African counterpart – including, for example, the tradition of child brides, the treatment of workers by a private organization, and lack of access to education or health care. Requiring a political motive would have limited the scope of these parts of our mandate in a way that would have undercut many of the purposes of creating a Kenyan TRJC in the first place.

The suspicion that the amnesty provisions of the Kenyan act were mostly cut and pasted from the South African legislation was also supported by the fact that many of the Kenyan provisions refer to the Commission "granting" rather than "recommending" amnesty. One of the references to "grant" was replaced with "recommend" as part of the first amendments to the legislation, but other such references remained in the legislation during our entire operational period.

---

[38] The Kenyan legislation differs from the South African in not including the requirement of proportionality and in not excluding acts that were committed for personal gain or out of malice, ill will, or spite.

Our amnesty powers were thus extremely limited. I was of the opinion that they should not have been included in our legislation as they created an unnecessary source of controversy that we frequently had to address. Some critics, including some sophisticated civil society organizations, mistakenly stated that we would be granting amnesty for massacres, assassinations, etc. One of the Kenyan commissioners, Professor Tom Ojienda, in an article published on a blog of a local radio station shortly after we were formed, confusingly suggested that our powers were similar to that of the South African commission: "As in the South African case, Kenyan applicants should apply for amnesty individually and make full disclosure in public. Shame will be the most effective punishment."[39] South Consulting, which was retained by the Panel of Eminent African Personalities to monitor the progress of reforms arising out of the National Accord, including the TJRC, mistakenly stated that our act was amended in 2009 "to the effect that there would be no amnesty for perpetrators of Post Election Violence who are guilty of international crimes."[40] As noted above, the 2009 amendments were much broader, not allowing us to recommend amnesty for any gross violation of human rights or international crime arising at any time during our mandate period, and not just out of the PEV. There was thus an understandable, though mistaken, perception among some that we had been established to provide amnesty to those most responsible for gross violations of human rights, which we could not do even if we wanted (which we did not). The fact that one of the commissioners seemed to suggest that we could provide such amnesty, and that the monitoring body of the Panel misunderstood our amnesty powers, contributed to such misperceptions. While the amnesty provisions thus provided fodder to our critics, we did not reap the benefits of an amnesty for truth deal as the South African commission had.

There were two areas within our mandate where we might have used our amnesty powers: corruption and violations related to land. One could argue that corruption – certainly grand corruption – and large land grabs can be characterized as gross violations of human rights and thus outside the scope of our amnesty powers.[41] There is no question that grand corruption and large

---

[39] "Ten Lessons for the TJRC," *Justice for Kenya* (Capital FM), July 28, 2009.

[40] South Consulting, FOURTH REVIEW REPORT ANNEX I (SUMMARY OF PROGRESS ON AGENDA 4: LONG-STANDING ISSUES AND SOLUTIONS) (October 2009), 9.

[41] Some have argued that corruption might rise to the level of a crime against humanity. In fact the former Kenyan Minister of Justice, Kiraitu Murungi, has made such an argument. This is ironic given the continued incidence of grand corruption in Kenya and the failure of any government to date to address the problem adequately. *See* Ruben Carranza, PLUNDER AND PAIN (New York: International Center for Transitional Justice, 2008) 328, at note 93.

land grabs were linked to, and in some cases direct causes of, gross violations of human rights in Kenya. If we were able to conclude that some of these violations did not themselves constitute gross violations of human rights, we could use our amnesty powers to try to elicit additional information concerning corruption and land.

We did enter into discussions with the national anticorruption agency in order to better coordinate our efforts with theirs in this area. We reached out to them (as we did with many other organizations working in areas related to our mandate) in order to determine what our best "value added" could be with respect to anticorruption efforts. Unfortunately, our efforts to work with the anticorruption agency did not bear much fruit. This was in part because a vocal section of civil society roundly criticized us for appearing to grant amnesty to those guilty of grand corruption (which, of course, we could not, and thus had not, done). Our partnership with the anticorruption agency also did not bear much fruit because the agency itself was highly politicized and itself vulnerable to corruption.

Although our amnesty powers were limited, the act did provide a strong incentive for individuals to provide us with information related to historical injustices and other gross violations of human rights. Like many truth commissions, as well as commissions of inquiry more generally, an individual's testimony before us could not be used against that individual in any civil or criminal proceeding. This testimonial immunity is not uncommon in most legal systems throughout the world. Our legislation, however, went further. In addition to providing that an individual's testimony could not later be used against the person testifying, any evidence *or information* provided by that individual could not be later used against him.[42] Thus, if an individual provided us with documents or other information related to a violation, that information could not be used later to prosecute or otherwise hold liable that individual for such violation.[43] This was, I thought, a very broad provision that might provide us with the opportunity to elicit information from individuals, including government officials, concerning their knowledge of historical injustices and other violations. We did not capitalize on this potential carrot, which was appropriate given its potential abuse by perpetrators.

---

[42] TJRC Act, *supra* Chapter 1, note 3, at Art. 24(3).
[43] Amnesty International correctly criticized this provision as violating basic principles of international human rights law and international criminal law. See AI Report, *supra* note 21, at 6.

PARTICIPATION BY WOMEN

One of the challenges identified by the Mutua task force when it recommended the creation of a truth commission was the low participation of
women in their process. In their report, the task force observed that while
their provincial hearings were "on the whole" well attended, the number
of women participating in the hearings was "low."[44] The experience of the
Mutua task force mirrored that of truth commissions generally. Female participation in truth commission processes worldwide has been low, leading more
recent truth commissions to create special units to encourage the participation
of more women.[45]

Feminist critiques of truth commissions tend to focus on two issues.[46] First,
truth commissions ignore or do not devote sufficient attention to systemic,
structural, and institutional violence that tends to affect women disproportionately. Second, truth commissions are not designed to encourage the participation of women, and thus perpetuate the silencing of women in those
societies. The drafters of our enabling act were sensitive to these critiques,
requiring that there be gender balance among the commissioners (we began
with five male and four female commissioners); requiring that the chair and
vice chair be of opposite gender, including sexual- and gender-based violence
in the violations we were to investigate; and suggesting that we put into place
special mechanisms and procedures to address the experiences of women.
During most of our operational period, our CEO was a woman, and during
the fourteen months when we conducted most of our external activities (statement taking, public hearings, investigations, and other outreach activities),

---

[44] TASK FORCE REPORT, *supra* note 8, at 14.
[45] *See* Kimberly Theidon, "Gender in Transition: Common Sense, Women, and War," 6 *Journal
of Human Rights* 453–478 (2007), which provides a good general discussion of attempts to
incorporate a greater gender sensitivity to transitional justice processes, focusing in particular
on Peru.
[46] For a good introduction to feminist critiques and transitional justice, *see* Christine Bell and
Catherine O'Rourke, "Does Feminism Need a Theory of Transitional Justice? An Introductory
Essay," 1 *The International Journal of Transitional Justice* 23–44 (2007). Bell and O'Rourke pose
three sets of questions. (1) Where are women (both representation and participation in
transitional justice design and process)? (2) Where is gender (where are the voices and
experiences of women with respect to conflict, human rights violations and justice)? (3) Where
is feminism (referring to the feminist critique of justice and its applicability to transitional
justice)? For another thoughtful discussion of feminist legal theory and transitional justice,
see Fionnuala Ní Aoláin, "Advancing a Feminist Analysis of Transitional Justice," in Martha
Albertson Fineman and Estelle Zinsstag, eds., FEMINIST PERSPECTIVES ON TRANSITIONAL
JUSTICE: FROM INTERNATIONAL AND CRIMINAL TO ALTERNATIVE FORMS OF JUSTICE
(Cambridge: Intersentia, 2013).

our acting chair was a woman – Tecla Namachanja Wanjala was the first woman to serve as the chair of a truth commission.

While we rightly point out in our report that women made up 50 percent of our senior leadership team, a look at the substantive areas led by men compared to women shows that we replicated the gendered bias of the professions found not only in Kenya but in most parts of the world. For example, the directors of our legal department, investigations, and research were all men. Women were directors of our media, special support, and administration and finance departments. This gendered distribution of leadership mirrored that found in the broader Kenyan society. For example, a chart we included in our final report shows, among other things, that the percentage of professionals in Kenya who are women is 13.3 percent, compared to 86.7 percent men.[47] A woman who participated in the women's hearing in Bungoma noted that "[i]f there is a seat being vied for, the one we can get is the position of Treasurer because they know women can take care of property. The men take the decision-making positions."[48]

During our first eight months, Kaari "Betty" Murungi was a commissioner (and for most of that time our vice chair). Commissioner Murungi brought a wealth of knowledge and experience to the Commission concerning human rights struggles in Kenya and internationally. In particular, she was one of the world's foremost experts on gender and transitional justice, having worked as a consultant on gender issues with the Sierra Leonean Truth and Reconciliation Commission. (She and I were the only commissioners who had previously worked for a truth commission; Judge Chawatama also had similar experience, having worked on a truth commission–like inquiry on torture in her native Zambia). Commissioner Murungi's insights and recommendations in general, but in particular with respect to incorporating a gendered perspective into the Commission, were instrumental in establishing policies and procedures that would benefit us throughout the life of the Commission. Unfortunately, because of our chair's conflicts of interest with respect to significant parts of our mandate and the delay (and ultimate failure) to have those conflicts addressed through an independent and legally sanctioned process, Commissioner Murungi resigned from the Commission in April 2010.

We adopted a three-prong approach to address gender-related issues. First, we "mainstreamed" gender by expressly including a gender focus in most of our activities. Second, we established a special unit that would both focus on

---

[47] "Gender Disparities in Employment Opportunities," TJRC FINAL REPORT, *supra* Chapter 1, note 9, at Vol. IIC, Ch. 1, p. 42, Table 1.

[48] RTJRC09.07 (Tourist Hotel, Bungoma) (Women's Hearing), July 9 2011, p. 14.

gender (as well as other systemic forms of discrimination) and facilitate the mainstreaming of gender in the rest of our work.[49] In addition, we developed partnerships with the largest women's organization in Kenya, Maendeleo ya Wanawake, and with the Gender Violence Recovery Center of the Nairobi Women's Hospital, to both increase women's access to our processes as well as to provide additional support to women, particularly those women who were victims of sexual violence. The result of this three-prong approach can be seen in our statement taking (which included a gender-related training component for all statement takers); our hearings (which included separate women's only hearings); and our final report, which includes an analysis of the gender dimensions of most of the violations we examined and also dedicates an entire chapter to gender and an entire chapter to sexual- and gender-based violence.

Addressing the first feminist critique – the failure to address systemic and structural violence that tends to affect women disproportionately – was easier for us to address compared to other truth commissions given our broad mandate and, in particular, the requirement that we investigate violations of socioeconomic rights. To better analyze systemic and structural issues, including those related to socio economic rights, we needed to address effectively the second critique – the failure to encourage active participation of women, a failure that had already been experienced by the Mutua Task Force.

In addition to dedicating specific parts of our statement-taking form to capturing the experience of women, training our statement takers on gender sensitivity, and ensuring a high percentage of female statement takers (43 percent), we also conducted thirty-nine of what we called women's hearings in each of the places where we held public hearings. Our challenge was not just to get women to participate and speak to the Commission, but also to get them to speak about violations and related issues experienced by them. The experience of previous truth commissions suggested that women who were willing to speak about past violations tended to speak as witnesses and observers concerning incidents that had happened to others, usually the male members of their family. The characterization of such testimony as indirect is itself problematic, as it tends to de-emphasize the secondary effects of violations on family members and community members and more fundamentally emphasize the individualistic, rather than community-oriented, aspect of violations. While women may testify about what happened to others in their

---

[49] In fact, this approach is the one recommended by a major study of gender and truth commissions published by the International Center for Transitional Justice. Vasuki Nesiah, et al., TRUTH COMMISSIONS AND GENDER: PRINCIPLES, POLICIES, AND PROCEDURES (New York: International Center for Transitional Justice) (July 2006) 4–5.

family or community because they are reluctant to testify about themselves, they may also focus on violations directly experienced by their family and community members because they see themselves as part of those larger social entities and, thus, are more likely than men to see such violations of "others" as affecting them, their families, and their communities directly.[50] Nevertheless, we were concerned that some women might feel reluctant to share their own direct experiences of violations out of fear rather than because of a more holistic approach to violations and their effects.

In addition to holding women's hearings in each place where we held public hearings, we often had a prominent woman activist from each community testify about the experience of women generally in that community. We were able to do this in part because of the strong working relationship we had developed with Maendeleo ya Wanawake, the largest women's membership organization in Kenya. We were thus able to explore at the local level some of the broader systemic, institutional, and cultural issues faced by women. To further broaden this analysis, we devoted one of our national thematic hearings to women. The purpose of the thematic hearing was to supplement the individual stories we had heard in the field – both from witnesses as well as local activists – with a more national and even international perspective on the broader systemic issues facing women in Kenya.

We collected and analyzed all of this information for inclusion in our final report. The report thus includes an analysis of gender-based persecution and systematic discrimination against women (for example, the preference for the boy child in some communities, and the marginalization that is then created from birth for the girl child). We discuss the link between traditional practices (bride price, female genital cutting, early and forced marriage, and widow inheritance) and other rights violations such as poverty, illiteracy, reduced life expectancy, and reduced access to education. We devote an entire section of our chapter on gender to the socioeconomic status of women, where we discuss the feminization of poverty, disparities in employment (including disparities across different employment categories); workplace abuse, including sexual harassment and violence; the lack of women's ownership or even co-ownership of land and the effect of this reality on other violations suffered by women; reproductive health and women's limited access to medical facilities and services; HIV/AIDs; leadership and political participation (including

---

[50] For a thoughtful discussion of women, silence, and testimony that discusses other factors that may explain the reluctance of some women to testify about themselves, *see* Theidon, *supra* note 45.

the link between systemic discrimination and the lack of female representation in government, and the effect of lack of female political leaders on perpetuating such systemic discrimination); women in armed conflict; and forced displacement and its impact on women and girls.

Sensitive to the common criticism of previous truth commissions that women are often portrayed as victims and not as agents in their final reports, we include stories of empowered women in the context of historical violations.[51] We also include discussion of the important role women have played in peacemaking in Kenya and the east African region.

We were also sensitive to the tendency of previous truth commissions to reduce women's experience with human rights violations to gender-based and sexual violence. We deliberately created separate chapters for the discussion of gender discrimination and for gender-based and sexual violence. In fact, the sexual violence chapter includes information we had gathered concerning sexual violence against men, a phenomenon also commonly overlooked not just by truth commissions but by many institutions dedicated to documenting and preventing human rights violations. Our gender chapter, titled "Gender and Gross Violations of Human Rights: A Focus on Women," is 161 pages long.[52] Our chapter on sexual violence is fifty-eight pages long and expressly discusses the linkages between gender- and sexual-based violence and other violations and consequences that previous truth commissions were criticized for ignoring. We thus include a discussion of the link between sexual violence and access to adequate healthcare; the effects of rape, including unwanted pregnancies, unwanted children, and the impact on the individual, family, and community of such "unwanted" or stigmatized children; and sexual violence committed against men.

THE CHALLENGE OF CAPTURING SOCIOECONOMIC RIGHTS AND THEIR VIOLATION

One of the most important developments in transitional justice practice adopted by Kenya was the inclusion of socioeconomic violations within our mandate. No previous truth commission had been given such a broad, or

---

[51] *See, e.g.,* TJRC Final Report, *supra* Chapter 1, note 9, at Vol. IIC, Ch.1, pp. 70–1, where we recount, from one of our women's hearings, the story in her own words of a woman who joined a public campaign against HIV/AIDs.

[52] Only one chapter was significantly longer: Unlawful Killings and Enforced Disappearances at 440 pages. Two others of equal importance to understanding historical injustices in Kenya were of comparable length: Land and Conflict (176 pages); and Economic Marginalization and Violations of Socio-Economic Rights (163 pages).

obligatory, mandate with respect to socioeconomic rights. While some previous truth commissions had briefly touched upon economic issues, those were often directly related to understanding more traditional violations. The Sierra Leonean TRC, for example, looked at diamond and other economic exploitation as a driver of the armed conflict in that country. The Liberian TRC looked at the relationship between the timber, mining, and telecommunications industries and that country's conflict.[53]

In contrast to this international practice with respect to truth commissions, the earliest debates in Kenya about establishing a truth commission included references to economic issues, including corruption and other economic crimes.[54] A fact-finding mission from OHCHR to Kenya near the end of the 2007 post-election violence noted the importance of historical violations of socioeconomic rights in Kenya, including lack of access to water, food, health, housing, and employment, in understanding the then-crisis facing Kenya.[55]

Scholars in the field of transitional justice have criticized the lack of examination of socioeconomic violations by truth commissions and other transitional justice mechanisms, and they argue that the failure to examine economic power and how it relates to oppression is a serious, if not fatal, lacuna in addressing an oppressive past.[56] The interference by the president's office to alter the discussion in our final report of the land holdings of the president's family, particularly concerning actions allegedly undertaken by the father of the current president, Jomo Kenyatta, to amass large tracts of land during his presidency, shows how sensitive, and thus perhaps how important, such analysis is. Our discussion of these matters led to no findings concerning the first family and land (an omission for which we could be rightly criticized), yet even this less threatening approach prompted interference from the most powerful office in the land. While we made no significant findings on land, we did establish that President Jomo Kenyatta was involved in the coverup of at least one political assassination and made a finding to that effect. The fact that merely reproducing allegations by a witness concerning the first family and land

---

[53] See also the reports of the East Timor Commission for Reception, Truth and Reconciliation (which looks at famine and forced displacement), the Liberian Truth and Reconciliation Commission, and the Chadian Commission of Inquiry into the Crimes and Misappropriations Committed by Ex-President Habre, His Accomplices and/or Accessories (which included within its mandate narcotics trafficking and embezzlement of state funds).

[54] *See* Musila, *supra* note 3, at 460.

[55] OHCHR, *supra* note 37, at 6.

[56] *See, e.g.,* Zinaida Miller, "Effects of Invisibility: In Search of the 'Economic' in Transitional Justice," 2 *The International Journal of Transitional Justice* 266–291 (2008). *See also* Ruben Carranza, *supra* note 41, at 310, for some suggestions on why, and how, a truth commission could incorporate economic issues into its mandate.

triggered such overt interference in our process, while a finding concerning involvement in a political assassination was barely noticed, underscores how economic power and interests lie at the heart of historical injustices, and thus how important it is for truth commissions to address economic violations, and their causes and contexts, to understand fully such injustices.

As with other parts of our mandate, our act uses inconsistent language to refer to socioeconomic rights and violations. There are references to "economic crimes,"[57] "violations and abuses of economic rights,"[58] "gross violations of economic rights,"[59] "economic marginalization,"[60] and "grand corruption."[61] None of these terms or phrases is defined in the definitional section of the act. When we asked those involved in the drafting of the legislation what was meant, for example, by the term "economic crimes," we were told that it was intended to cover all violations of socioeconomic rights as those rights are set forth in the International Covenant on Economic, Social and Cultural Rights.

In thinking about how to implement our mandate with respect to socioeconomic rights and related violations, we faced a number of challenges. First, how were we to define the scope of this part of our mandate? Second, what investigative and other activities should we undertake to further this part of our mandate? Third, what is the relationship between these violations and the rest of our mandate in, among other activities, the writing of our final report?

Socioeconomic violations can be the result of other violations, the cause of other violations, or freestanding violations independent of other human rights violations. A campaign of ethnic cleansing can (and often does) result in the destruction of housing, health facilities, and education facilities, thus resulting in or contributing to violations of the right to access to housing, health, and education. As illustrated by testimony we received concerning the Wagalla massacre, denial of access to food and water can lead to death through exposure, and thus a violation of the right to life. Denial of access to education or housing may lead individuals to protest such denials, which may, in turn, lead to a state response that rises to the level of a violation of other human rights, including the right to association or the right to life. Finally, barriers to access to health or educational facilities are violations irrespective of whether they result in death or other physical manifestations. Human dignity, and the ability to live a full and enriching life, is at the core of the promise of a human

[57] TJRC Act, *supra* Chapter 1, note 3, at Art. 5(f)
[58] *Id.* at Art. 5(a)
[59] *Id.* at Art. 5(b).
[60] *Id.* at Art. 6(p).
[61] *Id.* at Art. 6(n).

rights culture that protects an individual from violations of all of her inalienable rights. As we began to define the scope of our mandate and devise a strategy to fulfill its requirements, we focused on each of these manifestations of socioeconomic rights violations.

Initially, our plan was to fold our engagement with socioeconomic rights into our normal truth commission activities, most notably our statement taking, research and investigations, and hearings. We faced a number of challenges in this regard. First, we had a difficult time acquiring information concerning state expenditures and policies with respect to most social development programs. Not only was the government reluctant to provide such information to us (the reluctance of the government to share information with us – notwithstanding their legal obligation to do so – was not limited to issues related to socioeconomic rights, but also included information related to most areas of our mandate), but in many cases, we were told the information was never collected. For example, it was only in 2003 that national demographic studies included information on all regions of the country. Prior to 2003, such data was not collected for the North Eastern Province and northern section of the Rift Valley Province. This made it impossible to establish benchmarks and measure progress or regression with respect to poverty, health, and related areas. This made it difficult to determine whether a particular region was marginalized compared to other regions, which was a crucial part of our mandate. The fact that such statistics were only collected for some but not all regions of the country was itself an indicator of marginalization. Given that we had neither the resources nor the time to undertake our own detailed empirical work in this area, we reluctantly had to rely on the work of others, some of which was anecdotal and speculative. While such secondary sources often provided a good analysis of the overall political and economic policies and practices that led to marginalization and the denial of certain socioeconomic rights, they were less useful in providing specific or systematic data for us to undertake our own, particularly quantitative, analysis.

To compensate for this lacuna, we used testimony from our statement taking and public hearings to provide the perspective of, and to give voice to, those who experienced such marginalization, particularly in the North Eastern and northern Rift Valley regions. We discovered, however, that the traditional form of data collection employed by truth commissions – statement taking – was less well suited to capturing violations of socioeconomic rights.

HURIDOCS, an international organization that has assisted in the statement-taking process of numerous truth commissions, evaluated our statement-taking form, and found it to be the best such form they had ever evaluated. It was designed to cover the wide variety of violations, including violations of socioeconomic rights, included in our mandate. Notwithstanding this thoroughness, when we began to evaluate the statements we had collected in the first three months of our statement-taking process, we quickly discovered that we were capturing very little information on violations of socioeconomic rights. This was perhaps not surprising, as most individuals are more likely to remember, and talk about, exceptional acts of serious physical violence that they may have experienced or witnessed rather than what are sometimes viewed as the day-to-day challenges of living in many parts of Kenya. Based upon this preliminary analysis, we realized we needed to develop alternative methods for capturing the voices and experiences of those who suffered violations of their socioeconomic rights.

To better capture those voices and experiences, we developed a more discussion-oriented form of data collection – similar to the town hall–like process we used to capture the perspectives and experiences of women. We trained eight facilitators (one for each region of the country) on the mandate of the Commission, and, in particular, on the socioeconomic rights aspects of the mandate. We decided to focus the conversation they would facilitate in each region on economic marginalization. We did this for three reasons. First, economic marginalization (and the perception of economic marginalization) was a part of our mandate. Second, many Kenyans perceived themselves or their region as being marginalized (thus explaining the inclusion of *perceived* economic marginalization as part of our mandate). We discovered marginalization *within* regions based upon politics or ethnicity. Third, economic marginalization encompasses many of the socioeconomic rights within our mandate (from housing to health care to education). It thus provided a useful entry point for introducing a discussion of violations of those other, more specific rights. We held over eighty such discussions throughout the country, involving close to 1,200 participants. These discussions elicited information about specific violations and other challenges Kenyans face with respect to socioeconomic rights, their assessment of the reasons for those violations, and their recommendations for addressing such violations.

The results of our focus group discussions can be found throughout many sections of our report. We devote an entire volume of our report (Volume IIB) to socioeconomic rights and violations, with specific chapters on economic marginalization and violations of socioeconomic rights, land and conflict, and economic crimes and grand corruption. In addition, we include discussions of violations of socioeconomic rights in our chapters on the Shifta War, gender, children, and minority groups and indigenous peoples. These sections alone total 513 pages and do not include the references to the socioeconomic context of violations within our mandate that can be found throughout the other parts of the report. As a rough comparison, the East Timor commission has fifty-four pages devoted to socioeconomic rights and violations, while the Sierra Leonean commission report has a similar number of pages, primarily focusing on mineral resources and their relationship to the conflict. One interesting observation arising from our statements is that witnesses who spoke about bodily integrity violations and violations of civil and political rights often requested a more retributive form of justice as a recommendation.[62] By contrast, those who spoke about socioeconomic rights tended to prefer restitution and were less interested in retributive justice. This is perhaps not surprising, as many of the economic violations of which people spoke involved the theft of land or other things of clear financial value, whereas bodily integrity and other violations are less easily reduced to an economic valuation and thus tend to evoke more retributive notions of justice. In our recommendations, we tried to bridge this gap by requiring that any funds recovered from corruption or other economic crimes be paid into a general reparations fund, which would then benefit all victims, regardless of the violation they suffered.[63]

CAPTURING TRUTH

In implementing our mandate, one of our most important tasks was to capture as accurately as possible the voices of individual Kenyans throughout the country. We captured and made public 878 stories in our public hearings, recounted by 213 women and 665 men. We also heard the stories of over 1,000 women in our women's hearings, and one hundred individuals in our *in camera* hearings. We also captured over forty thousand such voices in our statement-taking exercise, the largest number of statements ever collected by a truth commission, and over a thousand in our focus group discussions. With respect to capturing the lived experiences and perceptions of Kenyans, we engaged with more individuals in more creative ways than perhaps any previous such commission.

Statement taking provides an opportunity to capture the narrative truths of far larger numbers of people than can be accommodated in a public hearing. Statement taking also provides an opportunity to create quantitative information that can be organized and analyzed through a database. Statement taking thus serves two important purposes: capturing the subjective truths

---

[62] This was brought to our attention by the monitoring report of KEWOPA and Action Aid (Fall 2010).

[63] The Liberian Commission made a similar recommendation.

of individuals with respect to violations and providing the raw material for a database that can be used to analyze quantitative trends with respect to such violations. There is a tension between these two purposes. On the one hand, individual experiences must be easily reduced to general categories – this facilitates the creation of a database and thus allows the creation of an aggregate picture of abuses during a particular period of time or in a particular region. On the other hand, statement taking must allow testators to "speak their truth" in their own words without being altered by the mediation of the Commission. Self-narratives, our individual truths related in our own words, do not usually fit easily into categories. Even those narratives that use precisely defined terms – such as torture or genocide – are not necessarily describing the same act. Thus, it became important for us to both preserve the subjective truths of those who shared their stories with us and to develop a method for classifying these experiences in a way that would allow us to make at least tentative quantitative statements about the information we collected.

Fiona Ross, in her fascinating book on women and the South African TRC,[64] tells the story of Yvonne Khutwane. Yvonne Khutwane told her story to the Commission through a statement taker, describing her life as an activist who had also been detained, tortured, and raped. Her story in the South African final report focused on the rape without much other detail about Yvonne and her life as an activist. The inclusion of Yvonne's rape story was important for the TRC, as it was one of the few stories of rape they had captured that could be included in their report. The rape narrative in the report, however, distorted Yvonne's own self-narrative of her experience, which involved far more than her experience as a rape victim.

To overcome the risk of reducing an individual's experience to one violation, we originally planned to have all of the interviews we conducted recorded on digital tape recorders – the recordings would then be made available so people could listen to an unedited version of a person's story (after, of course, the interviewees had given their consent to such public use). Recording the statements would also have allowed us to supplement what were often incomplete written narratives from the statement-taking exercise. While we did purchase digital recorders for our statement takers, for reasons that were never made clear to me, we neither received them back nor received the recordings that were made on them. This failure to capture on tape the over forty thousand interviews was unfortunate. During the statement-taking process, I read through a random sample of our statements – usually fifty at a time. Some of them were quite good and detailed, but more than I would have liked

---

[64] Fiona Ross, BEARING WITNESS: WOMEN AND THE TRUTH AND RECONCILIATION COMMISSION OF SOUTH AFRICA (London: Pluto Press, 2003).

had very little useful information. For example, some of the statements would, under the section for listing a violation, have only one word – such as land, torture, or rape – with little or no context or other narrative structure. While such a statement was useful for our quantitative purposes (though even for that purpose, it would have been useful to have more detail), it did little to contribute to the narrative truth we were collecting.

In order to create a quantitative record of our statements, we trained over fifty coders and data entry clerks. The coders read through each statement and determined what specific violations were being described. Each of the coders was trained and given a manual in the legal definition of the violations within our mandate. If a statement spoke of torture or genocide, the coder would read through the statement to determine if there were sufficient facts present to conclude that either torture or an act of genocide was being described. (Thus, for those statements that just listed "torture" without any more detail, we were forced to rely upon the assessment made by the statement taker in the field without any ability to verify the underlying factual premise that led to that conclusion.) If the details provided in the statement did not match the characterization provided by the statement taker, the coder would recharacterize the violation based upon the information provided. The data entry clerks then took the information created by the coders and entered it into our database. By the end of our process, every statement had been coded and added to our database, along with the over 1,800 memoranda we received. This data was then used to provide the quantitative information that is included in our report.

To better reflect the experiences of those who engaged with us, we were able to quote extensively from our statements and hearings. Sometimes these quotations were relatively brief and used to illustrate a particular point in a longer narrative. With these quotations, we did make choices about the emphasis to be placed on the stories presented to us. We also included more extensive narrative stories from our materials in an effort to allow individual stories to be heard in the report unmediated by our own judgments. These longer narrative quotations are highlighted in yellow, and in the entire report we included fifty-five of them. In addition, we have extensive quotations from witnesses embedded in the narrative of the report, many of which came from our women's hearings.

ACCOUNTABILITY

How does one hold accountable a commission that is meant to be, and should be, independent? While truth commissions are meant to engage with various stakeholders, mechanisms for holding the commission accountable to its diverse constituencies are limited and imperfect. As a temporary organization, a truth commission is not subject to traditional mechanisms of political accountability that one finds with respect to other government agencies. Traditionally, such accountability derives from the political process, most commonly through elections. Accountability is also provided through the checks that one branch of government has on the actions of another. A truth commission is more like a judicial institution in its independence. This is by design, as the commission, like the judiciary, is meant to be independent of the other branches of government and thus free from political direction or influence. Our enabling legislation makes clear (as did our oath of office) that we were not to take direction from any external source, including the government.

Yet we were accountable. We were accountable to the government in ways that were appropriate (complying with government procurement rules, for example). We were also accountable to a number of stakeholders, most importantly victims and survivors, but also civil society, the media, and donors.

Notwithstanding these appropriate forms of accountability and our independence under law, in practice we were dependent on the government for all of our finances. In and of itself, this dependence should not be a problem. Yet that dependence was used by the government to try to influence our work. In fact, during the first year of our existence, the Ministry of Justice completely controlled our money. The control was so extensive that we did not have a say in how our money was spent during the first year of our operations, and we were often not informed about where and how our money was spent. This led to a minor financial scandal within the Ministry of Justice, which I discuss in more detail in Chapter 3. During that first year of our existence, we were thus accountable to the Ministry of Justice with respect to our operations. Any activity that we wanted to undertake during that first year that required the expenditure of money had to be approved by the Ministry. This was an inappropriate form of accountability that seriously undermined our initial operational independence. After July 2010, we were given control over our finances, and thus could engage in activities without the approval and oversight of the government. This was to prove crucial as we geared up for our statement taking, public hearings, research, and investigations during the second half of 2010.

We were also to some extent accountable to civil society, or at least the more active and influential sectors of civil society. Our activities were scrutinized by civil society, and we were thus subject to public critiques (some justified, some not) that affected our ability to engage with other constituents. In addition, like most truth commissions, we sought to partner with civil society with respect to many of our activities. Partnering with civil society was important because (1) some civil society organizations had important information concerning some of the violations we were to investigate; (2) some civil society actors had experience and expertise with respect to investigations and outreach from which we could benefit; and (3) sympathetic civil society actors could, and some did, work closely with us with respect to statement taking (by seconding some of their staff to us for that purpose), research, drafting parts of our final report, and providing psychosocial and other support to individuals and groups who engaged with the Commission.

Kenyan civil society organizations varied in how accountable they were to their own constituents. Of particular concern to us was the relative lack of accountability some civil society organizations had to individuals and groups who qualified as victims under our legislation. We found ourselves at times in the middle of disputes between individual or organized groups of victims and certain civil society organizations that claimed to be representing them. Neither civil society nor we had any clear mechanisms by which we could be held accountable by the constituencies that we both claimed to be serving. If anything, civil society had slightly more accountability as they would, in most cases, continue to operate in this field and thus would benefit from developing both short- and long-term relationships with their constituents.

The Commission, like all truth commissions, was a temporary body. One might conclude that we would be less concerned about any long-term impacts, positive or negative, of our activities. Yet our ability to encourage engagement from important constituencies was dependent on our relationship with and accountability to those constituencies. A truth commission is limited in its ability to compel participation; instead it must rely on the soft power of persuasion and relevancy to encourage participation. While we were thus accountable for our actions during our operational period, we also wanted to create some form of accountability at the end of our process. As we traveled throughout the country, we heard from Kenyans that previous commissions and some of the Nairobi-based civil society organizations would travel out to meet with them, make promises about how they would assist, and then were never to be heard from again. This has also been true for most, perhaps all, previous truth commissions. Ever since the South African TRC, truth commissions have usually traveled to remote parts of the regions within their mandate to engage with victims and to hold public hearings. We certainly adopted this mode of operation. After we left an area, we might have further contact with the local community if they reached out to us. Otherwise, the next "engagement" between us and them would be our final report.

The final report, while an important part of a truth commission's legacy, is an imperfect vehicle for providing feedback and accountability to the people who engaged with the truth commission. This is true for at least two reasons. First, most truth commission reports are hundreds, and often thousands, of pages long. The Kenyan report is over 2,100 pages long. Leaving aside the important issue of literacy, it is unrealistic to assume that all but the most dedicated will read through such a report. The fact that the literacy rate among those who engaged with such a commission is probably quite low (and even if an individual is literate, she may not read English, which is the language of most such reports) makes a final report that much more ill suited for providing feedback and fostering accountability for a commission's activities and findings. Efforts have been made by previous commissions to address this issue by creating video and radio versions of the report, creating an executive summary, and by creating a child-friendly version of the report. In Kenya, we produced a twenty-page summary that was reproduced in all three of the major Nairobi newspapers. We also worked with a local television station to develop hour-long conversations about different aspects of the report. Finally, efforts are currently underway by a coalition of Kenyan and international NGOs to create a child-friendly version of the report.

Second, even in the best of circumstances, accessibility to such a final report is limited. In addition to the barriers of language and literacy, accessibility to a commission's final report is usually limited to those living in the capital and other major cities. In the case of Kenya, we posted the entire report online immediately after we handed it over to the president. Access to an online version is dependent on access to an internet connection, and given the size of the report, also dependent on a relatively fast internet connection. While Nairobi and some of the other major Kenyan cities have access to such a fast internet connection, most of the poor and those who live outside of the major cities do not. We had secured funding from the German government to print thousands of copies of the report, which we had planned to distribute to educational institutions and other relevant areas in remote parts of the country. The Government Printer refused to run the copies; we were told that high-level government officials had ordered them not to run them. Thus the only way for the average Kenyan to access our report was to secure a copy of the summary published in the national newspapers. The website on which we made available the final report was taken over by the government, and a few months later the website was taken down. At the moment, the only way to obtain a full electronic copy of our final report is through this book's website at Seattle University.

In reflecting on the accountability challenges of previous truth commissions, and anticipating some of the difficulties we were to encounter in making the final report available and accessible, we developed a plan to return to the places where we had held our public hearings, report back to those local communities, and engage with them about the overall narrative of their experience that we would include in our final report. This proposal was not universally embraced by all of the commissioners and senior staff. Some raised the concern that if we revealed our findings in advance, we would create confusion and, perhaps more importantly, an opportunity for named individuals to move to court to stop the release of the final report. I thought this was a legitimate concern and suggested that we not reveal our findings (or only reveal relatively innocuous findings) but instead engage with the local community concerning what issues we had identified as important ones for their community. My hope was that this process would allow us to "check in" with those who had shared their stories with us and for us to confirm with them that we had accurately captured their experience. In this manner, we would increase our accountability to the thousands of individuals who had engaged with us and entrusted to us their stories. Alternatively, we contemplated engaging in such activities after the report was published, both to disseminate the contents of the report and to begin what we hoped would be a national conversation about the content of the report. Many of the individuals we encountered in remote parts of the country had complained to us that individuals and organizations would visit them from Nairobi, take from them their stories, promise them remedies, and then never be seen again. We wanted to break that cycle.

Unfortunately, we were unable to travel back to the local communities either before or after our report was published. Near the end of our process, we had run out of money and thus were dependent on securing additional funds to undertake such a trip. Neither the diplomatic community nor civil society seemed particularly interested in supporting such a project, as much of their focus at the time was on the ICC process. The government refused to provide additional money for this purpose as well. In fact, the acting permanent secretary in the Ministry of Justice claimed that we did not have the legal authority to engage in such activities after the issuance of the final report and claimed that the government would make sure that the report was made available and discussed nationally. Five years after the report was handed over, no additional copies of the report have been produced, and the government-controlled website that included the report has been taken down. At the moment, no one, including the government, is being held to account for this failure.

3

The Elephant in the Room

The single largest challenge we faced in fulfilling our mandate was our chair, Ambassador Bethuel Kiplagat. His presence and actions divided the Commission; alienated important constituencies; hindered significantly our ability to pursue our mandate; and resulted in our recommending that he be further investigated and, if the evidence warranted it, prosecuted (the first and so far only time a truth commission has made such a recommendation regarding one of its own members). Ambassador Kiplagat was linked to three areas of gross violations of human rights we were to investigate: assassinations, land, and massacres. He adopted numerous, often contradictory, strategies to respond to these allegations. He admitted the truth of the allegations concerning his involvement in irregular or illegal land acquisitions. With respect to the worst massacre in the history of Kenya, he first denied that he had been present at a crucial meeting over twenty-five years earlier related to the massacre; then claimed he could not remember if he had attended the meeting; then acknowledged that he had attended the meeting and could assure us with certainty that nothing was discussed related to the security operation that resulted in the massacre. He claimed that he wanted a legal process provided for in our legislation to evaluate the allegations against him, but when it was created, he went to court to have it stopped. He agreed to abstain from involvement in Commission-related activities concerning the three areas in which he had a conflict of interest yet demanded that staff give him access to documents related to investigations involving his activities; demanded that we change parts of the report discussing those violations; and as recounted in the first chapter, provided crucial support to cleanse the report of allegations concerning improper land dealings by President Jomo Kenyatta, the father of the current president.

This chapter discusses the merits of the evidence we uncovered concerning Ambassador Kiplagat's involvement in these violations, the enormous challenge his presence posed for the Commission, and our efforts to create a credible process to address what began as a set of mere allegations against him. Some of what is revealed in this chapter can be found in the chapter of our final report concerning various challenges we faced; much of what I discuss here is being made public for the first time. I hope it will serve as a cautionary tale about the importance of choosing carefully those who will serve on such a commission and how one should address such conflicts as early as possible if they nevertheless arise.

While there were indications from the beginning that the appointment of Bethuel Kiplagat as our chair would pose a challenge, none of us, including me, anticipated how serious that challenge was to become or how his own actions would exacerbate rather than alleviate the challenges his presence presented for the Commission. The vast majority of the work we did – our statement taking, our public hearings, our major investigations – occurred during the fourteen months during which Ambassador Kiplagat was on leave from the Commission.[1] In fact, Ambassador Kiplagat did not participate in any of the more than one hundred public and private hearings we held across the country, and he only participated in a handful of hearings in Nairobi – most notoriously as a witness before us concerning allegations that he was present at an intelligence committee meeting during which the security operation that resulted in the Wagalla massacre was discussed.

Over the course of our operations and investigations, we were to acquire credible evidence implicating Ambassador Kiplagat in three sets of violations within our mandate. First, while he was a senior official in government, he took advantage of government schemes to transfer land reserved for poor and landless Kenyans to government officials and their allies. He eventually admitted to receiving at least two plots of such land. Second, he was an important witness to events leading up to the 1990 assassination of the minister of foreign affairs, Robert Ouko. At least four separate investigations concluded that he had knowledge of events that would assist their investigations and that he had refused to cooperate or had been an untruthful witness. Some of those investigations had recommended that he be further investigated. Third,

---

[1] Ambassador Kiplagat availed himself of the peculiarly Kenyan institution of "stepping aside" for fourteen months, which meant that he was on leave from the Commission but continued to receive his full pay. We even paid for his daily newspapers, which were still delivered each day to our offices. While he had "stepped aside," we devoted a staff person each morning to drive the newspapers to Kiplagat's home on the other side of town, a trip that could take more than an hour each way (and once took me three hours one way) depending on that morning's rush hour traffic.

he was present at a meeting between the Kenya Intelligence Committee (on which he served) and the local and regional security committees in Wajir in North Eastern Province in which the security operation that resulted in the 1984 Wagalla massacre was discussed. His presence at the security meeting in Wajir should have been enough to disqualify him from being a member of, much less the chair of, a truth commission. His link to questionable land dealings and the assassination of a government minister raise questions of the extent of his knowledge, and involvement, in these and perhaps other violations that were within our mandate. At the time of my appointment to the Commission, I was unaware of Ambassador Kiplagat's connection to these gross violations of human rights.

INITIAL DOUBTS

After my name and that of the other eight commissioners had been made public, but before we had been sworn in, I met a friend for coffee in a downtown coffee shop in Seattle. Priscilla Hayner is one of the foremost experts on truth commissions and transitional justice. She is the author of what many consider to be the best book on the subject of truth commissions and co-founded the International Center for Transitional Justice. More importantly, Priscilla had been present with Kofi Annan at some of the negotiations in Nairobi that resulted in the National Accord, which included the agreement to establish a truth, justice, and reconciliation commission. I was thus anxious to hear her views on the current state of affairs in Kenya, as well as her sense of the role I could play as part of the truth commission.

As we discussed my future in Kenya, Priscilla raised the appointment of Ambassador Kiplagat as our chair. I was only slightly familiar with one of the other commissioners, Kaari "Betty" Murungi, who was a prominent Kenyan human rights lawyer who had been a consultant to the Sierra Leone Truth and Reconciliation Commission; I knew nothing about the others, including Ambassador Kiplagat. Priscilla mentioned to me that some had raised concerns about the appointment of Ambassador Kiplagat because he had served as an official in the Moi government. Daniel arap Moi had served as the second president of Kenya, coming into office upon the death of the first president, Jomo Kenyatta. The government under Moi eventually became a de facto dictatorship (he served as president for twenty-four years, from 1978 to 2002), and during his presidency numerous gross violations of human rights that we were to investigate had been committed, including the creation of secret torture facilities like the one housed in the basement of Nyayo House, a prominent Nairobi skyscraper. Ambassador Kiplagat had served in the Moi government as ambassador to France and as high commissioner to the United Kingdom, as well as serving in the powerful position of permanent secretary in the Ministry of Foreign Affairs.[2]

I asked Priscilla if those raising concerns about Ambassador Kiplagat had any information linking him to human rights violations during the Moi government. She did not know of any, and I continued to receive the same response to that question from prominent civil society actors and others during my first few months in Kenya. During the extensive vetting of the Kenyan commissioners by members of civil society and Parliament, none of the evidence concerning his complicity in human rights violations we were to investigate came to light. In fact, I was told that no allegations against him were even raised during this process.[3] My view was, and still is, that the mere fact that Ambassador Kiplagat had been a member of a government that had committed gross violations of human rights was not in itself sufficient to disqualify him from serving on a truth commission. We were not a court of law. Appointing to the Commission someone who had served in the government but who was not himself implicated might assist us in encouraging members of that government to cooperate with the Commission, thus furthering all three pillars of our mandate: truth, justice, and reconciliation. I would have felt differently about the matter if there were some evidence linking him to serious violations of human rights within our mandate. None was forthcoming in these early days.

Initially, I and the other commissioners publicly defended him and his presence on the Commission. In the first month of our existence, we developed three specific arguments. First, we were not a court of law but a body that was equally dedicated to reconciliation, as well as truth and justice. Second, every Kenyan government had committed gross violations of human rights. If anyone who had ever served in government was disqualified from serving on the Commission, many otherwise qualified people would be precluded from participating in such an endeavor. The guiding criteria for appointment should be the specific actions, or inactions, of the individual in

---

[2] Many of my Kenyan colleagues have told me that under Moi's presidency the real power in the Ministry lay with the permanent secretary rather than the minister.

[3] For a critical discussion of the selection process, *see* Kimberly Lanegran, "The Kenyan Truth Justice and Reconciliation Commission: The Importance of Commissioners and their Appointment Process," 1:3 *Transitional Justice Review* 41–71 (January 2015). Lanegran recounts that members of the civil society panel that vetted the Kenyan commissioners complained that they were given only one week to review over 250 nominations (including Bethuel Kiplagat) and thus did not have time to engage in their own independent investigations regarding the candidates.

question, and not the actions of a government of which he was a part. Finally, we argued that even if Ambassador Kiplagat's service in government raised concerns about his judgment, bias, or integrity, he was only one among nine and only had one vote concerning matters presented to the Commission. In hindsight, I was naïve about some of the arguments we made – particularly about the assertion that he was only one of nine commissioners and thus had limited influence over the work of the Commission. As we were later to learn, even as one among nine he was able to create an enormous amount of trouble for the Commission.

In the absence of credible evidence to the contrary, I was willing to give Kiplagat the benefit of the doubt. As we were to discover, the allegations against Ambassador Kiplagat were supported by credible evidence, we became only eight Commissioners, and even with the remaining seven of us united against him, he was able to continue to cause serious damage to the process. One of the Kenyan commissioners, Tecla Wanjala, who was later to serve as our acting chair (becoming the first woman to chair a truth commission), did ask him in early August 2009 whether he had considered resigning. He immediately dismissed the idea, refusing to engage in a discussion about the best interests of the Commission and instead focusing on what he called his own rights, including what he characterized as his right to be part of the Commission. None of the rest of us pushed the issue, and in fact, at the time, given my outsider status and my unfamiliarity with the Kenyan political environment, I was comfortable with that decision.

As I began to engage with members of Kenyan civil society, some of whom I had known either directly or by reputation before moving to Nairobi, I began to realize how uneasy significant segments of Kenyan society were with Ambassador Kiplagat chairing the Commission. Yet each time I asked for specific evidence or even information concerning misdeeds of which he was a part, no one could point to any specific action or provide any specific evidence.

A GOVERNMENT AGENT?

Notwithstanding this lack of evidence, numerous people warned me that Ambassador Kiplagat had been appointed to the Commission to make sure the process was a whitewash, or to slow down the process to make sure we did not robustly pursue our mandate. We did receive express direction from officials in the Ministry of Justice that we should slow down our work. These directions were combined with the Ministry both controlling our finances during our first year of operations as well as refusing to provide us with more than a minimal amount of financing, thus making it impossible for us to engage in any substantial activity until our second full year of operation. It was unclear whether Kiplagat was coordinating with the Ministry to slow down our affairs. He did, however, exhibit a number of traits that had the effect of slowing down our process. First, our meetings under his chairman-ship were often disorganized and ineffective. Ambassador Kiplagat would often steer the conversation off onto issues not on our agenda or tangential to our current challenges of raising money and hiring permanent staff. He was prone to storytelling and long, discursive lectures. In addition to diverting us away from the core elements of our mandate, he had a difficult time reining in other commissioners, particularly some of the male commissioners who were prone to interrupt and to go off on their own tangents. At the time, this appeared to be attributable to a lack of organizational skills, but perhaps it was also a deliberate policy to slow things down.

Second, Ambassador Kiplagat also appeared to have preconceived notions about the work of a truth commission, some of which were in tension with the approach of the rest of us and with standard truth commission procedures. Two anecdotes illustrate this tension. First, Ambassador Kiplagat appeared to assume that we (or at least he) already knew which violations had occurred where. In our first months, Ambassador Kiplagat organized some of us into a reconciliation committee. The main activity of this committee consisted of a four-hour meeting during which Ambassador Kiplagat went province by province (Kenya at the time was divided into eight provinces) asking, though mostly telling, us what types of violations had occurred where, and the ethnic or other identifying features of the perpetrators and the victims. It was not clear what the purpose of this exercise was, but I was concerned that it would be used to limit how we would focus our energies in terms of investigating the truth of the wide range of violations we were to investigate. To illustrate how extremely he adopted this position, he noted at one point that no sexual violence had occurred in one (or maybe two) provinces. As this was in the early days of the Commission, I was hesitant as a newcomer to take a strong stand, so I tried to finesse the issue by observing that, notwithstanding the knowledge some of us had about past violations, we needed to approach our task with an open mind and not predetermine what violations had occurred where, by whom and against whom. While he seemed to acknowledge this, he continued on his province-by-province survey of violations. This approach of Kiplagat's was to foreshadow his far more damaging, and public, statement that "no government worth its salt would massacre its own people." He was to make this comment a year later during a televised interview concerning the massacre by the Kenyan security forces of approximately 1,000 people.

In hindsight it is significant that this first conversation, and approach to our task, took place under the rubric of reconciliation, which is an important part of our mission and that of most truth commissions but is unfortunately sometimes used to stifle the equally important goals of truth and justice.

The second example of Ambassador Kiplagat's unorthodox approach to our work occurred in early 2010 and concerned whether we would investigate and identify perpetrators at the end of our process. We had held numerous meetings with him in February to come up with a credible process to address his own conflicts of interest (more about that in a moment). At one of these meetings, he mentioned that while of course we would recommend investigations, we ourselves would not be identifying perpetrators. By this point, I had become less hesitant in asserting my views. I responded that I disagreed with his position and went on to note that if our investigations were to uncover evidence linking someone to a violation within our mandate, we might, in fact, identify that individual if we were satisfied with the sufficiency of the evidence. After this meeting, he had a further conversation with Commissioner Shava where he argued more forcefully that we should not identify perpetrators. Commissioner Shava was clear in her response that if we uncovered sufficient evidence, we would identify individuals we suspected of wrongdoing. Our legislation, in fact, empowered us to recommend prosecutions in cases in which we had sufficient evidence. After he had spoken with Commissioner Shava, Ambassador Kiplagat spoke with me, insisting that we would, of course, investigate; that we needed a strong investigative unit; and that the investigators should not be Kenyan – perhaps German or Dutch, but not British. When Commissioner Shava later discussed with me the very different conversation Kiplagat had just had with her, I was taken aback. It was an important moment, as we began to see firsthand his method of engaging with us individually, rather than collectively, in order to tailor his message to his audience, and in some cases to sow confusion. It is the first time I noted in my journal that I had serious concerns about his objectivity, integrity, and motives. I had no direct evidence that he was deliberately trying to sabotage the process, but his actions and approach to our mandate began to raise serious concerns among some of us, including me.

FIRST EVIDENCE AND FIRST CONFESSION

Notwithstanding these early signs, all of the commissioners were united in defending Kiplagat publicly, both as a member of the Commission and as our chair. That would begin to change in early February 2010, when a coalition of civil society organizations submitted documents to us purporting to link

Ambassador Kiplagat to three sets of violations within our mandate: land, assassinations, and massacres. With respect to land, the documents suggested that Ambassador Kiplagat had been the beneficiary of illegal or irregular allocations of land during his time in government. In fact, he had been mentioned as such a beneficiary of land in the report of a previous commission that had investigated illegal and irregular land acquisition.[4] He quickly admitted the truth of these allegations to us, though he continued to insist that he had done nothing wrong. With respect to assassinations, Ambassador Kiplagat had been permanent secretary in the Ministry of Foreign Affairs in 1990 when the minister for foreign affairs, the Honorable Robert Ouko, was assassinated. There had never been any allegations, much less credible evidence, that Ambassador Kiplagat had been involved in the murder of Minister Ouko; in fact, Ambassador Kiplagat appeared to have been genuinely distraught at the time by the death of his colleague. Ambassador Kiplagat had assured us that he knew nothing about the circumstances leading to Ouko's killing, that he was merely a minor witness, and that he had cooperated fully with the many investigations into the murder. In fact, his decision to testify before a judicial commission investigating the murder apparently led to his immediate dismissal from government service by President Moi. At the moment, his seemingly tenuous link to the assassination and the various subsequent investigations appeared innocuous.

With respect to massacres, it was alleged that Ambassador Kiplagat had been present over twenty years ago at a high-level security committee meeting just prior to the start of the security operation that resulted in the Wagalla massacre in February 1984. This was the most serious allegation, but the evidence presented to us was very weak, consisting of two typewritten pages of a list of names and dates that we were told were taken from the visitors' book in Wajir. The dates covered part of February 1984. Ambassador Kiplagat's name was on the typewritten list, suggesting he had visited Wajir on February 8, 1984. There were a number of problems with this evidence. First, the pages had no headings or titles indicating their source. The notations on the pages suggested they were from an appendix to a chapter of an unknown publication, raising the question of whether they were even from the visitors' book in Wajir. Second, visitors' books are signed by hand – in fact, we were later to do just that as we traveled throughout the country for our civic education and public hearings, including in Wajir. No one had an explanation for why these pages that were claimed to be from the Wajir visitors' book were typed

---

4   REPORT OF THE COMMISSION OF INQUIRY INTO THE ILLEGAL/IRREGULAR ALLOCATION OF PUBLIC LAND (Nairobi: Government Printer, 2004) [the "NDUNG'U COMMISSION REPORT"].

and not handwritten. Most of the commissioners thus dismissed this evidence. I was uneasy about the document and curious about its source and meaning. At the time, no one was able to answer adequately my questions about the meaning of these pages, so I, too, discounted the allegations of his involvement in the massacre.

On Thursday, February 11th, 2010, a few days after we had received this information, Ambassador Kiplagat called all of the commissioners together for a meeting at our offices at Delta House in Westlands. We sat around our large conference table, and Ambassador Kiplagat proceeded to discuss his land holdings. It was a candid discussion lasting more than two hours in which he revealed to us that he had acquired the plots of land attributed to him in the Ndung'u Report. He also confessed that he had acquired another plot of land in Trans Nzoia, which had been part of a land settlement scheme created under President Jomo Kenyatta to benefit landless individuals. During the Moi administration, much of the land set aside for poor, landless individuals had been divided up among high-level civil servants, including Ambassador Kiplagat. In his meeting with us, Ambassador Kiplagat claimed that he was landless at the time, and therefore was a legitimate beneficiary of the allocation. As Ambassador Kiplagat scrambled to justify how he had acquired land meant for poor and landless Kenyans, I started to appreciate the magnitude of the issues facing him and, by extension, us. Not long after this meeting, I was told that in the early discussions involving the creation of the Commission, even before any of the commissioners had been chosen, Ambassador Kiplagat had argued that land should not be included as part of our mandate. The fact that he was now defending his acquisition of land intended for poor Kenyans while he was a government official explained why he might have wanted to remove the issue of land from the Commission's mandate.

Within the span of a week, we had gone from publicly defending Ambassador Kiplagat's presence on the Commission to learning directly from him (after prompted by the evidence provided by the civil society organizations) that he had a direct conflict of interest with respect to illegal and irregular acquisition of land by government officials at the expense of poor and landless Kenyans. With respect to the assassination of Robert Ouko, we all realized that he was at least a witness to events leading up to that assassination, but there was no indication that he had played any role with respect to the killing itself, nor that he had been complicit in protecting those responsible. None of us, including me, viewed these two issues concerning land and assassinations as presenting insurmountable challenges for his presence on the Commission. They would require us to create procedures for us to restrict his involvement in those matters, and perhaps procedures for us to elicit his testimony concerning those matters, but such procedures had been adopted and used by many commissions of inquiry and similar bodies in the past. If that was the extent of the impact of his presence, we felt we could adapt without endangering our core mandate-related activities. Some in civil society strongly advocated the opposite, and with the benefit of hindsight, they were probably correct to take his conflicts concerning these two areas of our mandate more seriously than we initially did.

The allegations concerning Kiplagat's presence in Wajir right before the Wagalla massacre continued to worry me, notwithstanding the weak evidence presented to us. Ambassador Kiplagat initially had told us that he had never been to Wajir before in his life. A few weeks later, he revised his statement and informed us that he could not remember if he had been to Wajir in February 1984. He explained that, in February 1984, he would have just returned to Kenya after his diplomatic posting in the UK to take up the position of permanent secretary in the Ministry of Foreign Affairs. He argued that he, therefore, would not have traveled outside of Nairobi so soon after his return. The shift from certain denial (he had never been there) to uncertainty combined with speculation (I don't remember, but it would not make sense for me to have been there) heightened my concern. I was most concerned about these allegations for two reasons. First, if he had, in fact, been present at meetings related to the Wagalla massacre, that would place him directly at the center of one of the worst violations we were to investigate. Second, given his shift from a categorical denial to a speculative denial concerning his presence in Wajir, strong evidence to the contrary would, at best, throw into question his memory and credibility, and at worst, indicate that he had deliberately lied to us and others. Commissioner Murungi thought it very unlikely that he had, in fact, been in Wajir. I tended to agree with this assessment given the evidence we had seen so far but expressed my concern that, if the allegations turned out to be true, it would be devastating not only for him but for the Commission as a whole.

Ambassador Kiplagat exacerbated the tensions and disruption within the Commission and (perhaps intentionally) confused the public perception of the Commission and the allegations against him by speaking frequently to the press without our consent and often without our knowledge. The media coverage of the Commission in February focused primarily on the allegations concerning Ambassador Kiplagat. This was perhaps not surprising. First, he was our chair and thus viewed as having more control over the process than any of the other commissioners. Second, as our chair, he was empowered as the Commission's official spokesperson under our legislation. He thus spoke frequently to the press. While he was often asked by the media about the

FIGURE 3.1 Gado – Kiplagat and statement taking. Image courtesy of Gado (gadocartoons.com).

allegations raised against him, he was equally prone to make statements in his own defense irrespective of the question asked and irrespective of the impact such statements might have on the credibility of the Commission itself. While he was meant to be the spokesperson for the Commission and thus meant to communicate positions and decisions taken by the commissioners as a whole, he instead made statements and observations that did not necessarily reflect the views of the rest of us but were nevertheless perceived by the public as reflecting the official position of the Commission. This course of conduct raised reasonable doubts among many of our stakeholders about the position and integrity of all of us. Significant civil society organizations hardened in their resolve not to engage with us; donors were cautious in their approach to us; the government urged us to do our work but refused to provide us with any operational funds; and victims' groups split between those who were anxious for any process that might highlight their plight and those who wanted us replaced with a new, and presumably better, commission.

One example of how Ambassador Kiplagat hijacked his access to the press to serve his own personal interests occurred during the swearing into office of our newly hired CEO, Patricia Nyaundi, before the chief justice on

February 15. Patricia was a distinguished lawyer, having most recently been the executive director of the Federation of Women Lawyers – Kenya (also known as FIDA Kenya).[5] As we left her swearing in, which the press amply covered, Ambassador Kiplagat took the opportunity to speak directly to the gathering of reporters. This impromptu press conference quickly became a question-and-answer session about whether he would resign from the Commission, and he adamantly insisted that he would not. The major story about us in the papers the next day was thus not about our CEO and all that she brought to the Commission; rather, the media stories were about Ambassador Kiplagat and his insistence that he would not resign. As this anecdote illustrates, the story about the Commission was quickly becoming about him – not the substance of our work, how well we were performing our functions, or, most importantly, the issues of historical injustice that we were supposed to be addressing. It is easy to reevaluate with hindsight, but there is no question in my mind that had we immediately instituted a process to evaluate the allegations against Kiplagat, or if he had graciously agreed to resign, we would have accomplished so much more during our operational period and, leaving aside the political considerations that later came to influence most of the other commissioners near the end of the process, we would not have sought the numerous extensions we eventually received to finish our work.

IN SEARCH OF A PROCESS

In February 2010, six months into the life of the Commission, we faced credible allegations concerning links between Ambassador Kiplagat and three core areas of our mandate. I strongly felt that there needed to be an independent and credible process to investigate and evaluate the allegations raised against Ambassador Kiplagat. Although I deliberately never took a public position on whether he should resign, at times, I privately wished that he would put the interest of the Commission ahead of his own interests and offer to resign.

As a result of Ambassador Kiplagat's revelations about his land acquisitions, four of us realized that we needed to take the allegations concerning his past more seriously. Merely defending his presence without addressing the allegations about his integrity and credibility was no longer a viable strategy. We thus shifted from publicly defending the presence of Ambassador Kiplagat on

---

[5] FIDA is an abbreviation for the Federation International de Abogadas, the federation of women lawyers founded in 1944 by a group of women lawyers in Mexico with the aim of promoting women's rights globally.

the Commission to developing a credible plan to address the allegations against him. The four of us – Judge Gertrude Chawatama; our vice chair, Kaari Murungi; and Margaret Shava – began to meet regularly outside of the office to strategize. We usually met at Mercury, a local bar not far from the office, which I was quickly to learn made some of the best martinis in Nairobi. In the late afternoon and early evening, Mercury was relatively quiet with few customers, making it an ideal place for us to find a discreet table for our conversations. As the evening progressed, the bar became more crowded and noisy, and hosted both members of the Kenyan elite (often including the president's son) and members of the young and wealthy upper class that seemed to drink and dance late into the night, seven days a week. Needless to say, we had usually left Mercury by the time this younger crowd had begun to arrive.

On Monday, February 15, all of the commissioners met in the office without Ambassador Kiplagat. We had assembled for the purpose of candidly discussing among ourselves how to address Kiplagat's conflicts of interest. Ambassador Kiplagat had, in fact, suggested that he was comfortable with us meeting without him, though his subsequent actions quickly contradicted this expression of his position. Over the previous weekend, Ambassador Kiplagat had attempted to forestall us from meeting without him by speaking to most of us individually, although he did not reach out to either Kaari Murungi or me. This was to be a recurring tactic on his part. Rather than address us collectively, he generally preferred speaking to us, and others, individually in an attempt to both sway the individual over to his side and to tailor his remarks given his perception of which arguments would most resonate with his chosen target. While such one-on-one engagements are not unusual or improper in and of themselves, his continuing reluctance to have us engage in a collective discussion and craft a collective response further hampered our progress.

As we gathered to meet without him, Ambassador Kiplagat's assistant called to inform him that we had assembled in the office for a meeting. Very soon thereafter he appeared in the office, and we invited him to join us. There was clear tension among us as we tried to navigate what was quickly becoming a major challenge to our credibility and even existence. Ambassador Kiplagat informed us that he had spoken to individuals "at the highest levels" of both parties – people, he said, who directly speak on a regular basis to both the president and prime minister – and that those people had urged him not to resign. This was a curious argument, as our legislation and oath of office made clear that we were to act independently of any outside interests. We would later discover that this general feeling that he not resign was not widely shared within either of the major political parties. It is not clear if Ambassador

Kiplagat was mischaracterizing the conversations, or whether the individuals with whom he had spoken did not speak candidly to him. Nevertheless, he would continue to claim special access to those in power and insist he had received assurances of their full backing of him and our work. He never informed us of the identity of these strong supporters, nor did he ever include any of us in any of those conversations, which further fueled the growing feeling of uncertainty among us about our future and gave rise to numerous, sometimes farfetched, rumors and conspiracy theories. Ironically, it is this same lack of transparency and dissembling that has so plagued the Kenyan government response to many of the violations we were to investigate – for example, the multiple investigations into the Ouko assassination that have never been made public and that, therefore, have been cited by many to support their own, sometimes fantastical, theories of what really happened.

Even if one accepted Ambassador Kiplagat's claim that well-connected individuals from the two major political parties supported his continued presence at the Commission, the political elite were only one of a number of important constituencies with whom we had to engage and upon whom we depended for our legitimacy and accountability. It was clear that a number of victims' groups, civil society organizations, and media outlets felt strongly that Ambassador Kiplagat should not continue as a member of the Commission. The Kenyan commissioners were probably more attuned to the complicated political currents surrounding the Commission than I and perhaps the other two international commissioners. Kaari Murungi, who had close ties to important sectors of Kenyan civil society, was under increasing pressure to resign given the revelations about our chair. In fact, when I had arrived in the office on the morning of February 15, I found Kaari emptying her desk. She informed me that she was preparing to resign. I was alarmed at this turn of events and asked her to hold off resigning until she and I could speak privately and candidly, to which she agreed. I was very concerned that if she resigned we would lose much of our legitimacy internationally and among certain important sectors of civil society. I was also concerned because, besides me, she was the only commissioner with experience working with a truth commission. She was also, at least in those early days, a strong force for keeping us all together with a common purpose, though the tensions she had to navigate, particularly with respect to our chair, were clearly taking their toll. After further reflection that day, she decided to postpone her resignation.

With the increased, and critical, attention on Kiplagat and the Commisison itself, we realized we had to do something quickly. Our efforts to come up with an internal process were complicated by the fact that the Kenyan commissioners were unwilling to participate in such a process themselves given the complicated ethnic politics involved. Ambassador Kiplagat was a member of the Kalenjin community. Some of the other commissioners were reluctant to take a public role in raising questions about Kiplagat for fear that they would be accused of pursuing an ethnic agenda. To his credit, Ambassador Kiplagat was perceived (mostly correctly in my view) as someone who valued national unity over ethnic politics. In fact, I was told that many prominent members of the Kalenjin community were privately critical of him because he was not viewed as sufficiently committed to such ethnic politics. Nevertheless, the issues raised against him were often characterized as being motivated by ethnicity rather than ethics, and we were later to discover that he was not above manipulating such narratives to support his own personal agenda.

One of the Kenyan commissioners suggested that the three internationals form a committee to evaluate the allegations against our chair. The use of the internationals would minimize the perception that the process was motivated by ethnicity, and the internationals would be less likely to be influenced by ethnic and other political pressures that might otherwise be put to bear on the Kenyan commissioners. While a panel of the international commissioners to address the allegations against Kiplagat would not have been my first choice (I was concerned that the mere fact we were colleagues serving on the same Commission might create a perception of bias, and I would later oppose similar proposals for this reason), I was so desperate that something be done that I agreed to this proposal, which seemed to have the support of all of the Kenyan commissioners. Commissioner Chawatama also agreed to the proposal. Ambassador Dinka was opposed to the idea, however, stating that the three of us should not take such a prominent role in the matter. We consulted with the local office of the Panel of Eminent African Personalities (the body that had nominated the international commissioners), and they also counseled that we should not participate in such a process. The Panel representatives raised the concern, also shared by Ambassador Dinka, that this was a Kenyan political fight into which we should not insert ourselves; even more importantly, they argued, we should avoid being manipulated by each side in what was essentially a Kenyan matter.

The political nature of the dispute was unclear to me. Was it a disagreement between the two major political parties (PNU and ODM) as embodied in Kiplagat and Murungi? Some viewed Ambassador Kiplagat as an agent of the PNU because of his ties to the current president and his administration. Some viewed Vice Chair Murungi as an agent of the ODM because her husband was a prominent member of that party. Was it a disagreement among self-appointed leaders of various ethnic groups, and thus yet another incident of Kalenjins being pitted against Kikuyus, or perhaps some other constellation of ethnic tension? If these were the dominant political strands implicated in the dispute, did it mean that the underlying issues of Kiplagat's conflicts of interest and integrity were secondary or even irrelevant? As I struggled to understand the political environment that led some to counsel caution or inaction, I was quick to admit that I was less informed than others about the political and ethnic dimensions of the issues before us. It was, in fact, this political and ethnic overlay that made it even more important, in my view, for us to focus on the actual issue presented by Kiplagat's conflicts of interest and to focus on a solution tailored to that problem. These were matters that, at least on the merits, could be divorced from the political and ethnic dynamics in which they were admittedly embedded.

The concern that we might be manipulated was one that I took seriously, but the reality was that we, the three internationals, were already being used and manipulated. First, our mere presence in the Commission increased its credibility. That increased credibility certainly served Kiplagat's cause and, if one were to believe the political analysis of many commentators, it also served the current government and in particular PNU. Second, by not treating the allegations seriously *because* of the politics, we were being manipulated to ignore facts – and not just any facts, but facts concerning issues that were at the core of our mandate. In other words, we were playing into the hands of those who had a political interest in sweeping Kiplagat's conflicts under the rug.

As the public pressure on the Commission to do something escalated, we acquired more information concerning Ambassador Kiplagat's conflicts of interest. We were finally able to secure access to a copy of the Troon Report concerning the Ouko assassination. Detective Superintendent John Troon of Scotland Yard led the first of many investigations into the assassination of the Kenyan Foreign Minister Robert Ouko. Minister Ouko was found dead in a remote forest near his rural home in February 1990. He had a broken ankle, bruising on his body, a gunshot wound to the head, and his torso was badly burnt – a canister of petrol, among other items, was found near the body. Shortly after his body was discovered, the government floated the idea that Ouko might have committed suicide. As we said in our report, "The idea that Ouko somehow broke his own leg, shot himself in the head, doused himself in petrol, and then lit himself on fire was too far-fetched to be believable."[6] Nevertheless, the suicide hypothesis was periodically resurrected in the decades

---

[6] Lest one think that such outlandish stories are unique to Kenya, a US government investigation into the deaths of three detainees at Guantanamo Bay reached a similar outlandish conclusion:

after the killing. Shortly after the discovery of the body, President Moi contacted Scotland Yard to assist in the investigation, and they dispatched Detective Superintendent Troon. Troon's investigation was marred by the lack of cooperation of a number of suspects, the unwillingness of the government to assist in the investigation, and the existence of a parallel investigation by the Kenyan Special Branch designed to undercut the Troon investigation. Troon abruptly fled the country less than six months after his arrival when he was almost killed with poison. Nevertheless, he had compiled a report of his findings and recommendations. That report had been given to President Moi at the end of 1990 and, like so many such reports in Kenya, had never been made public.

We had been anxious to see a copy of the Troon Report as it was rumored that it recommended further investigation of, among others, Ambassador Kiplagat. The rumor turned out to be accurate. Troon and his team had recommended that Kiplagat be interviewed and investigated further, not because of any suspicion that he might have been complicit in the killing but because he was found to have been an untruthful witness who probably knew far more about the circumstances leading up to the assassination than he was willing to divulge. It became clear to me at this point that Ambassador Kiplagat's conflict of interest on the Ouko matter was far more complicated and serious than that of a minor witness as he had earlier suggested to us. We were later to learn that each successive inquiry into the Ouko matter (and there have been at least three or four others, depending on what you count) had concluded that Kiplagat was hiding information that could be relevant to identifying those responsible for the assassination.

Concern over the findings and recommendations of the Troon Report led four of us (Commissioners Shava, Murungi, Chawatama, and me) to invoke a provision of our legislation that allows any commissioner to request that the chair convene a meeting of the Commission. On February 17, we sent an email to Ambassador Kiplagat requesting that he call a formal meeting of the Commission. We also indicated that we would like to take him up on his

According to the NCIS documents, each prisoner had fashioned a noose from torn sheets and T-shirts and tied it to the top of his cell's eight-foot-high steel mesh wall. Each prisoner was able somehow to bind his own hands, and, in at least one case, his own feet, then stuff more rags deep down into his own throat. We are then asked to believe that each prisoner, even as he was choking on those rags, climbed up on his washbasin, slipped his head through the noose, tightened it, and leapt from the washbasin to hang until he asphyxiated. The NCIS report also proposes that the three prisoners, who were held in nonadjoining cells, carried out each of these actions almost simultaneously.

Scott Horton, "The Guantanamo 'Suicides': A Camp Delta Sergeant Blows the Whistle," *Harpers Magazine*, March 2010, page 27.

earlier offer to absent himself from our deliberations so that we could engage in a candid discussion about the effect of his presence on the Commission. In the two days between our February 15 meeting and our request for a Commission meeting without him, Kiplagat began to harden his position. He responded to our email stating that he would call a meeting of the Commission as requested, but that he insisted on being present and that he would be consulting his lawyer concerning recent developments.

In the meantime, Commissioner Ojienda reported that he had had an important conversation with Amina Mohamed, the then permanent secretary in the Ministry of Justice. As a result of that conversation, Ojienda requested a meeting restricted to Kenyan commissioners so that he could share with them certain "directions" from the Ministry of Justice. The directions from the Ministry apparently included adopting a vigorous public relations campaign to address the allegations against Ambassador Kiplagat in a way that would put the whole thing to rest. Tom Ojienda would prove to be one of the most erratic of the commissioners, and his ducking and weaving with respect to the allegations against our chair was to prove no different. During much of February, he had rarely come to the office. I was told that Ojienda often avoided politically contentious issues by absenting himself from any opportunity to discuss them. Certainly, his actions during this period were consistent with this assessment of his character. On the major issue concerning our credibility and viability, Commissioner Ojienda varied from being a close confidant, advisor, and defender of Kiplagat, to demanding that Kiplagat immediately resign, and everything in between. Kiplagat would at times convey to us Ojienda's views on an issue during the many times he was absent from our deliberations. I was told that, during this period, Ojienda was consulting with numerous political actors in order to assess whether he should stay or resign. His calculations had more to do with his assessment of the political advantage or disadvantage he would receive for remaining or leaving the Commission, rather than the substantive issues we were facing. The fact that he viewed his service on the Commission primarily through a political lens meant that it was often difficult to predict in advance his position on any issue we faced. In addition, as we would experience with the Kiplagat issue and later with the president's interference in our report, Ojienda's position often changed quickly and substantially, presumably as he reassessed the political implications of his position.

At the same time that Commissioner Ojienda was receiving these instructions from the permanent secretary, Commissioner Murungi ran into the minister of justice, Mutula Kilonzo, and Professor Makau Mutua at the Serena Hotel. Professor Mutua is an accomplished human rights advocate who, among other things, assisted in running the human rights program at Harvard Law School for a number of years. At the time of this encounter, he was dean of the law school at SUNY Buffalo, and he continues to be active with some of the major human rights organizations in Kenya. Commissioner Murungi, Minister Kilonzo, and Professor Mutua proceeded to discuss the TJRC and our credibility crisis. Shortly after this meeting, Commissioner Murungi sent an email to all of the commissioners in which she recounted her meeting with the minister and Professor Mutua; recounted Commissioner Ojienda's request for a meeting of only the Kenyan commissioners to share certain "directions" from the Ministry; laid out her specific concerns about the conflicts of interest of our chair concerning land and the Ouko assassination; and stated that she would not be attending to any TJRC-related business unless and until we resolved the issues around our chair. She also reacted to what was becoming an increasingly ugly smear campaign which alleged that she and others were opposing Ambassador Kiplagat for ethnic reasons and that she was hoping to become Chair of the Commission. After noting these allegations, Commissioner Murungi made it clear that she had never to date, and never would in the future, stoop to engage in ethnic politics; that she wanted to state categorically that she had no interest in becoming chair; and that, if on the remote chance it were offered to her, she would refuse it.

Joining Commissioner Murungi, I also circulated an email to all of the commissioners setting forth my concerns about the allegations concerning our chair: he had admitted to the land transactions; he was a witness with respect to the Ouko assassination and had been identified as an unreliable witness by at least one previous investigation; and he could not remember if he had been in Wajir at the time of the alleged security meeting leading up to the Wagalla massacre. I also indicated that, like Kaari, I would only be available to work on developing a process for addressing these allegations. In that spirit, I suggested that we consider asking an outside individual or individuals to investigate all three of these areas of conflict and make recommendations concerning how we could best address them and move forward with our work. It was important, I emphasized, that the individual or individuals chosen to perform this function be acceptable to the chair, acceptable to the rest of us, and enjoy a high level of trust and credibility with the Kenyan people.

We held a formal Commission meeting on February 18; the sole agenda item was how to address the allegations implicating Ambassador Kiplagat. This was the meeting that Chawatama, Murungi, Shava, and I had requested. Kiplagat began the meeting by noting that although he had offered not to be present, he now preferred to be present. We agreed that he could stay but noted that the discussion might be less candid because of his presence.

Commissioner Ojienda did attend this meeting, and repeated arguments he had made earlier that Kiplagat should not resign as, in his view, that would "kill us" as each of us would then be picked off in turn by different political interests. Ojienda did, however, change tack and argue quite strongly that the issues facing Kiplagat should be addressed head on and directly and that Kiplagat should address each of the issues to us in writing. Some agreed with this process, while others, including me, were concerned that we not be placed in a position of judging our own chair. Such a position could only hurt us. If we exonerated Kiplagat, it would raise the suspicion that we were complicit with him in trying to keep him and us in our positions; if we made a finding against him (whatever that might mean), then we would find ourselves in the awkward position of having to enforce our decision against him and we might be viewed as acting to further our own personal interests (as was alleged about Commissioner Murungi).

We were facing the classic situation where an independent and credible body was needed to investigate, evaluate, and recommend a course of action – in fact, exactly the sort of process that the South African TRC undertook with respect to allegations leveled against one of their commissioners, Dumisa Ntsebeza. Ntsebeza was one of seventeen commissioners on the South African Truth and Reconciliation Commission. He was in charge of the investigations unit of the Commission. In late 1997, an individual came forward and testified that he had evidence that Commissioner Ntsebeza had driven the getaway car after what became known as the Heidelberg Tavern massacre, a brutal attack on a pub (the Heidelberg Tavern) in 1993 in which four civilians were killed and a number of others critically injured. President Mandela immediately appointed a constitutional court judge, Richard Goldstone, to investigate the allegations against Commissioner Ntsebeza. A few weeks later the witness recanted, claiming he had been tortured by the police into make the incriminating statement. Judge Goldstone undertook a thorough investigation and after a little over a month submitted to President Mandela his report in which he cleared Commissioner Ntsebeza of any wrongdoing and recommended further investigations into the circumstances leading to the false accusations. What had threatened to undermine the credibility of the South African truth commission had been quickly investigated and resolved, and both Commissioner Ntsebeza and the TRC were able to continue the important work with which they had been entrusted. It was my recommendation that the Kenyan government undertake a similar process. This suggestion was summarily rejected by the other commissioners.

Our February 18 meeting did not bring us any closer to a consensus on how to move forward. Ambassador Kiplagat stated that he would recuse himself

from those areas in which he had a conflict and that he had no problem
appearing before us as a witness in the matter of the assassination of Minister
Ouko; he assured us that there could be no other surprises with respect to him
and the issues we were to investigate. His claim of full disclosure and promise
of no new surprises is, in hindsight, ironic given later revelations concerning
the Wagalla massacre and his possession of numerous documents concerning
the events leading up to the massacre. In other words, he refused to agree to
any process that would examine his conflicts of interest.

   With little agreement on how to move forward, two informal camps developed among the commissioners. As with every issue except our last (involving
the interference by the president in our report), the division among us was not
on ethnic or nationality grounds, but on politics and principle. Chawatama,
Murungi, Shava, and I felt that we could not move forward with our work
until we had agreed to some process to address the issues around Kiplagat.
Farah, Dinka, and, to some extent, Ojienda were not all in agreement but
were more of the view that we should just do our work and mostly ignore
the political storm surrounding Kiplagat. Wanjala stayed somewhat independent of both groups, though she more often leaned towards the position of
moving forward with our work rather than undertaking a process. Ojienda was
the most erratic and the most difficult to pin down, some days arguing that
Kiplagat should resign without any process at all (a position I was not willing to
take) or that Kiplagat should stay and we should just move on (which I also
opposed). During this period, he only seemed to view the issue in the context of these two extremes. Kiplagat himself also changed his position on the
nature of the process he wanted – ranging from having his lawyer make a
presentation to us, to us setting up an internal commission of inquiry, to
setting up a tribunal as provided for in our legislation, to his meeting with each
of us individually to convince us of his innocence. This last proposal underscored Kiplagat's lack of understanding concerning the challenge we faced
because of his presence. Kiplagat seemed to view the issue as one of our
individual assessment of his innocence or guilt. If he could prove that he
was not guilty of the allegations, he argued, he should not resign. That was
a defensible position, but it presupposed a credible process by which the
strength of the allegations raised against him would be tested. When we
suggested the creation of an independent process that would examine the
allegations and then recommend whether he should leave the Commission or
remain (and if he remained, what, if any, procedures we should put into place,
given his conflicts of interest), he immediately claimed we were assuming he
was guilty and rejected the suggestion.

Kiplagat's insistence that the issue was whether he was innocent or guilty of a crime also underscored his fundamental misunderstanding of the purpose and function of a truth commission and, in particular, the purpose and function of *this* truth commission. This misunderstanding can be illustrated with each of the three issues that had been raised about him: land, the Ouko assassination, and the Wagalla massacre. With respect to land, Ambassador Kiplagat claimed that his acquisition of land during his service in the Moi government was consistent with the then-existing laws and government procedures. Yet the Commission was not asked to evaluate whether the history of land transactions were consistent with the then-existing government rules and regulations. The Commission was required to examine whether such practices were unjust or not, and whether, and to what extent, they contributed to or were linked to other gross violations of human rights within our mandate. To do this, we would need to develop a set of criteria for judging whether certain practices with respect to land acquisitions were just or not, and then apply those criteria to the historical record. The result of this exercise could be that transactions like those of which Kiplagat was a part might be found to be unjust notwithstanding the fact that they were consistent with government policy at the time. Much, although not all, of the racial oppression committed by the apartheid government in South Africa was legal under South African law. That does not mean that it was right or just. The same could be said about much of the discrimination practiced in Nazi Germany and many other historical atrocities. An evaluation of the justness and impact of prominent government officials and their acquaintances acquiring plots of land "irregularly" – to use a Kenyan term of art – was a core part of our mandate. Given his participation in these "irregular" land transactions, Kiplagat clearly had a personal interest in whether, and how, we might find such transactions to be unjust.

With respect to the Ouko assassination, he was alleged to have been present during significant events that some believe explain why Ouko was assassinated. Kiplagat thus was a witness, and perhaps an important witness, to events that might explain why Ouko was assassinated and who might be responsible. In and of itself, the fact that Kiplagat was a witness, even an important witness, was not insurmountable. While it would be awkward to have him appear before us as a witness, if there were or had been no questions about his credibility, we could quickly take his testimony and then move on. The problem was that Ambassador Kiplagat's credibility with respect to his candor about events leading up to the Ouko assassination had been questioned by at least four previous investigations into the matter. This would mean that we as a Commission would have to come to a conclusion concerning a matter that was in dispute between our chair and four previous investigations. As with the land transactions, Ambassador Kiplagat had a personal interest in whether we found his testimony credible. If we found his testimony to be credible, we would be disagreeing with the conclusion of four previous investigations. We would thus need to provide cogent reasons why we disagreed with those previous assessments. Inevitably, such a conclusion on our part would be viewed with suspicion by the public, given that he was not only our colleague but also our chair. The alternative would be to find that he was not credible, which would, at a minimum, place a strain on our internal working relationship and, more likely, raise other questions about his credibility and integrity. In other words, given the history of his testimony concerning this matter, we would inevitably be placed in the position of judging his character and integrity in a way that would damage either our own credibility with the public or our working relationship with him. The dilemma had nothing to do with whether he was innocent or guilty of complicity in the assassination of Minister Ouko.

Finally, in the case of the Wagalla massacre, we did not at the time know that he had in fact been present at an important security committee meeting less than forty-eight hours before the start of the massacre. He was later to admit to us and to the public that he had in fact been present at that meeting. There is an important question about whether and to what extent those who are involved in the planning of an operation are legally responsible for crimes committed during its implementation. There is a sophisticated and complicated body of jurisprudence developed by the *ad hoc* international criminal tribunals and the international criminal court concerning the guilt or innocence of individuals who are involved in such meetings. The TJRC, like every other truth commission, was not empowered to determine the legal guilt or innocence of such individuals. This is understandable, as such evaluations require a searching review of all of the evidence, testimony from relevant witnesses including the accused, and robust legal representation both supporting the allegations and defending the innocence of the accused. As the handful of international trials that have addressed these issues illustrate, such inquiries are expensive and time consuming – understandably so, as they concern the guilt or innocence of an accused and thus whether that individual will be incarcerated for his or her actions. While we could and did recommend that certain individuals be further investigated and, if the evidence warranted, prosecuted, as a truth commission we did not have the power, time, or resources to determine whether an individual was guilty or innocent. With respect to the security meeting that Kiplagat attended before the Wagalla massacre, we would be evaluating the relationship between that meeting and the massacre itself: how that meeting fit into the overall planning of the massacre, what was decided at that meeting, whether participants in that meeting could have changed what later happened, etc. Based upon that evaluation, we then might recommend that the individuals who were involved in that meeting be further investigated if we thought there was sufficient evidence to suggest that they might be criminally liable for what later happened. We would not be determining the ultimate guilt or innocence of those individuals. Rather, we would be determining whether further investigations should be undertaken, which might then lead to a process that would determine the guilt or innocence of those individuals. Our conclusions with respect to that matter were something with which Kiplagat obviously had a personal interest.

Kiplagat's focus on his guilt or innocence made perfect sense from his own personal point of view. Like many individuals accused of wrongdoing, he wanted a process by which his responsibility could be determined conclusively. His assertion was that he was innocent of any wrongdoing; he understandably wanted this to be established publicly so he could put these many allegations behind him. As I attempted to explain to him a number of times, as a truth commission we did not have the power to determine whether he was guilty or innocent of the crimes he was alleged to have committed. We were not a court of law. Yet Kiplagat wanted us to perform that function for him. This misunderstanding of our powers and purposes lay at the center of the dispute between Ambassador Kiplagat and the rest of us from those early months of 2010 to the day we handed over our final report in May 2013.

Although we had insisted we would do no mandate-related work, both Kaari Murungi and I participated in meetings with consultants who had performed research for us, and we participated in meetings with various stakeholders. I found myself occupying multiple worlds – putting on a pleasant "we are all working together" face with stakeholders and others, while privately becoming more and more discouraged at the lack of progress of any proposal to address what we were now calling "the Kiplagat problem." Ambassador Kiplagat continued to engage in dissembling, manipulation, and political maneuvering to strengthen his own position, often at the expense of the Commission. It took all of my patience and energy to be civil to him in public, and I tried to avoid him as much as possible in the office. Like Kaari, I was beginning to find the situation intolerable and started to worry that my association with him would tarnish my own reputation unless we came up with a credible process. I was asked from time to time if I was going to resign. I certainly considered it but took the position, which I held throughout the four years of the Commission's life, that I would stay so long as I was convinced that I could achieve more good on the inside than on the outside, and so long as I felt comfortable defending my decision to stay. Until I no longer had a credible argument for staying, I would continue to do everything I could to further the process.

We met again on Monday, February 22. By this point, Kiplagat had clearly hardened his position and declared categorically that he would not step down, even temporarily, no matter what process, if any, we might undertake. He again proposed that he invite his lawyers to come and present the issues to us. He thus still viewed us as the appropriate decision-makers with respect to the issues around him, and the resort to lawyers showed that he also viewed the matter as an adversarial one between us and him, rather than a broader issue affecting the credibility and functioning of the Commission itself. During that meeting, I began to write out for myself the reasons I should resign.

PARLIAMENT WEIGHS IN

Our inaction with respect to our mandate-related functions during this period, along with all of the controversy surrounding Kiplagat's presence on the Commission, attracted the attention of Parliament. On Tuesday, February 23, the Parliamentary Committee on Justice and Legal Affairs discussed the challenges facing the Commission – challenges that the Parliamentary Committee noted "require urgent attention" – and invited us to a meeting with them on Friday, February 26. I had not received advance notice of our being called before the Parliamentary Committee and did not know what to expect. We had been told that the agenda was to discuss the challenges we were facing. While I assumed this meant the credibility issues surrounding Kiplagat, the communication was not that specific. We were also assured that the hearing, though public, would not be televised. To prepare for this important meeting, a number of us requested that we meet the day before in the office to discuss strategy. While some of us showed up for this meeting, we did not have enough members present for a quorum (which required six commissioners, including one international) and most importantly, and perhaps ominously, Kiplagat refused to attend. It later became clear that he was busy crafting his own strategy separate from that of the Commission.

On the eve of our meeting with Parliament, Archbishop Desmond Tutu and nine other former members of truth commissions from around the world issued a public statement urging Kiplagat to resign.[7] The statement was one of

---

[7] *See* International Center for Transitional Justice, "Desmond Tutu and Others Urge Kiplagat to Step Down as TJRC Chair," (February 25, 2010) and the attached statement of the ten former commissioners (on website). The ten included the chairs of the truth commissions of South Africa, Peru, and Sierra Leone.

the top stories on that evening's news and the Friday morning newspapers the next day, which were being peddled on the streets as we made our way to Parliament. Ambassador Kiplagat immediately raised questions about whether Archbishop Tutu had in fact endorsed the statement. Shortly afterwards, Kiplagat and Tutu spoke by phone. I did not hear Kiplagat's version of what was discussed but understood from Archbishop Tutu that Kiplagat was adamant that he would not resign.

As I was driving to the meeting at Parliament, Commissioner Ojienda called me and excitedly said that I would be very pleased with what was about to happen. I later learned that Kiplagat had indicated to Commissioner Ojienda earlier that day that he was going to announce his resignation during our meeting with Parliament. When we arrived at Parliament, Kiplagat was already in the room clearly preparing to make a statement to a large coterie of assembled press. He had clearly alerted the press that he would be making a formal statement. As the other commissioners arrived, Kiplagat read his statement to the press.[8] The statement was directed both to the public and to us, his fellow commissioners. It was a significant sign of our strained relationship with him that he addressed us on a number of issues for the first time through this press conference.

In his statement, Kiplagat lashed out at the "media lynch mob" that was behind the calls for his resignation. Vowing not to succumb to such pressure, he declared that he was "enjoining himself" to a lawsuit that had been filed months ago against the Commission by an organization called Kenyans Against Impunity. Kenyans Against Impunity consisted of a number of victims of the 2007 post-election violence. They had filed a lawsuit against the Commission just after we were formed, challenging, *inter alia*, the process by which we had been appointed and claiming that Ambassador Kiplagat's appointment as chair of the Commission was invalid because his oath of office had been administered prior to the publication of the *Gazette* notice appointing us as Commissioners.[9] None of the lawyers on the Commission had any clear understanding of what he meant by "enjoining" himself to that lawsuit. (I had initially thought this was a particular procedural move under Kenyan law, but the Kenyan lawyers I consulted said they did not know what it meant.) It was clear, however, that he had already decided upon a course of action without any consultation with the rest of us, and, from what we could tell, a course of action that would almost assuredly not

---

[8] *See* "Statement by Ambassador Bethuel Kiplagat" (on website).
[9] *Augustine Njeru Kathangu & 9 Others v. TRJC and Bethuel Kiplagat* (High Court Misc. App. No. 470 of 2009). We included a summary of the case in the TJRC Final Report, *supra* Chapter 1, note 9, at Vol. 1, Ch. 4, paragraphs 95–102.

address directly the issues concerning his conflicts of interest. As our official spokesperson, he had now publicly announced how we as a Commission would proceed without any discussion with, much less consent from, the rest of us. He had again used his position to avoid us and pursue his own self-interested agenda.

Commissioner Ojienda was visibly taken aback at Kiplagat's statement, as he was expecting Kiplagat to announce his resignation. Ojienda was the first to speak after Kiplagat read his statement to the press and asked Kiplagat if he wanted to clarify his statement – clearly thinking or hoping that Kiplagat had mistakenly omitted the language indicating his intention to resign. Kiplagat politely responded to Ojienda that he did not feel a need to clarify further his statement. Clearly Ojienda had misunderstood, or been misled by, Kiplagat concerning his intentions.

In yet another sign of the barriers Kiplagat was constructing between us, we were only able to secure a copy of Kiplagat's written press statement from members of civil society. Kiplagat never made the statement available to us, even after he had issued it, much less before he had made it public.

After Kiplagat read his statement, we turned to the meeting at hand and answered questions from members of the Committee. Ambassador Kiplagat was asked specifically if he had attended the meeting in Wajir two days before the start of the massacre. My notes of Kiplagat's response are as follows: "I do not recall. We are checking the records. I was on the national security committee. That committee *never* set out to deal with operations. I am confident I did not go, but I am checking."[10]

The minister of justice also made an appearance at this meeting. While we were still in the room, the minister stated that the government took no position on the matters affecting us other than that the rule of law should be followed. Notwithstanding his initial statement of government indifference, he did suggest that we conduct a public hearing with Kiplagat as a witness, including full cross-examination and other attributes of a judicial process. When I responded that such a process would take up precious time that we could otherwise spend on our mandate-related activities, he quickly responded that the government would provide us with more time, demonstrating that the government could adjust things quite easily if they saw it was in their interest to do so. After we left the Committee room, the minister remained behind. We were later told

---

[10] Kiplagat appears to have misspoken in placing himself on the National Security Committee. It would later come out that he was a member of the Kenya Intelligence Committee, which was the body that met in Wajir less than forty-eight hours before the start of the Wagalla massacre.

that after we left, the minister stated categorically to the Committee that if Kiplagat were no longer the chair then the entire Commission should be disbanded. So much for the government not taking a position.

THE US AMBASSADOR WEIGHS IN: "EVERYONE STEALS LAND"

After the Parliamentary meeting, I proceeded to the residence of the US Ambassador, Michael Ranneberger. Up until that morning, the US had officially adopted a hands-off approach to the Commission. Officials in the Embassy had confided in me that the US government believed that the Kenyan government had created the Commission to replace, rather than complement, the proposed special court to prosecute those responsible for the 2007 election violence. This was not an unreasonable assumption, particularly given that immediately after our creation, and shortly after Kofi Annan had handed evidence to the ICC prosecutor, the Cabinet met and proposed that our mandate be altered to allow us to prosecute those responsible for the post-election violence. We unanimously rejected this proposal and it was never raised again. The US government had been pushing hard for a credible process to hold accountable those responsible for the post-election violence. US officials feared that supporting the TJRC could be interpreted as supporting an alternative process to the ICC or other mechanisms of criminal accountability, such as the special tribunal recommended by the Waki Commission. In fact, we assumed that, like many other truth commissions, we would be operating alongside parallel processes of prosecution.[11]

Given the position taken by the United States, I was surprised when, as I was heading into Parliament that morning, I read in the morning newspapers that the US ambassador had made a strong public statement supporting Kiplagat and arguing that the Kenyan people should give him a chance to prove himself.[12] This statement was reported simultaneously with the statement by Archbishop Tutu and others calling upon Kiplagat to resign. I was surprised that the US position had apparently gone from, at best, indifference and, at worst, hostility, to one of supporting our chair in the face of the allegations that had been raised against him. The fact that the US government

[11] Truth commissions that have operated while criminal prosecutions have also been pursued include South Africa, Sierra Leone, and East Timor.
[12] *See* Lucianne Limo, "Why Tutu and Team Told Kiplagat to Resign," *The Standard*, February 26, 2010 (reporting that the US Ambassador "has defended the embattled TJRC chair," and "urged the commission to ignore calls for Kiplagat's resignation and move on with its work").

statement was issued at the same time as that of Archbishop Tutu made the US position even more puzzling.

I had been contacted by a number of people in the US Embassy who had become increasingly concerned that the US ambassador had not been briefed adequately on the issues raised about Kiplagat's past. They had arranged for me to meet with him to discuss the substance of the concerns. With the ambassador publicly taking a stand in defense of Kiplagat, these individuals now impressed upon me the importance of my upcoming meeting with him. Their hope was that I could at least convince him not to say anything more about the matter publicly (it was unlikely that he would publicly perform an about-face and say anything critical about Kiplagat or otherwise reverse his position).

I met with Ambassador Ranneberger at his private residence in Muthaiga, a suburb of Nairobi filled with large estates where many of the Kenyan elite and foreign diplomatic corps live. We met for a little less than an hour. I summarized for him the three areas of concern that had been raised about Kiplagat and provided him with a memorandum I had written analyzing each of the three issues. Over the course of our conversation, it became evident that the Ambassador and Kiplagat were acquaintances, and perhaps even friends. During our conversation, the ambassador pointed out, correctly, the positive role that Kiplagat had played in bringing calm to the country after the 2007 post-election violence, as well as the general role that Kiplagat had played as a peacemaker on the continent in the last two decades. I conceded that these were all admirable accomplishments but pointed out that Ambassador Kiplagat was implicated with respect to three specific areas of violations within our mandate and that, at a minimum, a process should be undertaken to evaluate those allegations. On the land issue, the ambassador somewhat surprisingly observed that "everyone" in Kenya had benefited from shady land deals, implying that Kiplagat's land dealings, which he had readily admitted, should not concern us. I was surprised by this reaction since the US Ambassador had been quite vocal – some thought too vocal – on issues of corruption in the current government.[13] His suggestion that we should just overlook Kiplagat's involvement in such land dealings – particularly when the propriety of such transactions was expressly within our mandate – was shocking. The US ambassador was, however, surprised by Tutu's statement calling for Kiplagat's resignation.

[13] *See, e.g.,* Nick Wadhams, "Kenya: US Ambassador's Crusade against Corruption," *Time Magazine,* January 28, 2011, http://content.time.com/time/world/article/0,8599,2044615,00.html (noting how outspoken, and controversial, Ambassador Ranneberger had been on raising the issue of corruption in Kenya).

I told him that Kiplagat and Tutu had recently spoken on the phone for approximately half an hour during which Kiplagat had apparently dug in his heels even more strongly, insisting that he was innocent and would not resign. In an effort to enlist the ambassador's assistance, I suggested that if he were close to Kiplagat he might try to convince him that his insistence that he remain on the Commission without any credible process to evaluate the allegations against him would not benefit him in the long run. The ambassador seemed open to the idea but then noted that he was not particularly close to Kiplagat. I left disappointed, realizing that the ambassador would probably not be that helpful in convincing Kiplagat to change course, and disillusioned by his matter-of-fact reaction to the land issue. I hoped, however, that as a result of our conversation the ambassador would refrain from making any more public statements on the matter. As far as I am aware, he remained silent publicly on the matter during the remainder of his tenure as ambassador.

KIPLAGAT'S DANCE

As I left the ambassador's residence, Kiplagat called me. This was to be the first of a series of phone calls we were to have over the coming weekend. He began by stating that he wanted to "run a few things by me." He floated the idea of "disengaging" from the Commission for the next three to four weeks. When I asked what he meant by "disengaging," he said that he would continue to come to work, attend Commission meetings and engage in Commission-related work but that he would keep a lower public profile. I thought this was a ridiculous suggestion and a curious use of the word "disengagement," but replied that I thought the idea should be raised with all commissioners at a proper meeting. My primary goal at this point was to have him engage with us collectively rather than individually, as had been his practice. By this point, I had learned that although he often spoke of collaboration and consultation, and equally often spoke approvingly of what he called African-based consensus decision-making, his preferred mode of operation was to engage each of us individually so he could control the conversation and minimize collaboration and consultation among the rest of us. I was careful during these one-on-one conversations not to commit myself to any position or course of action – though that did not stop Kiplagat from representing the reverse to others.

Kiplagat then complained to me about Tutu's statement, as he had now confirmed that Archbishop Tutu had, in fact, joined the nine other former truth commissioners in calling for Kiplagat to support the process by stepping aside. He mentioned to me that a local Anglican bishop had contacted him and complained that Tutu had not run his statement by him. I responded that

I did not think Tutu was speaking as a bishop, at which point Kiplagat interrupted me and said that there were important issues of protocol, even in matters involving the Church. As with so many of my conversations with Kiplagat, I realized that he was more interested in conveying information to me than engaging in a dialogue about the issues facing him, and us. So when he twice said to me that he "has not yet ruled out suing Tutu," I politely listened and said somewhat cautiously that I did not think suing Tutu would assist him in clearing his name, which, he claimed, was his primary concern. Sadly, by this point, and throughout this whole process, it was increasingly clear that the effect of his presence and actions on the Commission and our ability to undertake the important work with which we had been entrusted were not his primary concerns. He would dispute this at times, most famously when he had said earlier that week in a Commission meeting that he *was* the Commission and that what was good for him was good for the Commission. I remember trying to hide my astonishment at this blatant statement of personal power and importance; I looked down to avoid eye contact with my fellow commissioners and wrote in my notepad, "Louis XIV."

Over the weekend, there was a flurry of phone calls among us. Many rumors were passed about, including assurances from Commissioner Ojienda and others that Kiplagat would be announcing his resignation any day. I also heard that there was a conspiracy within the government to discredit Kofi Annan and the Panel, even including efforts to have Annan and the Panel formally censured by the African Union (rumors I had heard during the preceding few months). Kiplagat meanwhile called me numerous times to float various ideas, none of which included him doing anything meaningful with respect to addressing his conflicts of interest. From his conversations with me, I had no sense that he was even contemplating stepping aside, much less about to announce such a step. The weekend newspapers were filled with articles and opinion pieces about us, most of which either demanded that he resign or that the entire commission be disbanded.

At this point I was convinced that the whole project was doomed. I was tired and frustrated. Kiplagat continued moving from one idea to another and resisted any efforts to have us come together to discuss and design a strategy to which we could all agree. After ambushing us with his own press conference at the meeting with Parliament, our trust in him had decreased substantially. The statement by the minister – particularly his reported statement that without Kiplagat the Commission should be disbanded – made clear to me that there was, and probably always had been, a sinister objective on the part of the government with respect to the Commission.

FIGURE 3.2 Gado – I will not resign. Image courtesy of Gado (gadocartoons.com).

As the weekend came to a close, I resigned myself to waiting to see what others would do. There were a lot of ideas on the table. The questions were what, if anything, Kiplagat was willing to do, and what, if anything, the government was willing to do. I would wait, though I began to mentally prepare myself for returning back to the USA in a few months.

As we came out of the weekend, a Commission meeting was scheduled for Tuesday, March 2, which was then postponed until Wednesday, March 3. When we finally met, Kiplagat was as adamant as ever about staying with the Commission and seemed oddly reenergized either because of or despite the recent events. He announced that both PNU and ODM supported us and that we should move forward with our work. With respect to the issues raised about his presence, he announced that he was putting together a dossier that he would submit to court the next week. He spoke extemporaneously about the merits of the allegations raised against him, claiming over and over that they were not true. He also attacked the credibility of the Ndung'u Report (the land report in which some of his land transactions were mentioned), the chair of the Parliamentary Committee that investigated the Ouko assassination (which had found him to be an uncooperative and untruthful witness), and others.

While the events of the past few days may have emboldened Kiplagat, they had weakened his support within the Commission. Commissioner Dinka, who up until this point had been cautious in his approach, surprised me with his efforts during this meeting to get Kiplagat to see the advantages of stepping aside. Our newly appointed CEO, Patricia Nyaundi, quite passionately argued how his presence was distracting from our mandate and that until the issues around him were adequately addressed, he should step aside. Notwithstanding these pleas and the clear wish of now most of his fellow commissioners that he relieve us of the burden of his presence, Kiplagat continued to refuse to consider any alternative other than the *status quo*. In fact, he dismissively cut short our discussion and said that we should move on with our work and discuss other issues unrelated to the challenges raised by his presence.

Perhaps to convince us of the folly of our position, Kiplagat stated during this meeting that if he left we would receive no money from the government. This was somewhat curious, as at that point we had received minimal financial support from the government (and, as set out later in this chapter, the government continued to control our finances contrary to the clear requirements of our enabling legislation), thus raising a question about the credibility of this threat, not to mention its propriety. We were all deflated after this meeting. I was convinced more than ever that we would never be allowed to do our work. Without a credible process to address the Kiplagat problem, we would, at best, find little support for our work and us and, at worst, be met with outright hostility and active opposition. To pass the time and get my mind off of our increasingly untenable position, I read a popular mystery novel. At the start of one of the chapters is the following quotation that resonated with our current predicament: "I have never yet found Pride in a noble nature; nor humility in an unworthy mind."[14]

As we entered into March, it was clear that Kiplagat had decided to operate on his own, using the platform provided by the Commission to defend his own position. It was around this time that we were also informed that he had hired a public relations firm to assist him with his image. It was not clear who paid for the firm or whether it was meant to work on behalf of the Commission or just Ambassador Kiplagat. I was never consulted about hiring them nor about how they were used. He mentioned to us in passing that he had been meeting with various stakeholders, government officials, diplomats, and members of civil society. He was apparently meeting with them officially on behalf of the

---

[14] Attributed to Owen Felltham, RESOLVES (1623) vi. Of Arrogance, *quoted in* Michael Cox, THE MEANING OF NIGHT: A CONFESSION (New York: W.W. Norton, 2006).

Commission as our chair and spokesperson, yet we had neither advance knowledge of these meetings nor knowledge of their purpose or content, much less
any input into what message should be conveyed to these important stakeholders on behalf of the Commission. I was told that he had had a private
meeting with Kofi Annan during which he claimed that he had the support of
both parties in the coalition government. For the next few months, he was
often spotted hanging out in the lobby of the Serena Hotel[15] in the hope of
meeting influential politicians and others to whom he could plead his case.

In light of these meetings and of Kiplagat's decision to cut off any discussion
among us about his conflicts, I wrote an email to my fellow commissioners
setting out our current situation and suggesting that we come together to agree
on a strategy for moving forward that had the input, and agreement, of each
and every one of us. In my message, I reiterated that Kiplagat had every right to
defend himself but that his unilateral decision to use his position as chair to
pursue his private interest in order, to use his words, "clear his name," affected
all of us and our obligations to the people of Kenya.

In the midst of all of this, we received word that the government was not
going to provide us with any more money for the fiscal year 2009–2010. This
meant that our plans to hire professional staff and to begin our statement
taking that spring would have to be postponed. We would not be receiving any
additional money until after July 1 (the start of the new fiscal year), and even
then, we were not sure how much we would be receiving or when it would be
released to us. I was informed at this point that the prime minister appeared to
be indifferent to a genuine truth commission, and thus was not amenable to
spending political capital to support us in our work. We also heard, not
surprisingly, that the president was supporting Kiplagat in retaining his chairmanship. During this same period, former president Moi, who up until this
point had spoken out against the Commission as a whole, issued a statement
defending Kiplagat.

As we entered the second week of March, it was clear that we still had no
plan and that Kiplagat and his allies were mobilizing to keep him in place.
Communication among commissioners had broken down so badly that we
probably no longer knew our individual positions. Kiplagat continued to try to
engage with us individually rather than collectively. It was now seven months

---

[15] The Serena Hotel was the preferred hotel for both visiting dignitaries and prominent Kenyan
politicians. Kofi Annan always stayed there when he officially visited Kenya, and he often
held his meetings there. Consequently, the lobby of the Serena Hotel was a good place for
Kiplagat to station himself as he lobbied on his own behalf.

after we had been sworn in, and we had made very little progress on our mandate-related activities.

Commissioners Chawatama, Murungi, Shava, and I continued to meet outside of the office to strategize about a way forward. Given the breakdown in communications, we concluded that we should propose a retreat for all commissioners facilitated by a neutral outsider. We needed to hear each other's views on where we were and how, if at all, we could move forward. It was clear that we were unable to organize such a meeting ourselves, in part given Kiplagat's insistence that we just move on with our work.

The commissioners all agreed that a retreat would be useful, but we quickly got bogged down with the details. Ambassador Dinka sent a message to all of us in which he expressed the view that we should not have an outside facilitator. He argued that we could and should address our own issues among ourselves, and that retaining the services of a facilitator would provide support to the public's perception that we were "at each other's throats." A number of commissioners supported Ambassador Dinka's suggestion of a retreat without the benefit of a facilitator. Given our continued failure to discuss the issues constructively at numerous Commission meetings, and Kiplagat's refusal to allow such a discussion at our last formal meeting, most of us still felt that we needed an outside facilitator to ensure a productive conversation. Kiplagat had repeatedly demonstrated his inability to separate his own interests from that of the Commission in order to facilitate such a discussion. Each of the rest of us were already associated (whether accurately or not) with strong positions on the issue by the rest of us, so it was unlikely that any one commissioner would garner the support of the rest of us to facilitate such a discussion. For a week, we spent a good deal of time struggling to reach a consensus about the format of the process that we would use to come up with a process to address the issues raised by Kiplagat's presence on the Commission. This focus on the process for developing a process was not an auspicious sign.

With our inability to agree to the basic format of a retreat, I began to draft an open letter that we would release to the media concerning Kiplagat and the challenges we faced. We were no closer to a process or solution than we had been in early February. I had worked with a number of the other commissioners to come up with a way forward, but we were unable to bridge the growing divide that was developing among us. Publicly we had been portraying the Commission as productive and working through a number of issues, including the conflicts of interest of our chair. While I had agreed, and even in the early days supported, our public face of unity, our inability to come to any agreement on a way forward convinced me that such a policy was becoming counterproductive. My draft open letter noted that our public silence up until that point had been reasonably, but incorrectly, interpreted as indifference and that we were, in fact, "seriously and profoundly concerned about the allegations that have been raised against our chairman." Instead of arguing for his resignation (a position that still did not enjoy majority support among the commissioners), the letter stated that he should temporarily resign while a credible process was undertaken to address the allegations raised against him. As I did not want to act unilaterally, I circulated the draft letter to all of the commissioners, including Kiplagat. In yet another sign of his unwillingness to treat these issues seriously, he expressed shock that such a letter would even be contemplated as, in his words, we had all agreed to move forward with our work. In fact, others to whom he had confided reported to me that he was, in fact, dismissive of the concerns we had raised and suggested that if some commissioners were to resign, they would be replaced with others, and the process would move on. By this point, it was clear that he was not interested in a credible and independent process to address the allegations raised against him.

Notwithstanding, or perhaps because of, Kiplagat's expression of intransigence in response to my draft public letter, the commissioners all agreed to participate in a retreat facilitated by an outside mediator. On March 17, we assembled at La Mada in Nairobi for the retreat, the sole agenda of which was "the Kiplagat problem." After much debate internally, we had all agreed to have an external facilitator, Njoki Muhoho, who had successfully facilitated one of our initial orientation retreats. In addition to the nine commissioners, our newly appointed CEO, Patricia Nyaundi, also attended.

During the retreat, Kiplagat made clear again that his resigning was not on the table. Illustrating yet again how he refused to separate his own personal interests from that of the Commission and even the personal interests of other commissioners, he also stated at the retreat that Commissioner Murungi should not resign, for if she did, it would imply that he, Kiplagat, was guilty.

Kiplagat clearly wanted to come out of the retreat with an agreement that we had resolved any concerns we might have had about his past actions. In his effort to resolve the issues quickly, he stated to us that the only real issue was the Ouko matter. The land issue, he argued, he and his lawyers could address. He did not say anything about the allegations related to Wagalla.

Near the end of the retreat, Kiplagat pulled out of his briefcase a set of papers and suggested that he present his case to the commissioners, after which we would reach a decision concerning his innocence or guilt, and that would put an end to the matter. He stated that he was prepared to prove to us that he had acted legally when he acquired the plots of land in dispute. By acting legally, he apparently meant that he had followed the internal procedures set out by the government for individuals like him to acquire land that had been reserved for poor and landless Kenyans.

Kiplagat's suggestion that he present evidence to us concerning his land acquisitions, after which we would conclude whether he was guilty or not of wrongdoing, was fraught with all of the difficulties discussed above: we were not objective, we would not be perceived as being objective by outside consti- tuencies, and any decision we reached would be questioned and further erode our public credibility. In addition, Kiplagat was proposing that we base our decision solely on evidence collected by him and his lawyers. There was no provision for other evidence to be sought or presented, nor provision for other interested individuals to testify or present evidence. This was ludicrous. In response to this proposal, I stated to Kiplagat that we had no power to exoner- ate him of any of the allegations made against him. I pointed out to him that even if we felt he was innocent of all of the allegations, a judicial body such as a court could, if presented with the same evidence or, more likely, the same evidence supplemented with other evidence and arguments, reach a different conclusion. Kiplagat seemed profoundly shaken by this idea and immediately put his papers away.

THE TRIBUNAL IDEA

We came away from the retreat no closer to a solution to the Kiplagat prob- lem. This lack of progress, however, may have triggered an opportunity. His repeated inability to get us to drop the matter forced Kiplagat to consider other strategies. It was at this point that Kiplagat began to float the idea of requesting a tribunal as set forth in our enabling legislation.

Our enabling legislation sets out the procedures that must be followed in order to remove a commissioner.[16] The procedures were designed to make such removal difficult, which was appropriate given that our credibility was in part dependent on our ability to operate independently of the government and other outside actors. In making the removal of a commissioner difficult, the drafters of the legislation put in place a mechanism that increased our political independence. In fact, the subsequent desire on the part of the government to have me removed from the Commission would require a similar procedure, which they were apparently not willing to undertake. Ambassador Kiplagat had thus chosen a procedure that was designed to make it difficult to find him unfit to serve on the Commission.

---

[16] TJRC Act, *supra* Chapter 1, note 3, at Art. 17.

Only the president could remove a commissioner.[17] Before the president removes a commissioner, the Chief Justice must appoint a tribunal consisting of three current or former judges of the High Court. The tribunal would examine the relevant facts and make a recommendation concerning the removal of the Commissioner. That recommendation would go first to the chief justice, who in turn would communicate it to the president. Since the tribunal's conclusions constituted a recommendation, the president could either follow its advice or come to his own independent conclusion. Thus, there was the possibility that the three-judge panel could recommend that Kiplagat be removed, yet the president could still refuse to remove him. We would then face the situation of a public rebuke of our chair (by the three-judge panel) with the possibility that he would refuse to resign, which would ensure the death of the Commission.

The legislation provided only four bases for the removal of a commissioner: (a) misbehavior or misconduct; (b) convicted of an offense involving moral turpitude but not sentenced to a term of imprisonment; (c) inability to discharge the functions of the office by reason of physical or mental infirmity; or (d) absence from three consecutive meetings of the Commission without good cause.[18]

Kiplagat's new strategy of requesting a tribunal was not ideal. The legislation did not expressly mention conflicts of interest as a basis for removal, thus raising the question of how such a process could be used to address the allegations and conflicts of interest that Kiplagat claimed he wanted addressed. Nevertheless, this was the process that Kiplagat would eventually insist he preferred and that we would eventually embrace.

The retreat ended with little consensus on the way forward, other than that we would meet again in three weeks to take up the matter. One of the agreements we did reach was to have an independent and external lawyer join us in April to offer his or her views on the legal implications of Kiplagat's conflicts. There were two reasons we agreed to invite an independent lawyer. First, such an individual could provide an independent legal assessment for the non-lawyer commissioners who unfortunately found themselves being presented with conflicting interpretations of our act by the five lawyers on the Commission. Commissioner Ojienda was at that point taking the position that there was nothing in the act that raised questions concerning Kiplagat's conflicts of interest. This was difficult to understand, given that our legislation included express language requiring that none of us be "linked" to any human

---

[17] *Id.* at Arts. 16 and 17.
[18] *Id.* at Art. 17.

rights violations within our mandate. The other lawyers on the Commission (Chawatama, Murungi, Shava, and I) all pointed out this and other language that clearly raised questions about Kiplagat's presence on the Commission. Second, Kiplagat had insisted that his own lawyers make a formal, though private, presentation to us about the land issue. Given the unorthodox legal positions being taken by Commissioner Ojienda, we felt it would be useful to have a neutral outside lawyer present for this presentation.

As we prepared for the second retreat, which had been postponed until April 13–14, one of the names suggested as the external lawyer was Githu Muigai. Mugai was, in fact, representing Ambassador Kiplagat in some of the ongoing litigation related to the Commission and its creation. His ongoing representation of Kiplagat in related matters quickly led most of us to reject him as insufficiently neutral. Commissioner Ojienda and a few others took the remarkable position that Muigai's role in providing legal advice to Kiplagat made him an ideal candidate for such a role. Commissioner Ojienda appeared to believe that we should address Kiplagat's conflicts of interest by introducing a new conflict of interest with our "independent" outside lawyer. Those of us opposed to having such an interested party playing what was meant to be an independent role ultimately prevailed, and Muigai was never invited to join us. We could not agree on another individual to play this role, so we never received the advice of such an independent expert.

Although we had come out of the first retreat with no progress, both Kiplagat and our CEO were quoted in the press saying that everything was fine, that the commissioners were all reconciled, and that we were moving forward. The contradiction between our public statements and our internal reality was beginning to gnaw at me. I felt increasingly boxed in – others were conveying to the public a narrative that was far from accurate and that implicitly suggested I and the other commissioners were comfortable with the current state of affairs. When I saw the media reports indicating all was fine within the Commission, I immediately sent a message to our CEO noting how uncomfortable I felt misleading the public this way and how it, in fact, damaged us further as it gave the appearance that we were not concerned about the conflicts of interest raised by our chair. The CEO was in a difficult position, as Kiplagat often took the position that she was directly accountable to him, regardless of whether the rest of us agreed, or even knew, of his instructions to her. My concerns, shared by others within the Commission, did not change the media strategy that was largely driven by Kiplagat.

Part of our problem was that Kiplagat did not seem to appreciate the importance of public perceptions on the operation of a truth commission, particularly the perception of a lack of bias on the part of the institution and thus the perception of lack of bias on the part of individual commissioners. If he did appreciate the importance of the public's perception of us as an institution, he had clearly decided to subordinate that interest to his own personal agenda. I had been consistent in my arguments with him and with others that the important question was what a reasonable person would think of Kiplagat's objectivity given the allegations against him. Ironically, Kiplagat and some of the other commissioners seemed to accept implicitly the importance of perception by arguing at times that politically powerful people had assured them that the issues around Kiplagat were not a problem and we should just move forward. In fact, Kiplagat's tireless lobbying campaign among various elites in Nairobi was aimed at this perception. Neither Kiplagat nor the other commissioners who supported him on this, as far as I could tell, seemed to have any concern about the average Kenyan's perception of us, much less the perception of victims. Their assumption seemed to be that if the elites supported us, we would be fine.

In an effort to try to get Kiplagat to understand the power of perceptions of bias with respect to the administration of justice, I suggested to him that we constitute a panel consisting of myself and Commissioners Murungi, Shava, and Chawatama to determine whether he should stay on the Commission or not. He, of course, immediately rejected this suggestion, saying it would be unfair as we had already made up our minds about whether he should stay or not. I pointed out that we, in fact, had not made up our minds but that it was reasonable for him to perceive us as having done so, given our refusal to let the issue die. I expressed my agreement with him that it would be inappropriate for us to decide his fate regardless of how objective we thought we could be, given the reasonableness of his apprehension of bias. I then pointed out that this was exactly the issue his presence raised on the Commission for many victims and survivors, to which he immediately responded with claims of his actual innocence, thus entirely missing the point about the importance of perception. He either did not, could not, or would not try to understand the effect his presence on the Commission had on the reasonable perceptions and concerns of victims and other stakeholders.

GOING PUBLIC: THE OP-ED

Commissioner Murungi and I decided to go public. With no clear progress, Kiplagat acting as stubbornly as ever, and the public perception that we were ignoring the allegations raised about our Chair, Commissioner Murungi and I agreed to publish an op-ed piece setting out our concerns. The published piece was a toned-down version of my earlier draft open letter that had been circulated to all commissioners – we removed, for example, the suggestion in my original version that Kiplagat temporarily resign. In addition, we circulated to all of the commissioners the final version of the piece with an email informing them that it would be published in the local newspapers on Saturday, March 27. Instead of calling for his temporary resignation, we tried to strike a balance between the legitimate concerns of the credibility of the Commission with Kiplagat's legitimate concerns about his public reputation. We concluded the piece with the following:

> We support our Chairman's right to pursue a determination of his innocence or guilt in a court of law. That is his right, and we wish him godspeed as he undertakes it. It is not our fight. We were chosen to perform a specific task. As the Minister of Justice and others made clear at our creation, we were not chosen to serve as a court of law to determine the guilt or innocence of an individual. There are other institutions and other individuals far more qualified than we are to perform that role.

> It is our hope that our Chairman will find it in his heart to honor the commitment we know he has to Kenya and its people. We ask that he allow the Commission to continue with its important work while he pursues his own legal rights and interests vigorously in a forum of his choice.

While the op-ed was successful in making clear that at least two of us were committed to ensuring that some process was undertaken to address the Kiplagat problem, many of our fellow commissioners viewed our going to the press as a betrayal of our internal process. We found this somewhat ironic given that (1) we had come to no agreement with respect to speaking to the press; (2) other commissioners were freely speaking with the press; and (3) statements by, among others, our chair and CEO gave the impression that we were all in agreement about the way forward when, in fact, this was not the case. In fact, I had included in an earlier draft of our code of conduct (which at this point had still not been approved) a requirement that commissioners keep each other informed of interactions with the press. This provision was rejected and taken out of later drafts. Even more ironically, while Kiplagat had not given us notice, much less consulted with us, on a number of public statements he had made on our behalf, we had sent emails to all commissioners giving them more than forty-eight hours notice that our piece was being published and included in that notice a copy of our article.

In the face of mounting public and private pressure, and the perception that we were no closer to an agreed process than we were when we started our discussions months earlier, Commissioner Murungi resigned her position as vice chair of the Commission on the evening of March 28. The media mistakenly reported that Commissioner Murungi had resigned as a commissioner rather than her position as vice chair. Rumors began to circulate that I and Commissioner Chawatama would be resigning soon as well. I was interviewed on Citizen TV (the television station with the largest viewership in Kenya) where I denied that I had plans to resign. I also stated that I was not asking for Ambassador Kiplagat's resignation, though that was clearly an option, but that instead I and others wanted a credible and independent process to evaluate whether he should be a commissioner given the allegations against him and his conflicts of interest. Commissioner Chawatama had gone back to Zambia to deal with some personal issues. At her request, I mentioned during the interview that she had left the country, and it was unclear when she would return. Finally, I also noted that the government had made clear to us that we would have no money until July at the earliest. I was hoping that this interview and related activities would put increasing pressure on key stakeholders within and connected to government to move the process forward. My comments on Commissioner Chawatama led the media to immediately announce that she would be resigning shortly.

After Commissioner Murungi's resignation as vice chair, there began a flurry of activity within the Commission concerning her replacement. Under the Act, the vice chair must be Kenyan, and must be of the opposite sex of the Chair. This meant there were only two possible candidates: Commissioners Margaret Shava and Tecla Wanjala. Commissioner Shava immediately decided that she would not offer herself as a candidate given that she too was concerned with our lack of progress in addressing the issues around Kiplagat. We formally met as a commission on March 30. At that meeting, Ambassador Kiplagat formally accepted the resignation of Commissioner Murungi as vice chair. The discussion then turned to the election of a replacement. Commissioner Shava made clear that she was not offering herself. She, Commissioner Wanjala, and some of the rest of us argued that we should take time to consider whether and with whom we should fill the vacancy. Commissioner Wanjala specifically stated that she did not want to be considered at this moment. Commissioner Ojienda, however, insisted that we have an election and curiously argued that we could elect any of the eligible candidates even if they did not want to be elected. Commissioner Wanjala was clearly upset and was placed under enormous pressure by both Commissioner Ojienda and a few other commissioners. She finally relented and agreed to be considered. As there was no other candidate, there was no election, and Kiplagat immediately pronounced her as vice chair. It was a bittersweet appointment and an unfortunate beginning to Commissioner Wanjala's leadership role within the Commission – a role that she would later play with great distinction.

As we moved into April, we were five months into our twenty-four-month operating period, and we had only been able to hire one full-time member of our professional staff (our executive director); we were unable to pay consultants who were playing important roles with respect to communications, research, and planning; and our drivers and security personnel were not being paid. Ambassador Kiplagat continued to insist that the government would give us all the money we needed. He argued against approaching donors, as donor money, he claimed, came with strings attached. I argued that all money came with strings attached; as an example, I pointed to the government's continuous efforts to influence our activities by controlling our finances. It was unrealistic to assume that we would be given a large amount of money from any source without some expectation of a common interest or agenda, as well as some mechanisms of accountability that made sure the funds provided were used for the purposes intended. The important issue was whether there was a confluence of interests between the donor and the Commission. So if a donor was strongly pushing accountability for historical injustices, and that was their motivation for providing support to the Commission, then their interest and ours coincided. It was clear that the government of Kenya and the Commission had some areas of common interest but also significant areas of conflicting interest. The government provided more barriers, and had more conflicts of interest, with respect to our mandate than all of the other potential donors combined.[19]

Ironically, in meetings I was having with the Ministry of Justice and Ministry of Finance around this same time in my capacity as chair of our finance committee, the government was clear that resources for commissions (including the TJRC) must come from *outside* the government, and we were being encouraged by government officials in those meetings to seek donor funding for our operations. In fact, in early May we were informed by the government that we would be receiving approximately the same minimal level of funding for our second year of operations as we had the first – Ksh180 million (approximately US $2 million), which was less than 20 percent of our requested budget and would not even cover the cost of our proposed staff.[20]

---

[19] This is not to say that the Kenyan government committed more violations than some of those foreign donors had in the past. The atrocities committed by the British colonial powers are chillingly described in great detail in Caroline Elkins, IMPERIAL RECKONING: THE UNTOLD STORY OF BRITAIN'S GULAG IN KENYA (New York: Henry Holt & Co., 2005).

[20] While truth commissions are much cheaper than criminal tribunals, if properly staffed they are still relatively expensive institutions. This is even more so the case for a Commission like ours with such a broad mandate. As a matter of comparison, if adjusted for Kenyan inflation, the South African Truth and Reconciliation Commission cost US $51.8 million, and the Peruvian Truth and Reconciliation Commission cost US $28.6 million.

It is not clear if Kiplagat was simply being misled by his contacts in govern-ment concerning their financial commitment to us, or if he was deliberately trying to minimize the amount of funds available for our operations. His refusal to ever include any of us, including me as chair of our finance com-mittee, in any of these discussions meant that we were easily manipulated by the government, perhaps with the knowing participation of Kiplagat himself.

In addition to having no current prospect for securing money to hire our staff and engage in mandate-related activities, we appeared to be even further away from coming up with a process to address the credibility crisis we faced because of Kiplagat's presence. I was also informed that the government was seeking to retaliate against Commissioner Murungi and me because of our op-ed. The government had apparently contacted the local office of the Panel of Eminent African Personalities and complained that I was a "meddler." I was warned that the government might try to use a regulation concerning the terms and conditions of employment of foreigners in the civil service to expel me as a result of my recent activities. The regulation, known as Regulation O, provides that a foreigner who is employed in the Kenyan civil service may not publicly speak or write about their experience without the prior permission of an authorized officer. It was pretty clear that this regulation did not apply to me, as I was not employed as a member of the civil service but as a member of an independent commission. Nevertheless, the fact that the government was consulting such a regulation as a basis for disciplining, firing, or expel-ling me underscored the seriousness with which the government viewed our attempts to create a credible process to address the issues raised about Kiplagat. A few days later, I was told that the Minister of Justice had been working with Ambassador Kiplagat and others (apparently including one or two other commissioners) to draft legally binding regulations that would make clear that no commissioner other than the chair could speak to the press. As far as I am aware, those draft rules never went beyond the circle of those who drafted them.

I was also told that the Kenyan government might be filing a formal protest about me to the US government. In fact, I was told that the minister of jus-tice had asked both the US ambassador and the Panel of Eminent African Personalities to have me removed. Making such a request to the US Embassy was somewhat ironic, given that I was not representing the US and had had far less contact with the US ambassador and Embassy than our embattled chair. It was, however, consistent with the general Kenyan view that individ-uals represent their "tribe," which in my case would be my country. To the credit of each of them, neither the ambassador nor representatives of the Panel ever raised this issue with me or put any pressure on me to consider leaving. Around this same time Ambassador Kiplagat asked me about my ancestry.

In particular, he wanted to know if I was part Dutch – this was presumably to try to understand why I might be meeting with individuals from the Dutch Embassy. I had, in fact, met both formally and informally with a number of individuals from the diplomatic community, including individuals from the Dutch Embassy. His inquiry was either an effort to try to better understand my motivations or an attempt to intimidate me by letting me know he was aware of my movements. As I was not engaged in any consultations or other activities of which I had a reason to hide, the latter purpose would have been ineffectively served by such an inquiry.

THE STRUGGLE FOR A CODE OF CONDUCT

As we continued to seek agreement on a process for addressing the Kiplagat problem, we also struggled to agree to the provisions of our code of conduct. I had drafted a code of conduct in January, drawing upon a number of comparable codes used throughout the world. In many of our public conversations concerning the conflicts of interest presented by Ambassador Kiplagat, we had reassured our audiences that were developing a code of conduct that would preclude any commissioner from engaging with an issue in which he or she had a conflict of interest. As we entered April (eight months after we had been appointed), we had still not agreed to the terms of such a code of conduct.

We held a Commission meeting on April 6, during which we again discussed the code of conduct. Commissioner Ojienda raised a number of concerns with various provisions in the draft, including a provision restricting us from being affiliated with organizations with partisan views about the Commission (which was in fact a prohibition in the act itself); a provision requiring us to disclose our assets, including land, within Kenya; and a provision requiring that we disclose the professional activities of our spouse. As a result of this meeting, and under my objection which was duly recorded in our minutes, we removed provisions (1) prohibiting us from being employed by or earning money from any organization other than the Commission; (2) requiring that we be in the office or otherwise working for the Commission at least eight hours per day during a five-day work week; (3) requiring us to declare any interest or activity of our spouse that might present a conflict of interest with the Commission; and (4) requiring that we declare all interests we held in land in Kenya. The removal of these provisions significantly weakened our code of conduct and our ability to police ourselves for any conflicts of interest we might have with our mandate-related activities. The code of conduct did, however, provide that any commissioner with a known conflict of interest would be barred from any activities related to that conflict unless all of the other commissioners agreed otherwise in writing.[21]

ONE STEP FORWARD, TWO STEPS BACK

On Monday, April 12th, we met and finally came up with a unanimous plan to address the issues surrounding our chair: the establishment of a tribunal for the removal of a commissioner as set forth in our enabling legislation. It took a good deal of debate and discussion. Kiplagat looked tired and beaten at times and said on the one hand that he wanted the problem resolved but on the other hand that we should not move too quickly. He appeared confused and uncertain as he began to realize that he had lost control over how we would confront his issues. Both Commissioners Farah and Dinka pushed for a quick resolution – a position with which certainly I, and I suspect all of the other commissioners, agreed. Commissioner Dinka reiterated that if a tribunal was, in fact, created, Kiplagat should step aside to let that process run its course. Kiplagat pointedly did not respond to this proposal. After much discussion and debate, we agreed that we would write to the minister of justice requesting that he use his good offices to assist us in requesting that the chief justice establish a tribunal as provided for in our act to evaluate Kiplagat's conflicts of interest, and that in the meantime, Kiplagat would step aside. Faced with agreement among the rest of us, Kiplagat somewhat reluctantly relented and agreed to this course of action. It was 6:00 p.m.

I was tasked with drafting the letter to the minister of justice. We had been meeting around the conference table at our offices in Delta House, which was an open-plan office. I left the table and went to my desk to draft the letter on my computer. My desk was just around the corner from the conference table, so while I could not see the other commissioners, I could hear some of the resulting conversation. As I tried to concentrate on drafting the letter, I could hear Kiplagat complain about how quickly we were moving. Commissioner Dinka, fearing that Kiplagat might change his mind or leave without signing the letter, came over and stood behind me as I worked, urging me to write more quickly. I tried to get him to keep quiet as it was difficult for me to think with all of the conversations occurring around me, much less with Commissioner Dinka leaning over my shoulder and urging me to write faster. I drafted the letter; Commissioner Dinka edited it as I wrote. We quickly printed out the letter on Commission letterhead and we all signed it. We breathed a sigh

---

[21] A copy of the code of conduct can be found on the website.

of relief as Kiplagat appended his signature to the letter. Commissioner Dinka presciently insisted that we sign three originals of the letter.

In hindsight, I did not draft the letter as well as I should have. In particular, the letter was not as clear as it could have been about Ambassador Kiplagat's agreement to step down. The crucial paragraph read:

> We write this letter to you [the Minister of Justice] on the basis of a unanimous decision we have taken as a Commission at our meeting this afternoon, on 12 April 2010. We write to request this tribunal so that the Commission may move forward with its work. With that aim in mind, our Chairman has graciously agreed to step aside temporarily until the tribunal process has reached its conclusion.

The problem with the last sentence is that it is ambiguous with respect to whether Kiplagat would step aside immediately or only upon the creation of the tribunal. I was under the impression that we had agreed that he would step aside immediately, but the language is open to alternative interpretations. I am not sure, given subsequent events and the tenaciousness with which Kiplagat would continue to avoid any process to address his conflicts, whether drafting the sentence to indicate more clearly that he would immediately step aside would have mattered. Although he had signed the letter, he was clearly uncomfortable with this most recent turn of events. He expressed his anger to some of the other commissioners as we were signing the letter, noting that he could "spoil" the whole thing. Nevertheless, with his signature, we now had his written agreement that he would step aside (even if it was not clear exactly when) and his agreement to the creation of a tribunal.

I was immensely relieved at this turn of events. We had finally made some progress in addressing our impasse. I went to Mercury with Commissioners Chawatama, Murungi, and Shava. We began to discuss how to reenergize the process so we could begin to make progress on our enormous mandate. It was a daunting task, and I began to realize that while we had overcome a significant hurdle, we had an enormous amount of work still ahead of us. Nevertheless, it was the work I had anticipated doing when I agreed to serve on the Commission, and I was looking forward to finally engaging with the people of Kenya about the legacy of historical injustices that continued to plague their society.

After we had all signed it, the letter was sealed in an envelope and delivered the next morning to the Ministry of Justice. In a reckless, though perhaps well-meaning, move, one of the Kenyan commissioners leaked the letter to the press just after we had signed it. The existence of the letter was one of the top stories on that evening's television news. The networks repeatedly showed photographs of the letter, zooming in on Ambassador Kiplagat's signature. The leaking of the letter was viewed by Kiplagat as a breach of our agreed process. In addition, given that the letter was leaked before it was delivered to the Ministry, it put the Ministry and Kiplagat on the defensive.

The next morning, we all arrived at the office. We had scheduled a press conference for midday to announce the request for a tribunal and the fact that Kiplagat was stepping aside. We had been informed that Kiplagat was angry about the leak. As the rest of us assembled at the office for the press conference, he was at the Ministry speaking to the minister and senior Ministry officials. We waited for him, having no idea what he was discussing or planning with the Ministry. Shortly after we had assembled, both he and senior officials at the Ministry called to demand that we cancel our planned press conference. These senior officials claimed that we had no right to do what we had done and that if we proceeded, they would move to have us disbanded. We were clear in our response that we had agreed to a course of action as a Commission and would not defer to the Ministry. We began to strategize about how to handle the situation if Kiplagat did not show up. We prepared a press release announcing that we had requested that the chief justice establish a tribunal, that Ambassador Kiplagat had graciously agreed to step aside while the process ran its course, and that we commended Ambassador Kiplagat for taking this decision with us. In other words, we drafted a press release based upon our written and signed agreement from the day before. We also drafted a statement to be read on behalf of the Commission. In the absence of Ambassador Kiplagat, we unanimously designated Ambassador Dinka as our spokesperson.

As we were preparing to hold the press conference without him, Kiplagat returned to the office. At the time, our offices were on the fourth floor of Delta House and consisted of two large, open spaces, one to the left as you came up the stairs and the other to the right. The office suite to the right was where our small support staff had their desks and work areas. The office suite to the left contained a desk for each commissioner and a large alcove where we had our conference table. Glass doors separated the office from a small landing and the staircase leading to the lower floors. The press had assembled on the small landing outside our doors and down the staircase. There must have been at least fifty people on the landing and stairs waiting to be let in. We had already passed the scheduled time for our announcement, so the press continued to ask what was happening and when we planned to let them in. Kiplagat had passed through the assembled members of the press on his return, so they were now anticipating that the press conference would commence shortly. All nine commissioners and our CEO assembled around the conference table.

Kiplagat had spent the last five hours in intense discussions with officials at the Ministry of Justice, and we were anxious to hear what he had discussed and what, if anything, he had decided to do. Kiplagat started by expressing how shocked and surprised he was about the leak of the letter to the press the night before and how the leak had made things very difficult. As he then went on to describe his discussions at the Ministry, it became clear that he had been seeking direction from the Ministry on how to proceed. He conveyed to us three reasons the Ministry argued against our planned course of action. First, the senior lawyer at the Ministry – Gichira Kibara, who would later become the acting permanent secretary in the Ministry when Amina Mohamed left to become minister of foreign affairs – had advised him that he could not legally step aside. This was somewhat odd advice, as government officials had been "stepping aside" for a while in Kenya, and there was nothing in the act that prohibited any of us from stepping aside or coming to any other similar arrangement. Later, in November, Kiplagat would in fact "step aside," and as far as I am aware, no one at the Ministry, or even the entire government, raised a question about whether he was acting improperly, much less illegally. Nevertheless, at this point, the Ministry's senior lawyer and other senior officials were taking the position that he could not legally step aside.

Second, senior officials in the Ministry had also informed Kiplagat that a tribunal could not legally be established to address any misbehavior or misconduct that had occurred prior to his appointment as a commissioner. This was a matter of legal interpretation. The act speaks of misbehavior and misconduct as a ground for removal but is silent as to whether there is any temporal limitation on what misbehavior or misconduct is relevant. Third, Ministry officials advised him that by requesting an investigation he was acknowledging that there was a problem. While this was, of course, true – the whole point of requesting a tribunal was so that there could be a credible and independent process to address his conflicts of interest – presumably the Ministry was making the point that we, or at least Kiplagat, should not acknowledge that there was a problem.

I will leave it to those better versed in Kenyan law and practice to evaluate whether the nature of the Ministry's involvement in this stage of our proceedings violated the spirit, if not the letter, of the act requiring us to act independently and not to take direction from any outside body. Ambassador Kiplagat's consultation with the Ministry was yet another example of how he refused to work with his fellow commissioners over an issue of fundamental importance to the Commission itself, preferring instead to work with and take direction from the government. When we pointed this out to Kiplagat, he observed that he was not a lawyer and had thus sought advice from the Ministry of Justice, to which we pointed out that there were five lawyers on the Commission, including three Kenyan lawyers, all of whom were ready, willing, and able to walk him through the provisions of the act and their legal significance.

As Ambassador Kiplagat conveyed to us his position and that of the Ministry, the tension and frustration among the rest of us rose. This led our CEO to make an impassioned plea to Kiplagat. She lamented that less than a day after we had come together collectively to save the Commission, the whole project was being scuttled. She accused Ambassador Kiplagat of trying to ruin the Commission and pleaded with him to at least be up front with us and admit to us that he would stay with the Commission even if it meant we could not do our work, so that we would at least know where we stood. It was an emotional outburst that reflected what most of the rest of us in the room were thinking. Kiplagat just looked at her coldly but did not respond.

With Kiplagat clearly having made up his mind that he would not honor the written agreement from the day before, combined with the full support he had received from the Ministry, there was nothing more for us to discuss, so we called in the press. Approximately fifty members of the press squeezed into the area near our conference table, all jostling for position, particularly those with television cameras. At least twenty microphones were assembled in the middle of the conference table.

We immediately assembled around the conference table for the press conference. None of us had any idea what Kiplagat would say. Not surprisingly, he did not inform us, much less consult with us, about what he would be saying to the press on our behalf. As we gathered around the conference table with the press in attendance, Kiplagat began to speak and became increasingly strident and defiant. He did not mention the agreement we had reached or the letter he had signed. Instead he insisted that he was not resigning or stepping aside unless the law *required* him to do so. He also insisted that he was innocent, and that he had documents that would prove his innocence. He concluded by saying we had no more to say, and then got up and left the table.

To my surprise, Ambassador Dinka immediately motioned for the microphones to be moved in front of him and began to speak. Kiplagat, realizing that the press conference was not over, quickly returned to his seat. Ambassador Dinka calmly but deliberately recounted the agreement that we had all reached the day before, including Ambassador Kiplagat's agreement to step aside immediately while a tribunal did its work. As Ambassador Dinka was speaking, Ambassador Kiplagat interrupted him a number of times to clarify that he was in fact not stepping aside. Kiplagat tried unsuccessfully on numerous occasions to have the microphones moved back in front of him. It was an embarrassing moment: two wise and gray-haired African statesmen with more than 100 years of collective experience on the continent arguing with each other before the television cameras.

As the press conference ended, Kiplagat left the table without speaking to any of us and went to his desk. I asked Ambassador Dinka what we should do with the prepared press release that clearly stated that Kiplagat had agreed to step aside. He immediately responded that we should distribute it to the press, which we then did. The tension in the room was extremely high.

"I AM NOT A PARIAH!"

The next day, April 14, we all arrived at the office in the morning. There was a sense of foreboding that we had reached the end of the process. The euphoria I had felt Monday night after we had signed the letter had now been replaced with the dull dread that I had been living with for the last four months. All of the major newspapers had published editorials calling for Kiplagat to resign. Archbishop Tutu, no less, had urged him to resign. Perhaps Kiplagat thought that with the passage of time, all of the controversy around him would be forgotten, and we would then be able to move on with our work. He had even suggested at some point that he would stay but not go out in public with us. Staying was his focus. The work, the mandate, the important task entrusted to us by the people of Kenya – all of these were subordinate to his one abiding desire to stay, to not resign, to not give up. It had become clear to me that Kiplagat had dug himself into a deep enough hole that with each passing day it became more difficult for him to contemplate anything other than holding on to his position. The Ministry clearly seemed intent on keeping him in place. The phone conversations directing us to cancel our press conference the previous day were delivered with the tone of a superior giving orders to a subordinate, culminating in a threat to terminate us all.

The minister had also publicly ridiculed us when he heard about the letter we had written to him, claiming that he had no role to play in the establishment of a tribunal and, therefore, it was improper for us to write to him. He cited our decision to write to him and our internal disputes over Kiplagat as evidence of our incompetence and pledged to move to have the entire Commission disbanded. It was a nasty personal attack against each of us, freely conveyed to the press and thus repeated on the nightly news. He was, of course, correct about his role, as our legislation spoke of the chief justice, not the minister, creating such a tribunal. Notwithstanding this fact, we had decided to write to him out of courtesy and in an attempt to follow protocol. It was ironic that on the one hand he ridiculed us for attempting to involve him in matters to which he was not expressly assigned a role under the Act, but in other matters – stopping our press conference, advising Kiplagat that he could not step aside – he and his colleagues seemed to have no hesitation in involving themselves.

It was in this increasingly hostile environment that all nine of us assembled around the conference table on the morning of Wednesday, April 14. No one was willing to speak first. After a period of awkward silence, finally, in a very calm manner, I made three suggestions to Ambassador Kiplagat that most of the other commissioners and I had discussed informally that morning. First, we should move forward and submit a petition directly to the chief justice requesting a tribunal and copy the two principals – i.e., the president and the prime minister. Second, it was up to him to decide whether to honor the commitment he had made to us on Monday and step aside. Third, he should no longer be actively engaged with our work. He asked what we meant by him not being actively engaged with our work. I responded that this was something we should all discuss and agree on, but it could mean that he would no longer chair our meetings, that he would no longer be our official spokesperson, and that he would not appear publicly on behalf of the Commission. Others joined in this discussion and made different suggestions, making clear that we were all united on the general idea but open to discussion about the specific details. Commissioner Farah somewhat cryptically said, "there are many ways to kill a cat," and concluded that Kiplagat should leave us alone while we waited for a tribunal. Commissioner Ojienda said that Kiplagat should "lie low like an envelope." Both Commissioner Murungi and I said that we were close to resigning and that he had it in his power to save or destroy the Commission.

As I was trying to appeal to his conscience about the future of the Commission, he interrupted me and said that we all had the power to save or destroy the Commission. He was sitting at the head of the conference table, and I was sitting a few chairs away from him on his right. As he interrupted me, his voice began to rise and he started yelling at me, saying that I had never wanted him on the Commission, that I had always had it in for him, and that I had been plotting against him this entire time. He stood up and pointed his finger at me, literally screaming his accusations about my efforts to undermine him. His face was enraged and furious. I froze and did not look at him but instead looked straight ahead across the table at Commissioners Chawatama, Murungi, and Farah. A number of commissioners quickly stood up and approached him, attempting to calm him down. After a short time, they were able to escort him away from the table. We took a small break.

I was quite surprised, even shocked, at this turn of events. I had never seen him so angry, and while I knew he did not like some of the positions I had taken, I had never felt such profound, personal anger from him. As he was yelling at me, his face turned more and more red and furious, and I honestly thought he might be on the verge of having a heart attack.

I stayed at the table while others calmed him down. The other commissioners who remained at the table expressed shock at his performance. Ambassador Dinka, who had been talking with Kiplagat, came back and told me that Kiplagat had calmed down. I then went up to Kiplagat, who was now standing near the conference table, and said that I was sorry if I had said anything that had offended him, that I had not intended to make the issue personal but was instead focused on how we as an institution could move forward given recent events. He accepted my apology but continued to argue how unfair I was being and how I had convinced Archbishop Tutu to come out publicly against him. While I was uncomfortably flattered at the idea that he thought I had such enormous influence over Archbishop Tutu, I assured him that I had not asked, much less convinced, Archbishop Tutu to join the statement asking for his resignation.

After our mini-reconciliation, Ambassador Kiplagat and I joined the others at the conference table. The discussion continued as we tried to chart a way forward. Every single Commissioner in his or her own way tried to appeal to his sense of self and integrity to get him to honor the commitment he had made to us the other day in writing. His consultation with the Ministry, however, appeared to have hardened him in his position that he would not resign or even step aside. In an odd statement foreshadowing the future he was risking, he defiantly proclaimed that he was "not yet a pariah in this nation," and that he could still safely travel to places in the country. At the same time, he insisted that he had always wanted a tribunal. We thus came to an agreement with him that we would file a formal petition directly with the chief justice requesting a tribunal. He also agreed that he would not visit the Ministry alone, a promise that he quickly broke, and that I don't think any of us seriously thought he would keep for very long, if at all.

THE PETITION

For the next two days, I spent all of my time drafting our petition to the chief justice. Our act provided a limited number of circumstances that would merit a commissioner being removed:

(a) for misbehavior or misconduct;
(b) if the chairperson or commissioner is convicted of an offence involving moral turpitude but not sentenced to a term of imprisonment;

(c) if the chairperson or commissioner is unable to discharge the functions of his office by reason of physical or mental infirmity; or

(d) if the chairperson or commissioner is absent from three consecutive meetings of the Commission without good cause[22]

Clause (a) was the only provision that applied to our situation. I drafted the petition requesting the chief justice to determine whether Ambassador Kiplagat had engaged in misbehavior or misconduct by (1) signing a sworn affidavit as a condition of his appointment as a Commissioner indicating, as required by our legislation, that he "has not in any way been involved, implicated, linked or associated with human rights violations of any kind or in any matter which is be investigated" by the Commission; (2) both publicly and privately insisting since his appointment that he has not nor has he ever been involved, implicated, linked or associated with any human rights violation that is to be investigated by the Commission; and (3) acting contrary to Article 21 of our Act, which provides that "each commissioner... shall avoid taking any action which could create an appearance of partiality or otherwise harm the credibility or integrity of the Commission," by engaging in these and other activities.

In drafting the petition, I was mindful of the Ministry's position, as expressed to Ambassador Kiplagat, that "misbehavior or misconduct" could only apply to acts committed by a commissioner *after* being appointed to the Commission. While I did not agree with this interpretation, I did not want the petition to be dismissed on such a technical basis and felt that we could craft a strong enough petition consistent with that interpretation. Certainly, if it were revealed that one of us had intentionally murdered someone a week before our appointment, or that we had embezzled an enormous amount of money, or we had bribed individuals in order to secure our appointment, such actions should be a proper focus of inquiry with respect to our suitability to serve on the Commission.

By the morning of Friday, April 16, I had produced a final version of the petition that was approved by all of the commissioners.[23] We had discussed among ourselves whether it would be appropriate to have Ambassador Kiplagat sign the petition. Given that the petition was requesting a tribunal to enquire into his misbehavior or misconduct, we decided that it would not be appropriate to include him. He agreed with this position but wanted us to make clear that we were filing the petition with his full consent and approval. Thus, in our cover letter to the chief justice, as well as in the cover letters transmitting copies of the petition to the president, prime minister, minister of

[22] TJRC Act, *supra* Chapter 1, note 3, at Art. 17(1).
[23] A copy of the petition may be found on the website.

justice, and other relevant stakeholders, we indicated Ambassador Kiplagat's consent and approval to the filing of the petition.

As I was putting together fifteen packages of the petition with cover letters, Judge Chawatama arrived in the office. Out of the corner of my eye, I noticed her speaking with Commissioner Shava. Her voice began to rise, and she became more and more agitated until she was virtually screaming. It was an enormous outburst that resulted in her sitting at her desk for a good half hour without speaking as some of us tried to comfort her. I could not make out everything she had said, as I was trying to focus on putting the various packages together for our petition, matching the correct letter with the correct envelope. I was so distracted by Judge Chawatama's outburst that I had placed the letter to the president in the envelope addressed to the prime minister and vice versa. Luckily I had gone back to check each envelope and was able to correct the mistake.

From what I could hear, Judge Chawatama was complaining about the minister, emphasizing the importance of her reputation, and insisting that she should be treated with respect and not in the shabby way the minister had adopted.

The evening before, April 15, the minister of justice had continued his attack against us on television, arguing that the entire Commission should be disbanded, and that all of us were incompetent and should leave. He had clearly started to make the attacks more personal, and it was beginning to take its toll on all of us. Judge Chawatama had reached her breaking point. Her frustration and outrage echoed what was felt by many of us. The Ministry was clearly adopting a scorched-earth policy to discredit us personally.

The filing of the petition seemed to make little impact on Kiplagat (perhaps he knew it would take more than six months for the chief justice to respond to it). On Monday, April 19, I went into the office first thing in the morning and became caught up in a long conversation with Ambassador Kiplagat. He spoke to me in great detail about his work with the youth in Central Province, particularly on the issue of illegally brewed alcohol, known as Changa'a, which often leads to abuse and even death. He explained to me that if such informal alcoholic beverages were legalized, they could then be regulated and controlled. He suggested that this should perhaps be the subject of our first hearing. I sat there stunned. I really could not believe that he thought, given all of the massacres, assassinations, rapes, disappearances, displacements, and other gross violations of human rights we were to investigate, that he wanted us to devote our first public event on the legalization of unregulated alcohol production. I could just imagine the media response, not to mention the response of the victims and other important stakeholders, if we were to undertake such a course. Rather than argue with him, I suggested that he bring up the idea at a meeting with all of the commissioners. I learned that at a Commission meeting shortly after this conversation that I was unable to attend, he presented the idea to the others and said that I supported the idea. Luckily I had already told many of my colleagues about his idea and how I found it to be ridiculous given our mandate. The others agreed with my assessment, and the issue was never taken up again. It was yet another example of either how naïve he was about what a truth commission was or how blatant he felt he could be in trying to steer us away from the core of our mandate.

In the meantime, on that same Monday morning Commissioner Murungi tendered her resignation to the president. I was surprised at her timing, as we had finally all come together to file the petition with the chief justice, which, at least in the short run, suggested we had made some progress in addressing the Kiplagat problem. Yet I also knew that she had been under enormous pressure from her colleagues in civil society to make a clean break with the Commission. When I asked her if she thought I should also resign, she advised me to wait to see how things developed.

My euphoria from Friday's filing of the petition was replaced by trepidation, as I feared that with Kaari's resignation we were on the verge of collapsing. In her press conference announcing her resignation, Commissioner Murungi explained her decision: "The forces of impunity in this country are stronger than the forces that want a credible truth commission."[24] Losing Commissioner Murungi was a blow – both to our credibility and to our collective experience and skills.

FINANCING AND CORRUPTION: THE MINISTER MISSTEPS

Meanwhile, the minister of justice continued his attacks against us, but in his eagerness to destroy our reputations, he made a serious mistake. In one of his many public pronouncements against us, he announced that we had mismanaged and misappropriated funds allocated to the Commission. In particular, he stated that we "had misappropriated millions of shillings through illegitimate payments including elders' allowances and casual workers' payments."[25] The minister was publicly accusing us of corruptly misappropriating funds

---

[24] *See* "TJRC Crisis," *KTN*, April 21, 2010.
[25] *See* Anthony Kagiri, "Betty Murungi now Quits Keyna TJRC," *Capital News*, April 19, 2010, www.capitalfm.co.ke/news/2010/04/betty-murungi-now-quits-kenya-tjrc/; and Jacob Ng'etich, "Queries Raised over TJRC Funds," *The Daily Nation*, April 30, 2010, www.nation.co.ke/news/Queries-raised-over-TJRC-funds-/-/1056/909848/-/4s6qto/-/index.html.

entrusted to the Commission. Like Judge Chawatama, I was shocked and angry at the attack on our personal integrity. It appeared that the minister would stop at nothing to discredit not only the Commission but each of us individually in order to preserve a Commission with Kiplagat as its chair.

The allegation of misappropriation of funds was, in fact, almost certainly true. The problem, from the minister's point of view, was that the responsible parties were not the commissioners, or even the Commission, but his own ministry. Ministry officials had spent money on our behalf on a wide variety of activities, some of which clearly had nothing to do with our operations or mandate. All of these payments were made without our knowledge, much less our consent. In fact, up to the end of our operational life in 2013, we never received a satisfactory accounting from the Ministry concerning where and how our funds were spent during this period.

Since our creation in August 2009, the Ministry of Justice had exercised complete control over our finances. We required the Ministry's permission in order to spend any of the money allocated to us by Parliament. At the same time, the Ministry spent money on our behalf, not only without consulting with us but also without our knowledge. I had been tasked with developing our budget, and for months I had been requesting from the Ministry an accounting of the monies allocated to us from Parliament. It was only shortly before the minister made his accusations that I had finally received some information concerning funds that had been spent on our behalf, though the information provided was incomplete and extremely confusing. Yet the information was sufficiently detailed to raise concerns about how some of our money had been spent.

When we were first formed in August 2009, it was proper for the Ministry to have control over and responsibility for our money, as we did not have a CEO who, under Kenyan law, would be our accounting officer. In other words, he or she would be accountable under the law for our finances. Even though the Ministry was legally entitled, even obligated, to control our money when we were first created, there was no reason, legal or other, for them to withhold information from us concerning our finances, including how our money was being spent during this period.

We had hired our CEO in February 2010. With a legally responsible accounting officer on our staff, we had requested that our accounts be transferred to our control. After much delay and discussion with officials within the Ministry, we were eventually told that we would not be given access to or authority over our accounts until the start of the next fiscal year, July 2010. For the first year of our operations, we would thus not only have no control over money legally allocated to us, we would continue to require permission from the

Ministry for any expenditure we wanted to make, and we would continue to have no way of knowing what if any money was spent on our behalf by the Ministry. This obviously resulted in a very tight leash, making us completely dependent upon the government for any activity in which we wanted to engage – hardly an ideal situation for an organization that by law is supposed to be independent and impartial. Ironically, when the Minister was defending Kiplagat and criticizing us for writing to him to ask for his assistance in requesting that a tribunal be created, he was quoted in the press as saying with respect to our request, "the government cannot afford to make a mistake to own TJRC and my disappointment is that the commissioners do not have the understanding of that very important legal principle that the government must keep off."[26] It was not clear whether members of his own Ministry who were controlling our finances saw or heard this statement at the time, or if they did, whether they foresaw the firestorm that the minister would soon unleash on his own officials concerning our finances.

Up until this point we had pointedly not responded to the minister's increasingly personal and polemical attacks against us. With the assertion that we were at best incompetent and at worst corrupt with respect to monies entrusted to the Commission, we unanimously agreed to strike back. The allegation was not only an attack against us personally, it was also an allegation that could have serious consequences for many of us professionally if the record were not corrected. Judge Chawatama was concerned about her repu-tation as a judge in Zambia, and I was concerned about my bar memberships in the USA and the effect such an allegation might have on my position as a university professor.

We wrote a letter to the chairs of two important Parliamentary committees who would have jurisdiction over such allegations: the chair of the Public Accounts Committee, which oversees public spending, and the chair of the Parliamentary Committee on the Administration of Justice and Legal Affairs, which was the committee that operated as our main liaison with Parliament. We pointed out in that letter that even though our secretary had been sworn in on February 15, 2010, we had been informed by the Ministry of Justice that the money allocated to us by Parliament would not be placed into accounts over which we had control until after July 1. We also informed the committees that not only did we not have control over the monies duly allocated to us for our operations, but also that money allocated to us was spent on our behalf

<hr/>

[26] Judie Kaberia, "Kenya TJRC now faces Dissolution," *Capital News*, April 26, 2010, www.capitalfm.co.ke/news/2010/04/kenya-tjrc-now-faces-dissolution/.

without our knowledge or consent. We also recounted specific incidents of the Ministry refusing to allow us to use our money for mandate-related activities. For example, in January, when we undertook our outreach trip to the Coast Province, we had requested money to cover our expenses. Because the money was not forthcoming, individual commissioners lent money to the Commission to cover the expenses of the trip. In April 2010, we had again requested money for provincial outreach activities. Although the Ministry quickly acknowledged receipt of our letter, after two weeks we had still not received a response to our request, much less access to the requested funds. We also noted in our letter how expenses approved by the commissioners in formal Commission meetings had not been paid, and how our CEO, who had been hired on February 15, 2010, had still, near the end of April, not been paid her salary.

With respect to the allegations concerning misappropriation of funds, we noted that as early as October 2009, we had been requesting an accounting of monies spent on our behalf by the Ministry. We received some documents in January, and then in April, that purported to indicate how our monies had been spent. These documents were vague and contradictory. They included, for example, a line item called "Operational Needs of the TJRC," without any further explanation for what the Ksh396,182 (approximately US $5,000) had been used for. More specifically, we set out the following problematic expenditures made on our behalf by the Ministry:

- Approximately 16 million shillings (approximately US $200,000) had been spent on the Council of Elders, an organization that had no relationship with the TJRC. We had never been consulted about, much less given our consent to, these payments. We were later to learn that Ambassador Kiplagat had been involved with the Council of Elders.
- Rent payments listed for our offices that were inconsistent, and might have included rent for other commissions supported by the Ministry of Justice.
- Bulk payments to Ministry of Justice officials for nonexistent retreats, or for retreats that occurred six months prior to the payments.
- Monies had been spent on what the Ministry referred to as "casual workers." The Commission had only hired one staff person, our CEO, and two consultants – a communications consultant and a research consultant. None of them had been paid at the time we wrote this letter. Individuals had been seconded to us by the Ministry, but despite our repeated requests, we were unaware of the identities of those who were being paid on our behalf as "casual workers," their functions, or how much they were being

paid per month. The expenditure breakdown listed the "casual worker" payments in bulk form, making it impossible for us to ascertain who was being paid and for what activities.

Finally, we noted that we had submitted a two-year operational budget to the Ministry in December 2009 and a request for supplemental funding for the current fiscal year also in December 2009. As of April 2010, we had received no response to our two-year operational budget. With respect to our request for supplemental funding, we had first requested Ksh 630 million. That request went unanswered, and in January, we sent a second, lower, request for Ksh 480 million. It was only at the end of March 2010 that we were told that we would be receiving an additional Ksh 50 million, only 6 percent of what we had requested. That extra Ksh 50 million would still continue to be completely controlled by the Ministry.

In addition to sending information supporting the allegations of misfeasance by the Ministry to Parliament, we also issued a press release containing the same information. The press release triggered a flurry of news reports about the Ministry and the handling of our finances. The same people at the Ministry who were so reluctant to respond to our requests for authorization to spend money already allocated to us immediately called and complained to us about the information we had released. The minister became uncharacteristically silent on the issue. We were told that there was panic within the Ministry and that all TJRC-related financial documents had been placed in a room and were being scoured for information concerning these vague, and often inappropriate, payments. As far as I am aware, by the end of our operational life three years later, we had still not received a proper accounting of the money that was spent on our behalf. Incredibly, during this same period Ambassador Kiplagat gave an extensive interview on television during which he, among other things, stated that the Ministry had been supporting us all along. A western diplomat confided in me that this made Kiplagat appear to be complicit in a cover-up with respect to financial corruption within the Ministry.

BUSINESS AS USUAL: A ONE-PERSON COMMISSION

For the next few months, there was little movement on the Kiplagat issue as we waited for the establishment of a tribunal. We did not receive even an acknowledgment from the chief justice concerning our petition, much less a substantive response. After a month of silence, we wrote to the chief justice in May asking about our petition and offering to provide clarification or more

information if needed. Again, we received no response. Periodically, politicians, civil society leaders, religious leaders, or others spoke publicly either to
defend Ambassador Kiplagat or to call for his resignation. Major newspapers
ran editorials saying that he should resign,[27] and a number of prominent
individuals and stakeholders also called for his resignation.[28] One poll of
33,573 Kenyans found that 83.4 percent felt that Ambassador Kiplagat did
not command enough public trust to lead a truth and justice commission.
Only half of the remaining respondents, or 8.5 percent, thought that he did
command sufficient public trust.[29]

As we began our first statement-taking activity in Mt. Elgon in May 2010, we
read in the press that Kiplagat had held a number of TJRC-related meetings
with various constituencies, primarily in the Rift Valley. Based on the reports
we later received of these meetings, they consisted primarily (and perhaps
solely) of meetings with members of the Kalenjin community.[30] While it was
appropriate for the Commission to be reaching out to all communities in the
Rift Valley, including the Kalenjin, the fact that our embattled chair was
meeting primarily with individuals from his own ethnic group, and that such
meetings were not part of a larger Commission strategy to reach out to all
communities within the Rift Valley, further supported the argument that the
Commission was ill equipped to engage in a meaningful and even-handed
way with the conflicts of the region. These meetings unfortunately served to
exacerbate, rather than mediate, the ethnic conflicts in the region. We were
not given any notice of these visits, much less any input into whether and how
they might fit into our overall work plan or whether it would be prudent to
have more than one Commissioner attend such meetings. In fact, a number of
people from civil society and the diplomatic community contacted me expressing concern that the press coverage of the meetings was focused on Kiplagat

---

[27] See "It is Now Kiplagat's Turn to Resign," *The Standard*, April 21, 2010; "Kiplagat Must Now
Step Down," *The Star*, May 21, 2010; and "Why Kiplagat Should Leave TJRC," *East Africa
in Focus*, April 25, 2010.

[28] See "ICTJ Calls for Resignation of Kenya's Truth Commission Chairman," *APA-Nairobi*,
April 15, 2010 (International Commission on Transitional Justice); and "Kenyan Lawyers Tell
Kiplagat Time is Up," *Butterfly News*, April 15, 2010 (Law Society of Kenya).

[29] "Do you think that Ambassador Bethwel Kiplagat Commands Public Trust to Lead a Truth
and Justice Commission Successful [sic]," *Bunge la Mwananchi*, July 10, 2010. An earlier poll
had found a plurality supporting Kiplagat's continued tenure at the Commission. Confusingly,
that poll found that while 30 percent did not know who the chairman of the Commission was,
49 percent thought Kiplagat should stay while 41 percent thought he should leave. Samuel
Kumba, "Kiplagat Row Splits Kenyans," *Saturday Nation*, April 3, 2010 (reporting on poll
conducted by Synovate).

[30] The Commission's staff prepared summaries of these meetings, indicating that they took place
on May 24, May 26, May 27, May 29, and May 31.

and not the Commission itself – which was not surprising, as these meetings were clearly part of Kiplagat's campaign to keep himself in the public eye as embodying the Commission, and thus combat the public perception of him as a hindrance to the Commission and its work. Through his public relations firm, he issued press releases about the Commission and our work, often bypassing the Commission's own communication's department. It was reasonable for the media and others to assume that the statements he released reflected the views of the Commission.

Throughout the months of June and July, Kiplagat continued to organize public meetings in the Rift Valley in his attempt to bolster his reputation as a functional part of the Commission who was out and about and not a "pariah." This go-it-alone strategy on his part resulted in a number of news articles discussing splits within the Commission and confusion about the Commission's work plan. Much of the television coverage was of him meeting with prominent members of the Kalenjin community. The perception, if not the reality, of his focus on one ethnicity in the region further stoked the ethnic tensions that had been raised concerning the controversies surrounding him. I am told that some members of his family had been trying to push the ethnic angle, arguing that some people (or, somewhat unspoken, other ethnic groups, particularly Kikuyus) wanted Kiplagat out because he was a Kalenjin. The fact that I was publicly associated with pushing for a resolution of the issues surrounding him tempered this narrative a bit, though some claimed that I was either knowingly or unknowingly working with these other ethnic groups based on such an ethnic agenda.

In the meantime, I was told that acquaintances of mine were being threatened by members of Kiplagat's family who accused them of feeding negative information to me about Kiplagat. This was somewhat ironic as the only information I had was what had been given to the Commission, and all of my private and public statements, whether written or oral, had focused on that material and nothing else. At least one acquaintance informed me that he had been threatened and feared for his safety. He wanted me to know of his fears in case anything happened to him. I was also told that there was more information about irregular and perhaps illegal activities undertaken by Ambassador Kiplagat in the past. I informed the individuals who alerted me to the existence of evidence of other troubling activities by Ambassador Kiplagat that they were free to submit any information to me or the Commission, but I was not interested in seeking out or going out of my way to receive such information. There were three reasons I took this position. First, not being familiar with some of these individuals, I had no idea whether the offer was a trap, if the information would be credible, or what ulterior motives the individuals who would pass such information on to me might have. Second, my focus was on the Commission and not Kiplagat. Given the information we currently possessed, there was more than enough to warrant the creation of a tribunal or some other similar process. My primary interest was in protecting the Commission, not further discrediting Kiplagat. Third, given the threats against some of my Kenyan acquaintances, as well as the narrative that some of Kiplagat's allies were trying to peddle that I was trying to take over the Commission or "take down" Kiplagat, I did not want to give such fantasies any support by appearing eager to seek out more damning information about his past. As a result of my stance, I did not receive any additional information concerning Kiplagat, raising the question of whether these individuals had anything other than unsubstantiated rumors.

CIVIL SOCIETY: THE PERFECT AS THE ENEMY OF THE GOOD

Ever since our creation, some of the prominent Nairobi-based civil society organizations had called for the Commission to be disbanded. Some of these organizations focused their concern on the presence of Kiplagat, while others saw the entire Commission as tainted and ineffective. Unfortunately, these civil society organizations rarely spoke with a united voice and often gave conflicting rationales for opposing the Commission and our work. They rarely tried to work with sympathetic actors within the Commission, making their efforts to change or improve the process less effective than they might have been. Some worked with us openly and publicly while others worked with us privately while publicly calling for our disbandment. The head of one organization even lobbied to have us hire a relative while publicly criticizing the Commission as an agent of impunity that should be disbanded.

While many of the Nairobi-based organizations had been calling for Kiplagat's resignation, few of them publicly supported our petition to the chief justice for a tribunal to address the Kiplagat problem. Instead, on May 12th, the Kenya Section of the International Commission of Jurists and KEJUDE Trust filed a formal petition *to us* concerning Kiplagat. The petition urged us to use our powers to investigate and hold our own hearings with respect to the allegations raised against Ambassador Kiplagat. This was exactly the course of action that the Minister had suggested to us back in February, and one which we had thoroughly rejected. It was unfortunate that our relationship with some of these civil society groups in Nairobi was such that this petition was filed without any conversations with those of us on the inside trying to push the matter further. Nevertheless, it was one of the few constructive actions taken by civil society to address the Kiplagat problem.

Other efforts by civil society appeared to be designed more to create publicity than policy change. In what I am told was a common mode of activism on his part, Ndung'u Wainaina of the International Center for Policy and Conflict (ICPC) sent me an email on July 15, 2010. The email demanded that I resign, and stated that by continuing to stay at the Commission I was harming my own integrity and credentials. He had bcc'd a large number of people, including many members of the press, many of whom alerted me that they and others had been copied on the message. Many of those who had been copied on the message advised me to ignore the message, arguing that I was in a better position to judge the situation than much of civil society and that civil society, while critical of us, had not offered anything constructive as an alternative. Notwithstanding this advice, I sent a message to Wainaina saying that I would be willing to meet with him to discuss the content of his letter and more generally the TJRC. As though designed to confirm what others had told me, he never responded to my message.

Except for these isolated interventions, the campaign against us by some of the Nairobi-based organizations had died down during the summer as they shifted their focus to the newly drafted constitution and the referendum being held for its approval in August. After the constitutional referendum, the attention of some of the Nairobi-based organizations shifted back to the Commission. Unfortunately, there was again little communication with those of us inside the Commission who were potential allies of these organizations. Instead, we received periodic statements and demands that accused us of cronyism and corruption. As one prominent civil society member said, "the TJRC is irredeemably flawed and now needs to be disbanded."[31] Those civil society organizations that took a more constructive approach – for example, working with us to prepare our statement taking and hearing protocols – were put under increasing pressure to disassociate from us by those organizations demanding our dissolution. It was an unfortunately vitriolic, unplanned, and reactive campaign that did not provide any road map for addressing the concerns of the many victims who, we were later to learn, so eagerly awaited us throughout the country. In what was surely an unintended consequence of this scattershot approach to us, Kiplagat became more entrenched in his position, and given the attack against all of us the more moderate members within the Commission became more hesitant to take a bolder stand against Kiplagat.

On September 2 to 4, a coalition of civil society organizations convened a forum on the TJRC titled "National Dialogue Forum on the Truth, Justice

---

[31] *See* Otieno Otieno, "Truth Team Fights for Survival," *The Daily Nation*, September 4, 2010.

and Reconciliation: A Failed Promise?" Commissioner Shava and I attended and spoke at the meeting, as did various representatives from prominent civil society organizations and the United Nations. While the invitation to us to attend the meeting was described as an opportunity to learn and engage in a dialogue about the Commission, we learned that the organizers had already drafted a public statement denouncing the Commission and calling for a boycott of our activities. As an indication of where things were heading, the United Nations representative surprisingly (and uncharacteristically for a UN official) attacked the Commission and all but called upon civil society and others to boycott our activities.[32]

Around this same time, Ndung'u Wainaina's ICPC issued a report on the TJRC. It was a very weak and shoddy piece of work. It not only included typos, but also inaccurate statements about the Commission, some of which underscored the lack of contact the authors had had with the Commission, and others of which indicated how little they knew about the Commission and its mandate. For example, the report claimed that we could grant amnesty for acts associated with gross human rights violations, which was wrong on two counts: (1) we could only recommend, not grant, amnesty; and (2) the act expressly stated that we could not recommend amnesty for a gross violation of human rights. In compiling the report, the authors apparently looked at an earlier draft of our enabling legislation that had never been passed. Ironically, the changes to this draft legislation, which, among other things, made clear that we could not recommend amnesty for a gross violation of human rights, were the result of effective lobbying by civil society organizations. While the ICPC report claimed to be based upon firsthand monitoring and engagement with the Commission, it was difficult to believe that it was based on much, if any, engagement with us. In fact, some significant parts of the report appeared to have been taken from news stories, some of which were, in fact, inaccurate. It claimed, for example, that we had held public hearings in Mt. Elgon in May 2010. We had, in fact, begun our statement taking in Mt. Elgon around this time but had yet to hold a public hearing anywhere in the country.[33] The quality of this report was unfortunate, as we needed – as any truth commission does – a credible, and critical, civil society that would monitor us in a way that would move the process forward. The ICPC report failed to do this.

---

[32] Lucas Barasa, "UN Official Cautions TJRC over Handling of Past Injustices," *The Daily Nation*, September 3, 2010. For a response, *see* Godfrey Musila, "Take Heed: Truth and Reconciliation Train has Already Left the Station," *The Daily Nation*, September 8, 2010.

[33] The report even claimed that we were only seven commissioners by law. An early draft of the legislation did specify seven commissioners, but all of the legislation that finally passed indicated nine commissioners.

One of the more curious criticisms leveled against us by civil society was the fact that we had employed victims on our staff. We had, in fact, employed a wide variety of people on our staff, including those who self-identified as survivors or victims. The arguments against us hiring victims varied, but the most cogent were that (1) victims would be biased; (2) the presence of victims would discourage perpetrators from engaging with the Commission; and (3) because they were employees, they could no longer testify before us with respect to atrocities that they may have suffered or witnessed. Taking the arguments in reverse order, there was nothing in our rules or procedures that would preclude an employee of the Commission from also testifying as a witness before the Commission. I am not aware of any general legal or ethical principle that would preclude such a situation either.

Second, it is possible that some perpetrators might not want to engage with us because of the presence of victims on our staff. It is also possible that the presence of individuals knowledgeable about criminal law, or international human rights law, might also discourage such engagement, as might the presence of women, foreigners, and individuals of a particular ethnicity. The relevant question was not whether people might not engage with us because of the presence of particular types of individuals on our staff; rather the important question was whether the reasons for an individual's refusal to engage with us were reasonable and consistent with the values of democracy, human rights, and the rule of law.

Third, the question of bias, or even perceived bias, is a serious and important one. Because of the conflicts of interest of our chair we were particularly sensitive to this issue. We had therefore adopted a code of conduct that applied to commissioners and staff concerning such conflicts of interest and that could lead to an individual being recused from dealing with a matter in which she was perceived to have a conflict of interest. It is important to distinguish, however, between a conflict of interest and bias. Arguments have been made before international criminal tribunals that an individual who has argued that rape in an armed conflict should be prosecuted as a war crime is biased and should not sit as a judge on a case involving rape as a war crime. Such arguments have all been properly rejected by those tribunals. To use this specific example, if such an argument were to prevail, it would mean that only judges who had expressed no opinion about rape could sit in judgment over a suspected rapist. There is a distinction between being "biased" with respect to what the law is – i.e., that rape can be a war crime – and being biased with respect to a particular suspect before being presented with the evidence – i.e., I know this individual and I am sure he is (or is not) guilty of rape. It was never made clear to me what specific bias a victim employed by us might have, other than the bias to ensure that such violations did not happen again, that those individuals responsible be held to account, and that those who suffered be eligible for some form of reparations. There was no question, however, that some of these criticisms were articulated in a way that seemed to equate the conflicts of interest of our chair with the alleged conflicts of interest or bias of victims. As one prominent civil society actor noted:

> Impunity and lack of accountability also needs to be addressed via the Truth, Justice and Reconciliation Commission, which is unfortunately now turning into a bigger farce than could have been anticipated! How a potential witness – in a negative way – can Chair the TJRC beats comprehension! How someone who is supposed to lead reconciliation can be so arrogantly obstinate boggles the mind. If Bethuel Kiplagat does not get what conflict of interest is, his competence and integrity as Chair are marred *ab initio*. Worse, he has now gone out and hired other potential witnesses as staff for the TJRC! Which means that these survivors – and a large majority have been on the margins of society precisely because of the violations they suffered – who are now staff will not be testifying at the TJRC as that would be another conflict of interest! What better way to destroy an institution, and weaken it before it starts than this?[34]

The problem with this approach is that it equates the conflict of interest of an alleged perpetrator with the conflict of interest or bias (if any) of a victim/survivor. The problem with Kiplagat was that, absent an effective recusal system, he would be influencing decisions that directly affected his own personal interest (i.e., whether his acceptance of favorable land deals from the government was a violation or not). In the case of the staff we hired who identified as survivors, none would be or were involved in making decisions regarding findings and recommendations – those were decisions ultimately made by commissioners. To the extent that our work raised conflicts of interest with staff, our code of conduct for staff and commissioners provided a mechanism for addressing such issues.

There were, on the other hand, compelling reasons in favor of employing victims. First, such individuals were more likely to be knowledgeable and educated about many of the historical violations we were to investigate. Second, such individuals were more likely to be trusted by other victims who might otherwise be reluctant to engage with the Commission. Third, as was passionately argued to me by other Kenyans, many victims who had run afoul of the government in the past had been shut out of most employment

---

[34] Maina Kiai, "We are Not Out of the Woods Yet, Despite the New Constitution," *Maina's Blog,* August 31, 2010.

and education opportunities. Providing them with an opportunity to contribute to society in a meaningful way provided some measure of additional
dignity and purpose to their lives.

Leaving aside the positive arguments for a truth commission to employ
victims, prohibiting employment of victims raises the question of how one
defines a victim. Some have argued that most if not all Kenyans were the
victims of historical injustices committed by the government. Certainly, one
could say that all non-white people in South Africa were victims under
apartheid, and even, some persuasively argue, many white people. Archbishop
Tutu, who so ably chaired the South African Truth and Reconciliation
Commission, clearly suffered as a victim of apartheid. Under the arguments
made by these civil society groups, he should have been precluded from
playing that role. In addition, many of the Kenyan civil society leaders who
had lobbied for the TJRC and applied to be commissioners would themselves
also be disqualified from serving as Commissioners, as many of them had been
persecuted by the state. Such an expansive interpretation of conflicts of
interest is not only unworkable, it is also unwise. When I raised this issue
with some of my acquaintances within civil society, they suggested that the
concern was, in fact, something that was not being discussed publicly: that our
hiring of victims increased our political and moral legitimacy and effectiveness, a development that ran counter to attempts by some in civil society to
paint the entire Commission with a broad brush as a discredited institution
with no prospect of fulfilling our mandate.

THE PETITION, ACT 2

On September 10, the *Nation* published an editorial noting the credibility
challenges facing our chair, including the fact that a group of civil society
groups had finally – five months after we had – petitioned the chief justice,
asking for a tribunal to evaluate the appropriateness of Ambassador Kiplagat's
presence on the Commission.[35] Notwithstanding some of the earlier statements by some of the same civil society actors, their petition to the chief justice attributed "most of the legitimacy, credibility, and operational challenges
facing the TJRC to the questions related to its Chairperson's, Mr. Bethuel

---

[35] "Resolve the TJRC Row" *The Daily Nation*, September 10, 2010, reporting on *Public Petition to
the Chief Justice to Institute a Tribunal against Mr. Bethuel Kiplagat, the Chair of Kenya's
Truth Justice and Reconciliation Commission (TJRC)* (September 9, 2010) filed on behalf of the
Kenya Transitional Justice Network by the executive directors of the Kenya Human Rights
Commission, the International Centre for Policy and Conflict, and the International
Commission of Jurists.

Kiplagat, past record." The civil society petition also made reference to our earlier petition and noted that the current inaction on our petition might be a violation of the newly enacted constitution, which provides for expeditious and efficient administrative action. The reference to our petition and the chief justice's failure to act on it was, in retrospect, the most significant aspect of the civil society petition.

In clear response to this assertion of inaction, the chief justice responded to the civil society organizations and noted that he had been in touch with the Commission concerning the matter. This was news to us, as we had no record of the chief justice contacting us about the petition other than copying us on his response to civil society, which we had just received. Attached to the copy of the chief justice's response to civil society we had just received were copies of two additional letters, neither of which we had seen before. The first was a letter addressed to our CEO dated September 7 in response to our letter of May 14 inquiring about the status of our petition. In that September 7 letter, the chief justice informed us that he had written to the attorney general on May 3 concerning our petition. We had no record of receiving this letter prior to this copy being sent to us. In fact, the letter sent to us appeared to be the original letter, as it was signed by the chief justice and was not stamped "Copy." The second letter was a copy of the letter written by the chief justice to the attorney general on May 3. Unlike the September 7 letter, this letter was clearly marked "Copy" and did not include the signature of the chief justice. It is unclear whether the letter to us was written for the purpose of the response to the civil society organizations or whether it had, in fact, been written earlier but for bureaucratic reasons had only been sent to us four months after our inquiry in May.

The letter from the chief justice to the attorney general concerning our petition said, "In your role as the Principal Legal Advisor to the Government of Kenya. Kindly advise whether the listed grounds satisfy the requirements of the law precedent to setting up a tribunal as set out in S. 17(1) of the said Act." This was curious indeed. First, here was the head of one independent branch of government, the judiciary, asking for legal advice from the "principal legal advisor" of another branch of government. The act indicated no role for the attorney general in this or any other matter related to the Commission. As the head of the independent judicial branch of government, it would have been odd for the chief justice to have consulted even privately those in the executive branch about a strictly legal issue clearly entrusted to the chief justice under our enabling legislation. To have engaged in such consultations formally through a letter, and then to make that consultation known publicly through a letter to civil society organizations and copied to us, was particularly surprising. Second, the chief justice appeared to be asking the attorney general to make the legal determination of whether our petition satisfied the requirements for creating a tribunal. That decision was clearly one for the chief justice to make under our Act. The additional fact that the chief justice appeared to be unable to act until the attorney general responded to his letter (it had been four months since he apparently had requested the opinion) suggested that the chief justice either felt he could not make a decision without the attorney general or that he effectively wanted the attorney general to make the decision.

Given the new information contained in these letters, I thought we should write to the attorney general and (1) impress upon him how we were anxiously waiting a resolution of this matter and (2) offer our assistance in providing any additional information he might need in formulating his advice for the chief justice. Other commissioners felt we should not write to the attorney general but rather should wait and let the process play itself out. I was concerned that, at this rate, our operational period might end before a decision was made on whether to establish a tribunal, much less before such a tribunal could issue an opinion on the matter.

KIPLAGAT'S FOLLY: A NARROW ESCAPE

While we debated whether to respond to the letter from the chief justice, Kiplagat continued to engage in activities on behalf of the Commission without our knowledge. Over the weekend of September 18, he had apparently traveled outside Nairobi in an effort to mediate between the Mungiki and local communities. The Mungiki were a group who identified themselves as dedicated to correcting historical injustices suffered by the Kikuyu ethnic group. They were formed in response to the election-related clashes in the 1990s during which many Kikuyu were displaced from their land. They also identified themselves as furthering the legacy of the anticolonial Mau Mau movement. While their creation was based in part on legitimate grievances, over the years the Mungiki had also engaged in various criminal activities, including intimidation, assaults, and executions. They had also been the object of persecution from the state over the years, including losing members to extrajudicial killings. They were thus both perpetrators and victims with respect to many incidents within our mandate.

Ambassador Kiplagat had apparently taken it upon himself to try to mediate between the Mungiki and other groups in the region. In fact, in a meeting he attended in the Sudan, Ambassador Kiplagat mentioned to a member of the diplomatic community there that he was involved in secret mediations between the Mungiki and other groups, which was then reported to me by a member of the diplomatic community in Kenya. It would appear that Ambassador Kiplagat was a bit better about keeping foreign countries abreast of his (and thus our) operations than he was with respect to his fellow commissioners.

While the details of what exactly happened during Kiplagat's visit that weekend have never been made clear to me, at some point, a crowd of individuals turned on Ambassador Kiplagat, his driver, and one or two other people traveling with them. What ensued was described to me as a high-speed car chase as Ambassador Kiplagat's car was set upon by an angry mob. Apparently, the quick thinking and skills of his driver got them out of what appeared to be a lethal situation. The incident was reported in the press, although in only skeletal form. It again underscored the persistence of Ambassador Kiplagat in going it alone and the consequent risks to both himself and the Commission. The incident contributed to the perception of us as ineffective, being rebuffed yet again by communities to whom we were supposed to be reaching out.

"NO GOVERNMENT WORTH ITS SALT": ADMISSION
AND PUBLIC DENIAL

In early October, I was informed that one of the major television stations, KTN, had prepared a three-part series on the Wagalla massacre. Victims and others interviewed for the program apparently had mentioned Ambassador Kiplagat as involved in the planning of the massacre. Kiplagat had received advance notice of the airing of this series and had threatened to take KTN to court for libel and slander – as an observer of this dispute wryly noted, "I always thought K[iplagat] was in charge of searching for the truth?"

On October 14, the KTN series on Wagalla aired. It included an interview with Kiplagat. In fact, I had been in the office earlier that week when Kiplagat gave the interview. While I did not hear the entire interview at that time, I did hear enough to realize that he was now, for the first time, publicly acknowledging that he had been present at the meeting of the Kenya Intelligence Committee on February 8, 1984, in Wajir, less than two days before the start of the five-day security operation that resulted in the Wagalla massacre.

Ambassador Kiplagat's television interview was a remarkable event and became a major turning point in the life of the Commission. Up until this point, Kiplagat had repeatedly stated that he could not remember if he had attended this meeting of the Kenya Intelligence Committee twenty-six years earlier. In the interview, he revealed that a friend had recently reminded him that they had both attended this high-level security meeting. After being reminded of his attendance, his memory was sufficiently refreshed that he could now state with certainty that they had not discussed the security operation at all during their meetings with the local provincial security committee and the district security committee. In fact, he was later to claim in testimony before us that the purpose of the meetings held between the Kenya Intelligence Committee and the various provincial and district security committees in the region was to discuss economic development and only tangentially, if at all, security. In other words, Kiplagat wanted us to believe that a meeting among three different committees dedicated to security and intelligence did not discuss a pending security operation that involved the police, military, and other security services, and that would commence less than forty-eight hours later in the exact same provincial town in which they were meeting.

Leaving aside the plausibility of a national intelligence committee meeting with local security committees not discussing what was to turn out to be one of the largest security operations ever conducted by the government within the borders of Kenya, and Kiplagat's suddenly acquired memory of the details of meetings that took place a quarter of a century ago, what was equally troubling was the way Ambassador Kiplagat spoke about responsibility for the massacre. In short, he argued that the government not only was not but *could not* be responsible for the massacre. In particular, he stated on national television, "I doubt, now this is where I find it extremely difficult, no government worth its salt plans to massacre its own people. No."[36] Remarkably, the chair of the Truth, Justice and Reconciliation Commission, a body mandated to not only unearth the truth of what happened with respect to historical injustices but also to identify those individuals and organizations who were responsible for such injustices, publicly prejudged an issue that was clearly within our mandate and that we had yet to investigate. His conclusion that no government worth its salt would massacre its own people suggested that we as a Commission would not be identifying the government as a responsible actor for any of the many massacres we were to investigate, including the Wagalla massacre in which Kiplagat was now implicated. As a historical matter, claiming that no government "worth its salt" massacres its own people raises the unfortunate question of whether there is *any* government that can claim to be "worth its salt." In the United States, one need only look to the treatment, including massacres, of Native Americans, or the US Civil War, to conclude that the US government would not meet this standard. It is an unfortunate reality that few,

---

[36] "Inside Story, Wagalla Massacre pt. 4," *KTN*, October 14, 2010 (available on *YouTube*). The statement by Ambassador Kiplagat is found at 8:17–8:28 of that video.

if any, governments would pass Ambassador Kiplagat's test, including the Kenyan government. The fact that he was our chair, and under our legislation our official spokesperson, meant that his assertion that the government could not have been responsible for the massacre would lead a reasonable Kenyan to conclude that the Commission itself had concluded that the Kenyan government was not responsible for the massacre. Efforts by some of the other commissioners to get him to at least publicly clarify that his comments did not reflect the position of the Commission failed.

Ambassador Kiplagat's interview nicely illustrates the reason why we have rules and procedures concerning conflicts of interest. Taking his statement at face value, Ambassador Kiplagat was clearly interested in downplaying the responsibility of the government for this terrible massacre in part because of the accusation that he was linked to the event. Regardless of what, in fact, happened at that meeting on February 8, 1984, that Ambassador Kiplagat now so clearly remembered, the fact that there was a question about his involvement at least required him to abstain from being involved in anything related to that massacre. The fact that he now placed himself at a meeting so close to the operation that led to the worst massacre in Kenya's history, even with the uncertainty about what was discussed at that meeting, threw into even greater question his suitability for being a member of, much less chairing, the Commission. Even if his memory was correct that the pending security operation was not discussed during this unprecedented visit of the Kenya Intelligence Committee, it was reasonable for the average Kenyan to distrust his objectivity with respect to this, and perhaps other, matters within our mandate. Our legislation on its face disqualified him from being a member of the Commission, for it required that no commissioner be "linked" to any violation within our mandate. We were later to unearth documents and interview witnesses who were to tell a very different story about that meeting than the one that Kiplagat was telling with his newly revived memory.

MY THREATENED RESIGNATION

By early October, I had pretty much decided to resign from the Commission. After almost six months, there had been no movement on our petition to the chief justice. When the chief justice finally communicated to us (albeit indirectly) that he had been waiting for four months for advice from the attorney general (and apparently backdated a series of letters to justify his delay), many of my commissioner colleagues seemed content to continue to wait and see what the chief justice might eventually do rather than to try to nudge the process along. Organizationally, we were operating as though our challenges were minimal. A discussion paper prepared by our senior staff for donors stated that "despite a few challenges at the inception of the Commission's mandate, the Commission is now fully operational and has rolled out its work-plan."[37] In a separate section on risks, there was no mention of the conflicts of interest of our chair or of the protracted process undertaken by the chief justice to respond to our petition. Civil society continued to search for a viable and cohesive strategy concerning the Commission. Kiplagat appeared to be operating as he always had – using the Commission as a platform for his own agenda rather than working collectively with us. Finally, a good friend in the international human rights community outside of Kenya confided in me that some of my friends and colleagues were privately concerned that my continued presence on the Commission was hurting my reputation and had the potential to affect permanently my human rights credentials. I was beginning to agree with this analysis. At this point, I confided in a friend that I had decided to resign but was trying to figure out timing. I knew that if I resigned, the government would not pay my moving expenses back to the United States. Kaari Murungi had resigned in mid-April and she was still waiting to get her partial April salary and her gratuity payment, both of which were clearly owed to her under our contract. I would not be able to return to my university teaching until January at the earliest and might not be able to do so until the following August. With my apartment rented out in Seattle until the following August, I had no place to live even if were I to return to Seattle, and I was still losing money each month on my Seattle rental. It was clear that my financial loss in taking on this project would be even greater than I had originally anticipated.

When the interview with Ambassador Kiplagat – in which he admitted to being present at the intelligence committee meeting in Wajir and during which he opined that the government could not be held responsible for the massacre – was aired, I knew that I could no longer in good conscience continue to be a part of this process. I had no idea what else was out there that might now surface about Kiplagat's links to past atrocities. What was already revealed was, for me, enough. I could no longer associate myself with a Commission chaired by someone whose memory fluctuated so dramatically concerning crucial events within our mandate and who had now publicly expressed an opinion concerning responsibility for a matter within our mandate that we had yet to investigate.

[37] Kenya TJRC October Briefing Kit (October 2010), para. 3.3.

My decision to resign from the Commission was not the only reaction to Kiplagat's recent revelations. Parliament began to move more seriously to disband the entire Commission. I suspect that, like me, some members of Parliament had concluded that efforts to evaluate Kiplagat's suitability to be a member of the Commission, given the revelations of the past year, were going nowhere.

I crafted a press release that I sent to the major newspapers on Wednesday, October 20, and requested that it be embargoed until Friday, October 22. In the release, I announced my intention to resign and set out two main reasons for my decision. First, I highlighted the untenable position of our chair, given his recent revelations concerning his presence at the intelligence committee meeting in Wajir. Second, I mentioned the lack of support from the government, most notably the refusal to provide us with more than a token amount of money, making it impossible for us to fulfill the mandate entrusted to us by the people of Kenya.

On the same morning of Wednesday, October 20, the Commission met with the minister of justice. At the meeting with the minister, I did not speak, having already made up my mind to resign. Some of the other commissioners raised again the issue of our chair and asked for his support in moving towards a resolution. The minister deflected these appeals, citing to our independence and how he had no role to play in this matter. His position was, to put it mildly, quite ironic, given his earlier public statements concerning the matter back in April. He now seemed to be taking the same hands-off approach of every other responsible person in government: the chief justice, the attorney general, and the president. It just confirmed in my mind that my decision to resign was the correct one.

As we were waiting for the meeting with the minister to begin, people, including members of the press who were there for a brief photo op with us and the minister, began to whisper among themselves and started to look at me. I heard one of the commissioners whisper to Kiplagat, "Ron has resigned." Apparently one of the major newspapers, unable to sit on a scoop for more than a few minutes (much less the forty-eight hours I had requested and they had promised), broke the story of my announcement. The press asked the minister about my resignation. He was clearly annoyed and responded that people were obviously free to do whatever they wanted, including resign.

With the breach of the embargo on my announcement, the press began to report that I had *in fact* resigned. My statement began with the carefully chosen phrase of my "intention" to resign. I had neglected to say when I would resign but instructed the Commission's media office that, if asked, they should respond that I would formally resign on Monday, November 1. Given the problems that Commissioner Murungi had had with her salary and other related matters, it was my hope that by resigning as of the first of the month I would avoid such financially expensive loose ends. The impression in the press, however, was that I had, in fact, resigned. Under our Act, it was clear that a commissioner could resign "by writing under his hand addressed to the President."[38] I had drafted such a letter, had signed it, and had entrusted the letter with Ambassador Dinka.

The ten days between the announcement of my intention to resign and the date I had planned to resign were long and eventful ones. I suspect that the government, most particularly the minister, was happy that I would be resigning. I am told that on the day that he learned of my pending resignation, he immediately contacted the Panel of Eminent African Personalities to recommend a replacement for me. I was also told that the minister had been asking for a copy of my actual resignation letter – someone in his office even contacted the Commission to get a copy, only to be told that I had not written such a letter yet. I was also told that the president had been overheard to say something along the lines of, "We are finally rid of that American."

During this ten-day period, a number of crucial actors began to engage with the future of the Commission, including Parliament, the Panel of Eminent African Personalities, the media, and the Commission itself. On October 27, the chair of the Parliamentary Committee on Justice and Legal Affairs announced that the Committee was giving the Commission seventy-two hours "to resolve the question of integrity and credibility, failure of which the committee will move without delay to disband the Commission." The disbandment would only apply to the remaining commissioners; the staff was assured that they would be retained as new commissioners were sought. I was told privately that the Committee had told Kiplagat that he must resign, to which he said he would not.

The Panel of Eminent African Personalities released a statement noting my decision to resign and expressed regret at the circumstances that had led to my decision and concern about the issues I had raised, including our credibility and the lack of government funding.

The commissioners, faced with the possibility of imminent disbandment, drafted an urgent application to the chief justice demanding that he establish a tribunal pursuant to our April petition within the next seventy-two hours.

FINALLY, A TRIBUNAL

It was only after all of these actors had weighed in that the chief justice finally decided to act on the petition we had filed six months earlier. On the evening

---

[38] TJRC Act, *supra* Chapter 1, note 3, at Art. 16(b).

of Friday, October 29, the chief justice publicly stated that he would be establishing a tribunal to evaluate Kiplagat as requested by our petition and by Kiplagat himself. In April, Ambassador Kiplagat had stated that he would step aside when such a tribunal was formed and not when we had requested such a tribunal as we had all then assumed. With the announcement of the creation of the tribunal, the question was whether he would honor that earlier promise or, as he had done before, change the goal posts and insist that he stay in place until the tribunal had finished its work. I spent much of that weekend on the phone speaking to other commissioners, stakeholders, and the media about the possible ways forward and trying to discern what Kiplagat would do. Monday, November 1, was the day I was to hand in my resignation letter to the president. The United Nations had contacted me a number of times to get a copy of the resignation letter – they were anxious to remove themselves from supporting this process, which they successfully did in the last year of our operations.

By the morning of Monday, November 1, we had received no indication of Ambassador Kiplagat's intentions. I consulted with a number of friends and colleagues, most of whom counseled that I wait to see what Kiplagat did before making a decision about my own resignation. Ambassador Dinka, with whom I had entrusted the signed letter, persuaded me that I should wait at least until Kiplagat had announced what he would do.

As Kiplagat consulted with his family and friends, we waited. I drafted two public statements, one to be released if he stayed at the Commission, in which I would announce my immediate resignation, and the other to be released if he stepped aside, in which I would announce that I no longer intended to resign but that I continued to have serious concerns about the viability of the Commission given the lack of government support and funding.

On Tuesday, November 2, at about noon, we received a news alert that Kiplagat had released a public statement to the media to the effect that he was stepping aside while the tribunal did its work. As with previous such statements, we eventually received copies of his statement from the media rather than from Kiplagat himself.

Ambassador Kiplagat started his statement by welcoming the creation of the tribunal: "I would like to state clearly that I, indeed, very much welcome the decision of the Chief Justice to ascertain the truth concerning the allegations that have been made against me. Right at the beginning and repeatedly thereafter, I have maintained the need for this matter to be addressed **fairly and decisively, according to the rule of law.**"[39] He also stated that he "see[s] the

---

[39] *Media Statement by Ambassador Bethuel Kiplagat* (bold in original) (on book's website).

FIGURE 3.3 Gado – Stepping aside. Image courtesy of Gado (gadocartoons.com).

Tribunal as an opportunity to finally put any doubts about my credibility to rest once and for all." In light of the creation of the tribunal, he stated that "in order to allow the Tribunal to carry out its mandate, I am, therefore, as of today, stepping aside from my day to day responsibilities at the TJRC."

On its face, it was a good and positive statement, embracing the creation of the tribunal as a credible mechanism for addressing the allegations that had been made against him and appearing to separate his own personal interest in this matter from that of the Commission by "stepping aside." "Stepping aside" is an odd Kenyan institution whereby an individual temporarily leaves a position while still being paid their full salary. Some were critical that Kiplagat would continue to earn his salary even though he was not working with the Commission. I had argued from the beginning that, if necessary, the government should pay him the entire salary he would have received during the lifetime of the Commission in return for him leaving the Commission. It was a minor amount of money compared to the overall budget of the Commission and a price I thought worth paying if it would allow the process to move forward. It was, however, a lot of money for the average Kenyan, and thus such a compromise would have underscored yet again the inequities between well-connected government officials like Kiplagat and the people for whom much of our work was being done.

I was pleased that Kiplagat had finally agreed to put the interests of the Commission ahead of his own interests. I immediately issued my statement indicating that I would not be resigning, given the recent turn in events. The commissioners issued a positive and supportive statement commending Kiplagat on his course of action and wishing him the best in his search for vindication. Given our history with him, however, I was slightly uneasy about how he might approach the tribunal and related manners. We were to discover quite quickly that while Kiplagat had repeatedly expressed his desire for the creation of a tribunal, he was, in fact, opposed to its creation and would spend the next year undermining its work, ultimately making it impossible for it to do the job he so passionately had said he wanted it to do.

4

I am Kenyan: Voices of the Wananchi

*This is a Report. It is written with words, and printed on paper or converted into
electronic bits and bytes. Yet it is the product of, in some cases literally, the blood,
sweat and tears of the stories that were told to us as we travelled the country. The written
word, no matter how poetic, cannot convey accurately the passion with which people
demanded to tell their stories and the integrity and dignity with which they related their
experiences. It cannot convey the silence, the tears, and the emotions that engulfed
the venue at which a man described how he lost his entire family during the 2007/2008
Post Election Violence (PEV). It cannot convey the traumatic experience of a woman
who was raped during the PEV and her fear that the same could happen to her during
the 2013 elections. Nor can it convey the horrid experience of a woman who had to
carry the head of her slain husband all the way from Nakuru to Kisumu. It can neither
convey the tears that were shed before this Commission nor the tears that were shed
by the Commission's staff and Commissioners. The stories in these pages are horrid
but they did happen, here on our land. In a nutshell, there has been, there is, suffering
in the land.*

Kenyan TJRC Report[1]

The story of a nation arises out of the individual experiences of each person
who makes up that nation. Yet those experiences are not only diverse and
disparate; they can often be in conflict. This is an uncomfortable truth, as
each country has its own unifying narrative that is often anchored in a creation
story (e.g., revolution, independence) that, among other things, asserts that
all of its members share a common experience and legacy. These myths
are important for creating national cohesion and unity, notwithstanding the
fact (or perhaps because of the fact) that they are often selective, and sometimes distorted, versions of the lived experience of many of their members.

---

[1] TJRC FINAL REPORT, *supra* Chapter 1, note 9, at Vol. 1, pages iii–iv.

The reality is that nations are far more complex. There are winners and losers – those who wield power, and those who are subjugated and oppressed by that power.

The unifying story for Kenya starts with resistance to colonialism, moves to self-rule and then independence, and then, as President Uhuru Kenyatta recently said, "building a country that has been an island of peace and stability in this region and, indeed, in the continent of Africa."[2] Such unifying myths are less likely to be clearly false (though one may raise questions about describing Kenya as an island of peace and stability given its history of internal conflict and injustice), but instead present an overly simplistic version of history that tends to overlook important elements of a much more complex reality.

A truth commission can reveal that more complex reality. The purpose of a truth commission is not to establish the definitive truth about a country's history. Nor should it be. Instead, a truth commission should be judged on its effectiveness in revealing the complexity of a country's history, particularly with respect to violations of fundamental human rights. Much of the truth of what happened in the past, and its meaning for the present and future, will always be a contested area of public engagement for all societies, including (and perhaps especially) those emerging from conflict. This is not to claim that there are no definitive truths. We can, in many cases, determine who did what to whom and when.[3] A truth commission will ascertain some of those truths, and the Kenyan TJRC was required to establish such truth for a wide range of violations within our mandate. But a truth commission's purpose is far broader than determining who did what to whom and when. Truth commissions can, and should, play an important role in facilitating a public conversation about a country's past anchored in the lived experiences of the members of that country. Engaging with the truth of the past both sharpens the accuracy of the truth and increases the ownership of that truth by those in the present, whether or not they experienced or were active participants in that

---

[2] "Speech by His Excellency Hon. Uhuru Kenyatta, C.G.H., President of the Republic of Kenya and Commander in Chief of the Defence Forces During the 54th Madaraka Day Celebrations at Kabiru-ini Stadium, Nyeri on 1st June, 2017," *available at* www.president.go.ke/2017/06/01/speech-by-his-excellency-hon-uhuru-kenyatta-c-g-h-president-of-the-republic-of-kenya-and-commander-in-chief-of-the-defence-forces-during-the-54th-madaraka-day-celebrations-at-kabiru-ini-stadium-n/.

[3] Though we often associate a high level of certainty to such truths produced through the rigors of a formal judicial proceeding, our faith in the accuracy of such processes appears to be misplaced as more evidence emerges of those wrongfully convicted at the end of such a process. *See* The National Registry of Exonerations, EXONERATIONS IN 2013 (February 4, 2014) (discussing the 87 exonerations of convicted individuals achieved in 2013, and noting that the Registry has recorded 1,304 exonerations between 1989 and February 2014).

past. In addition, fostering such a critical conversation counters the tendency to view the past through a narrow self-fulfilling lens that often adopts a simplified binary analysis, such as good versus evil or us versus them. As Nanci Adler compellingly points out, a richer and more functional truth "emerges when *competing* narratives are reframed in a conceptual shift as *contributing* narratives."[4]

The South African TRC famously identified four different types of truths: (1) factual or forensic truth; (2) personal or narrative truth; (3) social or "dialogue" truth; and (4) healing and restorative truth.[5] Factual or forensic truth captures the objective nature of truth – who did what, when, to whom. Even here, however, our claim to objective truth can be overly simplistic. What was done may be described, *inter alia*, as a slap, a punch, an assault, severe ill-treatment, cruel and degrading, or torture. Objective truths have embedded within them subjective truths and judgments. The personal, or narrative, truth is the most important contribution that a traditional truth commission can provide. It is a subjective description of what happened, when, by whom, and to whom. More than a subjective description of an objective set of facts, personal or narrative truth also includes information about how individuals experienced that truth. For example, "I trusted him because he was a police officer. When he assaulted me, I was angry and surprised." This testimony reveals issues of trust and betrayal that are not revealed by the objective or forensic truth of the fact that a police officer assaulted an individual. Such truths are important for understanding the impact of a particular violation – which, in this case, might include a decreased trust in the police force or government generally – as well as for developing a program for addressing the harm suffered by the victim. Social or dialogue truth describes the public discourse around the different types of truths. The idea of social or dialogue truth hearkens back to the *agora* of ancient Greece and the premise that public engagement strengthens a society. This, too, is an area in which a truth commission can, and should, contribute greatly. The public hearings of a truth commission provide an entry point for various forensic and personal or narrative truths to enter the public space. Media coverage of a truth commission, as well as the commission's own statements and analysis (including its final report), also contribute to social or dialogue truth. One of the most important functions of a truth commission should be facilitating a

---

4   Nanci Adler, "Introduction: On History, Historians, and Transitional Justice," in Nanci Adler, ed., Understanding the Age of Transitional Justice: Crimes, Courts, Commissions, and Chronicling (Rutgers University Press, 2018).

5   SA TRC Report, *supra* Chapter 2, note 27, at Volume 1, Chapter 5, para. 29 (page 110).

public discussion of a contested past, and thus contributing to the creation of a process of social truth. Finally, healing and restorative truth describes truth that in its revelation contributes to the healing of victims and others affected by past violations. For example, discovering what happened to a loved one and who was responsible for her death can contribute to the healing of those left behind. Understanding why a particular person was targeted may also contribute to such healing. Such knowledge may also increase the pain and violation experienced by victims and their loved ones – thus a truth that may be healing or restorative for one victim may be a new violation for others.

The mandate of the TJRC incorporated a number of elements of these different approaches to truth. We were to establish "an accurate, complete and historical record" of violations within our mandate. This descriptive function included understanding violations within their broader context. Thus we were directed to establish the antecedents, circumstances, nature, factors, context, and extent of such violations. In addition to determining what happened, we were also to determine why such violations happened, and thus were directed to establish the causes of such violations. We were also directed to provide a safe space for victims and perpetrators to speak publicly, to share their truths. To fulfill these functions, we undertook a number of activities, including research, investigations, statement taking, and public and *in camera* hearings. We also built upon these traditional truth commission mechanisms by adding a women's hearing in each community we visited and conducting focus group discussions throughout the country on violations of socioeconomic rights. The product of these activities is most significantly found in our 2,100-page final report in which we synthesize much of this information to provide an account of historical injustices and violations. Its impact is also to be found among the thousands of people that participated in, or otherwise benefited from, these and other activities of the Commission. These activities and outcomes contributed to all four forms of truth. Our research and investigations contributed to forensic truth. The new information we discovered and revealed concerning a number of the assassinations and massacres that have plagued Kenya's history, including the involvement of high-ranking government officials, is an example of this contribution to forensic truth.[6] Our statement taking and public hearings contributed to personal and narrative truth. The Commission traveled widely throughout Kenya to provide Kenyans with an opportunity to tell their stories either publicly (in our public hearings) or privately (in our *in camera* or women's hearings). In some places, the TJRC was the first official

---

[6] See generally TJRC FINAL REPORT, *supra* Chapter 1, note 9, at Vol. IIA.

Commission to visit and provide this opportunity to some of the most marginalized regions of Kenya. Our public hearings, engagement with the media, and our final report all contributed to social or dialogic truth. Our hearings were often the subject of public discussion and debate – always within the communities we visited but often at the national level. The final report was subject to intense public debate and scrutiny during the first few weeks after its release. Finally, our public hearings, statement taking, community outreach, and other reconciliation-related activities contributed to healing or restorative truth.

While this chapter focuses on the personal and narrative truths provided to the Commission through our public hearing process, it also touches upon the other three types of truth that arose out of the public hearing process as well as other activities of the Commission. This chapter gives a flavor of the complex reality that we uncovered. It does not intend to, nor therefore should it be expected to, provide a full and accurate truth of what we found. Even our final report, which runs over 2,000 pages, could not do justice to the vast majority of stories and experiences we captured. This book, and even more so the Commission's final report, are contributions to an ongoing conversation about the history and future of Kenya, but neither should be viewed as the definitive version of that history.

CHALLENGES AND PREPARATIONS

With the creation of the tribunal and the stepping aside of Ambassador Kiplagat, the Commission's activities began to move forward in earnest. While some civil society organizations were still cautious about us – Kiplagat had only stepped aside rather than resigned, the credibility and effectiveness of the tribunal as constituted was an unknown, and there were concerns about some of the remaining commissioners and how we had handled the whole Kiplagat issue – many began to engage with us, and even some that would not publicly support us privately began to engage with us as well. At the same time, the government, for the first time, provided us with a substantial percentage of our budget.

Ambassador Kiplagat was away from the Commission for fourteen months. His absence allowed us to finally devote all of our attention to the enormous mandate that had been entrusted to us. During that time, we engaged in our largest statement-taking activities (ultimately collecting more of such statements than any other truth commission to date), held public and private hearings in every corner of the country, and undertook important research and investigations with respect to crucial issues within our mandate, including the Wagalla massacre and the Ouko assassination. All of our regional public hearings were conducted without the participation of Ambassador Kiplagat, except the public hearing for alleged perpetrators of the Wagalla massacre, during which Ambassador Kiplagat appeared as a witness before the Commission. (Ambassador Kiplagat was the only person who was given an entire day to testify before the Commission – in this case to describe and defend his participation in the events leading up to the Wagalla massacre.)

We had originally planned to start our public hearings within the first year of our operational period. This would have provided enough time to hold public hearings throughout the country, undertake a number of significant investigations, and finish all of our work by our original deadline of February 2012. These plans were soon to prove unrealistic as it became clear that neither the government nor any other donor would provide us with the necessary funds to plan and hold our public hearings, and as the paralysis created by our failure to address Ambassador Kiplagat's conflicts of interest deepened. The controversies surrounding our chair, and our inability to address them satisfactorily, made it difficult, and in some cases quite risky, for us to appear publicly in certain parts of the country. We decided to cancel a trip to the Rift Valley in early 2010, for example, after we were told that protesters would meet us with coffins representing the death and burial of the Commission.

During our first outreach trip to the Coast Province in January 2010, we experienced firsthand the turmoil that we would face if we engaged with the public without addressing the Kiplagat problem. We were met with an organized protest and demonstration in Mombasa. About ten to fifteen minutes into our presentation, approximately thirty or more individuals deliberately rose from their seats, hurled invectives at the Commission, and walked out of the hall. It appeared that the walkout had been planned in advance by a number of activist organizations, as the media had been alerted and captured much of the proceedings on film, which then became one of the major stories that night on the television news and in the next day's newspapers.

The reception in Lamu was even more disturbing than what we had experienced in Mombasa. Lamu is a small island off the northeast coast of Kenya, just south of the Somali border. Lamu Town is one of the best-preserved and oldest Swahili settlements in East Africa. There are no private cars on the island. People move around on foot, by boat, or on small donkeys. People say that Lamu Town today is what Stone Town in Zanzibar was like fifty years ago before it became a popular destination on the world tourist map. To get from the mainland to the island of Lamu one has to take a boat. We secured two large, open boats that could accommodate all of us and our luggage. As we sped across the channel, the two drivers appeared to be engaged in a race to see who would get to the island first. As we approached the main dock in the town, I could see from the distance a number of people milling about. As we came closer we changed course and the boats moved up the coast where they were able to dock right in front of our hotel. I had assumed that this had been planned all along, but I was told that the crowd on the dock had assembled to protest our arrival, and specifically to protest the presence of Ambassador Kiplagat. The concern was that we would be unable to disembark at the main dock because of the protestors, so we were diverted directly to the hotel.

The next morning, we were to proceed to Lamu Fort where we would hold our civic outreach and public education event. When I arrived in the lobby to walk with my fellow commissioners to the venue, we were told to wait as our advance team was still working with the local community at the fort. A thirty-minute wait quickly became an hour, and then two hours. Tea was arranged for us, and we were briefed on what was holding up the proceedings. Apparently, the local imams had taken offense at our failure to meet with them in advance, which was apparently customary for such meetings. In addition, the imams and many others in the local community were critical of the Commission. While their criticism included the presence of Ambassador Kiplagat, it was not limited to his presence.

The dominant Swahili community of the Coast Province is generally suspicious of Kenyans from other parts of the country, sometimes referred to as "Up Country" people. "Up Country" can refer to any non-Swahili Kenyan in the Coast Province but is often a coded way of referring to those of Kikuyu ethnicity. The suspicion of those from "Up Country," particularly those of Kikuyu ethnicity, was fueled by the history of land grabbing that had occurred on the Coast by prominent and wealthy Kenyans, many of whom are Kikuyu. Not least among these land grabbers was the first president, Jomo Kenyatta, and his family. The interference by the president in the content of our final report arose out of allegations we were to hear almost two years later when we returned to the Coast for our public hearings. There was thus a good deal of suspicion of not only Ambassador Kiplagat because of his ties to the Moi Government, but also some of the other Kenyan Commissioners.

Residents of the Coast and North Eastern Provinces were also suspicious of the Commission because of the Indemnity Act of 1972. The Indemnity Act provided amnesty to members of the armed forces and other state officials for atrocities committed during the so-called Shifta War. The newly independent president, Jomo Kenyatta, had declared a state of emergency in the north-eastern and coastal parts of the country shortly after independence in 1963 in response to a perceived threat of secession of those regions from Kenya to Somalia. While no one knows the number of people killed, assaulted, and injured, investigations undertaken by the TJRC and others suggest anywhere from 2,000 to 7,000 combatants and civilians were killed during the four-year-long Shifta War.[7] The harsh scorched-earth policy of the Kenyan military in the Shifta War was to become a common approach of the government in the region, resulting in numerous massacres of civilians, most notoriously the Wagalla massacre of 1984.

The lack of acknowledgment of these violations by the government, combined with the legalized impunity provided by the Indemnity Act, was a constant refrain of complaint from the residents of the Coast and North Eastern provinces. Residents of these provinces argued that the Indemnity Act would prevent the TJRC from investigating the atrocities committed during the Shifta War and would invalidate any reparations we might recommend for such violations. The Commission undertook an analysis of the Indemnity Act and concluded that it did not apply to the Commission and thus would not affect our work.[8] We also joined forces with leaders from both provinces to push for a repeal of the Indemnity Act. Parliament voted to repeal the Act, but President Kibaki vetoed the repeal. We thus included as a recommendation in our final report that the Indemnity Act be repealed within nine months of the issuance of the report. The government has neither complied with that recommendation nor indicated why it has failed to do so.

Finally, residents of the Coast joined many other Kenyans throughout the country who believed we could not and would not examine atrocities during the colonial period. The reality was that we could and did examine atrocities committed during the colonial period.[9] This was important for at least two reasons. First, a number of victims and survivors of the colonial atrocities were still alive and wanted to take advantage of the TJRC to tell their stories. Second, in order to understand the antecedents, institutional causes, and systemic nature of violations committed by successive Kenyan governments, it was crucial for us to understand and analyze the violations committed by the British during the colonial period.[10]

After waiting in the lobby of our hotel for a few hours, we were finally told that we could proceed to the fort. Lamu Fort was built in the early nineteenth century, and today houses a library and an environmental museum. During the colonial period, the British used the fort as a prison to house members of the Mau Mau resistance, and the Kenyan government continued to use the

---

[7] For more on the Shifta War, *see* TJRC FINAL REPORT, *supra* Chapter 1, note 9, at Vol. IIA, Ch. 3.

[8] *See* "Truth Commission Responds to the Indemnity Act," February 9, 2010 (on website).

[9] The Mutua Task Force in 2003 had recommended that a Kenya truth commission *not* include the colonial period in its mandate. *See* TJRC FINAL REPORT, *supra* Chapter 1, note 9, at Vol. 1, pp. 57–58.

[10] For an in-depth, and disturbing, description of the atrocities committed by the colonial government, *see* Caroline Elkins, IMPERIAL RECKONING, *supra* Chapter 2, note 19.

fort as a prison until 1984, when it was transferred to the National Museums of Kenya. The fort has a large interior courtyard surrounded on three sides by covered balconies. One side of the balcony is relatively narrow (about five meters wide), and the other two sides are much wider (fifteen or more meters). The local residents were in seats provided in the two wider sides of the balcony – one side for women, the other for men. When we arrived at the fort, we proceeded up to the balcony level, where a long table had been placed in the narrow balcony. We took our places behind the table facing the courtyard with our audience arranged in the balconies to our left and right. It was an odd arrangement, as directly in front of us was the open space of the interior courtyard. We were hemmed in behind the table, given the narrow balcony, leading me to wonder how we would exit if trouble erupted. Our only means of exit was to either move through the audience to the left or the right, or to jump off of the balcony into the interior, which was a drop of at least ten meters.

We had been warned that tensions were high among the members of the audience, with the local imams in particular suggesting they might disrupt or walk out of the proceedings. A friend who had been waiting with most of the audience for our arrival later observed that the tension in the venue was palpable. We quickly conferred among ourselves, and the consensus was that Ambassador Kiplagat would say a few words of introduction, and then he would hand the microphone over to me to discuss our mandate and plan of work, as well as to address the issue of conflicts of interest and our code of conduct, our ability to examine abuses during the colonial period, and the fact that the Indemnity Act would not affect our ability to do our work. As I stood to speak, I did not detect any serious level of hostility and noted that most people in the audience appeared eager to hear what I had to say. Later the friend in the audience told me that as I began to speak and to address the concerns in the audience (the presence of Ambassador Kiplagat, the Indemnity Act), the tension in the venue visibly lessened. After I finished, we took a number of questions from the audience, including further questions concerning Ambassador Kiplagat's presence and the Indemnity Act. Before we could respond, the imams publicly announced that they were leaving the venue and were going to boycott the rest of our visit. They had been present now for over an hour while Ambassador Kiplagat and I had spoken and were leaving at a few minutes before 1 p.m., which was when they were due for afternoon prayers.

Our trip to the Coast thus underscored some of the challenges we would be facing. Some were mandate related, such as public misperceptions about our ability to examine abuses committed during the colonial period and the effect of the Indemnity Act on our powers. Others were related to us personally, most specifically the presence of Ambassador Kiplagat. It was unfortunate that we had to expend time and energy addressing the controversial presence of our chair, but up until the end of the Coast trip, we were all united in defending his presence.

RESOURCE CONSTRAINTS, GOVERNMENT CONTROL

The government refused to provide us with more than nominal funds that would allow us to limp along without undertaking much of any substantive work. I chaired our finance committee during the first two years of our operational period. In that capacity, I worked with other commissioners, our skeletal staff, and a number of consultants to develop a budget to present to the government and other potential funders. We estimated that in order to do justice to the broad scope of our mandate, including traveling and holding hearings in all corners of the country, would require approximately 1 billion Kenya shillings per year, or approximately US $13 million per year. To put this in perspective, the actual expenses incurred by the South African Truth and Reconciliation Commission in the late 1990s were US $18 million. Adjusted for US dollar inflation from 1999 to 2009, this amount was the equivalent of US $23.6 million; if adjusted for Kenyan inflation during the same period the amount was the equivalent of US $51.8 million. In other words, the budget we presented for the Kenyan commission was substantially less than what was required for the South African Truth and Reconciliation Commission, a commission that operated for a comparable period of time but had a mandate that was far more narrow than ours.

While we estimated that we would require 1 billion Kenyan shillings per year to fulfill our mandate, the Government had provided us with only 100 million shillings for our first year of operations, or one-tenth of what we required. To be fair, the 100 million shillings had been allocated in early 2009 for the fiscal 2010 budget, before the Commission was created. At the point that the fiscal 2010 budget had been developed, it was not clear when the Commission was going to be created, if at all. Officials in the Ministry of Finance and the Ministry of Justice plausibly told me that the 100-million-shilling allocation was really just a placeholder, suggesting that if we put together a budget we would be allocated a more reasonable amount of money in line with our actual requirements.

I, along with other commissioners and senior staff, spent a good deal of time negotiating with various government officials to secure supplemental funding for our first year of operations. In the end, we were only able to secure an additional 50 million shillings for that first year, or a total of about 15 percent of our requested budget.

Perhaps even more problematic than the limited funds we had at our disposal was the fact that we did not have control over how our money was spent. Financial independence had been deliberately included in our enabling legislation in order to ensure political independence. Notwithstanding this clear legal requirement, the Ministry of Justice controlled our entire budget during the first year of our existence. This meant that we needed to secure specific approval from the Ministry to spend any of the 150 million shillings allocated to us during the first year. The Ministry used this power to keep a tight leash on our activities.

The requirement that we seek approval from the government before being able to undertake any activity that required the expenditure of money meant that we were beholden to the government in a way that threatened to undermine our operational independence. If we wanted to engage in public outreach and educational activities about the work of the Commission, we needed approval from the government. If we wanted to hire investigators to undertake investigations into historical injustices, we were required to secure approval from the government. If we wanted to hire interpreters for an *in camera* hearing with a witness who feared for her safety, we were required to secure approval from the government.

While we struggled to secure more funding from the government, we had even less success in securing funding from outside donors. The reaction of donors to our requests for support underscored the insidious relationship between the government's failure to provide us more than nominal funding and the cost we paid for not addressing adequately the controversies around our chair. There were two major reasons donors were reluctant to fund us: the presence of Ambassador Kiplagat and the miniscule financial and other support provided by the government. Many donors were unwilling to provide us with any funding so long as Ambassador Kiplagat was chairing the Commission. Others were willing to consider providing some funding if we or the government established a process to address the numerous conflicts of interest presented by Ambassador Kiplagat. Independently of the reluctance of donors to support the Commission while Ambassador Kiplagat was the chair, many donors were reluctant to provide funding to a Commission that had such little demonstrated support from the government itself. As one western diplomat said to me, if the government was unwilling to support the TJRC with more than nominal funding, it would be inappropriate for donors to fill that substantial gap. As this diplomat succinctly said to me, the TJRC should be a Kenyan-driven process, not a donor-driven process. I found it difficult to argue against this position.

Further complicating our efforts to seek donor funding – and underscoring the relationship between our funding challenges and our challenges arising from our chair – from the earliest days of our creation, Ambassador Kiplagat repeatedly told foreign donors that we did not need their money or other support as the government would provide us with all of the funds we needed. The rest of us tried to convince Ambassador Kiplagat to take a less negative view towards donor funding, particularly as the promised money from the government continued to fail to materialize.

At first I thought Ambassador Kiplagat's deliberate rejection of offers of donor support was based upon a naïve optimism concerning the government's willingness to provide us with adequate funds. Given all of the events that followed, I have to concede the possibility that, as some both within and without the Commission argued to me, he was at best deliberately trying to ensure that the Commission received minimal funding and at worst trying to ensure that the government would continue to exercise financial control over the Commission as a way to control our operations.

Our financial status changed dramatically after Ambassador Kiplagat agreed to step down in November 2010. For the second fiscal year of our operations (2010–2011), we had been allocated 190 million Kenyan shillings, or 40 million shillings more than our first year. This was still substantially below the approximately 1 billion shillings we had requested, and thus only covered a little under 20 percent of our budget. Shortly after Kiplagat left, the government notified us that we would be receiving approximately Ksh 500 million in supplemental funding for this second fiscal year. This was less than what we had requested but still a substantial amount of money and far more than we had ever been granted in the past. This about-face on the part of the government was surprising given that Kiplagat was no longer with the Commission. How can this change of heart by the government concerning our finances be explained? A dominant narrative, and one that I had become increasingly convinced was true, was that Kiplagat's presence on the Commission provided comfort to the government – he was someone whom they trusted and someone who could keep them apprised of our internal deliberations and plans. Providing us with significant funding after he left seemed inconsistent with this narrative. I could think of three possible explanations for this seeming contradiction. First, the provision of funding had nothing to do with Kiplagat's presence or absence. This explanation would discount the dominant narrative that assumed foresight and planning on the part of the government (a set of characteristics I rarely found in this government). In other words, the lack of government support was more a function of government inefficiency and lethargy rather than a deliberate attempt to control our activities. I had certainly seen and experienced enough bureaucratic inefficiency in my dealings with the Kenyan government to provide support for such a thesis. Second is an explanation that puts the government in a slightly more positive light. With the exit of Kiplagat, many other commissioners began to have direct contact with officials in the Ministry of Finance and Justice. While Kiplagat was chair, he excluded us from many of the meetings he held with such officials and even refused to share with us the content of those meetings (and in some cases even misrepresented to us the content of some of those meetings). This change in access allowed us to more directly, and presumably more effectively, make the case about the importance of our work (as well as what we were planning) and the importance of providing us with adequate financing. Third, it is also possible that with the loss of Kiplagat the government felt it had lost some of its influence over us. According to this theory, the government provided us with substantial funding as a means to try to control our activities. This would make even more sense if the fear was that foreign donors would step in to provide funding for our activities now that Kiplagat had left. I have no basis for determining which among these three narratives explains the government's decision to provide us with money at this point. I can confidently say that the provision of money did not provide the government with any leverage over our activities – in fact, it lessened their leverage as we had complete control over our money and freed us from lobbying the government for additional funds that might have led us to modify our plans to appeal to the interests of government decision-makers.

PUBLIC HEARINGS

With the influx of financing starting in January 2011, we were able to begin planning in earnest for our public hearings and other mandate-related activities. Our public hearings and related activities provided us with the opportunity to change the public perception of the Commission and its ability to engage with the violations within our mandate. We thus wanted to use the launch of our hearings to insert the Commission and its mandate into the public discourse. To do this, we needed to make our first hearing significant and important so the media would cover it. There were two ways to do this. One was to choose a significant event or issue that would capture the media's attention – a prominent assassination or massacre, or a searching examination of land or corruption. The second was to have prominent individuals present who would attract media attention. These two were strategies were not exclusive. Our initial hope was to have the president and prime minister attend our first public hearing. While neither had expressed strong public support for us or our activities, we hoped that with the provision of substantial financing they might now be willing to lend the power of their offices to support us. In terms of subject matter, we debated a number of possibilities, ultimately settling on beginning our hearings on violations related to North Eastern Province.

There were at least three reasons we chose the northeastern region of the country as the subject matter of our first public hearings. First, from colonialism to the present day, North Eastern was one of the most marginalized areas in Kenya. There were, for example, no paved roads in the entire province in 2010.[11] Second, some of the worst massacres in the history of the country, including the Wagalla massacre (which had been identified by the UN as the worst massacre in Kenyan history), had taken place in the province. Third, given the conflict of interest of Kiplagat with respect to the Wagalla massacre, we wanted to send a strong signal that we were not being influenced by him and his personal interests in determining our official activities.

Based on the above considerations, our initial plan was to start our hearings in the North Eastern Province with the presence of the president and prime minister. As we began to explore the possibility of the president and prime minister attending, however, it was conveyed to us that they were more likely to agree if the launch were in Nairobi. In addition, given that the major media outlets were all present in Nairobi, it was more likely that we would receive extensive media coverage if we launched in Nairobi instead of a more remote part of the country.

Unfortunately, neither the president nor prime minister was willing to attend the launch of our public hearings. It was never made clear to me why they did not want to publicly support the process. The prime minister only agreed to meet with us officially a few months later, in July 2011, after we had held months of successful public hearings. While this meeting was long overdue, at least the prime minister did finally meet and engage with us. We were never to meet with President Kibaki during the over three years that his presidency and the life of the Commission overlapped. We did meet with President Kenyatta, but that was only at the end of our process when we handed over to him our final report – a meeting that, as I recount in Chapter 1, I refused to attend.

Without the participation of both the president and prime minister, we quickly decided to hold the first set of hearings in North Eastern Province. If we could not use the hearings to generate positive publicity for the Commission through a show of bipartisan political support, we wanted to begin in one of the more marginalized areas of the country to emphasize the seriousness with which we approached our work. For each location where we held our

---

[11] The one exception was the paved road found at the military airport in Wajir.

public hearings, we sent advance teams that often included investigators, researchers, and our community outreach team to identify venues, engage in public education, and identify or confirm witnesses who would testify either in public or, if they so desired, in private. Representatives from our Special Support Unit, working with the Kenyan Red Cross and other partners, provided counseling and guidance to those who participated in our hearings. Our hearing rules, published in the *Kenyan Gazette* on April 8, 2011, set out the general conduct and procedures of our hearings.[12] Hearings were to be conducted by at least three commissioners, including at least one international commissioner. In addition, we required that each hearing panel have at least one commissioner of the opposite gender of the other commissioners. While any witness, including an adversely mentioned person, could retain counsel who could attend and advise the witness during the hearings, we did not allow witnesses or their counsel to directly examine or cross-examine any other witness. In this regard, our hearings drew more upon the inquisitorial civil law traditions than the adversarial common law tradition. Limiting questioning to the Commission was one way we ensured that the hearings provided a safe and productive space for witnesses to freely tell their stories.

The North Eastern Province is primarily an arid, desert-like region of Kenya. It's a little less than 50,000 square miles (roughly the size of Louisiana). Although its population is primarily Somali, many strongly identify with their clan, and clan disputes have often been as violent as ethnic disputes are in the rest of Kenya. The residents of the province were generally suspicious of the TJRC for at least two reasons. First, no Kenyan government up until that point had undertaken a concerted effort to address the many issues facing residents of the province, including cattle rustling, security, economic development, corruption, and land. In addition, the Kenyan government had been directly involved in numerous gross violations of human rights in the region, from the numerous massacres (including, but certainly not limited to, the Wagalla massacre) to the war crimes committed by the Kenyan military and security forces during the Shifta War, a war that was waged between the Kenyan government and the Somali residents of the region just after independence. The tragic story a woman recounted to us in Isiolo illustrates the intensity of that conflict and the far-reaching impact of the government's atrocities on its residents:

> I was 22 years old in 1967. I cry because of that day. Up to now, I have tears in my eyes because of that day. All our livestock were taken on that day and my

---

[12] The hearing rules can be found in TJRC FINAL REPORT, *supra* Chapter 1, note 9, at Vol. 1, Appendix 6.

husband was murdered. My children do not have a father now. They killed my husband and took the animals too. They separated me from my children. I am not the one who brought up all my children. I do not know where my first son was brought up. I heard that he was in Marsabit. When my husband died I had a five days old child. We ran away. I did not know where my eldest son was. He ran away separately and I ran away for my dear life too. The Kenyan Government did those things to us. My husband was taken away and I heard that he was killed. Up to now, I have never seen his body or bones. I lost my animals, children and husband. I can say this is my country, but I did not get justice in my country. Where else will I get justice?[13]

Residents of the region often said that they did not feel that they were a part of Kenya, often referring to the rest of Kenya as "Kenya." The basis for this perception was underscored by the reception I and other commissioners received upon flying from Wajir (in North Eastern Province) to Nairobi one day. Upon landing on the tarmac, we were directed to enter the Nairobi airport through the international arrivals building where we were promptly asked for our passports. Since we had not left the country, we were not traveling with our passports. It took a few hours of phone calls to various government officials to finally clear up the mess so that we could "reenter Kenya." We were government officials with access to other government officials, and still we faced barriers traveling from North Eastern Province to the rest of Kenya. Imagine the effect of the same barriers imposed on others without such access to power.

Yet many of the residents, notwithstanding the atrocities committed and tolerated by the government since the Shifta War, passionately argued that they were Kenyan and not, as they felt others in Kenya believed, Somali. A woman who testified *in camera* about the atrocities she suffered during the Shifta War proudly asserted her Kenyan citizenship and the obligation of the Kenyan government to protect and provide for her:

This is what I wanted to tell you. It is upon the Government to help its citizens. We were born in Kenya. We do not know Somalia. We never went to Somalia. We were born here. We gave birth to our children here. We do not know Somalia. Even if I went there, my Government would be in Kenya. So, it is up to the Kenya Government to take care of us and stand for our needs. I do not know of any place that could be better than Kenya, because Kenya is where I grew up to old age. I do not know anywhere else.[14]

---

[13] RTJRC10.05 (Isiolo, Wabera Primary School Dining Hall) (Women's Hearing), May 10, 2011 p. 1.

[14] RTJRC10.05 (Isiolo Wabera Primary School Dining Hall) (*in camera*), May 10, 2011, p. 22.

On Saturday, April 9th, all commissioners and some of our senior staff and much of our hearings support group arrived in Garissa, the provincial capital of North Eastern Province. Garissa is approximately two hundred miles east and slightly north of Nairobi. The drive takes from four to five hours on mostly paved roads. As one approaches Garissa, however, the paved roads end, and the last few miles are on dirt roads, underscoring the sense that one is entering a place separate from "Kenya."

Over that weekend, we oversaw preparations for the launch of our hearings on Monday, April 11th. We had already placed numerous advertisements in local and national newspapers and on local radio. We hired sound trucks to drive throughout the neighborhoods in the region to announce the launch on Monday. On Sunday, April 10th, a few of us met with the provincial commissioner (often referred to as the PC). He was apparently angry with us as his name was listed in the newspaper as someone who might be mentioned adversely by witnesses at our public hearings. I was volunteered to explain to him why we had mentioned him. I explained that we had been informed that some who would speak at our public hearing would identify him as a responsible party. We had previously provided him with notice of this fact in order for him to decide whether to attend the hearings and, if he wished, an opportunity to respond to any allegation that might be raised by others against him. He said he was satisfied with the explanation, but I could tell that he was still annoyed at us and the situation in which we had put him. This was yet another example of the delicate position we occupied – on the one hand, an independent agency, but on the other, dependent upon government officials to ensure our security and other logistical needs as we traveled throughout the country. Often, as was the case here, those same individuals would also be identified as alleged perpetrators. This dynamic was similar to what we faced with the government generally, but as we moved around the country, the consequences of this dependence on alleged perpetrators became more evident and contributed, not unreasonably, to some local Kenyans viewing us with suspicion. The PC or district commissioner (DC) was often one of our first stops in a town. The first view residents had of the Commission was frequently a fleet of cars driving through town to meet with the local head of government, who in some cases was the source of many of the complaints of the local population.

On Monday, April 11th, we launched our hearings with a mass meeting at a large open-air field in Garissa. Hundreds of people were in attendance. The large open-air venue, crowds of people, and the music and other entertainment that preceded our formal launch made the event feel like a political rally. A senior official from the Ministry of Justice spoke about the importance of the Commission and its work, and a number of us discussed the Commission, its mandate, and our work plan. Students from Garissa High School recited a poem, "I Call for Justice."[15]

Justice! I call for justice
Fear is in my heart

In the street, I pass calling for justice
In the police station, I pass calling for justice
In the court, I pass calling for justice

When I saw streams of blood flowing down the road
I could not believe my eyes
For what man had done
Killing innocent people mercilessly
Fear is in my heart
Justice! I call for justice

Children are left orphans
Rolling on the street meaninglessly
Sleeping on the street hungry
And the cold breaking their ribs
I am afraid of losing my life
Fear is in my heart
Justice! I call for justice

The widows are stressed
Recalling the love of their husband
Recalling the loss of their children
Fear is in my heart
Justice! I call for justice

Justice! Where are you?
In the police?
In the court?
In the local tribunal?
In the ICC?
Justice! Where are you?

Truth be told
Justice to prevail
Justice! Justice! Justice!
I call for justice.

---

[15] Reprinted in TJRC Final Report, *supra* Chapter 1, note 9, at Vol. IV, p. 69.

For the next year we traveled to each province in the country, often visiting communities that had rarely, and sometimes never, been visited by an official investigative body. The picture of daily life in Kenya painted by those who engaged with the Commission is a bleak one. Over forty thousand Kenyans submitted formal statements to the Commission. We received over one thousand memoranda prepared by community groups, members of civil society, and other collectives. While the picture painted by those who engaged with the Commission is authentic and an important indicator of some of the dominant narratives circulating in Kenya concerning historical injustices, it would be inaccurate to assume that it either captures all of the important experiences of Kenyans with respect to violations or that it accurately reflects the relative frequency of different violations. There are a number of reasons to be careful about the conclusions drawn from the data and narratives we collected. First, as with most truth commissions, very few alleged perpetrators cooperated with the Commission. Some did, often after being subpoenaed, although not all required such legal compulsion to appear before us. Except for our own chair, Ambassador Kiplagat, every individual we subpoenaed appeared before us. Second, some groups of survivors were well organized and proactively reached out to the Commission, such as the survivors of the 1982 coup attempt and its aftermath, the survivors of the Wagalla massacre, and the survivors of the Nyayo House torture chambers. Many others were not so well organized or supported by the many civil society organizations operating in the country. Third, grassroots membership organizations and organizations focused on peace, and conflict resolution were more likely to encourage and support their constituents engaging with the Commission compared to the Nairobi-based human rights organizations. As a result of these and other factors, the picture presented to the Commission was incomplete. Nevertheless, we were provided with an enormous amount of information concerning not only details about past violations, but also about the subjective experiences of many of the victims of such atrocities. The rich and nuanced picture this information painted can be found in great detail in our final report.

I have chosen four thematic areas to discuss arising out of our hearings, statement taking, research, and investigations. Each of them illustrates a different aspect of our work. The thematic areas chosen illustrate some of the challenges we faced and some of the successes we achieved. First, property- and land-related violations were consistently identified by Kenyans in every region of the country as the most important set of violations for us to address. Second, although many of the massacres and assassinations in Kenyan history have been subject to prior investigations (in some cases, numerous investigations), it was in this area that we contributed the most in terms of forensic truth. Third, as with most truth commissions, our ability to engage with perpetrators and to capture their narratives was limited. Our failure in this area was due in part to our own limitations but also to the environment in which we operated. Fourth, the women's hearings provide one of the most detailed records of the views and experiences of women arising out of a truth commission process and, in their operation and design, they provide a useful counterpoint to the more formalistic and legal nature of our public hearings.

PROPERTY AND LAND

The most frequent set of violations identified by most people in each of the eight provinces concerned property and land. In seven out of the eight provinces, property violations, including those related to land, constituted the highest number of reported violations.[16] During our women's hearings, violations related to property or land numbered 89, exceeded only by violations related to sexual violence and gender-based discrimination at 114. This is perhaps unsurprising. Land has been, and continues to be, a major source of historic and current injustices in Kenya, and has been a driver of ethnic conflict since the colonial period. The TJRC was the latest of many government initiatives that were created to address the issue of land in Kenya as a driver of conflict.[17] The most recent such initiative, prior to the TJRC, was the Ndung'u Commission.[18] The report of the Ndung'u Commission was released in June 2004 and set forth specific information concerning allegations of powerful individuals receiving illegally or irregularly[19] plots of land. Ambassador Kiplagat was listed in the Ndung'u Report as having been allocated land that had been dedicated to the poor and landless under a government scheme. Illegal and irregular allocations of public land had become so commonplace that the US Ambassador at the time dismissed my concerns regarding Ambassador Kiplagat's involvement in such a practice by noting that "everyone" in Kenya steals land. The Ndung'u Report was controversial in part because it

---

[16] The one exception is Nairobi, where violations related to the post-election violence of 2007 were more frequently cited than land.

[17] For more discussion of previous efforts by the Kenyan government to address land as a driver of conflict, see the TJRC FINAL REPORT, *supra* Chapter 1, note 9, at Vol. IIB, pp. 328–341.

[18] The formal name of the commission is the Commission of Inquiry into the Illegal/Irregular Allocation of Public Land (2002), chaired by Paul Ndiritu Ndung'u.

[19] An irregular allocation of land is, according to the Ndung'u Commission Report, an allocation of land that is available for allocation, "but in circumstances where the standard operating or administrative procedures have not been observed." NDUNG'U COMMISSION REPORT, *supra* Chapter 3, note 4, at p. 49.

was perceived to be skewed against members of the Kalenjin community, and because some individuals were named in the report without being given the opportunity to respond to the allegations against them.[20]

While one may rightly raise concerns about some of the specific findings of the Ndung'u Report, there was no question that the problem it was designed to address – injustices related to land – was in need of addressing. The drafters of the legislation establishing the TJRC recognized this need, listing land as a specific issue that we were to address as part of our mandate. As we began to solicit information from Kenyans through our statement taking, research, hearings, and investigations, it became clear that issues around land ownership and use were one of the highest concerns of Kenyans, regardless of their ethnicity, community, religion, or location. We heard numerous stories of people being evicted from their land and homes by powerful people (usually politicians, government officials, or individuals closely connected to them). The lack of a stable property recording system contributed to these injustices, making it difficult for those who had occupied a particular parcel of land to prove their ownership and, thus, difficult to reclaim ownership if forcibly evicted. In addition, it was explained to me by a land law expert on the Commission, Professor Tom Ojienda, that the Kenyan judiciary had developed a legal doctrine of "absolute title," by which an individual who is in possession of a formal title document cannot be challenged with respect to his ownership of that property, even in a court of law. In other words, as Professor Ojienda explained to me, even if the title document was obtained through fraud or other illegal activity, the general acceptance among most lawyers and judges in Kenya was that such title could still not be challenged.[21] The combination of an ineffective recording system and the doctrine of absolute title makes it easy to understand how the powerful and well connected in Kenya can seize land and continue to retain ownership of it. All it requires is securing a formal title from a proper authority (which can be achieved with a strategically placed bribe or two) which gives the holder of that formal title absolute ownership of the land regardless of how long someone else has occupied and used that land and regardless of who in the past may have purchased the land. Combine this corruption, which pervades various government agencies devoted to land and land ownership, with corruption in the judiciary and the numerous barriers to

---

[20] For additional concerns raised about the Ndung'u Commission Report, see TJRC FINAL REPORT, *supra* Chapter 1, note 9, at Vol. IIB, pp. 336–340.

[21] For a brief, and critical, summary of this phenomenon in Kenya, see NDUNG'U COMMISSION REPORT, *supra* Chapter 3, note 4, at pp. 15–17.

accessing justice by the average Kenyan, and it is not difficult to see how and why land ownership has become such a contentious issue within Kenya.

We received numerous reports of government officials and other powerful individuals "grabbing" land that had been reserved for public use. Land that had been set aside for parks, schools, hospitals, housing for the poor, and other socially beneficial uses was instead given to politically powerful individuals. Our chair had been the beneficiary of just such a practice while he was serving in the government of Daniel arap Moi. While in government, he was allocated land from a development scheme reserved for poor and landless Kenyans that had previously been owned by white settlers. This was unfortunately not atypical; valuable land that had been grabbed by the British during the colonial period often ended up in the hands of powerfully connected individuals in the Kenyan government and not to their original owners or to poorer, more deserving Kenyans. The most valuable white settler land was in the richly fertile Rift Valley, parts of which became notoriously famous as Happy Valley, depicted (somewhat inaccurately) in the film *White Mischief*.[22] By far the largest number of statements we received concerning property and land violations came from the Rift Valley (7,780 out of 21,982).[23] Two of the plots that were allocated to Ambassador Kiplagat while he was in government were mentioned in the Ndung'u Report. In a private conversation with commissioners, Ambassador Kiplagat disclosed that he had been allocated a third plot of land in a similar fashion. As with all of the allegations facing him, Ambassador Kiplagat claimed that he was innocent. As part of his defense, he noted, correctly, that many of the individuals identified in the Ndung'u Report had not been given the opportunity to respond to the allegations leveled against them. We thus found it somewhat ironic that Ambassador Kiplagat refused our summons to appear before us concerning the allegation that he had received plots of land illegally. He was the only person who refused to honor a subpoena from the Commission. Failure to honor a Commission subpoena was a criminal offense, though Ambassador Kiplagat was never prosecuted or otherwise held to account for his action.[24]

---

[22] *White Mischief* (Directed by Michael Radford, 1987). More accurate descriptions of Happy Valley can be found in Juliet Barnes, THE GHOST OF HAPPY VALLEY: SEARCHING FOR THE LOST WORLD OF AFRICA'S INFAMOUS ARISTOCRATS (London: Aurum Press, 2013), and Frances Osborne, THE BOLTER (New York: Alfred Knopf, 2009).

[23] Eastern Province was a distant second with 2,806.

[24] The relevant section states "[a]ny person who, without lawful cause, fails to appear before the Commission pursuant to any summons by the Commission commits an offence and shall on conviction be liable to a fine not exceeding one hundred thousand shillings [approximately US $1200], or to imprisonment for a term not exceeding one year, or both." TJRC Act, *supra* Chapter 1, note 3, at Art. 7(6)

Land-related violations, like many of the violations we examined, spiked during national elections. As Francis Munoko testified before us in Bungoma, ". . . it has been the tradition that when we are approaching election time, many people use such chances to grab land and to destroy other people's property."[25] An elder in Mt. Elgon testified that while there was a good deal of violence in the region during the 2007 elections, the violence was not because of the elections but rather because of land.[26] Forced evictions by the government, starting as early as 1913 by the British settlers, have resulted in generations of displaced families who have, in extreme cases, taken up arms to reclaim their land. According to some in the region, as represented by the elder who testified before us, elections are the spark, not the cause, of much of the violence that people have experienced in Mt. Elgon. As Richard Wasilwa told the Commission in Mt. Elgon, "When it is elections time, politicians promise to evict certain tribes from the area so that they can get votes."[27] This narrative is supported by the scores of testimonies we received concerning violence by the government and militia groups such as the Sabaot Land Defence Force (SLDF) in the years before the 2007 elections. The very name of one of the more prominent, and notorious, militias, the Sabaot *Land* Defense Force, underscores the common perception of the primary driver of the conflict in this region.

The importance of land to the powerful in Kenya, and their sensitivity to any attempt to discuss, much less investigate, the issue of illegal land acquisitions is illustrated by the reaction of the president's office to the inclusion of the public and sworn testimony of a Kenyan who alleged that the first president, Jomo Kenyatta, had stolen land from the witness. The Office of the President cajoled, threatened, and bribed the Commission to have that testimony removed. Such efforts were undertaken to have a mere allegation removed (we had not determined whether the allegations were true or not).

The president's heavy-handed tactics to have references to his father's land dealings removed from the final report, and Ambassador Kiplagat's refusal to testify before us concerning his land dealings, underscores the importance of land, and more generally socioeconomic violations, to understanding gross violations of human rights and historical injustices. This observation is further strengthened by noting that we made a factual finding that the first President Kenyatta had covered up a major political assassination to protect members of his own government (a finding that was allowed to remain in our final report), and Ambassador Kiplagat testified for an entire day about his attendance at a

---

[25] RTJRC08.07 (Bungoma County Council Hall), July 8, 2011, p. 38.
[26] RTJRC23.05 (Kibuk Catholic Church, Mt. Elgon District), May 23, 2011, p. 22.
[27] RTJRC23.05 (Kibuk Catholic Church, Mt. Elgon District), May 23, 2011, p. 31.

security committee meeting, held just before the Wagalla massacre. It was involvement with illegal or irregular land dealings, not assassinations or massacres, which motivated powerful Kenyans to obstruct and subvert our process.

MASSACRES AND ASSASSINATIONS

Kenya's post-independence history is marred by numerous incidents of political assassinations, massacres, and organized torture. Thanks to the hard work of our investigators and researchers, we were able to uncover new information concerning high-level responsibility for some of the political assassinations and massacres. In fact, in the case of the assassination of politician and champion of the poor, Josiah Mwangi "JM" Kariuki, we made a finding that President Kenyatta "deliberately interfered in the [contemporaneous] independent investigation undertaken by the Parliamentary Select Committee" by removing the names of two people who worked in his office and who were implicated in the assassination and its subsequent cover up.[28] This was significant, as our findings were factual assertions for which we had gathered enough evidence to be more certain than not that the assertion – in this case a presidential cover-up – was in fact true.[29] In other words, our findings are part of our contribution to "forensic truth."

We were able to obtain and make public previously undisclosed documents that shed light on the decisions leading up to the Wagalla massacre. The documents we discovered included previously undisclosed minutes of key meetings of local, provincial, and national security and intelligence bodies that shed light on which government officials were aware of the security operation that resulted in the massacre, and who later contributed to the official distortions and lies regarding that massacre. In addition to our public hearings in Wajir, we devoted a number of days in Nairobi where those same government officials, including Ambassador Kiplagat, testified and were questioned about the massacre. A thorough description of the new information we uncovered, the narrative we were able to construct concerning the events surrounding the massacre, and our findings concerning government and individual responsibility can be found in the final report.[30]

While our formal investigations into political assassinations focused on politically prominent individuals, we heard scores of stories of extrajudicial

---

[28] TJRC Final Report, *supra* Chapter 1, note 9, at Vol. 4, p. 25.
[29] This is sometimes referred to as the preponderance of the evidence test, and is the level of proof usually required for a civil, as opposed to criminal, judgment.
[30] TJRC Final Report, *supra* Chapter 1, note 9, at Vol. IIA, pp. 221–366.

executions by government officials. A participant at our women's hearing in Hola recounted an unfortunately typical story concerning the summary execution of her husband:

> He went to the toilet, washed his hands and came back into the house and put on a shirt. He told me to stay at home but he told me, "I have not wronged anybody and I am a free man in a free country." He told me he was going to see what was happening. He opened the door and stood by the door. The DO [district officer] and his police men had already arrived. They came and took him from the door. We were following them. He kept asking what was happening but they continued beating him. He was asking, "What have I done?" The DO took a pistol from one of the police officers and shot my husband there and then and he fell down. He was then taken to hospital but he did not survive.[31]

While the Wagalla massacre is the most well-known both in Kenya and internationally, there have been an unfortunate number of incidents of the Kenyan government killing large numbers of its own people. Most, though not all, of these massacres occurred in the North Eastern and Eastern provinces. The large amount of attention paid to the Wagalla massacre has often been at the expense of other similarly atrocious massacres. The Bagalla massacre, for example, in which approximately two hundred people were killed, is rarely discussed and some of the survivors resent that it often plays second fiddle to the Wagalla massacre.[32] The Bagalla massacre was committed in the context of a dispute between the Boran and Degodia ethnic groups. These disputes often included interventions by the Ethiopian kin of the Borana, though the Borana community of Ethiopia deny that they have ever been involved in the conflicts involving their community in Kenya. One witness that we heard *in camera* indicated that the perpetrators of the massacre were all Kenyan and included members of the Kenyan Army (or at least individuals wearing the uniforms of the Kenyan Army). Our investigations also revealed that the conflict included cross-border abductions of children from Kenya into Ethiopia, with attendant killings, sexual violence, and torture. We heard a

---

[31] RTJRC13.01 (Hola County Council Hall) (Women's Hearing), January 13, 2012, p. 15.

[32] For one of the few scholarly treatments of the Bagalla massacre, *see* Gunther Schlee, "Brothers of the Boran: On the Fading Popularity of Certain Somali Identities in Northern Kenya," 1:3 *Journal of Eastern African Studies*, 417–435 (2007). The origin of the name "Bagalla" is unclear. Schlee notes that it is a name "not known to the Boran, and the reasons for its selection by the media remain somewhat obscure." *Id.* at 421. It appears to be a play on Wagalla, with the "B" standing in for Boran. The implicit nod to the Wagalla massacre underscores the iconic nature of that massacre and the dominant role it plays in the self-identity of the region.

young man testify about his own abduction when he was six years old, along with that of three girls, during one of our *in camera* hearings:

> I was still young when the Boran people came one morning, at about 5 a.m. At that time, we were reciting the Quran. When the Boran people came, there was an exchange of gunfire but, at that time, I could not tell what war was. So, they killed people. All the pupils who were there escaped, but I was very young and I could not run away. They killed everybody who was there. So, I tried to hide in the bushes. After they finished killing all the people, they abducted me. One person said something which I did not understand, but someone else said: "Let us not kill this one. Let us take him to Ethiopia." It was their leader who said that I should be taken to Ethiopia. They detained me for ten years. They cut off my fingers. They shot me and stabbed me with a knife.[33]

While we undertook some preliminary research on the Bagalla massacre, going so far as to identify a few key witnesses who could testify to the massacre and its context, we failed to include them in our public hearings, thus perpetuating the public neglect and ignorance of this important massacre and the conflict out of which it arose.[34]

PERPETRATORS AND ADVERSELY MENTIONED PERSONS

Our mandate required us to establish "the motives and perspectives of the persons responsible for [the] commission of the violations" within our mandate;[35] "provid[e] victims, *perpetrators*, and the general public with a platform for non-retributive truth telling that charts a new moral vision and seeks to create a value-based society for all Kenyans;"[36] and "provid[e] repentant perpetrators or participants in gross human rights violations with a forum to confess their actions as a way of bringing reconciliation."[37] We were also to "identify any persons who should be prosecuted for being responsible or involved in human rights and economic rights violations."[38] As with most truth commissions, we had limited success in capturing the experiences and expressions of responsibility from perpetrators.

---

[33] RTJRC20.04 (Kenya Red Cross Hall) (*in camera*), April 20, 2011.

[34] In fact, we barely mention the Bagalla massacre in our final report, though we do provide a list of victims of the massacre.

[35] TJRC Act, *supra* Chapter 1, note 3, at Art. 5(a)(iii); Art. 5(b)(iii).

[36] *Id.* at Art. 5(g) (emphasis added).

[37] *Id.* at Art. 5(i).

[38] *Id.* at Art. 6(f).

In order to entice the engagement of alleged perpetrators with a truth commission, at least one of three conditions must exist: (1) an enticing carrot, usually in the form of amnesty or immunity; (2) a punitive stick, usually in the form of a credible threat of prosecution; or (3) confidence that such engagement will be positive and affirming. None of these conditions existed in the Kenyan context.

The one truth commission that did collect extensive narratives from perpetrators was the South African Truth and Reconciliation Commission. The South African Commission's amnesty process provided a carrot that enticed individual perpetrators to come forward and testify concerning violations for which they were responsible. The South Africa process had its own limitations. First, while a large number of people did come forward to take advantage of the amnesty, the vast majority of those who were responsible for gross violations of human rights refused to participate. There are thus still major human rights violations in South Africa's past for which we do not know who was responsible. Second, the amnesty process was structured as a quasi-judicial process and was operated like an adversarial court proceeding. Applicants, often with the help of highly paid lawyers, revealed only the bare minimum and, it is alleged by some, deliberately hid or distorted the truth about wrongs they had committed.

The Kenyan Commission did have some amnesty powers, but as discussed in Chapter 2 on the mandate, these powers were extremely limited. We did have, however, a very generous provision granting an individual immunity from any civil or criminal liability "in respect of any evidence or information given to the Commission by such person."[39] This language is open to an expansive interpretation that would provide close to the equivalent of an amnesty. The provision goes beyond providing for the inability to prosecute an individual based upon any information they provide to the Commission; instead it provides such immunity with "respect to" any such evidence or information. As far as I could discover at the time no court in Kenya had interpreted such language with respect to a commission of inquiry. Despite the potentially expansive nature of this immunity, no adversely mentioned person or alleged perpetrator took advantage of it. To be fair, we did not highlight this provision for fear that it would be abused and support the criticism of the Commission as a vehicle for providing amnesty to those responsible for the worst violations in Kenya's history.

---

[39] *Id.* at Art. 24(3).

While the carrot provided by our amnesty and immunity provisions was limited in its appeal, the stick of possible prosecution was, at best, weak, and at worst, nonexistent. The history of impunity in Kenya is a long and sordid one. No significant prosecutions or convictions have ever been undertaken with respect to the numerous assassinations and massacres throughout Kenya's history, not to mention various corruption scandals and land grabs. The risk of not seeking amnesty or immunity from the Commission was thus quite low. There was very little possibility that those most responsible for the violations we were investigating would be indicted, and even if they were, the history of impunity, combined with the corruption endemic to the judicial system, all but guaranteed that such individuals would never be held to account. Without a credible threat of prosecution, there was little incentive for perpetrators to cooperate with the Commission. While we did have subpoena powers, we were dependent upon the same legal system for the enforcement of those powers. Nevertheless, we did subpoena a number of alleged perpetrators, including individuals identified as responsible for some of the worst massacres and assassinations in Kenya's history. As noted, except for our chair, all of the individuals we served complied with our subpoena. We spent, for example, more than a week holding public hearings with members of the various security committees implicated in the Wagalla massacre. The resulting information gleaned from those hearings can be seen in the extensive discussion of the Wagalla massacre in our final report.[40]

Many of the Kenyan commissioners had contact with people who were adversely mentioned to us. The most prominent of those was our chair, Ambassador Kiplagat, who not only knew many of the people who were alleged to have been responsible for some of the violations we were to investigate but was himself an adversely mentioned person. While some had criticized his inclusion in the Commission given, among other things, his ties to the government of Daniel arap Moi, I continue to take the position that his inclusion was not only appropriate but desirable. My position was premised on the fact that he was not directly linked to any violation that we were to investigate (a premise that was to prove incorrect) and on the hope that he would reach out to alleged perpetrators and encourage them to participate in our process (a hope that turned out to be misplaced). Ambassador Kiplagat's reaction to the allegations that were leveled against him provided a model to other suspected perpetrators that substantially undercut our ability to encourage the participation of such individuals. Rather than striking a posture of

---

[40] TJRC Final Report, *supra* Chapter 1, note 9, at Vol. IIA, pp. 221–366.

contrition and a willingness to work with victims to move beyond the violations of the past, Ambassador Kiplagat instead retreated into a defensive posture that focused on his own self-interest rather than the broader project of truth, justice, and reconciliation, and in the process seriously undermined the credibility of the Commission and his own credibility. If the chair of a Commission dedicated to truth, justice, and reconciliation was unwilling to engage with the process in a meaningful way, why would any other alleged perpetrator?

More people who engaged with the Commission identified nonstate actors as perpetrators. Fifty-nine percent of perpetrators were identified as non-state actors, while 41 percent were identified as state actors. This binary distinction between state and nonstate actors does not adequately capture the responsibility of the state for even those violations presented to us. First, the large number of violations committed by nonstate actors indicates that the state was failing in its obligation to protect the safety and security of its citizens. Scores of individuals testified before us about the failure of the police or other government authority to protect them from the violence of others or to provide them redress for such violations. Lucy Lolosoli testified concerning a number of specific incidents of child kidnapping, murders, and disappearances in the Samburu community, "I also blame the Kenyan Government because when that incident was reported, instead of it coming to check about the incident and get the details, some of the leaders never took any opportunity to come and find out more about this."[41] We received reports of 9,838 incidents of victims requesting some form of legal redress only to have nothing happen.

Second, the largest category of identified perpetrators consisted of youth groups and various ethnically organized groups (such as the Mungiki or SLDF). As we learned through our statements, hearings, research, and investigations, state agencies and officials often supported such groups both directly and indirectly. As in most societies with a high level of conflict, the line separating state and nonstate actors in the Kenyan context is often a blurry one. We heard testimony, often *in camera*, of specific politicians who sometimes indirectly, but also directly, supported the work of groups like the SLDF and Mungiki.

As a result of our statements, public hearings, investigations, and research, we identified 154 individuals who should be investigated and, if the evidence warranted, prosecuted. We also exonerated six individuals who were accused of wrongdoing before us. In those cases, we acquired enough evidence that we

[41] RTJRC09.05 (Isiolo, Agricultural Training Centre – Multipurpose Hall), May 9, 2011, p. 39.

were comfortable asserting that the allegations presented to us were false.[42] As far as I am aware, none of the individuals we identified has been investigated or prosecuted. This is perhaps not surprising, given the government's historical failure to hold any individuals to account for the worst crimes committed in Kenya's history.[43]

WOMEN'S HEARINGS

We held women's hearings in each location we visited. These hearings provided a rich insight into the experience of women with respect to historical injustices. They also provide an alternative model of how truth commission hearings could be structured to create a space more conducive to capturing the lived experiences of victims.

Our women's hearings – really more town hall–type conversations – were designed to provide a safe space for women to speak freely about their experiences with respect to violations within our mandate. The hearings were women-only – only female commissioners and staff were present[44], and only women were allowed to participate. These events were extremely popular – over 1,000 women participated in them throughout the country. They typically lasted four to six hours, and sometimes much longer. At these hearings, women spoke quite candidly about violations they had experienced, including quite graphic and heartbreaking stories about sexual and other gender-based violence they had suffered. The commissioners and staff who attended these hearings were often quite exhausted and even traumatized themselves by the

---

[42] For the list of those individuals recommended for further investigation and those exonerated, *see* TJRC FINAL REPORT, *supra* Chapter 1, note 9, at Vol. IV, Appendix 2. That appendix also includes individuals for whom we requested investigation not by the prosecuting authorities for possible prosecution, but investigations by the National Land Commission of allegations of land grabbing, the National Environmental Management Authority for allegations of environmental harms, and the Ministry of Labor for alleged labor violations. As with the recommendations concerning the director of public prosecutions, as far as I am aware, none of these investigations has occurred.

[43] As one example, the individuals identified through numerous investigations (including Scotland Yard, and judicial and Parliamentary commissions of inquiry) as having been responsible for the assassination of the Honorable Robert Ouko has never been seriously investigated or prosecuted.

[44] This was not always strictly the case. In at least some cases, men who operated our video cameras and male Hansard personnel were present. We have no reason to think that their presence silenced any woman in the room, but future truth commissions might ensure that they have adequate female staff to perform all of the functions required in holding such an event.

end of the day, given the often intense stories that were related at the hearings. While I never attended these hearings, I often had the opportunity to hear immediately afterwards what had transpired from commissioners and staff who had attended, and I was later able to read the verbatim transcripts of these hearings.

The existence of the women-only hearings created a dilemma for us as we tried to mainstream gender into our activities. We typically held three days of hearings in each place that we visited. Most of the women's hearings occurred on the same day as one of our three "regular" public hearings for that region. Usually on the second day of those hearings, the male commissioners would preside over the public hearing while the female commissioners attended the women's hearing. This meant that on those days, our hearings were heavily gendered. Very few women attended the public hearing; most understandably chose to participate in the women's hearing. This meant that the male members of the local community were often the only ones to hear issues highlighted during our second day of hearings. The issues raised during the women's hearings were, of course, also not heard by the male members of that community. It is also certainly the case that women who might have testified during our public hearings chose instead to speak about their experiences at the women's hearings. Only 213 women testified before us at our public hearings, compared to the more than 1,000 who participated in the women's hearings. A few, however, courageously testified before us at our public hearings about sexual and other gender-based violence while men from their community sat and listened.[45]

The women's hearings thus created an unfortunate bifurcation of our activities along gender lines. This bifurcation was, however, unavoidable given the limited time and resources made available to us to conduct our work. The amount of information we gathered from the women's hearings, in addition to the immediate benefits women experienced in being able to speak freely among themselves, far outweighed the fact that the male members of a community (some of whom were directly or indirectly responsible for many of the violations discussed) were not present. A woman in Kapsokwony underscored this reality:

> We are grateful that you have separated us from men because yesterday we listened to what the men were saying and we could not talk. This is because you would say one thing and leave the rest as we were oppressed in very many things. We could be punished in many aspects. Thank you for the knowledge

[45] *See, e.g.*, the public testimony of Magdalene Wangui Wambugu and Rhoda Njiru Muguika, RTJRC18.11 (Meru Municipal Hall), November 18, 2011.

and the wisdom you used to decide that women should be separated in order for them to say their own things.[46]

Yet creating women-only spaces did not always make the space safe for everyone. In at least one such hearing, a woman who broke down into tears when recounting her story elicited laughter from some of the women in the hall.[47] Ideally, had we more time and, more importantly, more money, we would have devoted an additional day to just the women's hearings which would have allowed the women to attend all of our public hearings if they desired. To compensate for the fact that most of the experiences related by women were not heard by the men in the community, we devoted a number of sections of our report to the experiences of women and made sure to include women's voices in most parts of the report.

The women's hearings were significantly different than our integrated public hearings and provide a useful contrast to how most truth commissions conduct their hearings. Our hearings, like those of most truth commissions, had many of the trappings of a more formal legal process. A number of monitoring reports of our hearings raised this concern.[48] We referred to the witnesses we were going to hear as "cases." When the commissioners who presided over the day's hearing entered, all in the hall rose. Witnesses and their advocates often referred to us as "Your Honor" or "My Lord." Witnesses were sometimes interrupted when their testimony was not considered relevant to the "case." While such a narrow focus on the relevance of a particular witness's testimony might be warranted, it also made it more difficult for witnesses to tell their story in their own words. In contrast, the women's hearings were much less formal and were often punctuated with episodes of singing and dancing.

Which of these models is more appropriate depends on the purpose of the public hearing. If the purpose of the hearing is to provide witnesses with a platform for "non-retributive truth telling,"[49] or to provide a forum for victims "to be heard and restore their dignity,"[50] then a less structured hearing along the lines of our women's hearings is better tailored to such purposes. If instead

---

[46] RTJRC24.05 (Mt. Elgon County Council Hall, Kapsokwony) (Women's Hearing), May 24, 2011, p. 7.

[47] RTJRC13.01 (Hola County Council Hall), January 13, 2012, p. 13. The story the witness was recounting did not, however, involve sexual or gender-based violence, but instead concerned her being forcefully evicted from her home by people connected to the local government.

[48] See TJRC Final Report, *supra* Chapter 1, note 9, at Vol. 1, pp. 108–110.

[49] TJRC Act, *supra* Chapter 1, note 3, at Art. 5(g).

[50] *Id.* at Art. 5(h).

the purpose of the hearing is more investigative, such as probing a reluctant witness who is alleged to be responsible for a gross violation of human rights, then a more formal hearing along the lines of our regular public hearings is more appropriate. Unfortunately, we did not take the time to strategize about the different types of hearings we could have held given the different purposes we wanted to achieve. Public hearings are some of the most public acts of a truth commission. They provide an opportunity for the commission to communicate with a broader audience, often unfiltered by the media. We did not take advantage of the flexibility and discretion we had with respect to our hearings as much as we could have, or should have.

The picture painted by the testimony and other information we received is of a Kenya struggling with the weight of generations of gross violations of human rights. It is not difficult to see why a young Kenyan living in a refugee camp in Uganda continued to refuse to return to Kenya. At our women's hearing at the Kenyan refugee camp in Kiryandongo, Uganda, one of the mothers described to us the attitude of the young Kenyan refugees: "When you say 'Kenya' to them, they say: 'Policemen in Kenya kill people. Houses are being burnt in Kenya. People are killing each other.'"[51] One could see the effect of this history on the children we encountered at refugee camps, in schools, and in our outreach activities. Children from the community of Kibera wrote and sang a song called "This Is Our Land" at our children's hearing.[52] They sang: "Why did people fight while corrupt leaders watched? Why did innocent men, women and children die? Why was property destroyed while leaders watched? Is this land ours?" At the same hearing, Cynthia Rebecca from Mombasa sang "Dunia Inatutesa" ("The World Is Mistreating Us"): "Let children raise their voice and cry tears of blood, because we want to be heard. Let's cry loudly, even if just a few will hear us." An eight-year-old boy spoke at the hearing. His parents were killed during the 2007 post-election violence. His message? He wanted to personally kill the people who had killed his parents. That was probably one

---

[51] RTJRCo1.11 (St. Patrick Catholic Youth Center, Kiryandongo Uganda) (Women's Hearing), November 1, 2011, p. 15.

[52] The Children's Hearings were held from December 13 to 14, 2011, in Nairobi. At the hearing, individual children who testified spoke from a room separate from the public hearing venue. The children were seated around a table with commissioners and staff. They were given pens, pencils, and paper to draw if they wanted. Commissioners and staff asked questions in this informal setting. The audio was broadcast into the other room where other commissioners, the press, and the public were gathered. Close to forty children participated, ranging in age from four to eighteen.

of the most depressing pieces of testimony we heard during our year of hearings. Violence and revenge, inculcated at such a young age, do not bode well for the future of conflict in Kenya. It was difficult to see how the cycle could be broken without a level of commitment from the government and political elite that was clearly not evident then, and even less evident today.

5

The Elephant Returns

While we were busy with our public hearings and related activities, Ambassador Kiplagat began to organize his attack against the same tribunal he had so passionately requested. While he eventually succeeded in neutralizing the tribunal so that the issues raised in our petition were never addressed, we still benefited from the year that it took him to maneuver around any formal inquiry into his conflicts of interest. While Ambassador Kiplagat continued to lobby on his own behalf both privately and in the press, the fact that he had left the Commission (if only in the form of "stepping aside") meant that his issues were viewed as separate from the Commission. We spent most of the year conducting our public hearings and other related activities without him, further underscoring our independence from him and his issues.

THE TRIBUNAL'S SLOW START

The tribunal did not get off to a smooth start. The chief justice had given the tribunal six months to do its work, yet it took over a month for him to successfully appoint the three members of the tribunal. The *Gazette* notice establishing the tribunal was published on Monday, November 1, three days after the chief justice had publicly announced his intention to create it. Curiously, the notice itself, though published on November 1, was dated October 21,[1] suggesting that either the chief justice decided to create the tribunal prior to Parliament's threat to dissolve us and my threat to resign or, as we suspected with the earlier letters delivered to us, the chief justice or someone in his office had backdated the notice. The fact that the chief

---

[1] Gazette Notice 13203, *The Kenya Gazette*, Vol. CXII, No. 111, p. 3974 (November 1, 2010).

justice announced the creation of the tribunal a week after he had allegedly decided to create it, and prior to the publication of the notice, supports the latter suspicion.

Pursuant to the TJRC legislation, the tribunal members were required to be current or former judges of the High Court. One of the judges appointed in this first *Gazette* notice, Justice (Rtd.) William Shirley Deverell, declined to serve. Thus on November 19, a new *Gazette* notice was issued replacing Justice Deverell with the same Mwanaisha Saida Shariff. Unfortunately, Mwanaisha Saida Shariff was not a current or former judge. In a separate *Gazette* notice dated December 2 but with a publication date of November 30, 2007 (presumably it should be 2010), the same Mwanaisha Saida Shariff and Perpetual Wangeci Waitere were appointed as joint secretaries to the tribunal. On December 10, the chief justice issued another notice replacing Mwanaisha Saida Shariff as a member of the tribunal with Justice Wanjiru Karanja. As the back and forth over membership had taken up all of November and some of December, and as the December holidays were fast approaching, not much work was accomplished through the end of the year. I was to later hear that as late as February 2011 (three months into its six-month lifespan), the tribunal was still awaiting money from the government so it could begin its work in earnest.

This delay in appointing members and providing financing was particularly worrisome, given that the chief justice had given the tribunal only six months to do its work. Initially, I had been quite concerned that the tribunal might last as long as six months. This meant yet a further delay in resolving the conflicts of interest presented by Ambassador Kiplagat, and thus the prospect of six more months of victims and others not trusting us because of his presence (or the possibility of his future return) given the outstanding allegations against him. Given the delay in appointing the initial members and the government's failure to provide operational funds in a timely manner, the six months quickly began to look like an insufficient amount of time for the tribunal to perform properly its intended function.

The mandate of the tribunal was curious – curious because it was unusually broad and did not reflect what was requested either in the petition filed by the commissioners or in the petition filed by civil society. We had requested that the tribunal examine the link and conflicts of interest between Ambassador Kiplagat and three things: the Wagalla massacre, the Ouko assassination, and the irregular and illegal acquisition of land. We drafted the petition with due regard to the objections raised by the Ministry of Justice: that the tribunal could not look at the conduct of a commissioner prior to his or her appointment to the Commission. We thus focused on Kiplagat's continued assertions since his appointment that he had no conflicts of interest, that he was not present at a meeting during which the security operation in Wagalla was discussed, and that he had always served as a reliable witness with respect to investigations into the death of Robert Ouko. To the extent that any or all of these and other related statements were untrue, they could arguably constitute "misbehavior or misconduct" committed after our appointment. Separate from this legal argument concerning the interpretation of the provisions of the Act, Ambassador Kiplagat had made it clear that this was his preferred process for addressing the allegations of his conflicts of interest, suggesting that he, too, agreed that such a tribunal could and should have jurisdiction over such matters.

The chief justice did not interpret the provisions for the establishment of a tribunal so narrowly. Instead, he entrusted the tribunal with the following mandate:

> To investigate the conduct of the Chairman of the Truth, Justice and Reconciliation Commission, Ambassador Bethwell Kiplagat including, but not limited to, the allegations that the said Chairman's past conduct erodes and compromises his legitimacy and credibility to chair the Commission; his past is riddled with unethical practices and absence of integrity; he has been involved in, linked to or associated with incidents considered to be abuse of human rights; is likely to be a witness in the same matters that the Commission is mandated to investigate.

This was an incredibly broad mandate that appeared to bring into its purview any questionable incident within Ambassador Kiplagat's past. Notwithstanding this broad mandate, the tribunal began to examine the three issues that we and (we were led to believe) Ambassador Kiplagat wanted it to address: the Wagalla massacre; the assassination of Robert Ouko; and Kiplagat's irregular or illegal acquisition of land.

The tribunal did not start to engage with the substance of its mandate until February 2011. At that point, Ambassador Kiplagat wrote to the Commission noting that the tribunal was about to start its work and that he had retained Githu Muigai (who was later to become Kenya's attorney general) as his legal counsel and requested that the Commission pay his legal fees for that representation. This request was consistent with Kiplagat's view that he and the Commission were one. We met to consider this request and decided that the Commission should not pay Kiplagat's legal fees as the issues were ones of a personal nature to Ambassador Kiplagat and did not concern the Commission itself.

KIPLAGAT SHUTS DOWN THE TRIBUNAL

Although the conflicts of interest raised by these three issues were the ones that Ambassador Kiplagat had agreed should be the subject of the tribunal's inquiry, he quickly challenged the tribunal's power to inquire into *any* of his past conduct, including those three areas. His challenge first took the form of a formal motion before the tribunal. The tribunal (not surprisingly) rejected this motion and cited, among other things, the terms of reference duly established by the chief justice. Ambassador Kiplagat immediately went to the High Court requesting an order to either disband the tribunal or, in the alternative, to restrict the tribunal's inquiry to acts that occurred after he had been appointed to the Commission.

On April 27, 2011, Judge Muchelule of the High Court issued a stay of the proceedings of the tribunal while it prepared to hear Ambassador Kiplagat's arguments challenging the creation and jurisdiction of the tribunal. Judge Muchelule, in his opinion, succinctly articulated the dilemma facing the Commission and Ambassador Kiplagat:

> For me, [Ambassador Kiplagat] is faced with a serious moral issue. His appointment was on the basis that his conduct, character and integrity were beyond reproach, and that he was going to be an impartial arbiter in whatever proceedings that were going to be conducted by him. It was expected that he was not involved, implicated, linked or associated with human rights violations of any kind or in any matter which the Commission is supposed to investigate. But now, he is faced with a situation where his past has allegedly been dug out and his own Commission may very well be seeking to investigate him. The issue is not whether the allegations being levelled against him are true. What is material is that the Commission will want to investigate the circumstances surrounding the death of Robert Ouko, the Wagalla Massacre and the Ndungu Report on Illegal/Irregular Allocation of Public Land and in each case he is being adversely mentioned. He cannot sit in judgment when the issues are being discussed. Justice will cry if he were allowed to sit in judgment, be a witness and an accused, all [at] the same time. My advise [sic] is that he should do the honourable thing.[2]

The "honourable thing" is a turn of phrase in Kenya that, at least in this context, was meant to suggest that Ambassador Kiplagat should resign. The Judge also noted that although the Tribunal's term was about to expire, "experience has shown that such terms may be extended."[3]

On May 10, 2011, the tribunal reached the end of its six-month life. During its brief lifespan, it had issued one opinion, ruling against Ambassador Kiplagat's claim that the tribunal did not have jurisdiction over his conflicts of

---

[2] *Bethuel Kiplagat v. Chief Justice of the Republic of Kenya and Four Others* [2011], Misc. Application No. 95 of 2011, eKLR (Judge A. O. Muchelule) (April 27, 2011).

[3] *Id.*

interest. With the expiration of the life of the tribunal, we awaited a decision from the High Court concerning Ambassador Kiplagat's claim that the chief justice erred in its creation.

For the next seven months, there were no significant developments in Ambassador Kiplagat's legal case challenging the creation of the now-expired tribunal. On December 1, 2011, Ambassador Kiplagat withdrew his legal challenge to the creation of the tribunal. At the time of his withdrawal, the High Court had yet to rule on the merits of Ambassador Kiplagat's challenge to the tribunal. The withdrawal was not surprising, however, given that the tribunal no longer existed and there was no sign that it would be reconstituted. While Ambassador Kiplagat's challenge against the tribunal was pending, the chief justice prudently decided not to reconstitute the tribunal as, given the temporary stay, it would be unable to do any work unless and until the High Court ruled on Ambassador Kiplagat's challenge. With the withdrawal of Ambassador Kiplagat's lawsuit, however, the tribunal could be reconstituted and proceed with its work as the temporary stay, with the withdrawal of the case, was no longer in effect.

A NEW CHIEF JUSTICE STAYS THE COURSE

In February 2011, Johnson Evans Gicheru stepped down as chief justice and was replaced in June 2011 by Willy Mutunga. Although Justice Gicheru had eventually established the tribunal, the fact that it had taken almost seven months from the time we had submitted our petition made us cautiously optimistic about his retirement and replacement by Chief Justice Mutunga. Willy Mutunga came from a strong human rights background, both in Kenya and internationally. Central to some of the most important human rights campaigns in Kenya from the 1970s onwards, Mutunga was one of the founders of the Kenyan Human Rights Commission (one of the most important independent human rights organizations in Kenya) and served as a human rights officer and then executive director of the East African office of the Ford Foundation. I was heartened by the fact that there was now a chief justice who would understand the importance of a credible truth commission and would also understand the legal issues raised by Ambassador Kiplagat's conflicts of interest. Given his background and my assumptions concerning how he would view these issues, I was thus quite surprised at how disinterested he eventually revealed himself to be with respect to the Commission and the conflicts of interest of our chair.

When Ambassador Kiplagat withdrew his lawsuit, we expected that the original tribunal would be reestablished, or a new tribunal established, in response to our original petition. The creation of a tribunal was premised on the assessment that our petition was meritorious. That assessment had already been made by the previous chief justice and resulted in the creation of the original tribunal. If Justice Gicheru had felt that our petition was frivolous or misplaced, he would have rejected our petition and not established the tribunal. Given that the original tribunal had expired without concluding its work, the new chief justice had three options. First, he could reconstitute the original tribunal, thus giving legal effect to the removal of the injunction issued by the High Court pursuant to Ambassador Kiplagat's withdrawal of his legal challenge. Second, he could create a new tribunal pursuant to our petition. He might have chosen this path if the original members of the tribunal were no longer available or willing to serve or if he wanted to modify the mandate of the tribunal given, among other things, Ambassador Kiplagat's legal challenge. Third, he could reverse the decision of his predecessor and reject our petition based upon his assessment that it did not provide a basis to establish such a tribunal under the relevant provisions of our Act. It was our view that our petition was still alive and had already been found sufficiently meritorious to trigger such a process. The current chief justice was thus faced with deciding between the first and second options.

We waited two months to see what the new chief justice would do. During that time, I was hearing from mutual acquaintances that the chief justice was inclined to do nothing. I requested through a number of intermediaries that he meet with me, or with me and the other international commissioners, either officially or informally. Those entreaties were rebuffed. Given that Ambassador Kiplagat continued to stay away from the Commission, we did not pursue the establishment of the tribunal with much vigor. We were busy with our public hearings, our ongoing investigations, and the drafting of our final report. While there was no existing process to evaluate Ambassador Kiplagat's conflicts of interest, his continued absence pursuant to his "stepping aside" meant that he was effectively doing "the honourable thing" as earlier suggested by Judge Muchelule.

"HE'S BACK WITH A BANG"

In early January 2012, some of the commissioners traveled to the Coast region to prepare for our public hearings. I had remained in Nairobi to engage with some of our Nairobi-based stakeholders and to work on the final report. During the first week of January, Ambassador Kiplagat returned to the Commission offices unannounced to reassert his position as chair of the Commission. This was a complete surprise to all of us, as the last communication on the matter we had received from Ambassador Kiplagat was his public statement in November 2010 that he was stepping aside so the tribunal could do its work. We could not understand why he was now returning when there had been no decision from the tribunal (or any other body for that matter) concerning his conflicts of interest. Our surprise turned to alarm when we received reports from our staff in the office concerning Ambassador Kiplagat's activities. First, he took over the office of our acting chair, Tecla Wanjala, without informing her of his intention to do so. We did not know whether there were documents related to investigations concerning those three areas in which he had a conflict of interest in her office. Up until this point, we had been able to assure victims and other stakeholders that any information we had received from them concerning those three areas of investigation had been kept from Ambassador Kiplagat. Second, we were informed that Ambassador Kiplagat had called in members of the staff and demanded that they give him access to documents related to the three areas in which he had a conflict of interest, including our investigations related to the Wagalla massacre. The commissioners had instituted a number of internal procedures with respect to access to sensitive documents within the Commission, including those related to investigations. These were procedures that all of us, including commissioners, were to follow – and had followed. We had adopted these procedures in order to assure those who had given us sensitive information that we were able to keep their identities confidential as we had promised. When the staff refused to hand over those and other materials – citing our existing internal procedures for access to such documents – Ambassador Kiplagat apparently responded that the staff worked directly for him as chair, and not for the other commissioners or the CEO, and that if they refused to obey his orders he would call the police and have them arrested. Third, Ambassador Kiplagat was reported to have declared a number of times that he had returned to the office "to shape the final report." As he told a reporter, "I am back with a bang."[4]

None of the commissioners were present when Ambassador Kiplagat reportedly said these things to members of the staff, but many of us received contemporaneous communications from the staff recounting these and other conversations as they were happening.

Upon receiving reports of Ambassador Kiplagat threatening the staff in order to get access to sensitive documents, we quickly consulted each other by phone and agreed that at least two of us should immediately return to the office to ensure the security of the Commission's documents. We also agreed

---

[4] Wahome Thuku, "Kiplagat Back at Truth Commission," *The Standard*, January 5, 2012.

to write a letter to Ambassador Kiplagat immediately requesting that he honor his earlier commitment to step aside until a credible process evaluated his conflicts of interest as he himself had requested. Commissioner Shava and I volunteered to return to the office and draft the letter.

We were concerned that upon our return to the office, Ambassador Kiplagat would adopt a belligerent attitude towards us, given the reports we were receiving about his confrontational interactions with staff who had the courage to question his authority. When we entered the office, we did not see him and were later told that within twenty minutes of his being informed that we were in the office he quietly exited through the back door. This was something of a relief, suggesting that while he was willing to confront and intimidate the staff, he was not yet willing to adopt a similar strategy with his fellow commissioners.

Commissioner Shava and I immediately drafted a letter to Ambassador Kiplagat noting his earlier commitment to refrain from active engagement with the Commission while his matter was being determined by the tribunal and the courts. We also noted that we had existing internal policies governing access to Commission documents, which, if what had been reported to us were true, he was threatening to ignore. Finally, we noted that it had been reported that he had stated that he had returned to "shape the final report," and we reminded him that the final report was a product of the entire Commission and thus was not amenable to being "shaped" by any one person.

In addition to writing to Ambassador Kiplagat, we also immediately wrote to the chief justice requesting that he urgently either reconstitute or constitute anew a tribunal to evaluate Ambassador Kiplagat's conflicts of interest. We informed the chief justice that Ambassador Kiplagat's recent actions threatened to undermine the integrity of our process and breach the confidentiality of individuals who had entrusted sensitive information to the Commission (indeed in some cases information that, if revealed, might place those individuals at risk). In our letter to the chief justice, we enclosed a copy of our letter to Ambassador Kiplagat.

We never received a response to our letter to the chief justice. Instead people in his office apparently engaged in a number of informal conversations with our office. I was never a part of those conversations, and, as far as I am aware, neither were any of the other commissioners. It is my understanding that those conversations made clear that the chief justice saw no reason to create a tribunal. I again tried to arrange an informal meeting with the chief justice, either alone or with some of the other commissioners. It was my hope that there was perhaps a misunderstanding about the issues at stake or confusion about the history of the legal proceedings. The issue, at least to me, seemed relatively simple. Ambassador Kiplagat had clear conflicts of interest. Those conflicts of interest not only threatened the credibility of the Commission but had, up until his stepping aside, seriously undermined our efforts to perform the functions entrusted to us by the people of Kenya. Our legislation provided a clear process by which a commissioner could be evaluated for misbehavior or misconduct. Ambassador Kiplagat himself had insisted that such a process be undertaken. The commissioners unanimously requested such a tribunal through the submission of a formal petition to the prior chief justice. The chief justice had eventually responded favorably to the merits of our petition and established such a tribunal. The tribunal was unable to finish its work as the High Court, at the request of Ambassador Kiplagat, had stayed its proceedings. Ambassador Kiplagat had withdrawn his legal challenge to the tribunal. The logical next step was for the chief justice to constitute the tribunal. In the end, I never had an opportunity to explain this history to the chief justice, as my efforts to secure even an informal meeting with him were again rebuffed.

KIPLAGAT'S ASSERTION OF ABSOLUTE POWER

Given Ambassador Kiplagat's refusal to confront us when we had returned to the office, we hoped that our letter would convince him to at least refrain from trying to interfere with the work of the Commission. This was not to be the case. Less than a week later, Ambassador Kiplagat wrote a four-page open letter to all commissioners and staff with the heading, "Chairman's Resumption of Office,"[5] the tone and content of which supported what we had been hearing from the staff. The letter was posted in the office for all of the staff and commissioners to see and was copied to the chief justice, the secretary of the Cabinet and head of the civil service, and the permanent secretary in the Ministry of Justice. The letter began with an incorrect statement of the legal proceedings to date, asserting that the High Court had found valid his claim that the tribunal's mandate to inquire into his past conduct was improper. The High Court had in fact not ruled either way on whether his claim challenging the mandate was valid or not. In this letter, he also for the first time indicated that he had stepped aside in November 2010 not only to assist the work of the tribunal, but also to assist the "easy and expeditious determination" of a case that had been filed against the Commission by a number of NGOs at the start

---

[5] For a copy of the letter *see* TJRC FINAL REPORT, *supra* Chapter 1, note 9, at Vol. I, Appendix 7.

of the Commission's life in late 2009. This was the same case that Ambassador Kiplagat claimed he would be "enjoined to" in February 2010 when we had met with Parliament.

The case filed by the NGOs in 2009[6] was a broad challenge to the creation of the Commission under the Kenyan Constitution (the main claim of which was that our mandate was unconstitutionally restricted to exclude the colonial period);[7] a challenge to the creation of the Selection Panel that chose each of the Kenyan Commissioners, including Ambassador Kiplagat; and a challenge to Ambassador Kiplagat's oath of office since it had been administered before the publication of the *Gazette* notice indicating his appointment as chair. The case did not concern the specific conflicts of interest that were the subject of our petition to the chief justice. The constitutional claims alleged that Ambassador Kiplagat was not qualified to be a member of the Commission because, *inter alia*, he was "a senior member of an oppressive regime," "he has no record of any sustained struggles or fights for human rights in Kenya," and "he has something to explain to the Commission regarding the disappearance of the late Robert Ouko."[8] The last reference to Ambassador Kiplagat's conflict of interest with respect to the Ouko assassination was the only reference (and a passing one at that) to the three issues that were the subject of the tribunal's inquiry. The legal bases for these challenges were, in fact, quite weak and in some cases improperly pled, all of which eventually led the court to dismiss each and every claim. In its decision dismissing the case, the court did not even address the merits of the constitutional claim, including Ambassador Kiplagat's conflict of interest with respect to the Ouko assassination, concluding that the claims related to those matters were improperly pled. The court also dismissed the challenge concerning the Selection Panel, and dismissed the challenge to the validity of the timing of Ambassador Kiplagat's oath of office. Finally, in its decision, the court was very clear that it was not ruling either way on the suitability of Ambassador Kiplagat as a member of the Commission but limited itself to the process by which he, and the rest of us, were appointed.[9] Interestingly, the court noted that Ambassador Kiplagat had argued

> that the proper procedure for removal of chairman or member of the Commission is set out under Section 17 of the TJRC Act. That procedure

[6]   A full copy of the decision can be found on the website.

[7]   Our mandate was not so restricted. *See supra* Chapter 2.

[8]   *Republic v. Truth Justice & Reconciliation Commission & Another Ex-parte Augustine Njeru Kthangu & 9 Others* [2011] Misc. Application No. 470, eKLR, para. 10.

[9]   *Id.* at para 47.

having not been followed, judicial review cannot be used to supplant the specific statutory procedure provided for the removal of commissioners and chairman of the Commission.[10]

In other words, Ambassador Kiplagat had argued successfully before the court that the only proper procedure for evaluating whether he was suitable as a member or chair of the Commission was the creation of a tribunal by the chief justice pursuant to our Act, a procedure that he had requested along with the rest of us in April 2010 and that he subsequently succeeded in blocking.

Notwithstanding the limited nature of the original claims and the limited nature of the court's decision, Ambassador Kiplagat now claimed that the court in this decision had thoroughly addressed each of the issues that had been raised concerning his conflicts of interest and dismissed them on the merits. This was patently false.

For those who did not find his rewriting of the past persuasive, Kiplagat made clear that he would resort to legal and other disciplinary proceedings. His open letter declared that any commissioner or staff member who did not recognize his authority as chair of the Commission should go to court otherwise, any action taken contrary to his directions "will be treated as insubordination, to be dealt with in accordance with the relevant legal and disciplinary procedures."

It was now clear that Ambassador Kiplagat was prepared to be as confrontational with his fellow commissioners as he had been with the staff. To underscore the absolute authority he was now claiming, he asserted that decisions duly made by the Commission did not apply to him. This was particularly disturbing when it came to his conflicts of interest, and it was with respect to our policy on protecting our sensitive and confidential information (including information related to his own alleged wrongdoing) that he asserted that he was *sui generis* within the Commission:

> [T]he Commission and its staff are legally incapable of formulating any *"existing policy"* to withhold the Commission's documents from the Chairman. Any such *"policy,"* assuming one was put up in the absence of the Chairman, is *ultra vires* the TJRC Act and hence null and void. Accordingly, the Chairman expects every Commissioner and staff member to avail to him all such of the Commission's documents as the Chairman may from time to time require in the execution of the functions of his office. Any Commissioner or staff member who defies any such request shall be deemed to be

---

[10] *Id.* at para 7.

engaging in insubordination, to be dealt with in accordance with the relevant legal and disciplinary procedures.[11]

It was clear that Ambassador Kiplagat no longer felt bound by any principles concerning conflicts of interest and was intent upon gaining access to all of the Commission's documents, including those involving investigations in which he had a direct interest. This was quite alarming. Over the last fourteen months, we had solicited and received confidential testimony from individuals. We had repeatedly assured them that we had procedures in place to ensure that such information and their identities would remain confidential. A number of witnesses were particularly worried about whether Ambassador Kiplagat would have access to such materials. We were able to assure those individuals that first, Ambassador Kiplagat was not currently participating in the work of the Commission and thus could not access the materials; second, that we had instituted internal procedures to keep track of and limit access to such sensitive information; and third, given his conflicts of interest, Ambassador Kiplagat would not have access to confidential documents related to investigations in which he had an interest even if he were to return. Notwithstanding these assurances, some individuals still refused to provide us with testimony or other information. Some, however, did. We were now faced with the possibility not only that our representations and promises to such individuals would be broken, which in and of itself was of concern, but also that such individuals might be exposed to the risk of being identified publicly, which could place them or their loved ones in danger.

The fact that the letter was copied to government officials, including the chief justice, meant that Ambassador Kiplagat was intent upon soliciting external support for his demand for confidential documents within the possession of the Commission. While we hoped that the chief justice would be equally alarmed by the content of this letter and thus act quickly to constitute a tribunal, this was not to be the case.

WE APPEAL TO THE JUDICIARY

Faced with this increasingly dire situation, the Commission immediately went to court requesting (1) an injunction preventing Ambassador Kiplagat from accessing the Commission's offices unless and until a tribunal was appointed to evaluate whether he should remain a commissioner or not, and (2) a writ of mandamus directing the chief justice to respond to the petition we had filed

---

[11] The emphases in the text are from the original.

almost two years earlier by either reconstituting the previous tribunal or constituting a new tribunal.

The commissioners also wrote a public letter to the staff on January 11 indicating that we had (1) gone to court to request that the chief justice create a tribunal to investigate Ambassador Kiplagat; (2) written a letter to Ambassador Kiplagat requesting that he refrain from coming to the office until the process we initiated with respect to the tribunal had run its course and (3) directing all staff to ignore the memo from Ambassador Kiplagat and to continue to refuse his requests to access official documents or other sensitive materials without following our internal procedures or without the express authorization from the other commissioners.

The letters and court filings, along with our united stand against him, appeared to be sufficient to keep Ambassador Kiplagat away from the Commission. While we continued our public hearings, investigations, and drafting of our final report, we worked with our lawyers to provide sufficient evidence to the court to support our case. We also reached out to numerous stakeholders – victims, civil society, the media, government agencies, and the diplomatic community – to update them on the current state of affairs and to ensure them of our commitment to preserving the integrity of the process. It was time that we would have preferred to have spent on our mandate-related operations. As with the beginning of our mandate period, we spent far too much time fighting about a process for the Kiplagat problem. Two years after the issues about Kiplagat had been brought to our attention, we had still made no progress on addressing the problem, in no small part because of Kiplagat's clear intent to block any possible process. His actions continued to undercut the credibility of the Commission and its work.

On Friday, February 24, we were informed that Judge M. Warsame would be issuing an opinion in our case. Our lawyers informed us they would be present at the court when the judge issued his opinion. Judge Warsame read out his judgment in open court in front of our lawyers and the media. It was clear from this reading that the judge had ruled against us and refused to enjoin Ambassador Kiplagat from coming to our offices and refused to request that the chief justice respond to our petition. While the judge was clearly reading from a written text, our lawyers were informed that the written ruling was not yet available as certain typos and other minor edits needed to be made before the text could be released. I and a number of commissioners immediately went to the court so that we could read a copy of the judgment so that we could respond intelligently to the numerous media inquiries we were beginning to receive. By the end of the day on Friday, we had not received a copy of the ruling. The media carried the story of the judgment against us on Friday and throughout the weekend, including airing excerpts from the opinion as read in open court by the judge. As we did not have access to that video footage or access to the opinion itself, we were unable to respond to the media concerning the reasoning of the judge and our reactions to it. At the end of the day on Friday, we were told that the judgment would be ready on Monday.

On Monday, we returned to the judge's chambers to receive a copy of his judgment. We were told again that the judgment was not ready but that it would be ready that afternoon. When we returned that afternoon, we were told it would not be ready until Tuesday morning. As we were patiently waiting in the judge's chambers for the minor edits to be made, we learned that Ambassador Kiplagat had been given a signed copy of the final judgment that same Monday morning. When we pointed out this anomaly to the court staff, they continued to refuse to give us a copy of the judgment. It was only after we had made a number of phone calls to other judges and government officials that finally, in the early evening of Monday, February 27, we were given a copy of the judgment.[12] We were never to learn why we were not given a copy of the judgment at the same time as Ambassador Kiplagat nor who, if anyone, was behind refusing us a copy. It was, however, a relatively minor example of the barriers to justice that many other Kenyans had recounted to us, and their stories were often far more dire in their consequences than ours.[13]

In our final report, we diplomatically state that we found "it difficult at times to follow the reasoning of the learned Judge" in this judgment. It was, in fact, a terribly reasoned opinion – so poor that at times the judge's own biases with respect to the issues before him were made glaringly apparent. I would have expected more from a first-year law student. First, the judge appeared to indicate that the judgment in the suit brought by the former members of Parliament and NGOs (Misc. No. 470 of 2009, summarized briefly above) had addressed the issue of Ambassador Kiplagat's suitability and credibility as chair

---

[12] *Truth Justice and Reconciliation Commission v. Chief Justice of the Republic of Kenya & Another* [2012], Judicial Review 7 of 2012, eKLR.

[13] While we do not know what typos and other minor edits may have been changed between the time of the reading of the Judgment in open court and the issuance of the final decision, it is in fact the case that the Judgment we eventually received did contain numerous typos and other mistakes – for example, in at least two places referring to the applicants before him (i.e., the Commissioners) as the "tribunal" (see page 6 of the opinion); or using the word "prove" instead of "proof" in the following sentence on page 15: "Indeed it was necessary for me to state that nobody should be allowed to indulge in wild and reckless allegations besmirching the character and authority of others without prove and/or evidence;" or the following sentence on page 21: "It is also clear that the allegation since not determined were unproven allegations." It is unclear whether the original draft had so many typos that the editing process failed to catch them all, or whether there were other reasons the opinion was withheld from us.

of the Commission. The judge also stated that that suit (i.e., Misc. No. 470 of 2009) "was heard and fully determined"[14] in Ambassador Kiplagat's favor, and that the allegations against him "were conclusively and finally determined."[15] While this was certainly the public opinion expressed by Ambassador Kiplagat, it was a conclusion that could find no support in the actual judgment of that case. The judge's analysis of this earlier case led many of us to wonder if he had even read the opinion.

Second, the judge also appeared to feel it necessary to determine whether Article 17 of our act "empowered" the chief justice to appoint a tribunal in response to the allegations raised against Kiplagat. This was a curious inquiry given that the chief justice had already decided that he was empowered to create such a tribunal when he did just that in November 2011. In finding that the chief justice was not so empowered, Judge Warsame appeared to be overruling a legal determination already made by his judicial superior, the chief justice.

Third, the judge concluded that because Ambassador Kiplagat was appointed a commissioner, "it can only be assumed" that he was not "in any way involved, implicated, linked or associated with human rights violations of any kind."[16] It was as though being appointed as commissioners had miraculously removed any transgressions from our pasts. This was a curious turn of logic, not least of which was that the entire basis for establishing the tribunal was that Ambassador Kiplagat was in fact linked to, and perhaps even involved in, human rights violations that we not only were to investigate but had already investigated. Ambassador Kiplagat had on numerous occasions acknowledged that he was so linked, while at the same time vigorously proclaiming his innocence. Rather than engage with the factual allegations underlying the dispute (many of which were uncontested), the judge decided to assume them away.

Fourth, the judge appeared to argue that because Ambassador Kiplagat had been vetted already through the Parliamentary process, he could not be subjected to a fresh process "on matters which ought to have been raised at the time he sought the public office."[17] In other words, if the Parliamentary process was flawed, there was no remedy – a curious position for a judge to take in a system without Parliamentary supremacy. The judge also argued that any allegations against Ambassador Kiplagat should have been raised prior to

---

[14] *Id.* at 6. Note that there are differently formatted versions of the opinion, and thus the pagination depends on the version being consulted. The version to which I cite can be found on the book's website.

[15] *Id.* at 12.

[16] *Id.*

[17] *Id.*

his appointment "to avoid the apparent existence of double jeopardy."[18] The use of a criminal law concept – double jeopardy – in connection with an appointment of public trust is itself curious, though it does mirror the position argued by Ambassador Kiplagat – viz. that this was primarily about his rights and not the larger public interest in a credible truth commission. Double jeopardy refers to the principle that an individual who has been tried and legitimately acquitted or convicted of a criminal offense will not be tried again for the same offense. Its purpose is to protect criminal defendants from being tried for the same crime twice. It was not clear how this principle applied, if at all, to Ambassador Kiplagat's situation. Was the selection process by which he was chosen the trial, and his appointment the acquittal or conviction? Neither Kiplagat nor the judge ever made it clear how double jeopardy applied to a non-criminal (and even non-judicial) process.

The judge's argument that any matter concerning the integrity or suitability of any of the appointed commissioners could not be raised after appointment was problematic, particularly given the situation here where Ambassador Kiplagat first denied that he was even present at the meeting of the Kenya Intelligence Committee in Wajir and then later admitted that he had been present. Such an approach to government appointments would create a clear incentive to dissemble and conceal at the appointment stage. In addition, the judge's argument that any such issues could not be raised after appointment seems to undercut the purpose of Article 17 and the procedure for removing a commissioner for misbehavior or misconduct. What is even more curious about this is that later the judge, in apparent *dicta*, stated that "[t]here could also be flaws and lacuna in the way [Ambassador Kiplagat] is going back [to the Commission] after he agreed to step aside for allegations against him to be investigated and determined."[19] It is not clear to which flaws or lacuna the judge is here referring, but presumably he found these flaws and lacuna to be of little legal significance given his ultimate decision.

Fifth, the judge also included a fair amount of *dicta* in his opinion, including assertions that seemed to have led to his ultimate determination of the outcome of the case. For example, he stated that Ambassador Kiplagat "cannot ... disrupt and/or destroy the work of the Commission, for he holds one vote."[20] This was a factual issue that was not argued before the judge and, given our experiences up until this point with the challenges we had faced because of Ambassador Kiplagat's go-it-alone approach, was factually

---

[18] *Id.* at 13.
[19] *Id.* at 17–18.
[20] *Id.* at 16.

incorrect. Ambassador Kiplagat had ably demonstrated that he could single-handedly disrupt the work of the Commission. The judge also indicated that the commissioners should have sought the "advice, guidance and concurrence" of the attorney general before filing the suit.[21] This was a curious statement for a number of reasons. First, the act made no reference to the Commission being required to seek the advice or approval of the attorney general before embarking on *any* activity, including whether to request a tribunal. Second, the act made clear that we were to act independently of any outside influence, which presumably would include the attorney general. Third, the attorney general had made clear back in 2010 when the chief justice had sought his advice with respect to our petition that he had no role to play in the matter.

It would seem that our failure to seek the advice of the attorney general contributed to the judge's ultimate conclusion that our lawsuit was "frivolous and vexatious," and that it diverted from the court spending time on cases brought by "genuine litigants."[22] The judge's view of the merits of the suit and the motives of the Commission in requesting a process to address our chair's admitted conflicts of interest, is nicely captured in the following two sentences:

> Though as courts we spare no efforts in fostering and developing liberal and broadened litigation, yet we cannot avoid but express our opinion that while genuine litigants with legitimate grievances relating to matters which is [sic][23] dear to them must be addressed, the meddlesome interloppers having absolutely no grievances for personal gain or as a proxy of others or for extraneous motivation break the queue by wearing a mask of public interest litigation and get into the court corridors filing vexatious and frivolous cases. This criminally wastes the valuable time of the court and as a result of which genuine litigants standing outside the court in a queue that never moves thereby creating and fomenting public anger, resentment and frustration towards the courts resulting in loss of faith in the administration of justice.[24]

The decision ended with a remarkable, and confusing, set of statements that appeared to acknowledge that the issues concerning Ambassador Kiplagat had not been determined or even investigated, and that again criticized us for not approaching the attorney general concerning this matter:

---

[21] *Id.* at 17.

[22] *Id.* at 17.

[23] The numerous misspellings, grammatical mistakes, and awkward phrasing throughout this excerpt are as found in the published opinion.

[24] *Id.* at 17.

> I will like to make it clear that I am not saying that [the Commission] cannot
> ask the court to interpret or address a particular issue which they feel is
> important for the performance of its statutory function and objectives. There
> could also be flaws and lacuna in the way [Ambassador Kiplagat] is going
> back after he agreed to step aside for allegations against him to be investigated
> and determined. What I am saying is that the [Commission] could and
> should have sought the opinion and advice of honourable Attorney General
> by listing of all relevant issues and seeking a cogent and clear request,
> reconsideration of their mandate in view of the return of their Chairman. It
> is not for fellow Commissioners or the Commission to question the return of
> the Chairman and put obstacles and hurdles into the path of his return when
> none of the allegations have been considered, investigated and determined.[25]

Notwithstanding this apparent concession by the judge that there were clear
issues concerning our chairman that had not been dealt with, he concluded
that the commissioners in our individual capacity were to pay the legal fees of
Ambassador Kiplagat because our suit was so "frivolous and vexatious." This is
a stunning, and outrageous, conclusion. The judge appeared to be saying that
(1) we should have approached the attorney general with this matter even
though (a) our act expressly provided for a judicial process through the
creation of a tribunal, (b) the act provided no role for the attorney general,
and (c) the attorney general had already made clear that he saw no role for
himself with respect to this matter; (2) we should have known that requesting
a tribunal in response to our petition was frivolous even though the chief
justice himself had found enough merit in our petition to establish just such
a tribunal a little over a year ago; and (3) that given that we knew or should
have known those two sets of facts, we acted so frivolously that we should
be sanctioned individually, notwithstanding the fact that the act makes clear
that we are entitled to immunity for any act we perform in good faith in our
capacities as commissioners.[26]

Shortly after the judge issued the opinion requiring us to pay Kiplagat's
legal fees, Kiplagat's lawyers claimed that the fees to which they were entitled
amounted to approximately US $70,000, or about US $10,000 per commissioner. Eventually, however, the court approved fees in the amount of approximately US $600 per commissioner. Ambassador Kiplagat never pursued the
matter, and we never paid his fees.

---

[25] *Id.* at 17–18.
[26] TRJC Act, *supra* Chapter 1, note 3, at Art. 24(1). What is even more remarkable is that the judge
does not even address this issue of our official immunity in his decision.

KIPLAGAT'S SECOND RETURN

With this judicial defeat, we had little leverage to argue that Ambassador Kiplagat should not return to the office. We were concerned that he might continue to try to gain access to sensitive documents that might put some of our sources in danger. We were also concerned that the failure to address his conflicts of interest meant his return would affect the credibility of our report, including our findings and recommendations. Some of us grasped at straws, hoping that we could appeal to his sense of justice and fairness and request that he not return until some process had been undertaken to address his conflicts of interest, or that he agree to limit his future involvement with the Commission given those conflicts.

All of the commissioners met with Ambassador Kiplagat on March 30. At that meeting, we reiterated our concerns arising from his conflicts of interest and how the failure to have those conflicts resolved through an independent and credible process threatened to endanger the work of the Commission, including the final report. We asked that he continue to honor the pledge he had made to us and to the people of Kenya in his public statement of November 2010 – that he would stand aside until such a process was undertaken. We concluded that until such a process was undertaken and completed, none of the commissioners would agree to work with him. We were quite clear that we would not – in fact, we could not – prevent him from coming to the office. Our CEO had vacated her office in order to provide him with a separate office – in fact that office was the largest of any of our offices and was one of only two offices that included a separate office for a dedicated personal assistant. He refused to step aside and insisted that he had every right to be back chairing the Commission. He also he refused to agree to any restrictions on his activity or on his access to documents related to matters for which he had a conflict of interest. As one of the other commissioners was later to decry, he appeared to feel that he had a divine right to lead the Commission.

The commissioners were divided about how to handle this new development in the Kiplagat saga. Some wanted to come down hard, publicly rebuke him, and indicate that we would have nothing to do with him. Those holding this position became more committed against working with Kiplagat when he became the first and only person to refuse a summons to appear before us. We had summoned him to testify before us concerning allegations that he had illegally acquired land while he was in government. Given that we were planning to have our report completed by May 3, merely two months away, I argued that we should not divert too much attention to a public campaign around Kiplagat. Instead, we should finish the report and remain vigilant about keeping him away from sensitive information, particularly informa-tion related to investigations around the three areas in which he had a conflict of interest.

A NEW MINISTER BRINGS NEW OPPORTUNITIES

Meanwhile, a significant change occurred in the Ministry of Justice at the end of March. Mutula Kilonzo, who had been an ardent and public supporter of Ambassador Kiplagat, was replaced as minister of justice by Eugene Wamalwa. While we were relieved that Kilonzo would no longer have jurisdiction over us, we did not know how his replacement would view our situation. Minister Wamalwa had been a vocal critic against the ICC efforts to provide accountabil-ity for the PEV. I was concerned that this might reflect an anti-accountability, pro-impunity position that would not augur well for us. I remained open minded about this, however, as Minister Kilonzo had been a vocal *supporter* of the ICC process, while at the same time opposing many of our efforts to address the Kiplagat problem.

Shortly after our unsuccessful meeting with Ambassador Kiplagat on March 30, the then acting permanent secretary of the Ministry, Gichira Kibara, requested a meeting with us. It was an unproductive, and at times heated, meeting, as the one item on his agenda was to insist that we welcome Kiplagat back to the Commission. While he acknowledged that nothing had been done to address Kiplagat's conflicts of interest, he said that we should just move on and finish the report. He repeatedly referred to our differences with Ambassador Kiplagat as personal and urged us to not be so "emotional" about the issue. Each of us tried to make clear that our differences with Ambassador Kiplagat were not personal but rather matters of principle concerning the integrity and credibility of the process. At one point, Kibara shifted gears and spoke a number of times about the importance of the community from which Ambassador Kiplagat came[27] and the effect on that community of Ambassador Kiplagat being shut out of the Commission. This was, he noted, of particular concern to the execu-tive branch, which, he explained, had as one of its primary concerns the pre-servation of political stability. He even went so far as to say that because our investigations had focused mostly on the Kalenjin community, losing Ambas-sador Kiplagat would increase the likelihood that our report would be viewed as a witch-hunt against Kalenjins. He indicated that if Kiplagat was not part of the

---

[27] He meant the Kalenjin community. The irony, as noted earlier, is that Kiplagat generally did not publicly identify himself as a Kalenjin – as he usually decried tribalism – and many Kalenjin leaders did not trust him for exactly that reason.

process the executive branch would refuse to stand behind the credibility of the Commission or our report. The resort to ethnic stereotypes and tribalism was not that surprising (the disease of viewing everything through a tribal lens pervades almost every aspect of Kenyan society), and the assumption that our investigations were primarily focused on the Kalenjin community was just another manifestation of that mindset. Unless the Ministry had infiltrated our investigations department, there was no way that Kibara could know whether our investigations were skewed in favor of or against any particular ethnic group. Our investigations had focused almost exclusively on individuals and organizations regardless of ethnic identity. While we did not monitor the ethnic identity of those we investigated as perpetrators (we used objective criteria concerning the nature of the violations instead of the ethnicity of the participants to drive our investigative decisions), I have no doubt that such an analysis would not reflect any ethnic bias. We had, for example, devoted a substantial amount of investigations to historical injustices and human rights violations committed during the government of Jomo Kenyatta (who was a Kikuyu). In fact, the executive branch through the president's office was later to intervene directly in our process to censor parts of the report concerning the Kenyatta family; no similar effort was undertaken with respect to the Kalenjins or any other ethnic group or individual.

The meeting with Kibara was frustrating, as he continued to describe our issues with Kiplagat as personal ones, though we knew that as a trained lawyer he appreciated the concept of conflicts of interest. At the same time, the meeting was somewhat enlightening with respect to the past and current position of the Ministry and the Office of the President concerning the Commission. Kibara insisted repeatedly during our meeting that the executive branch had consistently taken the decision not to interfere with the Commission. This was his response each time we tried to solicit ideas from him about the best way to move forward, and each time we suggested to him that the government provide a political solution to the problem – for example, by promoting Ambassador Kiplagat to another position, such as an ambassadorship and replacing him with another individual from the Kalenjin community who was not linked to any of the violations within our mandate. Kibara's assertion that the executive had consistently taken the position to not interfere with the Commission was ludicrous given the repeated meddling in our operations by the executive branch, most often through the Ministry of Justice. At the same time, Kibara revealed that the Ministry and the Office of the President had been in close touch with Kiplagat during all of the controversies surrounding him, particularly, according to Kibara, when Ambassador Francis Muthaura was in the Office of the President. Kibara revealed to us that there were a number of meetings and discussions that he was not at liberty to disclose to us. He did reveal that he and others (including Muthaura) had insisted a number of times that Ambassador Kiplagat should resign. I had heard that Ambassador Kiplagat had told at least one diplomat in Nairobi that Ambassador Muthaura had urged him to resign and he had refused, lending credence to this assertion by Kibara. Kibara went on to argue that our lawsuit against Ambassador Kiplagat had undercut their efforts to have him resign, thus suggesting that we were responsible for the government's inability to do anything at the moment. It was difficult to understand how we could give any credibility to the assertion that the government had and would always adopt a hands-off approach to us given these revelations.

There are a number of curious things about the revelation that the government had asked Kiplagat to resign. First, it indicated that the Ministry and the Office of the President had been (and presumably continued to be) in close touch with Ambassador Kiplagat and, at least according to Kibara, had been exerting its power to push a possible solution. This was hardly the course of action of an executive branch that had decided not to interfere in our operations (though, in this case, it would be an interference that we would welcome). Second, it was also curious that while the Ministry and president's office were apparently engaged in such conversations with Ambassador Kiplagat concerning not only his future but also the future of the Commission, no one from those offices communicated to any of the rest of us concerning these efforts and possible ways forward. We had repeatedly asked for their assistance in these and other matters and each time, as reported to me, we were rebuffed. Third, back in April 2010, Ambassador Kiplagat had reported to us that Kibara (who at the time was the chief legal officer at the Ministry) had asserted that Kiplagat could not legally resign. Kibara's assertion that the Ministry had pushed Kiplagat to resign threw into question the accuracy of Ambassador Kiplagat's reports to us concerning the position of the Ministry with respect to this issue, providing further evidence that he had been less than candid with us concerning his conversations with the government and perhaps with respect to his other activities. It was also possible that Kibara was now misrepresenting that earlier conversation to us.

As we debriefed among ourselves after this meeting and reviewed the messages it was meant to convey from the Ministry, we received a letter from Francis Kimemia, the secretary to the Cabinet, inviting the Commission to attend a meeting of the National Security Advisory Committee. What was particularly significant about the letter was that although it was dated April 2 (after Kiplagat had returned to the office), it was addressed to Tecla Wanjala as the acting chair. This suggested that Kimemia, and thus probably the president's office, did not view Ambassador Kiplagat as the current chair of the Commission. It was unclear whether this indicated a difference of opinion between the Ministry and the Office of the President on the relationship between Ambassador Kiplagat and the Commission at that time.

Meanwhile, the new minister of justice wanted to meet with the commissioners without Ambassador Kiplagat. He had had a number of meetings with Ambassador Kiplagat, who, as it was reported to us, would just show up unannounced at the minister's office. We had it on pretty good authority that the minister was not a big supporter of Kiplagat's and would thus not go out of his way to keep him at the Commission. His feelings about Kiplagat, however, were less important than his obvious desire to be seen to be succeeding in his new position. He was a bright and relatively young minister, who was increasingly being discussed as an eventual presidential candidate. He wanted to get the TJRC process moving, if only so that he could take credit for succeeding where his predecessor had failed. Perhaps he was also attuned to the fact that if the TJRC was perceived to have been a failure or a whitewash, it would undercut the political argument the government was trying to make regarding the ICC, viz., that Kenya should be allowed to address violations committed on its territory using its own domestic process. I was, and continued to be, amazed at how little the government tried to use us for that purpose. Perhaps the absence of Kiplagat led them to avoid that strategy, but even while he was with us, we were starved of funds and frustrated over and over again in our dealings with the Ministry, hardly a strategy designed to present us as a viable alternative to the ICC.

We met with the minister on April 10. The tenor of the meeting could not have been more different than our interactions with his predecessor. While Kilonzo often lectured us about what we should and should not do, Wamalwa came across as a more studious listener and appeared to be genuinely interested in engaging with us about the process. We had prepared a document for the meeting – an "aide-mémoire"[28] – that set out the history of our efforts to address the problems raised by the conflicts of interest of Kiplagat, and that set out four conditions for us to continue working with Ambassador Kiplagat. Those conditions were:

(1) Ambassador Kiplagat will review drafts of the final report in the same manner and at the same time as other commissioners. The final report is being prepared by a technical team of experts under the supervision of

---

[28] The full text of the aide-mémoire can be found at TJRC Final Report, *supra* Chapter 1, note 9, at Vol. I, Appendix 10.

a committee of the Commission. Once a draft of the report is ready, commissioners will be given an opportunity to review and comment on the draft. The technical team will then redraft the report taking into account the comments of the commissioners.

(2) Ambassador Kiplagat will not be allowed to review those sections of the report that concern areas in which he has a conflict of interest, including those parts of the report concerning massacres, political assassinations, and land. Ambassador Kiplagat will be given the same rights and opportunities as any other adversely mentioned person. Thus, if the report includes an adverse finding concerning Ambassador Kiplagat, he will be given the same opportunity as other adversely mentioned individuals to respond to that finding and to have his response taken into account in the final drafting of that finding.

(3) Ambassador Kiplagat has refused to honor a summons to testify before the Commission. He is the only person to date who has so refused a summons. Unless Ambassador Kiplagat agrees to testify before the Commission pursuant to this summons, the Commission reserves the right to pursue legal enforcement of its summons as provided for under Section 7(6) of the Act.

(4) Ambassador Kiplagat must agree to comply with the decision-making processes of the Commission set forth in the act and as established by resolutions of the Commission. The Commission has operated successfully for over fifteen months with these procedures, and all of the other commissioners to date have abided by them.

Part of our purpose in meeting with the Minister was to discuss the challenges we faced in issuing our report by May 3, which was the current statutory deadline. We argued that we could finish the report sometime between May 3 and August 3, which was the day the Commission would be dissolved after its three-month winding-down period. We wanted to use the three-month winding-down period provided for in the act as part of our operational period, thus giving us an additional three months to finish the report. In other words, we were not asking for additional time. Kibara, who was also at the meeting, argued that we did not have legal authority to work on the report after the statutory deadline of May 3, as working on the report constituted "operations," and we did not have the authority to "operate" between May 3 and August 3, only to "wind down" our affairs. This could be remedied by amending the act to make clear what we could and could not do during that period and also to clarify what was meant by operate – for the act obligated us to engage in a number of activities during our three-month winding-down period.

The minister and his staff appeared more comfortable giving us an additional three months (rather than reallocating our existing time), thus moving the deadline for issuing the report to August 3 and providing a winding down period of three months between August 3 and November 3.

In order to obtain support for such an extension, however, the minister stated a number of times that we needed to show that we were no longer a divided Commission – in other words, that we had "reconciled" with Ambassador Kiplagat. We all agreed that our aide-mémoire would be the basis for such an agreement. Kibara had already informed us that Ambassador Kiplagat was agreeable to the provisions set out in the aide-mémoire.

We concluded the meeting with an agreement to attend a follow-up meeting with all of us, including Ambassador Kiplagat, chaired by the minister, the next afternoon. The purpose of that meeting would be to explore the possibility of us reaching an agreement with Ambassador Kiplagat based upon the four requirements set out in the aide-mémoire. Notwithstanding the fact that Kibara and others had represented to us that Kiplagat had already agreed to what we were asking in the aide-mémoire, many of us were skeptical – skeptical that he had in fact agreed, and even if he had agreed, that he would stick to the agreement given his past record of reneging on previous promises.

DEFINING KIPLAGAT'S CONFLICTS

At the meeting the next day, April 11th, we faced a potential stumbling block concerning the scope of Ambassador Kiplagat's conflict with respect to issues related to land. Ambassador Kiplagat took the position that he should only be excluded from any discussion or decisions related to the specific plots of land that he had acquired but not any other issue concerning land, including how one might define irregular or illegal acquisition. Tom Ojienda, who continued to assert his expertise as a land lawyer, very forcefully supported Ambassador Kiplagat and took the same position. The rest of us expressed concerns about this approach, noting for example that given the allegation that Ambassador Kiplagat had "illegally or irregularly" acquired these plots of land, he would understandably have an interest in how we defined and interpreted the concept of illegal or irregular acquisition of land. The minister was clearly intent on being able to announce an agreement. Commissioner Shava picked up on this and cleverly suggested that the question of the scope of the restriction on Ambassador Kiplagat was a detail that we could work out internally but that we could say that we had reached an agreement in principle. The minister was quick to accept this characterization. After some additional discussion on this and other matters, the minister called in the media and announced that we had come to an agreement, that we had reconciled among ourselves, and that our work was so important that the minister would be asking Parliament for an additional three-month extension to allow us to finish the work as a united team.

While there is very little, if any, precedent with respect to conflicts of interest and truth commissions, there is a good deal of jurisprudence with respect to conflicts of interest of public officials, including judges and members of commissions of inquiry and investigation. There are two approaches to such conflicts of interest with respect to public officials and members of commissions of inquiry: (1) resignation, and (2) recusal with respect to the matter for which there is a conflict of interest. While many, both within and outside the Commission, had argued that he should resign, Ambassador Kiplagat was adamant that he would not agree to such a remedy. While he had "stood aside" – effectively a temporary resignation – for fourteen months, the fact of his return and the manner in which he had conducted himself since then made clear that he was not open to resigning. With the refusal of the chief justice to reestablish the tribunal, there was no possibility of any credible and definitive ruling on the seriousness of his conflicts of interest, much less what he or we should do as a result.

We were thus left with the second option, which is recusal. The question then is how to define the scope of the conflict of interest. This was the issue Ambassador Kiplagat himself had raised with respect to his personal interest in the land issue. One could raise a similar issue with respect to assassinations and massacres – should he be recused only from any discussions related to the Wagalla massacre, or perhaps even just any discussion of the meeting he attended of the Kenya Intelligence Committee just before the massacre? With respect to land, Commissioner Ojienda had argued that Kiplagat should only be recused with respect to any determination we might make concerning his specific acquisition of the disputed parcels of land. This was clearly too narrow a definition of his conflict of interest. If we adopted Commissioner Ojienda's approach, then Ambassador Kiplagat would have input into a number of matters that would touch upon his personal interest. For example, we had not decided whether, and to what extent, we would discuss or opine on the various land transactions that had been brought to our attention. It would clearly be within his interest to have us not discuss specific land transactions. We had also not decided what criteria we would use to label a land acquisition as illegal or irregular. Whether Ambassador Kiplagat's acquisitions of parcels of land were illegal or irregular would depend on what criteria we used and how we interpreted, and then applied, those criteria to his specific transactions. A similar set of issues applied to our treatment of massacres generally and the Wagalla massacre specifically. The criteria we would use to determine whether a particular incident qualified as a massacre; our evaluation of the level and extent of government complicity in such incidents, and how we defined such complicity; our decisions concerning who we would recommend for further investigation and possible prosecution; these and many other similar decisions facing us would affect our ultimate evaluation of his involvement in the Wagalla massacre.

There are three standards for determining when recusal is warranted. First, a recusal is warranted when there is an actual and direct conflict of interest. For example, a specific decision that would directly benefit or harm the decision-maker. In Ambassador Kiplagat's case, this would be a specific decision concerning whether a plot of land he acquired from the government was acquired illegally or irregularly and what, if any, penalty should be imposed if the acquisition was found to be improper. The formulation of the Commission's test concerning what qualifies as an illegal or irregular land transaction would also be a direct conflict, for our decision concerning the propriety of Ambassador Kiplagat's acquisition of a parcel of land would depend to a large extent on the standard we applied to that transaction. Second is an objective test concerning a perception of bias. In other words, an individual should recuse himself from a matter if there is an objective and reasonable basis for doubting his impartiality. There are a number of ways in which different legal systems have articulated this test. Third is a subjective test concerning a perception of bias. This subjective test would require that an individual recuse himself if any party to a matter believed the individual would be impartial, no matter how unreasonable that belief.

One can discern from these different approaches to bias and conflicts of interest a set of rules on recusal that is grounded in certain basic, fundamental human rights, including the right of an individual to have her claim adjudicated by an impartial decision-maker and the importance of preserving public confidence in the administration of justice. While courts of law, at least in domestic legal systems, may avail themselves of the power of the state to enforce their judgments, it is often the case that such enforcement actions are unnecessary since the judicial process is widely viewed as fair and impartial. This confidence in the integrity of the judicial system results in a high level of compliance with its judgments. This is summed up in the trite expression: Justice must not only be done; it must be seen to be done.[29]

---

[29] The exact quotation is "justice should not only be done, but should manifestly and undoubtedly be seen to be done." *R v. Sussex Justice ex parte McCarthy* [1924] 1 KB 256, 259.

Truth commissions, unlike domestic courts, are much more limited in their power to issue binding decisions that are enforceable by the police power of the state. Truth commissions rely upon their stakeholder's perception of their integrity and impartiality. The government of Kenya had this reality in mind when it made sure that the Kenyan commissioners were broadly representative of Kenyan society, and thus included individuals from many of the major ethnic groups of Kenya. This was part of the concern raised by the government in response to the pressure to have Kiplagat removed – if he were removed, his ethnic group, the Kalenjin, would no longer have a representative on the Commission, and this would give rise to a perception of bias or partiality.

Ironically, the reaction of Ambassador Kiplagat to concerns raised by his conflicts of interests increased the reasonableness of the perception that he would be biased. For example, his legal challenge to the authority of the tribunal to evaluate his conflicts of interest is in stark contrast to his earlier claim that he welcomed such a process, and raised a reasonable inference that he did not want such a process. His actions suggested that he did have something to hide. His assertion that the internal rules of the Commission concerning access to sensitive information did not apply to him similarly raised questions about his commitment to the integrity of the process.

THE MORE THINGS CHANGE, THE MORE THEY STAY THE SAME

Our "reconciliation" with Kiplagat facilitated by the minister of justice was, as we had feared, more of a one-way street. Ambassador Kiplagat continued to speak publicly and engage in activities on our behalf without our knowledge, much less our consent. Shortly after we had come to an agreement that he would recuse himself from the three areas in which he had a conflict of interest, he immediately lobbied individual commissioners to give him full access to the discussions and drafting of the parts of our report concerning the Ouko assassination, land, and the Wagalla massacre. He had made some statements during our meeting with the minister that suggested his concern with our agreement went far beyond how we defined his conflict of interest with respect to land. While he had indicated his agreement that he should have nothing to do with our deliberations concerning Wagalla, Ouko, and land, he had also said that he "could not cut himself off from Wagalla," for he had certain documents that might help us in understanding that massacre. This was an outrageous position for the chair of a truth commission to take. His saying that he had documents related to the Wagalla massacre – presumably documents in addition to those he had already submitted to us when he testified before us – suggested that he had been withholding important information from us. He was now trying to use his claim that he possessed additional documents relevant to our investigations to blackmail us into allowing him to influence that part of our report. This only further underscored why he could not be a part of our substantive discussions about how we would describe and evaluate the Wagalla massacre.

Kiplagat also indicated that he had certain views about land that he wanted to share with the Commission. This was puzzling as he had refused to honor our subpoena to testify before us concerning land. In both of these examples (Wagalla and land), he was conflating his ability to provide information to us concerning an issue within our mandate with his participation in our internal deliberations concerning the same issues. He either was unable to grasp that distinction or was trying to use his possession of information relevant to our work as a lever to force us to give him access to those sections of the report involving him. While we resisted this pressure from him until the end, he never gave up his desire to influence these sections of the report. He even suggested at one point that he provide us with documents concerning the three areas so that we could examine them and clear him, which was ironic given that he had been saying for a while now that he had been "cleared" already by the courts. This was, in the end, yet another example of his dancing around the issues with which he had an interest, as he never did submit such materials to us. While the other commissioners and I held firm to our original agreement, it is a credit to our staff, particularly those safeguarded with shepherding the writing of the report, that he was kept from altering the content of those sections of our report with which he had a clear personal interest.

We could not, and I fear did not, prohibit him from sharing parts of the report with others outside of the Commission contrary to our express internal rules. While this was disappointing, it was not surprising, as he had already made it clear that he did not recognize the validity of any of our internal procedures – at least as they purported to apply to him. He was at times quite open about his willingness to share our internal deliberations inappropriately with those outside the Commission. At a meeting we attended with the National Security Advisory Committee (NSAC),[30] he confidently stated that

---

[30] The NSAC is chaired by the secretary to the Cabinet, which was Francis Muthaura until he resigned in February 2012, and then, during the remainder of the Commission's life, Francis Kimemia. The NSAC consists of senior members of the security services, including the military, the police, and the intelligence services. It provides advice to the Cabinet Security Committee, and direction and intelligence to the provincial and district intelligence committees. *See* REPORT OF THE COMMISSION OF INQUIRY INTO THE POST ELECTION VIOLENCE (Nairobi: Government Printer, 2008) [the "CIPEV REPORT"], page 358, for a brief description of the Kenyan security intelligence machinery, including the NSAC.

we would of course share advance copies of the report with the members of that Committee. This was worrying both for the substance of the decision and because he had taken this decision without consulting with, much less informing, us.

The promise by Kiplagat that we would share our report prior to its being made public was made when we were meeting with the NSAC at the end of April 2012. The NSAC had asked to meet with us because they were concerned about the potential political fallout from the report. This was a legitimate concern, and one that all of us were willing to discuss with the NSAC. There is a difference between working with the government both to minimize the politicization of our report and to increase constructive engagement with its content, and changing the content of our report because of political concerns of the government (no matter how well founded). In offering to share advance copies of the report to the NSAC, Kiplagat was indicating his openness to the latter position.

The NSAC had other concerns with respect to the report based on misinformation they had received concerning the report-writing process. In particular, they were concerned with the role Ambassador Dinka and I were playing. The report was being written by a large team of researchers and outside consultants. The Commission had tasked Commissioner Wanjala, Ambassador Dinka, and me to oversee this process, which included editing drafts of chapters as they were completed by the staff writers. Once we had approved a chapter, it was then circulated to other commissioners for their comments, suggested changes, or approval. We undertook this process both for reasons of efficiency, but also to create a structure that would keep Ambassador Kiplagat away from those parts of the report with which he had a conflict of interest.

The NSAC was concerned that the report was being primarily written by foreigners – i.e., Ambassador Dinka and me. We had been warned about "foreign interference" in our activities since the early days of our creation – which was a bit ironic given the important role that foreign actors had played in facilitating the end of the post-election violence, a role that had enjoyed the support of all of the major political parties at the time. When Ambassador Muthaura was the permanent secretary in the Office of the President, he had warned us about foreign influences on our work. He was particularly concerned about foreign influence with respect to our investigations. This was perhaps not surprising, as at the time he expressed these concerns he was being investigated by the ICC prosecutor. Now his replacement, Francis Kimemia, was warning us about such foreign influences and expressed his concern that two foreigners were overseeing the report writing. We responded that while the two of us were assisting in the drafting and editing of the report, there were twenty-six Kenyans who were writing the report. We also noted that our director of research, a Kenyan, was the primary person overseeing the drafting; that we were a Committee of three that included a Kenyan (Commissioner Wanjala) as its chair; and that our role was not to finalize but to get chapters in readable shape for review, debate, and modification by commissioners and to ensure that our findings were supported by sufficient evidence.

As a descriptive matter, therefore, it was patently false to say that the report was being drafted by foreigners. To the extent that the NSAC was concerned that the report would include unsubstantiated allegations, their focus would have been more appropriately directed at some of the Kenyan writers. Ambassador Dinka and I quickly discovered that many of the younger Kenyan writers were quick to include strong, and usually unsubstantiated, allegations against prominent Kenyan officials in their drafts. If there was no authority provided for such claims, Ambassador Dinka and I would remove them. For example, one draft claimed that President Jomo Kenyatta had ordered the assassinations of Pio Gama Pinto, Tom Mboya, and J. M. Kariuki. We had no evidence (much less conclusive evidence) pointing to such direct involvement by President Kenyatta and thus removed those assertions. In fact, the educated Kenyans we had hired seemed to assume the worst about their own government. Perhaps because we were from the outside, both Ambassador Dinka and I were meticulous in making sure our written report accurately reflected the evidence and other information we had received during our operational period.

THE REPORT AND OUR FINDINGS: KIPLAGAT'S ENDGAME

While the last few months of our lifespan were dominated by the president's interference in the content of our report (see Chapter 1), Ambassador Kiplagat continued to push for access to and influence over those sections of the report that implicated him. The additional year's extension we had received provided him with ample time to try to influence those sections of the report.

As we approached our new deadline of May 3, 2013 for the handing over the report, we decided to formalize in writing our procedures for commissioners to review and approve chapters of the report. We had already, in March 2011, adopted certain policies regarding our findings and recommendations.[31] As with many such things, these policies were drafted in reaction to challenges faced by other truth commissions in developing their findings and recommendations. We were informed, for example, that in Sierra Leone some

---

[31] *Commission Decision-Making by Email, and for Findings and Recommendations* (March 14, 2011), available on book's website.

Commissioners refused to vote for or against a particular finding or recommendation. We were told that abstaining allowed such commissioners to later claim that they did not approve of a particular finding or recommendation. We thus drafted procedures that provided for the opportunity to approve of findings or recommendations by email if we could not secure a quorum for three consecutive meetings. The procedures also provided that silence by a Commissioner was to be interpreted as consent. Finally, we agreed that if consensus could not be reached on a finding or recommendation, then we would decide by a vote of the majority, and the record of the vote would include how each commissioner had voted. As it turned out, none of the issues these provisions were designed to address were raised in our case. The challenges we faced concerned the narrative content of the report and not our findings and recommendations.

In April 2013, we were in the final stages of the report writing. Commissioners had reviewed most of the chapters. Pursuant to the aide-mémoire we had prepared for the minister of justice and that formed the basis for our "reconciliation" with Ambassador Kiplagat, he had not been given the chapters on land, assassinations, and massacres for comment and review. While he was not to have input on the content of those chapters, he was entitled to see the final versions of each so that he could decide if he wanted to sign the report, or sign the report and write a dissenting opinion, or not sign the report. We had adopted general procedures for a commissioner to dissent or not sign the report. First, we adopted a rule that a commissioner would have to exercise her right to dissent within forty-eight hours of receiving the chapter or chapters from which she wanted to dissent. Second, we tied the filing of a dissent with the obligation to sign the report. In other words, if a commissioner decided to dissent from a part of the report, she was then obligated to sign the report. If a commissioner did not want to sign the report, then she was free to abstain from signing it, but she could not then also have a dissent included in the report. Third, we decided that both the dissent and any response by the majority to the dissent would be appended to the relevant chapter of the report.[32]

Pursuant to this policy, Ambassador Kiplagat was given the final version of the chapters on land, assassinations, massacres, and the chapter on challenges (a substantial part of which discussed the challenges we faced because of his presence on the Commission). Based upon his review of these chapters, he indicated that he would be drafting a dissent to the chapter on challenges. He also requested that he be able to contribute substantively to those chapters

---

[32] *Final Report Procedures* (April 16, 2013) on website.

from which he was not dissenting (i.e., the chapters on land, assassinations, and massacres). We declined the latter request. At this late stage of the process, he continued to threaten us if we did not accommodate him. He threatened, for example, to go public concerning allegations of corruption within the Commission unless we removed the discussion of him in the challenges chapter. This was outrageous on a number of levels, not the least of which was his implicit offer to cover up evidence of corruption if we acceded to his demands. We refused, and encouraged him to make public any evidence he might have concerning corruption within the Commission. To my knowledge, he never produced any credible evidence of corruption as he had threatened. In the end, Ambassador Kiplagat's dissent consisted of us appending to the chapter on challenges the open letter he had written to the commissioners and staff in January 2012 upon his unexpected return to the office.[33] While we felt that the letter illustrated one of the many challenges his presence created for us (e.g., his refusal to abide by internal Commission rules on access to sensitive documents), he apparently saw his letter as vindicating his position.

In the end, I can confidently state that Ambassador Kiplagat had no influence over the content of the chapters of the report in which he had a conflict of interest. As an indication of our commitment to the integrity of the process, one need only point to our recommendation that Kiplagat be barred from ever holding a position of public trust, and that he be investigated for possible prosecution for his involvement in the Wagalla massacre.[34]

Kiplagat is reported to have told a number of people that he was a long-distance runner. The implication is that he would be in this for the long run, far after all the rest of us had departed the scene. While the metaphor of a long-distance runner has some appeal as a message of ultimate vindication if the other "runners" do drop off, its meaning becomes quite different when the "runners" continue to race. And, of course, this is not a race. It is a process that involves the people of Kenya, and they are not about to give up. Eventually one has to stop running, and when that happens, it is the weight and judgment of history that takes over. I suppose Kiplagat thought he would have the power to craft that history, and thus succeed in drafting history's judgment of himself. It was a tragic fight, which not only crippled the Commission, but more importantly diminished the process of truth, justice, and reconciliation in a country that so clearly needed and wanted it. It was also tragic at a personal

---

[33] TJRC FINAL REPORT, *supra* Chapter 1, note 9, at Vol. I, Appendix 7 ("Ambassador Kiplagat's Statement on Resumption of Office").

[34] *Id.* at Volume IV, Chapter Four, p. 133.

level. Ambassador Kiplagat entered this process with a generally positive public image, particularly given the important role he had played as peace-maker during the 2007–2008 election violence. His stubbornness and prevari-cation on, among other things, his attendance at the intelligence committee meeting in Wajir less than two days before the massacre, imprinted an indelible stain on his character that will be difficult to remove.

6

Ships Passing in the Night: The ICC, the Kenyan Government, and the TJRC

In June 2012, a month before I was to leave Kenya to return to Seattle, I was staying at a hotel in Mombasa with the other commissioners and senior staff of the TJRC drafting and reviewing sections of our final report. I received a message from a friend from my law school days who was working in the Office of the Prosecutor at the International Criminal Court. He wrote to ask if I would be willing to meet confidentially with investigators from his office who were currently in Kenya. Up until this point, there had been only sporadic, and informal, conversations between the ICC and the Commission. During the first year of our existence, we had discussed meeting with the ICC to establish a framework for the fulfillment of our two mandates that would complement each other and avoid potential conflicts. No such meeting between the two institutions ever took place. From our side, the majority of commissioners (along with some of the senior staff) were at best indifferent and in many cases hostile to the ICC. From the point of view of the ICC, it appears we were viewed as tainted and irrelevant given the unresolved issues surrounding our chair. The ICC had been involved in Kenya for the same amount of time as the Commission. While many Kenyans had initially greeted the ICC with enthusiasm and high expectations, support for its activities was slowly eroding as little progress had been made in holding individuals accountable for the atrocities committed just after the December 2007 elections. The fact that the prosecutor's office was reaching out to us for assistance was a further sign of the challenges facing efforts to hold those most responsible accountable. It was a rare moment when the two institutions – the ICC and the TJRC – engaged with each other, albeit unofficially. Nothing was to come from that meeting.

Notwithstanding the lack of engagement between the TJRC and the ICC, we owed much of the timing of our creation to the activity of the latter. Although the political parties agreed during the negotiation of the National

Accord in March 2008 to create a truth commission, it was only after the threat
of ICC intervention over a year later that the government moved to establish
the Commission. The legislation establishing the TJRC was first drafted in
May 2008. After undergoing various revisions, some of which civil society
initiated, the bill was passed into law in October 2008, though it was amended
a few times after its initial passage. It took almost another year, until August
2009, for the commissioners to be chosen and sworn in. It was the completion
of the work of another Commission arising out of the National Accord, the
Waki Commission, that led to the involvement of the ICC and the creation of
the TJRC.

The Commission of Inquiry into the Post-Election Violence (CIPEV, also
referred to as the Waki Commission after its chair, Judge Philip Waki) was one
of the three *ad hoc* commissions created as part of the National Accord that
ended the near-genocidal violence that arose out of the disputed 2007 presidential election between the incumbent, Mwai Kibaki, and his challenger,
Raila Odinga.[1] The 2007 election-related violence (or "PEV") engulfed most
of the country from late December 2007 until the end of February 2008 when
the peace agreement facilitated by the Panel of Eminent African Personalities (chaired by former UN Secretary General Kofi Annan) resulted in the
National Accord and the creation of a coalition government. The coalition
government divided power between the two contesting parties: the presidency
remained with Mwai Kibaki, and Raila Odinga was given the newly formed
position of prime minister.

The Waki Commission consisted of three individuals – Judge Philip Waki
of Kenya, Gavin McFadyen of New Zealand, and Pascal Kambale of the
Democratic Republic of the Congo – who were sworn into office on June 3,
2008. It is not clear why the government moved somewhat quickly to establish
the Waki Commission (a mere four months after the agreement creating the
coalition government), while the TJRC had to wait an additional year before
its creation. Perhaps it reflected the government's recognition of the need to
address the most recent, and therefore what was perceived to be the most
crucial, violence that had engulfed most of the country and had almost resulted
in a genocide. More cynically, perhaps the government felt that the Waki Commission would be relatively weak in its operations and recommendations, and

---

[1] The other two *ad hoc* commissions were the Independent Review Commission on the General
   Elections held in Kenya on December 27, 2007 (also known as the Kriegler Commission, after
   its chair, South African Judge Johann Kriegler); and the Truth Justice and Reconciliation
   Commission. The National Accord also created the Committee of Experts, which successfully
   drafted the 2010 Kenyan constitution, and a permanent commission, the National Cohesion
   and Integration Commission, to address the ethnic and other divisions that plague Kenya.

thus appointing such a Commission would create the appearance of addressing the more recent past without risking the reputations and careers of those still in power. This would not have been an unreasonable assumption on the part of the government – Judge Waki was a long-serving judge in the notoriously corrupt Kenyan judiciary, having joined the High Court bench in 1994 and then been elevated to the Court of Appeals in 2004. His appointment to head CIPEV was probably viewed with indifference by those in power, who may have assumed (reasonably so) that they had little to fear from a commission chaired by this long-serving establishment judge.

The Waki Commission was given very little time to do its work. Its term was originally set to expire on August 22, 2008, which was less than three months after its commissioners were sworn in. Judge Waki and his colleagues immediately lobbied for extensions, which were granted piecemeal by the government. The piecemeal nature of the extensions meant that the Commission could not adequately plan for its activities – a problem that we, too, at the TJRC were to experience. The Waki Commission did have the advantage, however, of financial support from the United Nations, which covered the expenses of its staff. By the time the TJRC was formed, the willingness and ability of the United Nations and its member states to provide such financial support had shifted dramatically, and we were to receive very little direct financial support from any of them.

Despite the short amount of time allocated to its activities, the Waki Commission handed over its report to the president and prime minister on October 15, 2008, a little over four months after its commissioners had been sworn in.[2] Given the short amount of time it was given to do its work, its accomplishments were impressive.

The report of the Waki Commission was to have a major impact on the future of the country, not least of which was the eventual decision of the Prosecutor of the International Criminal Court to request, and then to be granted, authority to open an investigation to prosecute those most responsible for the post-election violence. In a relatively short period of time, the Waki Commission had collected testimony and other evidence concerning the post-election violence, some of which was set out in its over 500-page report. Based upon its investigations, the Waki Commission identified a number of alleged perpetrators, though as the Commission itself acknowledged in its report, the evidence implicating these individuals was preliminary and required further investigation:

[2] *See* South Consulting, *The Kenya National Dialogue and Reconciliation Monitoring Project, Agenda Item 2, Report on Statute of Implementation*, para. 15 (January 2009).

The evidence the Commission has gathered so far is not, in our assessment, sufficient to meet the threshold of proof required for criminal matters in this country: that it be *"beyond reasonable doubt"*. It may even fall short of the proof required for international crimes against humanity. We believe, however, that the Commission's evidence forms a firm basis for further investigations of alleged perpetrators, especially concerning those who bore the greatest responsibility for the post-election violence.[3]

Although the Waki Commission recognized the need for further investigation of those it had preliminarily identified as candidates for prosecution, it also made clear that the current Kenyan justice system did not enjoy the level of credibility and integrity necessary to perform such further investigations. In a part of its report remarkable for its candor, CIPEV set out the deficiencies of the Kenyan justice system. Its view can be summarized in one sentence taken from the report: "The elements of systemic and institutional deficiencies, corruption, and entrenched negative socio-political culture have, in our view, caused and promoted impunity in this country."[4] This analysis was all the more remarkable coming from a Commission chaired by a prominent and established court of appeals judge from within the Kenyan judicial system who had an insider's view of the challenges facing the Kenyan justice system. The report pointed fingers at a number of domestic institutions that had contributed to this state of affairs, including the attorney general for his lack of progress on prosecuting those responsible for previous incidents of election-related violence: "In view of the lack of any visible prosecution against perpetrators of politically related violence, the perception has pervaded for sometime now that the Attorney General cannot act effectively or at all to deal with such perpetrators and this, in our view, has promoted the sense of impunity and emboldened those who peddle their trade of violence during the election periods, to continue doing so."[5] In addition, evidence was tendered before the Waki Commission that the commissioner of police had ordered that powerful individuals arrested for involvement in election-related violence be unconditionally released from custody.[6]

Given this state of affairs, CIPEV recommended that Kenya establish a hybrid tribunal – consisting of both Kenyan and international judges and staff – to investigate and, where the evidence so warranted, prosecute those

---

[3]　CIPEV Report, *supra* Chapter 5, note 30, at p. 17 (emphasis in original).
[4]　*Id.* at 444.
[5]　*Id.* at 453. *See also* pp. 448–454.
[6]　*Id.* at 458–459.

individuals responsible for the PEV.[7] The proposed special tribunal was loosely modeled on other similar hybrid tribunals that had been established in Sierra Leone and Cambodia.

In order to ensure that the suspects the Commission had identified were properly investigated by a credible process, CIPEV also handed over to Kofi Annan, in his capacity as chair of the Panel of Eminent African Personalities, a sealed envelope with a list of suspects, along with six boxes of supporting evidence. The Panel was instructed that if the government did not establish a hybrid tribunal as recommended, then "consideration will be given by the Panel to forwarding the names of alleged perpetrators to the special prosecutor of the International Criminal Court (ICC) in The Hague to conduct further investigations in accordance with the ICC statutes [sic]. This is a major recommendation made by the Commission."[8]

"DON'T BE VAGUE, LET'S GO TO THE HAGUE"

CIPEV set up a timeline for the creation of its recommended hybrid tribunal. Within sixty days of the handing over of the Waki Commission Report, the president and prime minister were required to sign an agreement to establish the special tribunal. Within forty-five days of the signing of such an agreement, the Waki Report directed that a statute for a special tribunal should be enacted into law and come into force.[9] On December 17, 2009, which was sixty days after the handing over of the envelope to Kofi Annan and sixty-two days after the handing over of the CIPEV Report, the president and prime minister signed an agreement to establish a special tribunal as required by the Waki Commission. Notwithstanding this agreement at the highest levels of government, the required legislation was never passed, and such a tribunal was never created.

There were at least three formal attempts to establish such a tribunal through legislation. Two successive ministers of justice, Martha Karua and Mutula Kilonzo, requested that Parliament pass the required legislation. Political parties and prominent politicians shifted back and forth between support and opposition, mirroring the shifting positions the same politicians and parties would later take with respect to the ICC investigations and

[7] *Id.* at 472–475.
[8] *Id. at* 18. While the language quoted here from the report says that the Panel is to "consider" handing over the envelope and its supporting documentation to the ICC Prosecutor, later in its section on recommendations the Commission says that the envelope and supporting material "shall" be handed over if such a hybrid tribunal was not established. *Id.* at 473.
[9] *Id.* at 473.

FIGURE 6.1 Gado – ICC then and now (Don't be vague). Image courtesy of Gado (gadocartoons.com).

prosecutions. Prominent politicians coined the phrase, "Don't be vague; let's go to The Hague."[10] Ironically the then minister of agriculture, William Ruto, who would later be one of the six Kenyans indicted by the ICC prosecutor, argued publicly that it would be better to have the PEV investigated by the ICC rather than a local tribunal.

While the agreement between President Kibaki and Prime Minister Odinga provided for a Cabinet committee to draft a tribunal bill, such a draft was never presented to Parliament. Instead, the first attempt to create a special tribunal was led by the then minister of justice, Martha Karua, in January 2009. Karua drafted two pieces of legislation: a bill to amend the constitution to allow for the creation of a special tribunal along the lines recommended by the Waki Commission, and a bill that would create such a tribunal.[11] The constitutional amendment was required in order to establish a *sui generis* court

---

[10] *See, e.g.*, Statement by Major Sugow, the Assistant Minister of State for Public Service, who stated during a Parliamentary debate, "To conclude, let me say this: Let us not be vague in this House; let us go to the Hague." Hansard, National Assembly, February 5, 2009, p. 43.

[11] *The Constitution of Kenya (Amendment) Bill, 2009* (which would amend the constitution to allow for the creation of a special tribunal), and *The Special Tribunal for Kenya Bill, 2009* [the "Karua Bill"] (which would create the special tribunal itself). A copy of both of these Bills may be found on the book's website.

outside of the normal Kenyan judiciary, something that was not allowed under the constitution. As an amendment to the constitution, the first bill required a majority of 65 percent to pass. The vote on this first bill failed on February 12, 2009, with 101 MPs voting in favor, and 93 against, falling short of the 65 percent required for passage.[12]

Gitobu Imanyara, a seasoned human rights activist, was one of the most vocal opponents of the Karua bill in Parliament. Imanyara feared that a local tribunal would be vulnerable to political pressure and manipulation and thus preferred prosecutions before the ICC. Similar concerns were raised by a number of the major human rights groups based in Nairobi.[13] While fears of political manipulation motivated one set of opponents to a local tribunal, others opposed a local tribunal (and thus supported the ICC option) assuming that the ICC would take a long time to get to the Kenya situation[14] given the perception that it worked slowly and was already busy with other situations. The ICC option was thus viewed by this second group as a vehicle to delay justice and further impunity. The prime minister later identified these two sets of arguments as motivating some of those who opposed the creation of a local tribunal.[15] While it is difficult to know why certain members of Parliament opposed the bill to create a local tribunal, some who voted against the local tribunal were later quick to raise concerns about the ICC when it appeared that the ICC was moving quickly to identify and indict powerful Kenyans for the post-election violence,[16] suggesting that their votes may have been motivated more by a desire to further impunity rather than accountability.

---

[12] Hansard, Kenya National Assembly, February 12, 2009, pp. 33–34.

[13] *See* Human Rights Watch, "Turning Pebbles": Evading Accountability for Post-Election Violence in Kenya ["Turning Pebbles"] (December 2011), 22–23.

[14] "Situation" is a term of art under the Rome Statute. While it is not defined in the Rome Statute, "situation" refers to a group of crimes (or "crime base") within the Court's jurisdiction committed within a particular geographic and temporal context. Usually a situation encompasses a state (e.g., Kenya), but not always (e.g., Darfur, which is only one part of the state of the Sudan). The ICC prosecutor then brings cases against individuals accused of committing crimes as part of a situation that is before the Court.

[15] Hansard, Kenya National Assembly, December 16, 2010 (P), p. 23 (statement before Parliament of Prime Minister Raila Odinga conveying the government's position on the ICC).

[16] Isaac Rutto, for example, voted against the creation of a local tribunal, and then raised concerns about the ICC process once the names of six suspects were released. In fact, Rutto moved in Parliament to repeal the recently enacted International Crimes Act (by which Kenya had incorporated the Rome Statute into its domestic law) so that, in the words of his motion, "Kenya be immediately released from any obligation to implement the Rome Statute and further that any criminal investigations or prosecutions arising out of the post election violence of 2007/2008 be undertaken under the framework of the new Constitution and that the Government suspends any links, cooperation and assistance to International Criminal Court forthwith." Hansards, Kenya National Assembly, December 16, 2010 (A), p. 30.

There were two additional attempts to create a special tribunal. First, in July 2009, the Cabinet attempted to draft a new bill that would have a higher chance of passage in Parliament.[17] The Cabinet, however, was unable to reach a consensus on a draft, and thus nothing was presented to Parliament. Second, in August 2009, one of the earlier opponents of the bill, Gitobu Imanyara, submitted his own draft bill to create a special tribunal. Imanyara's bill was never discussed in Parliament for lack of a quorum, and died in December 2009.[18]

Imanyara's bill differed from the earlier government bill in a number of respects. First, and most significantly, the Imanyara bill acknowledged the involvement of the ICC, making clear that the special tribunal was to coexist with, and not replace, the ICC process. The bill went so far as to contemplate the tribunal referring cases to the ICC for prosecution, though any decision with respect to an individual ICC prosecution would rest in the first place with the ICC prosecutor, and ultimately with the ICC judges.[19] The Karua bill had made no mention of the ICC. Second, compared to the Karua bill, the definitions of international crimes set out in the Imanyara bill more closely reflected the definitions found in the Rome Statute.[20] Third, the Imanyara bill was more favorable to victims, allowing them to appeal decisions of the tribunal that affected them. Fourth, while the Karua bill included a provision that the prosecutor could "seek" the assistance of relevant government agencies, the Imanyara bill added that such agencies and government officials were obligated to provide such assistance notwithstanding any other legal obligation that might apply.[21] Fifth, and somewhat curiously, the Karua bill imposed permanent lustration from public office for those convicted by the tribunal,

---

[17] See summary of events presented by the PM in Parliament on December 16, 2010. Hansards, Kenya National Assembly, December 16, 2010 (P), at 23. According to the prime minister, a draft was rejected by the Cabinet on July 14, and again on July 30, 2009.

[18] At the scheduled debate on the bill on November 11, 2009, only eighteen of 222 members of Parliament were present. A similar failure to amass a quorum occurred in December. *See* Human Rights Watch, TURNING PEBBLES, *supra* note 12, at p. 24, note 71.

[19] *See* Imanyara Bill, Art. 7(5), which empowers the Tribunal "to invoke Article 14 of the Rome Statute." Article 14 allows a state to refer a *situation* to the Court, not a specific case. (A copy of the bill is on the book's website.)

[20] In the Karua Bill, the definition of crimes against humanity included a discriminatory motive requirement (on national, regional, political, ethnic, racial, cultural, or religious grounds) that is not included in the Rome Statute definition.

[21] Compare Karua Bill, Article 35(4), with Imanyara Bill, Article 32(4). The Imanyara Bill carved out an exception from this obligation, making clear that a government official could invoke the privilege of "non-self-discrimination," which presumably is a typo and meant to refer to the privilege against self-incrimination.

while the Imanyara bill imposed such lustration for "at least ten years," implying that after ten years such individuals might be eligible to hold public office.[22]

THE ICC TAKES AN INTEREST

As these bills were being drafted, debated, and rejected by either the Cabinet or the Parliament, the ICC prosecutor moved forward with his investigations. Shortly after the 2007 election-related violence began, the ICC Prosecutor, Luis Moreno-Ocampo, announced on February 5, 2008, that he was undertaking a preliminary examination to determine if crimes within the jurisdiction of the ICC had been or were being committed in Kenya. Preliminary examinations may be undertaken by the prosecutor with an eye to requesting authority from the Court to open a formal investigation into a situation.[23]

While the International Criminal Court has jurisdiction over some of the worst crimes in the world, it does not have unfettered authority to investigate and prosecute individuals responsible for those crimes. The ICC *complements* the work of national jurisdictions; it does not supplant them.[24] Even if crimes within the Court's jurisdiction have been committed, the Court does not have the power to assert its jurisdiction unless certain requirements are met. First, the situation within which the crimes were allegedly committed must be brought before the Court. This is done in one of three ways: a referral by the Security Council, a referral by a state, or authorization by a panel of judges at the request of the prosecutor. At the time the prosecutor began his preliminary examination of Kenya in January 2008, he had yet to invoke his power to request authority for the initiation of a formal investigation into a situation. Most of the situations up until that point had been referred to the ICC by the states on whose territory the alleged crimes had occurred, and the Security Council had triggered the others.

---

[22] Compare Karua Bill, Article 53(5), with Imanyara Bill, Article 50(5).

[23] In addition to undertaking a preliminary examination to determine if he should request authority to initiate a formal investigation into a situation or case, the prosecutor may also undertake a preliminary examination when a state or the Security Council refers a situation to the Court.

[24] This is one of many differences between the ICC and the earlier *ad hoc* tribunals for the former Yugoslavia and Rwanda, which preempted national jurisdiction rather than complementing it. In other words, the ICTY and ICTR had primacy over national jurisdictions – if the ICTY or ICTR asserted jurisdiction over a case, a competing national jurisdiction would have to defer to the international tribunal. By contrast, the ICC is generally subordinate to national jurisdictions. In other words, if a national jurisdiction is investigating or prosecuting an international crime the ICC cannot assert its jurisdiction except in certain narrow circumstances.

Second, the situation must be found to be "admissible." Admissibility is a term of art under the Rome Statute, and involves two separate inquiries: complementarity and gravity. The complementarity inquiry ascertains whether a genuine investigation or prosecution of the alleged crimes has been undertaken by a state with jurisdiction over the matter. In this case, the question was whether the Kenyan government had undertaken a genuine investigation or prosecution of individuals suspected of responsibility for the PEV. Admissibility of the Kenya cases was thus tied directly to the creation of the special hybrid tribunal recommended by the Waki Commission. The gravity inquiry evaluates whether the scale, nature, manner of commission, and impact of the alleged crimes are sufficiently grave to warrant intervention by the Court. Both of these inquiries are designed to ensure that the Court's limited investigative and prosecutorial resources are only expended on situations that most require them. Thus if a state is already genuinely investigating or prosecuting crimes arising out of a particular situation, or if the crimes are not sufficiently grave, the Court should not intervene.

It is not surprising then that the prosecutor in February 2008 did not immediately ask for approval from a pre-trial chamber to open a formal investigation into whether international crimes had been committed in Kenya. First, he obviously needed time to collect sufficient evidence to persuade a judicial chamber that such crimes might have been committed and that they satisfied the gravity requirement. Second, given the fundamental principle of complementarity, it was proper to wait to see whether Kenya would undertake a credible domestic process to investigate and, if the evidence warranted, prosecute those responsible.

With the successive failures of Parliament to establish a special hybrid tribunal as recommended by the Waki Commission, a high-level bipartisan delegation of the Kenyan government (including the minister of justice and the attorney general) visited Kofi Annan and the ICC prosecutor, Luis Moreno-Ocampo, in early July 2009 to request more time to establish a local mechanism. The Kofi Annan–led Panel of Eminent African Personalities had already agreed that they would wait until the end of August 2009 before handing over to the ICC prosecutor the evidence entrusted to them by the Waki Commission.[25] The Kenyan delegation and the ICC prosecutor jointly issued a public statement noting that if the Kenyan government undertook genuine judicial proceedings against those most responsible for the PEV, the prosecutor would

---

[25] Hans Corell, "Statement by the Legal Advisor to the Panel of Eminent African Personalities," *ReliefWeb* (July 29, 2009), http://reliefweb.int/report/kenya/kenya-statement-legal-advisor-panel-eminent-african-personalities.

have no basis for intervening in the Kenyan situation. As part of this agreed statement of affairs, the Kenyan delegation also agreed to submit to the prosecutor by the end of September "a report on the current status of investigations and prosecutions arising out of [the] post-election violence and any other information requested by the Prosecution [sic] of the ICC to perform its preliminary examinations."[26] In addition, the Kenyan delegation would provide to the prosecutor information concerning measures put into place to ensure the safety of victims and witnesses. Most significantly, the Kenyan delegation agreed to provide to the prosecutor by the end of September:

> information on modalities for conducting national investigations and prosecutions of those responsible for the 2007 violence through a special tribunal or other judicial mechanism adopted by the Kenyan Parliament with clear benchmarks over the next 12 months; in the alternative, if there is no parliamentarian agreement, and in accordance with the Kenyan commitment to end ... impunity of [those] most responsible of the most serious crimes, the Government of Kenya will refer the situation to the Prosecutor in accordance with article 14 of the Rome Statute.

The Kenyan delegation thus recommitted itself to the establishment of a special tribunal despite Parliament's repeated rejection of such a course of action and the failure of the Cabinet to develop its own draft legislation. More significantly, the delegation agreed to refer the Kenyan situation to the ICC if such a tribunal could not be established. This agreement to refer the matter to the ICC meant that the prosecutor would not have to invoke his own powers to initiate an investigation into the situation. This was particularly important as he had never invoked such powers before, and the ICC was coming under increasing criticism as a Court that was "targeting Africa." The "targeting Africa" charge was a bit unfair at the time. While it was true that all of the situations before the Court were in Africa, the vast majority of those situations were before the Court because the African states themselves had requested the Court's intervention. If the prosecutor were to use for the first time his power to initiate an investigation into the Kenya situation, he would provide support to those critics who saw the Court as disproportionately focused on Africa. By securing the agreement of the Kenyan delegation to refer the matter to the Court if it failed to create a special tribunal, Moreno-Ocampo appeared to have forestalled the necessity of using his own powers to bring the Kenyan

---

[26] ICC Office of the Prosecutor, "Agreed Minutes of the Meeting between Prosecutor Moreno-Ocampo and the Delegation of the Kenyan Government," The Hague, July 3, 2009. (A copy may be found on the book's website.)

situation before the Court, thus preserving the argument that, far from the Court "targeting" Africa, the Court was instead accommodating the requests of African states for assistance.

NEGATIVE COMPLEMENTARITY

Less than a week after this agreement between the Kenyan delegation and the prosecutor, Kofi Annan announced on July 9, 2009, that the Panel of Eminent African Personalities had transmitted the envelope and six boxes of support-ing documentation entrusted to them by the Waki Commission to the ICC prosecutor.[27] Less than two weeks after Kofi Annan announced the transfer of the evidence to the ICC, on July 22, President Kibaki created the TJRC by formally appointing the nine commissioners.[28] The chief justice, Evans Gicheru, swore us into office on August 3.

The TJRC was thus created in the context of a struggle between the Kenyan government and the ICC prosecutor over whether and how to hold account-able those most responsible for the PEV. This tension over accountability for PEV informed the Kenyan government's view of the TJRC from our incep-tion, and its effects were to resurface a number of times in our dealings with the highest levels of the Kenyan government.

The creation of the TJRC in reaction to the possibility of ICC involvement may be viewed as a successful example of positive complementarity – that is, the ability of the ICC to foster or encourage domestic mechanisms of account-ability. There is no question that the ICC played a role in the creation of the TJRC, though the agreement to create the Commission was a product of the earlier mediated peace agreement arising from the PEV. The government's commitment to an effective and robust truth commission, however, was as problematic as their commitment to creating a domestic tribunal. As the weakness of the ICC cases became more apparent, the government's commit-ment to accountability lessened even more. The disintegration of the ICC cases eventually emboldened the government's commitment to impunity, suggesting that the ICC's influence on domestic accountability in Kenya was ultimately negative. First, some of those who supported accountability voted

---

[27] It appears that while Annan announced the transfer of the evidence on July 9, the prosecutor only received it on July 16. *See* International Criminal Court, *Situation in the Republic of Kenya*, Case No. ICC-01/09, Pre-Trial Chamber II, Office of the Prosecutor, "Request for Authorization of an Investigation Pursuant to Article 15" (November 26, 2009), para. 15. It is not clear what prompted Annan to hand over the evidence when he did.

[28] Gazette Notice 8737, *The Kenya Gazette*, Vol. CXI, No. 70, dated July 22, 2009 (published August 14, 2009).

against the creation of a special tribunal in the belief that the ICC was the better option. While one cannot be certain, there is the possibility that such a tribunal would have been created if the ICC had not been a viable option. Whether such a tribunal would have been more effective than the ICC is, of course, speculative. At the time, I tended to agree with critics like Imanyara who feared that such a local tribunal would be vulnerable to political manipulation and control and thus would give the false appearance of accountability while effectively protecting those most responsible.

Second, the presence of the ICC probably diverted domestic resources away from the TJRC and efforts to increase other domestic mechanisms for accountability. An analysis based on interviews with civil society actors concluded that the ICC intervention in Kenya did not create the dynamics of positive complementarity predicted by the court and some scholars, and it suggested that the intervention of the ICC diverted resources away from efforts to create a credible domestic alternative.[29] We at the Commission saw the effects of this diversion as many civil society groups focused their limited resources on the ICC process rather than the TJRC. While the relationship between the Commission and civil society was complicated, there is no question that the presence of the ICC made it easier for some of the key human rights organizations to focus on supporting the ICC process rather than engaging with the Commission or other similar domestic processes.

The government initially saw the TJRC as a vehicle to prevent ICC intervention. Before we had taken our oath of office on August 3, 2009, the Cabinet was already moving to alter our mandate and powers in response to the threat of ICC intervention. On July 30 (three weeks after Kofi Annan had transmitted the Waki materials to the ICC), the government issued a "Cabinet Statement on the National Mechanism for Dealing with Post Election Violence."[30] The statement revealed that the Cabinet had discussed "extensively and exhaustively" the various options for addressing those responsible for crimes committed during the PEV. The options considered included withdrawal from the Rome Statute and repeal of the International Crimes Act of 2008 (which was the legislation implementing the Rome Statute in Kenya).

---

[29] Christine Bjork and Juanita Goebertus, "Complementarity in Action: The Role of Civil Society and the ICC in Rule of Law Strengthening in Kenya," 14 *Yale Hum. Rts. & Dev. L.J.* 205 (2011). For a detailed and empirically based study of the effect of the ICC on Kenya, and in particular on efforts within Kenya to combat impunity, *see* Lionel Nichols, INTERNATIONAL CRIMINAL COURT AND THE END OF IMPUNITY IN KENYA (Cham: Springer 2015). Nichols concludes that the ICC had little if any effect on combatting impunity, a conclusion consistent with my own experience during this time in Kenya.

[30] A copy of the statement may be found on the book's website.

In addition, the statement noted that "while it will not stand for impunity in the pursuit of justice, the country should equally pursue national healing and reconciliation." The statement concluded with a reaffirmation of the Cabinet's commitment to the Rome Statute and the ICC (notwithstanding the earlier reference to withdrawal); a promise to undertake far-reaching reforms in the judiciary, police and other investigative arms of government "to enable them [to] investigate, prosecute and try perpetrators of post-election violence locally"; and an announcement that the Cabinet "will propose amendments to the Truth Justice and Reconciliation Act that will make the TJRC more representative and effective."

The Cabinet statement threatened to change the fundamental nature of the Commission even before we had been sworn in to office. The reference to making the Commission more representative was not surprising. Kenyan politics is unfortunately dominated by a fetishism of ethnicity. There is an assumption in the political discourse that individuals are first defined by their ethnicity, and thus members of a particular ethnicity will not benefit from a government process unless a member from their tribe is represented in that process. While there is, not surprisingly, some truth to this assumption, there are far more examples of individuals steering government benefits to their immediate family or friends, or even political allies from a different ethnic group, rather than to their larger ethnically defined community. Nevertheless, the public perception of ethnic representation in a process like the TJRC was very important. The six Kenyan commissioners came from six different ethnic groups: Luhya, Somali, Luo, Kalenjin, Kikuyu, and Meru. Kenya contains anywhere from forty-one to over seventy ethnic groups, depending on whom you ask. It is difficult to get accurate information about the ethnic breakdown of the Kenyan population, as there have been few censuses, and those that have been conducted are considered inaccurate. The largest ethnic groups are the Kikuyu (around 22 percent); Luhya (around 14 percent); Luo (around 13 percent); and Kalenjin (around 12 percent).[31] Somalis and Merus each make up approximately 6 percent of the population. While the Commission was thus quite diverse in its ethnic composition, we acknowledged political pressures to make the Commission even more representative. Consequently, in a press release we issued in response to the Cabinet statement (our first public act as a Commission), we stated that we were open to an increase in our membership in order to increase representation on the Commission, though we noted that the membership should continue to be an odd number, and

---

[31] These numbers come from Index Mundi (www.indexmundi.com).

that our numbers should not be expanded so much as to make our operations unwieldy (we recommended not going beyond a total number of fifteen commissioners).[32]

The reference to "effectiveness" in the Cabinet statement was far more worrying. We had heard rumors that the Cabinet wanted to give the TJRC more court-like powers, including the power of prosecution, to address the PEV.[33] We were unanimous in rejecting any modification to our mandate that would make us a criminal court rather than a commission focused on truth, justice, and reconciliation. While we were careful not to take a position on whether the ICC, a special hybrid tribunal, or a local court should handle the PEV cases, we were clear in our press statement that we did not want to take on that task ourselves.

After we issued our press release and held informal discussions with the government, and after a large outcry about the proposed amendments from civil society, the government backed down and did not try again to transform us into a substitute for the hybrid tribunal recommended by the Waki Commission. We were later to learn that some within the government were reluctant to give us the power of a criminal court in part because of the presence of the international commissioners who the government felt could not be trusted to perform the role in a way consistent with the interests of those in control of government. A few months later, in February 2010, the government submitted a report to the Human Rights Council of the United Nations indicating that the TJRC was "not expected to handle perpetrators of post election violence but will only deal within its mandate of correcting injustices."[34]

PEV AS A CRIME AGAINST HUMANITY

With the handing over of the evidence to the ICC prosecutor, and the failure of Parliament to establish a special tribunal as recommended by the Waki Commission, Moreno-Ocampo indicated in early November 2009 that he

---

[32] To place this proposed expansion into perspective, the South African Truth and Reconciliation Commission had seventeen commissioners.

[33] For one report suggesting something sinister in the efforts to make us more effective, *see* "A Government of National Impunity," 50:16 *Africa Confidential* 7 (August 7, 2009). *See also*, The Kenya National Dialogue and Reconciliation (KNDR) Monitoring Project, *Status of Implementation of Agenda Items 1–4: Fourth Review Report*, 8–9 (October 2009) (noting efforts to expand the TJRC mandate to try the PEV suspects).

[34] *National Report Submitted in Accordance with Paragraph 15(a) of the Annex to Human Rights Council Resolution 5/1: Kenya*, A/HRC/WG.6/8/KEN/1 para. 78 (February 22, 2010).

would be requesting authorization to investigate the Kenyan situation under his *propio motu* powers.[35] To authorize such an investigation, the Pre-Trial Chamber had to find that there was "a reasonable basis to believe" that crimes within the jurisdiction of the court had been committed. There was no question that killings, rapes, and other atrocities had been committed during the PEV. In order for such crimes to fall within the jurisdiction of the ICC, however, the prosecutor was required to show that these acts were committed as part of one of three international crimes within the court's jurisdiction: war crimes, crimes against humanity, or genocide. In this case, the prosecutor argued that the killings, rapes, and other atrocities committed in Kenya were part of a crime against humanity.

Crime against humanity was for the first time prosecuted before the international tribunal at Nuremberg established by the victorious Allied powers after World War II. Much of what constituted the Nazi genocide was prosecuted as a crime against humanity; at the time the concept of genocide had yet to be codified as a crime. In order to fall within the jurisdiction of the ICC as a crime against humanity, the killings, rapes, and other atrocities had to be found to be part of "a systematic attack against a civilian population."[36]

In his submission to the Pre-Trial Chamber, Moreno-Ocampo provided evidence that crimes against humanity had been committed in the context of the PEV. At this stage, the prosecutor relied heavily upon the evidence presented in the CIPEV Report (presumably including the confidential evidence he received from the Waki Commission via Kofi Annan), as well as reports from various agencies of the United Nations (including the Office of the High Commissioner for Human Rights) and reports of various Kenyan and international human rights organizations. In his submission, Moreno-Ocampo also noted that there was an "absence of national proceedings related to those bearing the greatest responsibility for these crimes."[37] While he initially did not identify who he thought – or who the Waki Commission thought – might be those most responsible, the Pre-Trial Chamber requested that he

---

[35] *See generally*, International Criminal Court, *Situation in the Republic of Kenya*, Case No. ICC-01/09, Pre-Trial Chamber II, Office of the Prosecutor, "Request for Authorization of an Investigation Pursuant to Article 15" (November 26, 2009). This announcement followed a last attempt on the prosecutor's part to convince the Kenyan government to self-refer the situation to the Court. *Id.* at para 20.

[36] Rome Statute of the International Criminal Court, UN Doc. A/CONF. 183/9; 37 ILM 1002 (1998); 2187 UNTS 90 ["Rome Statute"], Art. 7.

[37] International Criminal Court, *Situation in the Republic of Kenya*, Case No. ICC-01/09, Pre-Trial Chamber II, Office of the Prosecutor, "Request for Authorization of an Investigation Pursuant to Article 15" (November 26, 2009) p. 3.

reveal the names of those being investigated. Moreno-Ocampo thus submitted a confidential list of twenty names of possible suspects.[38]

While the question of whether the PEV qualified as a crime against humanity had important consequences for accountability in Kenya, the ICC's answer to that question also had a significant impact on the development of international criminal law. What constitutes a systematic attack against a civilian population divided the judges of the Pre-Trial Chamber in the Kenya cases, and the division centered on the nature of the organizational require-ment. While two of the judges found that there was a reasonable basis to believe that a systematic attack against a civilian population had occurred, the third judge in dissent argued that the prosecutor had not presented sufficient evidence supporting the assertion that the violence was organized by the state or by an organization that was similar in nature to a state. The majority and dissent divided over what type of organization would satisfy the organizational requirement under the definition of crimes against humanity.

One of the debates during the negotiation of the Rome Statute was whether an attack against a civilian population must be widespread *and* systematic to qualify as a crime against humanity, or whether such an attack would qualify if it were *either* widespread *or* systematic. The definition in the Rome Statute clearly adopts the latter approach, defining crimes against humanity as "a widespread *or* systematic attack directed against any civilian popula-tion . . ."[39] This choice, which suggests that an unorganized but widespread attack against a civilian population would qualify as a crime against humanity, was modified by including in the definition of the phrase "attack directed against any civilian population" the requirement that such an attack must be "pursuant to or in furtherance of a *State or organizational policy* to commit such attack."[40] While it may appear that this was bringing in through the backdoor an absolute requirement for such an attack to be systematic, the drafting history from the Rome negotiations indicates that the formulation resulted from a compromise between those who wanted "and" rather than "or" in the definition of the crime itself. The organizational policy require-ment was not meant to add a systematic requirement to the definition of crimes against humanity. Rather, it was added to distinguish between a situa-tion involving unrelated criminal acts and a situation involving a group of

---

[38] See International Criminal Court, *Situation in the Republic of Kenya*, Pre-Trial Chamber II, Case No. ICC-01/09, "Prosecution's Response to Decision Requesting Clarification and Additional Information," (Public) (March 3, 2010). As part of this submission, the prosecutor submitted a confidential annex (Annex 2) that listed twenty names of potential suspects.

[39] Rome Statute, *supra* note 36, at Art. 7(1) (emphasis added).

[40] *Id.* at Art. 7(2)(a) (emphasis added).

such acts that are united through a policy such that in the aggregate they form a coherent "attack." In other words, the policy element is meant to require some connection among the criminal acts that make up the crime against humanity. As two scholars who have studied the issue have observed, the organizational policy element is intended to be "a flexible test, of a lower threshold than the term 'systematic,' which was understood as a much more rigorous test."[41]

The majority of the Pre-Trial Chamber judges, drawing upon precedent both before the ICC as well as the early jurisprudence of the *ad hoc* tribunals for the former Yugoslavia and Rwanda, held that a group of persons utilizing public or private resources to engage in an attack "which is planned, directed, or organized – as opposed to spontaneous or isolated acts of violence ..."[42] would qualify as an organization for purposes of establishing the existence of a crime against humanity. These same judges also held that the policy need not be expressly articulated but could be inferred from the nature and pattern of the individual acts of violence. To determine whether an organization qualified, the majority adopted a case-by-case approach that "may" take into account a number of considerations, including: "(i) whether the group is under a responsible command, or has an established hierarchy; (ii) whether the group possesses, in fact, the means to carry out a widespread or systematic attack against a civilian population; (iii) whether the group exercises control over part of the territory of a State; (iv) whether the group has criminal activities against the civilian population as a primary purpose; (v) whether the group articulates, explicitly or implicitly, an intention to attack a civilian population; [and] (vi) whether the group is part of a larger group, which fulfills some or all of the abovementioned criteria."[43]

To make clear that they were not setting forth a precise legal definition, the majority concluded the previous list of considerations by noting, "It is important to clarify that, while these considerations may assist the Chamber in its determination, they do not constitute a rigid legal definition, and do not need

---

[41] Herman von Hebel and Darryl Robinson, "Crimes Within the Jurisdiction of the Court," in Roy S. Lee, ed. THE INTERNATIONAL CRIMINAL COURT: THE MAKING OF THE ROME STATUTE – ISSUES, NEGOTIATIONS, AND RESULTS (Cham: Springer, 1999) 97.

[42] International Criminal Court, *Situation in the Republic of Kenya*, Case No. ICC-01/09, Pre-Trial Chamber II, "Decision Pursuant to Article 15 of the Rome Statute on the Authorization of an Investigation into the Situation in the Republic of Kenya" (March 31, 2010) para 84, *quoting* International Criminal Court, *The Prosecutor v. Germain Katanga and Mathieu Ngudjolo Chui*, Case No. ICC-01/04–01/07–717, Pre-Trial Chamber I, "Decision on the Confirmation of Charges" (October 13, 2008) para. 396.

[43] *Id.* at para. 93.

to be exhaustively fulfilled."[44] Nevertheless, the majority was later to find that some of the acts of violence committed during the PEV did not reflect the presence of such an organization, dismissing, for example, many of the first killings and other acts of violence that had been committed in the Nairobi community of Kibera.[45]

Judge Kaul in his dissent disagreed with this analysis and argued for a more precise definition that would exclude some acts of widespread or systematic violence from the jurisdiction of the ICC. Judge Kaul argued that the organization should be "state-like" in its structure, functions, and capabilities in order for its acts to qualify as a crime against humanity. For Judge Kaul, local politicians banding together to foment violence, even with the assistance of criminal gangs, "is an indicator of a partnership of convenience for a passing occasion rather than an 'organization' characterized by structure and membership,"[46] and thus could not meet the organizational requirements for a crime against humanity.

While these debates may seem somewhat technical or academic, they concern foundational issues at the core of international criminal law, and international law generally. One of the world's pre-eminent scholars of crimes against humanity has observed that the disagreement between the majority and the dissent in the Kenya case "is nothing less than a struggle to shape the future jurisdiction and direction of the [International Criminal] Court."[47] A fundamental question for both international law and international criminal law is whether, and why, a particular matter rises to the level of international concern. Like most legal systems, international law adopts the general principle of subsidiarity. In other words, within a hierarchical legal system, issues should be addressed at the lowest level of the hierarchy possible, given the nature of the issue. This preference for subsidiarity in international law serves a number of purposes. First, judicial efficiency: It is more efficient to have local courts address local events rather than to have many or all of them

---

[44] *Id.*

[45] International Criminal Court, *Prosecutor v. Kenyatta et al.*, Case No. ICC-01/09-02/11, Pre-Trial Chamber II, "Decision on the Prosecutor's Application for Summonses to Appear for Francis Kirimi Muthaura, Uhuru Muigai Kenyatta and Mohammed Hussein Ali" (March 8, 2011). A similar conclusion was reached in the same decision with respect to much of the election-related violence in Kisumu.

[46] International Criminal Court, *Prosecutor v. Kenyatta et al.*, Case No. ICC-01/09-02/11, Pre-Trial Chamber II, "Dissenting Opinion by Judge Hans-Peter Kaul to Pre-Trial Chamber II's 'Decision on the Prosecutor's Application for Summonses to Appear for Francis Kirimi Muthaura, Uhuru Muigai Kenyatta and Mohammed Hussein Ali" (March 15, 2011) para 82.

[47] Leila Sadat, "Crimes Against Humanity in the Modern Age," 107 *Am. J. Int'l L.* 334, 335 (2013).

"bumped up" to an international court. A liberal approach to international-izing disputes would risk quickly overwhelming the international system. Second, judicial effectiveness: Local decision-makers are usually in a better position to adjudicate a dispute. Parties and local observers are more likely to trust a familiar, local institution over an unfamiliar, distant one. (This was one of the challenges that faced the ICTY, for example.) Evidence is more accessible at the local level, as are potential witnesses. Local decision-makers are also more familiar with local issues and practices, making it more likely that they will resolve a dispute in a way that better addresses the needs of the local community and that is more likely to be accepted by the local com-munity. These advantages point to some of the risks of depending on local processes: local elites may capture the process, and decision-makers may be biased in favor of one party over another. Third, deferring to local processes acknowledges the importance of national sovereignty. In the case of the ICC, the principle of admissibility ensures that it is only when the local government is unwilling or unable to investigate and prosecute those responsible for an atrocity that the ICC may intervene.

A HISTORY OF INACTION AND IMPUNITY

Regardless of how one defines the requirements of organization and policy for crimes against humanity, and thus where the line should be drawn between purely domestic organized criminal activity and international crimes, it was extremely unlikely that the Kenyan government would hold accountable those most responsible for the PEV. Although Kenya has a history of ethnically based election-related violence, there has been virtually no accountability for those responsible for such violence. One of the motivations for creating the TRJC was to address a wide range of historical injustices, including election-related violence, which had never been adequately addressed.

There were significant ethnic clashes in Kenya in the early 1990s leading up to the first multiparty elections in December 1992. In response to this violence, a Parliamentary Select Committee to Investigate Ethnic Clashes, chaired by Kennedy Kiliku, was created. The recommendations of that Committee were ignored, and no one was prosecuted or otherwise held to account for that violence. The next multiparty election in 1997 was also marred by ethnic violence. In response, a Judicial Commission of Inquiry into Tribal Clashes in Kenya, chaired by Judge Akiwumi, was created. While the Akiwumi Report was submitted to the president in August 1999, it was not made public until the end of 2002. We were unable to get a copy of that report from the gov-ernment despite our repeated requests. We finally received a copy of the report after it was "leaked" to us by a former official who had a copy. The report, needless to say, did not result in any accountability or reforms to prevent future outbreaks of election-related violence. This is perhaps not surprising given that many former and current politicians were named in the report, including Mwai Kibaki, who was president during much of the life of the TJRC.

Lack of accountability in Kenya has not been limited to election-related violence. Individuals responsible for the numerous political assassinations and massacres, along with scores of other violations, have rarely, if ever, been identified, much less held to account. The assassination of Foreign Minister Robert Ouko in 1990 has been the subject of at least four formal investigations: by Scotland Yard (1990), the Kenyan Police (1990), a Judicial Commission of Inquiry (1990), and a Parliamentary Commission of Inquiry (2003). To this day, no one has been prosecuted successfully for the assassination despite these numerous investigations.[48]

In addition to this robust track record of impunity, at the time that the ICC prosecutor was requesting authority to investigate, close to two years had passed without any prosecutions of individuals alleged to have been most responsible for the PEV. Today, over ten years since the PEV, only a handful of very junior individuals have been prosecuted for their participation in the violence, and no one has been identified, much less prosecuted, for any leadership role in the violence.

KENYA'S CAMPAIGN AGAINST THE ICC

On March 31, 2010, the Pre-Trial Chamber of the ICC, for the first time in its history, authorized the prosecutor to initiate an investigation on his own motion – in this case, those most responsible for the PEV in Kenya. Notwithstanding its failure to make any progress in investigating and prosecuting those most responsible, the Kenyan government began a well-organized campaign to argue that Kenya was able and willing to provide accountability and that the ICC should cease interfering in what the government and their supporters characterized as a purely domestic affair. This campaign was multifaceted and had domestic, bilateral, and multilateral components. Domestically, the

---

[48] In fact, there is a lack of clarity concerning how many investigations have been undertaken into the Ouko murder. *See, e.g.,* David William Cohen and E.S. Atieno Odhiambo, THE RISKS OF KNOWLEDGE: INVESTIGATIONS INTO THE DEATH OF THE HON. MINISTER JOHN ROBERT OUKO IN KENYA (Athens: Ohio University Press 1990), 33 (noting five formal investigations and many "lesser" investigations, and that the number of investigations conducted "is a matter of dispute").

Kenyan government appeared to initiate or reinitiate investigations into the PEV from time to time, though none of these efforts led to any significant investigations, much less prosecutions. Bilaterally, the Kenyan government challenged the admissibility of the Kenyan cases before the ICC multiple times, and used its diplomatic presence at the United Nations to urge the Security Council to use its powers under the Rome Statute to intervene and stop the ICC investigations. Multilaterally, the Kenyan government undertook a concerted campaign with the support of the African Union to issue critical resolutions against the ICC, push for amendments to the Rome Statute, and to threaten the withdrawal of African states from the Rome Statute.

In order to argue that a specific case is not admissible before the ICC, a suspect or interested party needs to show that a state is willing and able to investigate and, if the evidence warrants, prosecute the same individuals who are being investigated and prosecuted before the ICC for the same conduct. In the absence of the identity of specific suspects (which is often the case at the preliminary stage of proceedings), one must show that a state is investigating or prosecuting individuals who qualify as those most responsible for the international crimes under investigation by the ICC. At the early stage of the Kenya proceedings, when no suspects were identified, the Kenyan government only needed to show that it was investigating or prosecuting individuals who would qualify as those most responsible for the PEV.

The legal test for the ICC to defer to a local process, clearly laid out in a number of early court decisions, requires domestic investigations or prosecutions of the same suspect for substantially the same conduct as the proceedings before the ICC. An exception to this clearly articulated test arises during court proceedings undertaken prior to the identification of any individual suspects. This exception applied at the early stage of the Kenya cases. When the prosecutor received authorization to initiate an investigation into the Kenya situation in March 2010, he had not yet identified individual suspects. He did, however, at the request of the judges, provide a sealed list of possible suspects that to date has not been made public.[49] At that point, when the prosecutor was only requesting authority to investigate the *situation* in Kenya and not to investigate or prosecute a specific individual, the

---

[49] For the request, *see* International Criminal Court, *Situation in the Republic of Kenya*, Case No. ICC-01/09, Pre-Trial Chamber II, "Decision Requesting Clarification and Additional Information" (February 18, 2010) para. 14; for the prosecutor's response *see* International Criminal Court, *Situation in the Republic of Kenya*, Case No. ICC-01/09, Pre-Trial Chamber II, "Prosecutor's Response to Decision Requesting Clarification and Additional Information" (March 3, 2010).

complementarity inquiry concerned whether the Kenyan government (or any other government that had jurisdiction) was conducting "national proceedings in relation to the *groups of persons* and the crimes allegedly committed during those incidents, which together would likely form the object of the Court's investigation."[50] The Waki Commission had recommended that a special tribunal be created to investigate and prosecute those most responsible for the PEV as an alternative to ICC involvement. Had Parliament established such a special tribunal, it would have been difficult to justify ICC intervention. After noting the failure of the Kenyan government to create a special tribunal as recommended by the Waki Commission, the Pre-Trial Chamber concluded in its March 2010 decision that because there were no "pending national proceedings against 'those bearing the greatest responsibility for the crime against humanity allegedly committed,'"[51] there was no complementarity bar at that stage to authorizing a formal investigation. The Chamber acknowledged that there were ongoing investigations and prosecutions with respect to "minor offenses," but noted that they did not include the category of individuals (i.e., those most responsible) that were the focus of the ICC prosecutor's investigations and thus did not satisfy the requirements of complementarity.[52]

Had the special tribunal been created and initiated investigations into those most responsible for the PEV, there is a good possibility that the Pre-Trial Chamber would not have authorized an investigation. It is even more likely that the prosecutor would not have requested such an authorization. At this early stage of the proceedings, the Kenyan government was not required to show that they were investigating or prosecuting a particular individual for a particular type of conduct. The existence of domestic proceedings through a special tribunal, no matter how weak, would have made it politically, and perhaps legally, more difficult to argue for ICC involvement. As the ICC process progressed, however, the specific showing the Kenyan government would have to make to argue against ICC involvement on the basis of complementarity would become more specific and thus, given the stature and political power of the eventual suspects, politically more difficult.

---

[50] International Criminal Court, *Situation in the Republic of Kenya*, Case No. ICC-01/09, Pre-Trial Chamber II, "Decision Pursuant to Article 15 of the Rome Statute on the Authorization of an Investigation into the Situation in the Republic of Kenya" (March 31, 2010) para. 52 (emphasis added).

[51] *Id.* at para. 183.

[52] *Id.* at para. 185.

With the failure to create a special tribunal, the focus shifted to the domestic criminal justice system for signs of relevant investigations and prosecutions. There had been some, though limited, investigations and prosecutions related to the PEV by the Kenyan government. It is difficult to get credible information concerning the number of investigations and prosecutions – which is, in itself, a sign of the challenges facing the Kenyan criminal justice system. In a report issued in December 2011 (thus four years after the violence), Human Rights Watch found that while the Department of Public Prosecutions had compiled lists of thousands of cases related to the election violence, "there have been few prosecutions and fewer convictions, as well as a near total lack of investigations of those who organized and financed the violence. Hundreds of files literally gather dust in police stations."[53]

The reliability of government statements on PEV-related investigations became open to question as the government proceeded to report wildly conflicting numbers to the ICC in an attempt to force the ICC to drop the cases. In March 2011, the Kenyan Department of Public Prosecutions claimed that there had been ninety-four convictions related to the PEV. At the same time that this department was reporting ninety-four convictions, the chief prosecutor publicly stated that 50 percent of 700 completed PEV-related trials had resulted in a conviction (in other words, there had been 350, not ninety-four, convictions). Nine months later, in January 2012, the government reported that there had been 258 PEV-related convictions instead of the 350 reported nine months earlier.[54] Human Rights Watch's analysis of the ninety-four convictions reported in 2011 revealed that only a small handful of them were for serious crimes related to the violence: two for murder, three for robbery with violence, one for assault, and one for grievous harm.[55] Human Rights Watch also found that despite the estimate of over 400 fatal police shootings and dozens of reported rapes by the police, not one police officer

---

[53] Turning Pebbles, *supra* note 12, at p. 3. For a more detailed critique of Kenyan efforts domestically, *see* Sostenes Francis Materu, The Post-Election Violence in Kenya: Domestic and International Legal Responses (Cham: Springer 2015), 106–115.

[54] *See* Lionel Nichols, *supra* note 29, at p. 97 (citing to various media reports).

[55] Turning Pebbles, supra note 12, at 4. In addition, according to Human Rights Watch, many of the cases included in this list of ninety-four are not related to the election violence at all which, according to Human Rights Watch, is "either intentionally misleading or is the unintended outcome of sloppy work." *Id.* at 25. Human Rights Watch also found that four of the cases on the list of forty-nine convictions for sexual and gender-based violence were, in fact, acquittals. Even more remarkably, the information indicating that these cases were acquittals and not convictions was included in the same government report. *Id.*

had been convicted. While twenty-one victims of police shootings had succeeded in securing civil judgments against the police and thus were entitled to money damages, the government had failed to pay any of them.[56]

While one may question whether any of these numbers accurately reflect the full extent of investigations and prosecutions related to the PEV, there is no evidence that any investigations had been undertaken with respect to prominent politicians, business people, and others who were alleged to have financed and organized the violence. While there may have been such investigations with respect to high-level suspects (notwithstanding the absence of any public evidence of such investigations), there is no question that there have been no prosecutions of such high-level suspects close to ten years after the violence. In March 2015, President Kenyatta announced in his State of the Nation Address that he had received a report from the national prosecuting authority that there was insufficient evidence to pursue further PEV cases, and thus no more would be pursued.

In December 2010, the ICC prosecutor revealed the names of the six Kenyan suspects he was investigating. The six suspects, who were to become known colloquially as the "Ocampo Six," were divided into two separate cases based upon their political affiliation during the 2007 election. The first set of suspects that made up Case One had been affiliated with the Orange Democratic Movement (ODM), the political party whose candidate was Raila Odinga. Those suspects were William Ruto (who in December 2010 was minister of higher education, and who, as of this writing, is deputy president); Henry Kosgey (who in December 2010 was minister of industrialization); and Joshua arap Sang (who is a radio personality with KASS FM, one of the ethnic radio stations that were alleged to have fueled the violence).

The second set of suspects that made up Case Two were individuals from the Party of National Unity (PNU), which was the party of the then-incumbent, Mwai Kibaki. Case Two consisted of Uhuru Kenyatta (who in December 2010 was the deputy prime minister and minister of finance, and who as of this writing is the president of Kenya); Francis Muthaura (who in December 2010 was the head of the civil service, permanent secretary in the Office of the President, and reported to be one of the most powerful men in Kenya at the time); and Mohammed Ali (who was the police commissioner during the 2007 election and who was transferred to the Postal Commission as chief executive in late 2009).

---

[56] *Id.* at 4.

On March 31, 2011, the Kenyan government submitted an application to the court challenging the admissibility of both cases.[57] In its submissions to the court challenging the admissibility of the specific cases against the Ocampo Six, the Kenyan government appeared to misunderstand the change in the legal test for admissibility now that specific suspects had been identified.

With the release of the names of the Ocampo Six in December 2010, the issue of complementarity shifted from whether the Kenyan government was investigating or prosecuting *any* individual for being most responsible for the post-election violence to the more specific question of whether the government was investigating or prosecuting *these six individuals* for their alleged involvement in the post-election violence. Previous decisions of the court had clearly stated that admissibility determinations in the context of a specific case are not based on "hypothetical judicial determination[s]" of the possibility of future prosecutions,[58] but rather on investigations or prosecutions actually "taking place" at the time of the determination.[59] The Kenyan government and its legal team appeared to be unaware of or deliberately ignored these previous decisions as illustrated by the arguments they tendered before the court. The generic "we are reforming our judicial system and thus will be able and willing to prosecute cases like those before the Court" argument offered by the Kenyan government was quite similar to that offered by the defense against the prosecution of the Ugandan commander of the Lord's Resistance Army, Joseph Kony. The Pre-Trial Chamber in the Joseph Kony case noted that notwithstanding the reforms undertaken by the Ugandan government, there was still inaction with respect to the domestic prosecution of Kony himself, which was the relevant focus of the inquiry.[60] That decision was made in 2009, and thus readily available to the Kenyan government. Notwithstanding this clearly applicable precedent, there was no attempt by the Kenyan government to argue that its situation was somehow different from that of the

---

[57] International Criminal Court, *Situation in the Republic of Kenya*, Case Nos. ICC-01/09-01/11 and ICC-01/09-02/11, Pre-Trial Chamber II, "Application on Behalf of the Government of the Republic of Kenya Pursuant to Article 19 of the ICC Statute" (March 31, 2011).

[58] International Criminal Court, *The Prosecutor v. Joseph Kony et al.*, Case No. ICC-01/04-01/05-377, "Decision on the Admissibility of the Case under Article 19(1) of the Statute" (March 10, 2009) paras. 47–52.

[59] International Criminal Court, *Prosecutor v. Germain Katanga and Mathieu Ngudjolo Chui*, Case No. ICC-01/04-01/07-1497 OA 8, Appeals Chamber, "Judgment on the Appeal of Mr. Germain Katanga against the Oral Decision of Trial Chamber II of 12 June 2009 on the Admissibility of the Case" (September 25, 2009) para. 75.

[60] International Criminal Court, *The Prosecutor v. Joseph Kony et al.*, Case No. ICC-01/04-01/05-377, "Decision on the Admissibility of the Case under Article 19(1) of the Statute" (March 10, 2009).

Ugandan government or any indication that the Kenyan government or its lawyers were even aware of the guidance provided by this already existing jurisprudence.[61]

The government did not even attempt to argue that there were existing investigations or prosecutions of the Ocampo Six. Instead, the government argued that general legal reforms – including the adoption of a new constitution – somehow made these specific cases inadmissible. The government argued, for example, that the passage of the new constitution cured the deficiencies in the Kenyan judicial system that had led the Waki Commission to recommend the creation of a special tribunal. While the constitutional and other legal reforms might have convinced the Waki Commission not to recommend that a special tribunal be created and might have satisfied the requirements of complementarity prior to the identification of the six suspects had they happened earlier, the argument that such developments were relevant for determining the admissibility of specific cases before the ICC underscored the government's fundamental misunderstanding of the doctrine and requirements of complementarity. The government's submission went so far as to claim that Kenya had "managed to put in place the necessary reforms to investigate and try all cases at whatever level arising from the post-election violence."[62] The government thus appeared to be conceding that prior to these reforms it had been unable to undertake such investigations and prosecutions.

The government's submission addressed questions concerning the government's "ability" to investigate and prosecute those responsible for the PEV.[63] While the ability of a government to investigate and prosecute is part of the complementarity inquiry, the other prong is whether the government is "willing" to investigate or prosecute, and at this stage of the proceedings, the relevant question was whether the government was *in fact* investigating or prosecuting the specific individuals charged by the ICC prosecutor. As a policy matter, the focus on specific investigations or prosecutions of suspects

---

[61] Curiously the Kenyan government does cite to the Kony admissibility decision, but for reasons having nothing to do with the substantive test established in that decision. *See* International Criminal Court, *Situation in the Republic of Kenya*, Case Nos. ICC-01/09-01/11 and ICC-01/09-02/11, Pre-Trial Chamber II, "Application on Behalf of the Government of the Republic of Kenya Pursuant to Article 19 of the ICC Statute" (March 31, 2011) para. 34, note 24.

[62] *Id.* at para. 8.

[63] Ironically, the government in the same submission acknowledged that the process of reform on which it was relying was not complete, and that existing tensions within the government concerning such reforms "may continue to an extent to characterize the unfolding process of reform." *Id.* at para. 9.

before the ICC makes sense. If the mere promise and ability to investigate or prosecute was sufficient, states could easily make such representations to remove ICC involvement and then not follow up with actual investigations or prosecutions. The Kenya cases certainly underscore the strength of this argument, as more than seven years after the government made these representations to the ICC, there have been no prosecutions of any senior person for the PEV, no evidence that the government has undertaken a serious investigation of the suspects charged before the ICC, and hardly any prosecutions of any individual for the numerous acts of violence committed during the 2007 election period. As already noted, President Kenyatta announced in March 2015 that there would be no more domestic prosecutions arising from the PEV.

The Kenyan government supplemented its admissibility challenge a month later with twenty-two annexes filed with the court on April 21, 2011. This was the first of three such additional submissions, each of which consisted of a hodgepodge of documents and news reports. The Kenyan government appeared to have adopted a kitchen-sink approach, throwing anything at the problem in the hope that at least one would hit its mark. Unfortunately, few, if any, of these documents were relevant, and those that were did not come close to supporting the government's argument of admissibility. The first additional submission in April contained a curious collection of documents. It included a letter from the attorney general, Amos Wako, to the commissioner of police, Matthew Iteere, dated April 14, 2011, directing that all pending cases concerning the PEV be "concluded expeditiously," and that investigations of others alleged to be involved, including the six suspects before the ICC, be investigated.[64] As the prosecution observed in its response, the April 2011 instruction to initiate an investigation against the six suspects suggested that there currently was no such investigation.[65] This was a damaging concession by the Kenyan government as it suggested that such an investigation had not yet commenced, which could be fatal to a claim of inadmissibility. The annexes also included a March 2011 progress report on PEV-related prosecutions that had already been discredited in a lengthy report by Human Rights Watch.[66]

---

[64] *Id.* at Annex 1 (Letter dated April 14, 2011, from S. Amos Wako, Attorney General, to Matthew Iteere, Commissioner of Police).

[65] International Criminal Court, *Prosecutor v. Ruto et al*, Case No. ICC-01/09-01/11-69, Pre-Trial Chamber II, "Prosecution Response to 'Application on behalf of the Government of the Republic of Kenya pursuant to Article 19 of the ICC Statute'" (April 28, 2011) para. 25.

[66] The report was submitted as Annex 3. The Human Rights Watch Report, TURNING PEBBLES, was discussed *supra*, and notes internal inconsistencies within the report (including acquittals listed under convictions). Human Rights Watch also reviewed some of the case files

Many of the remaining annexes consisted of press releases, reports, and resolutions issued by the ICC itself, some on general issues relating to complementarity that had no clear relevance to the Kenyan situation.[67] Others included the text of the new constitution and other pieces of legislation, such as the International Crimes Act and the Witness Protection Act. One annex, ironically, was an article from a Kenyan paper that included a quotation from the US State Department that argued *against* ICC deferral of the cases,[68] and a statement by Human Rights Watch noting (correctly) that for an admissibility challenge to succeed, the government would have to show that there were "genuine national proceedings encompassing both the person and the conduct that is the subject of the case before the ICC."[69]

The Kenyan government continued its scattershot approach, submitting seven additional documents on May 13, 2011, including a reference to an ongoing investigation against one of the suspects, William Ruto.[70] The reference to the Ruto investigation was made in a brief, five-page report concerning investigations into the PEV compiled by the director of criminal investigations and dated May 5, 2011. Coincidentally, the only specific investigation mentioned in this report is the one against William Ruto, which appears to have been based upon allegations made three years earlier, just after the end of the PEV. In addition, the letter also ironically indicated that the police investigators were "taken by surprise" at the identification by the ICC of the six suspects as, except for Ruto, none of the six had been the subject of any ongoing investigation, further undercutting the government's claim for inadmissibility.

mentioned in the government's report and found inconsistencies between the actual file and the government's description of its content.

[67] *See, for example,* Annex 4 (a screen shot of the ICC website with a press statement by the chair of the Assembly of State Parties encouraging Kenya to undertake investigations and prosecutions), Annex 5 (a report by the ICC prosecutor to the Assembly of States Parties from September 2003), Annex 6 (a report to the Assembly of State Parties on the general issue of complementarity, with no direct reference to the Kenya cases), and Annex 15 (an overview of Kenyan efforts to prosecute piracy committed on the high seas).

[68] Kevin J. Kelley, "Local Trials Possible, US Says," *The Daily Nation,* January 29, 2011, included as Annex 8. The State Department is quoted in this article as stating "Deferral or suspension of the ICC process could call into question the political will to ensure accountability for post-election violence and potentially defer or subvert justice for Kenyan victims of the violence."

[69] *Id.*

[70] *See* International Criminal Court, *The Prosecutor v. Ruto et al.,* Case No. ICC- 01/09–01/11–89, Pre-Trial Chamber II, "Reply on Behalf of the Government of Kenya to the Responses of the Prosecutor, Defence, and OPCV to the Government's Application pursuant to Article 19 of the Rome Statute" (May 13, 2011) Annex 2.

Even more curiously, a short three days later, the government submitted documents indicating for the first time that investigations into all six of the suspects before the ICC had been undertaken shortly after the end of the PEV (i.e., in February 2008).[71] This was in direct conflict with the letter written a week earlier by the director of criminal investigations in which he had stated that the police investigators had been "taken by surprise" at the identity of the ICC suspects. It was not made clear why the government had not indicated earlier that such investigations against all six of the ICC suspects had been initiated back in 2008, and no further details were provided concerning those investigations other than the reference to the opening of a case file concerning William Ruto. At best, these filings and the narrative they portrayed indicated a government in disarray – the left hand not knowing what the right hand was doing. At worst, they indicated a government scrambling to create retroactively a record that would support a claim for inadmissibility.

On May 30, 2011, the Pre-Trial Chamber rejected the government's challenge to the admissibility of the cases, expressly rejecting the government's argument that it did not need to show that it was investigating the same individuals the ICC prosecutor was investigating. The Chamber raised the question of whether the government was deliberately ignoring or rejecting clearly applicable precedent, going so far as to call the government's interpretation of precedent as "misleading."[72]

Notwithstanding this clear rebuke of its general reform approach to complementarity, the government attempted to submit a number of investigative updates to advance this now-discredited legal strategy as part of its appeal of the Pre-Trial Chamber decision. The first of these updates was filed with the court on July 4, 2011. The court rejected the update as irrelevant to the appeal of the decision of the Pre-Trial Chamber and as a disguised attempt by the government to convert the appeal into a new challenge on admissibility.[73]

In this appeal, the government continued to argue that it was not required to show that it was investigating the same individuals for the same conduct.

---

[71] International Criminal Court, *The Prosecutor v. Ruto et al.*, Case No. ICC-01/09–01/11–307, Appeals Chamber, "Judgment on the Appeal of the Republic of Kenya against the decision of Pre-Trial Chamber II of 30 May 2011 entitled 'Decision on the Application by the Government of Kenya Challenging the Admissibility of the Case Pursuant to Article 19(2)(b) of the Statute,'" para. 59.

[72] International Criminal Court, *The Prosecutor v. Ruto et al.*, Case No. ICC-01/09–01/11–101, Pre-Trial Chamber II, "Decision on the Application by the Government of Kenya Challenging the Admissibility of the Case Pursuant to Article 19(2)(b) of the Statute" (May 30, 2011) para. 54

[73] International Criminal Court, *The Prosecutor v. Ruto et al.*, Case No. ICC-01/09–01/11 OA "Decision on the 'Filing of Updated Investigation Report by the Government of Kenya in the Appeal against the Pre-Trial Chamber's Decision on Admissibility'" (July 28, 2011).

Despite precedent to the contrary, and despite the express statements of the Pre-Trial Chamber, the Kenyan government continued to argue for the test applicable *before* specific suspects were identified, viz. that the national investigations must "cover the same conduct in respect of persons at the same level in the hierarchy being investigated by the ICC."[74] The Kenyan government's arguments at this stage appeared to center on the importance of state sovereignty, and in part argued that national jurisdictions should have discretion to determine who to investigate and prosecute domestically. The test proposed by this new line of argument would lead to even more uncertainty with respect to whether a case was admissible, as the focus would inevitably shift to whether a specific individual being investigated or prosecuted at the domestic level would qualify as someone "at the same level in the hierarchy" as the person being investigated and prosecuted by the ICC. Such a test might also result in states investigating other high-level individuals in order to shield the persons being investigated or prosecuted by the court. It is clear that the drafters of the Rome Statute did not have such a broad definition of complementarity in mind. Article 17 concerning admissibility clearly refers to "the case" at issue and also makes reference to the "person concerned" who is a part of that case. It is difficult to imagine how one could interpret the plain language of Article 17 in the way the Kenyan government was urging. While complementarity is a doctrine that in part is meant to accommodate state sovereignty, it is fundamentally a doctrine that supports accountability. The Kenyan government's proposed test would make it easier for states to shield individuals from accountability; all that they would have to do to shield person A from being prosecuted by the ICC would be to investigate person B, so long as one could argue that person B was "at the same level in the hierarchy" as person A.

Notwithstanding its challenge to the same person/same conduct test, the Kenyan government did again suggest on appeal that it was starting (yet again) to investigate the Ocampo Six. On July 4, the Kenyan government submitted an update to the court that included assertions that a number of witnesses related to the PEV had been interviewed and expressed the government's intention to interview all six of the ICC suspects as suspects under Kenyan law. The update also stated that an investigative team created after the identification of the Ocampo Six dedicated to investigating those same six suspects had unearthed no evidence implicating them in crimes as alleged by the ICC prosecutor. The exception was the allegations against Ruto, which the

---

[74] *Id.* at para 28, *quoting from* the Pre-Trial Chamber decision at para. 32.

government had already indicated was the subject of an ongoing investigation. The update also indicated that the reports of the Waki Commission and the Kenya National Commission on Human Rights would be reviewed for possible leads, suggesting that in the over two years since those reports had been issued, no effort had been made to use them to investigate those responsible for the PEV.[75] Finally, the update indicated that evidence presented before the TJRC would be examined for any reference to the six ICC suspects. As far as I am aware, this was never done,[76] though we had received some testimony (and some of it *in camera* and thus confidential) concerning some of the ICC suspects and other prominent government officials concerning the PEV.

Even an observer sympathetic to the Kenyan government's position noted that "the suggestion that mere expression of an intent to proceed against an amorphous group of unidentified suspects that may or may not include the suspects presently before the Court swings the pendulum too far ..."[77] This sentiment was later affirmed by the Appeals Chamber and reiterated what had been made clear before, viz. that in order for a case to be found inadmissible, it must be shown that national investigations "cover the same individual and substantially the same conduct as alleged in the proceedings before the Court."[78]

Regardless of how genuine one finds this flurry of investigative activity at the domestic level, there is no question that even the minimal efforts undertaken by the Kenyan government would not have occurred absent the involvement of the ICC.[79] In fact, up until the Pre-Trial Chamber decision at the end of

---

[75] International Criminal Court, *The Prosecutor v. Ruto et al.*, Case No. ICC-01/09-01/11, Appeals Chamber, "Filing of Updated Report by the Government of Kenya in the Appeal against the Pre-Trial Chamber's Decision on Admissibility" (July 4, 2011) Annex 1 (Letter dated July 1, 2011, from Ndegwa Muhoro, Director Criminal Investigations, to the Director of Public Prosecutions).

[76] At least one of the Kenyan commissioners was reported to have met with the head of the CID around this time. When confronted, this commissioner said that his visit had nothing to do with the TJRC and ICC.

[77] Charles Chernor Jalloh, "Kenya vs. The ICC Prosecutor," 53 *Harv. Int'l L. J. Online* 227, 236 (August 2012).

[78] International Criminal Court, *The Prosecutor v. Ruto et al.*, Case No. ICC-01/09-01/11-307, Appeals Chamber, "Judgment on the Appeal of the Republic of Kenya against the Decision of Pre-Trial Chamber II of 30 May 2011 entitled 'Decision on the Application by the Government of Kenya Challenging the Admissibility of the Case Pursuant to Article 19(2)(b) of the Statute'" (August 30, 2011) para. 1.

[79] For a detailed and informative analysis of the Kenyan government's efforts with respect to forestalling ICC involvement, see Lionel Nichols, *supra* note 29. See particularly pages 161–162, where Nichols persuasively argues that the Government of Kenya's arguments for declaring the cases inadmissible were really an attempt to protect the ICC suspects from any accountability.

May 2011, the government studiously declined to speak about any investigations of the six suspects, suggesting that there were no such investigations. Within less than a month, however, the government was now claiming that such investigations were ongoing and, in fact, had begun three years earlier. Curiously, the investigation reports indicated that individuals other than the Ocampo Six had been identified as potentially responsible for incitement, though it does not appear that further investigations were conducted with respect to those individuals.

WITNESSES UNDER THREAT

The increased activity by the government in identifying relevant witnesses in connection with investigating the ICC suspects appears not to have increased the security of those witnesses. In fact, it appears that this increased attention by the government and the ICC made such witnesses even more vulnerable to intimidation, threats, physical violence, and even death. In fact, the ICC prosecutor has alleged that the government itself, as well as individuals aligned with some of the suspects, have been involved in intimidating and even killing some of the ICC witnesses.[80]

As their arguments on admissibility were rejected by the court, the government began to shift its strategy to elicit from the ICC prosecutor the evidence it had amassed against the Kenyan suspects, including the identity of crucial witnesses who, to protect their security, had remained confidential. In order to learn the identities of key witnesses, the government requested that the ICC

[80] The ICC recently made public a number of decisions indicating a direct link between revealing the identity of witnesses to the Ocampo Six and the intimidation of those witnesses. *See, e.g.*, International Criminal Court, *The Prosecutor v. Muthuara and Kenyatta*, Case No. ICC- 01/09–02/11–574-Conf, Trial Chamber V, "Public Redacted Version of Decision on the Second, Third, and Fourth Application for the Authorization of Redactions" (December 17, 2012) para. 25 (Trial Chamber agreeing to prosecutor's request to deny the defense access to certain witness information as it found that "disclosure of the information to the accused persons would present an objectively justifiable risk to further or ongoing investigations and that this risk could not be addressed by less restrictive means."); International Criminal Court, *The Prosecutor v. Muthuara and Kenyatta*, Case No. ICC-01/09–02/11–464-Conf, Trial Chamber V, "Public Redacted Version of Decision on the Prosecution's Application to Authorize Redactions to a Statement of Witness 4 and to withhold Documents from Disclosure" (August 16, 2012) para. 8; International Criminal Court, *The Prosecutor v. Muthuara and Kenyatta*, Case No. ICC-01/09–02/11–569-Conf, Trial Chamber V, "Public Redacted Version of Decision on the Prosecution's First Request for the Authorization of Redactions" (December 13, 2012) para. 29. For allegations set out by the Prosecutor, *see* International Criminal Court, *The Prosecutor v. Kenyatta*, Case No. ICC-01/09–02/11–796-CONF-Anx A, Trial Chamber V(B), "Public Redacted Version of 'Second Updated Prosecution Pre-Trial Brief (August 26, 2013)'" (January 19, 2015).

prosecutor provide it with all of the information it had collected on the six suspects. The Kenyan government ironically argued that it required this information in order to undertake its own investigations, undercutting its own argument that it was able to undertake such investigations on its own without international assistance. The government's formal request to the ICC for its investigative materials was quite broad, and included "all statements, documents, or other types of evidence obtained by the Court and the Prosecutor in the course of the ICC investigations into the Post-Election Violence in Kenya, including into the six suspects presently before the ICC."[81] The request was based upon Article 93(10) of the Rome Statute, which provides that the court may provide assistance to a state party "conducting an investigation into or trial in respect of conduct which constitutes a crime within the jurisdiction of the Court or which constitutes a serious crime under the national law of the requesting State."[82]

The Kenyan government's request raised an important issue concerning the court's relationship with states endeavoring to investigate and prosecute crimes within the court's jurisdiction. Article 93(10) is written in broad language, and thus could apply to a number of scenarios, including situations in which a state party is investigating suspects other than those before the court or a situation in which the court declines to assert jurisdiction (i.e., for reasons of complementarity or gravity) and a state party wants to pursue the same suspect for the same or different crimes. In both of these hypothetical cases, the state would be requesting assistance to investigate and prosecute an individual who is not currently being investigated or prosecuted by the court itself. The Kenyan government's request for cooperation raised a different scenario, viz. a state claiming to be pursuing the same suspect for the same crimes investigated by the court. This last scenario places the court and the state party in competition, each pursuing the same individual for the same crime. The scenario presented by the Kenyan government was exactly the focus of the numerous decisions on admissibility in which the Court had unanimously found that the government's claims of willingness and ability to pursue the same investigation was without merit.

Not surprisingly, therefore, the Kenyan government attempted to combine its request for cooperation with its challenge to the admissibility of the Kenyan

---

[81] International Criminal Court, *Situation in the Republic of Kenya*, Case No. ICC- 01/09–58, The Government of the Republic of Kenya, "Request for Assistance on Behalf of the Government of the Republic of Kenya pursuant to Article 93(10) and Rule 194" (April 21, 2011) para. 2.

[82] Rome Statute, *supra* note 36, at Art. 93(10)

cases. In fact, the Kenyan government argued that the request for cooperation be decided prior to its admissibility challenge,[83] presumably because the
government wanted to use the results of the ICC's investigation of the suspects
before the court to support its argument that the cases are inadmissible. The
Pre-Trial Chamber refused to cooperate with this strategy. First, the Pre-Trial
Chamber refused to link the cooperation request to the admissibility challenge. Second, in a decision issued on June 29, 2011, the Pre-Trial Chamber
denied the request for cooperation, noting that, by the terms of Article 93(10),
such cooperation is contemplated only if the state requesting such cooperation is conducting an investigation with respect to conduct that is a crime
within the jurisdiction of the court or is a "serious crime under the national
law of the requesting State." The Pre-Trial Chamber noted that the Kenyan
government had failed to provide any information or evidence concerning
such an investigation in its request for cooperation.

Perhaps in response to the Kenyan government's argument that they were
now initiating investigations into the Kenyan suspects, the court also clarified
that a state challenging the admissibility of a case "must provide the Court
with evidence of a sufficient degree of specificity and probative value that
demonstrates that it is indeed investigating the case. It is not sufficient merely
to assert that investigations are ongoing."[84] If all it took to make a case
inadmissible was a statement by the government that they were investigating (such as the brief report that referred to the case opened with respect to
William Ruto)[85], or even a letter instructing such an investigation (along the
lines of the letter of April 14, 2011, from Attorney General Wako to Director of
Public Prosecutions Tobiko filed before the court),[86] then complementarity
would effectively eviscerate the ability of the ICC to assert jurisdiction for the
crimes within its jurisdiction. The requirement for more specific evidence of
an asserted investigation makes sense given the second prong of the admissibility test – whether a particular investigation or prosecution is designed
to shield an individual from accountability. More is required than a mere

---

[83] International Criminal Court, *Situation in the Republic of Kenya*, Case No. ICC-01/09–58, The
Government of the Republic of Kenya, "Request for Assistance on Behalf of the Government of
the Republic of Kenya pursuant to Article 93(10) and Rule 194" (April 21, 2011) para. 7.

[84] International Criminal Court, *The Prosecutor v. Muthaura et al.*, Case No. ICC-01/09–02/11
OA, Appeals Chamber, "Judgment on the Appeal of the Republic of Kenya against the
Decision of Pre-Trial Chamber II of 30 May 2011 Entitled 'Decision on the Application by the
Government of Kenya Challenging the Admissibility of the Case Pursuant to Article 19(2)(b)
of the Statute" (August 30, 2011) para. 2.

[85] *See supra* note 70.

[86] *See supra* note 64.

assertion that there is an investigation, or an official instruction that there be such an investigation, in order to evaluate the genuineness and quality of such an investigation.

In addition, the Kenyan government argued, or at least raised the possibility, in its appeal on admissibility that it might not have evidence implicating some of the six suspects in order to justify its lack of progress with respect to investigating or prosecuting any of them.[87] This is a curious argument, and one that again moves outside of the framework of the Rome Statute. If the government had no evidence implicating the suspects, then it would be reasonable for the government not to investigate, much less prosecute, those individuals. This is an explanation for the lack of investigation by the state, and therefore an admission that no such investigations exist, thus making the cases admissible before the ICC. Within the framework of the Rome Statute, this was yet another fatal admission on the part of the government. The Pre-Trial Chamber had already concluded that the ICC prosecutor had amassed sufficient evidence to authorize an investigation into the Kenyan situation (and later found sufficient evidence to support the prosecution of four of the Ocampo Six). Whether this evidence was sufficient to secure a conviction would be determined after a trial during which the prosecutor and the suspect's defense lawyers would present and challenge the relevant evidence. The Kenyan government appeared to be arguing that because it did not have sufficient evidence to prosecute the Ocampo Six, the ICC evidence should be ignored. It was an argument premised less on the law as set out in the Rome Statute and more a broader political campaign to reduce international jurisdiction (at least as exercised by the ICC) to extremely rare circumstances. Through its admissibility challenges and requests for access to the evidence collected by the ICC, the Kenyan government was trying to reassert its control over the investigations. Its argument appeared to be that because it was claiming a willingness to investigate the ICC suspects, notwithstanding its apparent inability to discover inculpatory evidence, the ICC should halt its own investigation and hand over all of the information it had collected to the government.

MULTILATERAL CHALLENGES TO THE ICC

At the same time that it was arguing unsuccessfully before the ICC to have the cases declared inadmissible, the Kenyan government undertook a major

---

[87] *See* International Criminal Court, *The Prosecutor v. Ruto et al.*, Case No. ICC-01/09–01/11, Appeals Chamber, "Document in Support of the 'Appeal of the Government of Kenya against the Decision on the Application by the Government of Kenya Challenging the Admissibility of the Case Pursuant to Article 19(2)(b) of the Statute'" (June 20, 2011) para. 55.

multilateral political and diplomatic initiative to counter ICC involvement. This initiative was twofold, focusing both on preventing the specific intervention in Kenya and on diminishing the authority and legitimacy of the ICC, including pushing to reverse long-held principles of international criminal law that were developed at Nuremberg. The government thus not only challenged the legitimacy of the Kenyan cases before the ICC but also the legitimacy of the ICC and international criminal law.

The first public indication that the Kenyan government was willing to challenge the ICC outside of the courtroom was ironically, though perhaps appropriately, at the celebration in Nairobi of Kenya's newly promulgated constitution. For over a decade, Kenya had struggled to adopt a new, more modern, constitution that would incorporate a broad range of universally recognized human rights and empower local communities through a more decentralized national government. Each of those attempts had failed for various reasons, including, in one case, the assassination of one of the constitutional delegates.[88] The PEV provided a new impetus for the political elite to recommit themselves to constitutional reform. A committee of experts, consisting of six Kenyans and three internationals, spent a good part of 2009 and 2010 drafting, and then securing public approval for, a new constitution. The newly drafted constitution was approved by a substantial majority of the voting population on August 4, 2010.[89] On August 27, 2010, President Mwai Kibaki signed the constitution in front of a standing-room-only crowd of dignitaries at Uhuru Park.[90] Those present included Kofi Annan, members of the committee of experts (who ironically did not have seats assigned to them so had to scramble for places to sit or stand during the ceremony), numerous heads of state from the African continent, most of the Nairobi diplomatic community, and most of the commissioners and senior staff from the TJRC. As we settled into our seats (we had arrived at the venue early and were able to find seats), we watched as dignitary after dignitary arrived. At some point, there was a murmur in the crowd, and walking into the arena, accompanied by senior Kenyan government officials, was the President of Sudan, Omar al-Bashir.

President al-Bashir enjoys the distinction of being the first sitting head of state indicted by the ICC. The ICC had issued two warrants of arrest for al-Bashir, the first on March 4, 2009, and the second a little over a month

---

[88] See TJRC FINAL REPORT, *supra* Chapter 1, note 9, at Vol. 1, page 10, para. 27 (referring to the assassination of Professor Odhiambo-Mbai).

[89] Over 72 percent of those eligible to vote participated in the referendum, and 67 percent of those voted in favor of the new constitution. South Consulting, *The KNDR Monitoring Project: Review Report* (October 2010), para. 41.

[90] Uhuru Park is a major park in downtown Nairobi which has hosted a number of significant political events in Kenya's history. Uhuru is the Swahili word for peace.

before his Kenyan appearance, on July 12, 2010.[91] He was indicted for genocide, crimes against humanity, and war crimes arising out of the conflict in
Darfur. Al-Bashir's presence at the Kenyan celebrations as an honored head
of state, instead of a fugitive from justice, was thus a surprise to many in
attendance. At the end of the ceremony, as the large crowd began to disperse,
the numerous ambassadors in attendance huddled together to discuss this turn
of events, resulting in numerous statements by governments around the world
criticizing Kenya for its failure to enforce the international arrest warrant
against al-Bashir.

Whether states are obligated to arrest al-Bashir if he sets foot in their territory
is an issue that has divided international lawyers. While there is no question
that states are generally obligated to enforce international arrest warrants,
including those issued by the ICC, al-Bashir's status as a sitting head of state
has led some to claim that he is immune from such enforcement actions, or at
least immune from enforcement action by another state, as opposed to an
international body like the ICC or the UN Security Council. The problem is
that the ICC does not have its own police force to enforce its orders, and thus
is dependent on state parties for enforcement of its arrest warrants. The Rome
Statute makes clear that heads of state, along with other government officials,
may be indicted by the ICC,[92] and that state parties to the Rome Statute,
which include Kenya, are to cooperate fully with the investigations and prosecutions of crimes by the court.[93] While a recent opinion of the International
Court of Justice reaffirms the immunity of a limited number of government
officials, including heads of state, from legal process initiated by other *states*,
that same opinion also makes clear that such immunity would not apply with
respect to a legal process initiated by an international court such as the ICC.[94]
In other words, certain government officials may still be entitled to immunity
from legal process by other states, but such immunities do not apply to an
international legal process like the ICC, and thus would not apply to states
enforcing an ICC arrest warrant, which, if they are parties to the Rome

---

[91] The two warrants were necessitated by the initial denial by the Pre-Trial Chamber to find
enough evidence to support a claim of genocide. The first warrant thus concerned claims
against al-Bashir involving war crimes and crimes against humanity. The Appeals Chamber
later reversed the Pre-Trial Chamber's denial of the genocide claim, leading to the issuance of
a second warrant of arrest to cover the genocide claim.

[92] Rome Statute, *supra* note 36, at Art. 27 ("...official capacity as a Head of State or
Government....shall in no case exempt a person from criminal responsibility under this
Statute...")

[93] *Id.* at Art. 86.

[94] International Court of Justice, *Case Concerning the Arrest Warrant of 11 April 2000 (Congo
v. Belg.)*, 2002 I.C.J. Report 3 (Feb. 14).

Statute, they are obligated to do. Upon learning of al-Bashir's visit to Kenya, the ICC immediately sent a formal notification to the UN Security Council noting Kenya's obligation to arrest al-Bashir under both the UN Security Council resolution referring the Darfur matter to the ICC and the Rome Statute itself.[95]

While international lawyers debated whether Kenya was obligated to arrest al-Bashir during his previous visit to Kenya, President Kibaki announced that an important meeting of the Intergovernmental Authority on Development (IGAD)[96] concerning the situation in South Sudan would be held in Kenya in October or November, and it was suspected that al-Bashir would attend representing the Sudan.

Under the provisions of the Rome Statute, a state party is obligated to enforce a warrant of arrest issued by the ICC or inform the court of what further documents or other information is required under its domestic law to enforce such a warrant. Consequently, when it was announced that al-Bashir might visit Kenya again in October or November 2010, the ICC requested that the government of Kenya inform it of any conditions that might prevent the Kenyan authorities from arresting al Bashir. Rather than argue that it could not or would not arrest al-Bashir, the Kenyan government formally informed the court that the IGAD meeting on South Sudan would, in fact, not be held in Kenya (it had been quickly moved to Ethiopia which is not a party to the Rome Treaty), and thus that al-Bashir would not be traveling to Kenya. Therefore, the response from the Kenyan government did not answer the question posed by the ICC, viz. whether there was any impediment to the arrest of al-Bashir if he were to return to Kenya. Curiously, a few months later, the Kenyan government argued before the ICC that the provisions of the Rome Treaty were "binding law in Kenya," though this representation was made, not with respect to Kenya's obligation to arrest al-Bashir or otherwise cooperate with the court, but as part of the Kenyan government's argument that the ICC cases could and should be prosecuted in Kenya and not before the ICC.[97]

---

[95] International Criminal Court, *Prosecutor v. Al Bashir*, Case No. ICC-02/05-01/09-107, Pre-Trial Chamber I, "Decision Informing the United Nations Security Council and the Assembly of State Parties to the Rome Statute about Omar Al-Bashir's Presence in the territory of the Republic of Kenya" (August 27, 2010).

[96] IGAD is a regional trading bloc consisting of states in Northeastern Africa, including Kenya and the Sudan.

[97] International Criminal Court, *Situation in the Republic of Kenya*, Case No. ICC-01/09-02/ 11-26, Pre-Trial Chamber II, "Application on Behalf of the government of the Republic of Kenya Pursuant to Article 19 of the ICC Statute" (March 31, 2011) para. 58.

Meanwhile, the Kenya chapter of the International Commission of Jurists went to court to request that it issue, under Kenyan law, a warrant of arrest against al-Bashir and that it issue an order obligating the Kenyan government to effect such warrant if and when al-Bashir next set foot in Kenya. Clarifying the legal obligation of the Kenyan government with respect to the international arrest warrant was particularly important given al-Bashir's then-pending visit to Kenya for the IGAD meeting. The high court of Kenya took a year to issue a decision in the case. In a convoluted and somewhat confusing opinion, the high court concluded that the Kenyan government was obligated to implement the ICC arrest warrant against al-Bashir were he to return to Kenya, and even seemed to suggest that if the government failed to arrest al-Bashir, then any legal person (including the ICJ) could also execute the arrest warrant.[98]

Since al-Bashir never returned to Kenya, the issue of government compliance with this domestic decision upholding the ICC warrant of arrest was never tested. Nonetheless, the government continued its campaign against the authority of the ICC through the attorney general, who immediately appealed the high court decision and argued, among other things, that al-Bashir was immune from legal process in Kenya by virtue of his position as head of state of the Sudan.[99] That appeal is still pending.

The Kenyan government's reaction to the arrest warrant against al-Bashir foreshadowed its approach to cooperation with the ICC in the Kenya cases. At no point did the Kenyan government expressly refuse to cooperate with the ICC. At the same time, the government never went out of its way to assist the court, and, in fact, the government pursued numerous legal and political strategies to delay, halt, or undermine the court's ability to pursue the Kenya cases.

The identification of specific suspects by the ICC so soon after the Pre-Trial Chamber had authorized the investigation spurred an intensive shuttle diplomacy by a number of high-level government officials, most notably the vice president, Stephen Kalonzo Musyoka. Government officials began to lobby other African states, members of the Security Council, and other relevant actors to postpone or even drop the ICC cases. The government efforts to have the ICC cases deferred was generally not supported by the ODM wing of the

---

[98] *Kenya Section of the International Commission of Jurists v. Attorney General* [2011] Misc. Criminal Application 685 of 2010 (November 28, 2011).

[99] See *Attorney General v. Kenya Section of ICJ*, Civil Application No. Nai. 275 of 2011 (UR. 179/2011) (February 17, 2012).

coalition government and, significantly, was not supported by the then justice minister, Mutula Kilonzo.[100]

This diplomatic push resulted in a number of statements in support of the Kenyan effort to end the ICC cases; the first of which was a statement by IGAD on January 30, 2011, supporting "Kenya's deferral of the ICC investigations and prosecutions in line with Article 16 of the Rome Statute to enable affirmation of the principle of complementarity."[101] Article 16 of the Rome Statute provides for a twelve-month suspension of any ICC investigation or prosecution if the Security Council passes a resolution to that effect under its Chapter VII powers under the UN Charter. Chapter VII of the UN Charter empowers the Security Council to pass resolutions that are binding on all UN member states in order to maintain international peace and security in the face of a "threat to the peace, breach of the peace, or act of aggression."[102] Deferral of an ICC investigation at the request of the Security Council is thus dependent on a finding that such a deferral is in response to a threat to the peace, breach of the peace, or act of aggression.

In its campaign for Security Council deferral, the Kenyan government did not attempt to argue that the ICC involvement in Kenya threatened or would threaten international peace and security.[103] Instead, in a five-page bullet-point memo sent to all UN member states in January 2011 the Kenyan Ministry of Foreign Affairs tried to relitigate the issue of complementarity that had been rejected by the Pre-Trial Chamber the previous March. The memo argued that the government had already made significant progress on the reform front that would allow investigations and prosecutions of PEV suspects. In addition, the memo noted that since the referral of the Kenyan cases "there had been intensified efforts to implement the reform agenda" (thus suggesting that without ICC involvement such reforms might not have been pursued as

---

[100] International Crisis Group, *Kenya: Impact of the ICC Proceedings*, Africa Briefing No. 84 (January 9, 2012), page 8, note 56.

[101] IGAD, *Communique of the 17th Extraordinary Session of the IGAD Assembly of Heads of State and Government on Sudan, Somalia and Kenya* (Addis Ababa, January 30, 2011).

[102] UN Charter, Art. 39.

[103] During his campaign for the presidency in the lead up to the March 2013 elections, Kenyatta played down the significance of the ICC cases, repeatedly arguing that his trial in the Hague would not affect his ability to govern, and that the trial was a personal issue. *See, e.g.,* James Verini, "Debate Night in Kenya," *New Yorker* (February 20, 2013); Al Jazeera, "Uhuru Kenyatta Says He Will Run Kenya from The Hague if Elected President," *Kenya Stockholm Blog* (January 20, 2013) (http://kenyastockholm.com/2013/01/20/uhuru-kenyatta-says-he-will-run-kenya-from-the-hague-if-elected-president/); Dominic Burbridge, "Kenya's First Presidential Debate," *Democracy in Africa* (February 12, 2013) (http://democracyinafrica.org/kenyas-first-presidential-debate/).

"intensively"); that a local judicial mechanism would facilitate the trial of "**ALL** PEV suspects and not just those bearing the highest responsibility" (emphasis in the original) (without indicating whether the suspects before the ICC were or would be investigated); and, while noting that the Kenyan Parliament had voted for withdrawal from the Rome Treaty, the government was not currently pursuing that option (suggesting that it might in the future).[104] Attached to the memo was a copy of the IGAD resolution of January 30 indicating support for Kenya's request for a Security Council deferral. On March 4, 2011, the Kenyan government wrote to the Security Council formally requesting a deferral of the Kenyan cases pursuant to Article 16 of the Rome Statute.[105]

Perhaps in an effort to demonstrate the increased "intensity" of the government's reform efforts, and thus in support of the argument for Security Council deferral, in January 2011, President Mwai Kibaki nominated a new attorney general, director of public prosecutions, and chief justice. Ironically, these appointments were made in a manner that bypassed the vetting procedures required under the new constitution that the Kenyan government was simultaneously praising before the ICC. In addition to not following the constitutional procedures for such nominations, the president chose the three nominees without consulting his coalition partner, resulting in the ODM publicly opposing the nominations. To make matters worse, two of the three nominees (for attorney general and director of public prosecutions) had been on record as attorneys for two of the ICC suspects, and the third (the chief justice) had recently been identified as a suitable judicial candidate by a panel chaired by one of the ICC suspects. The basis for the uproar over these unilateral appointments was threefold: the unconstitutional procedure by which they were chosen, the relationships and even conflicts of interest they had with respect to the ICC suspects, and the quality of the nominees. The president was forced to withdraw their names. The incident raised additional questions about the genuineness of the government's commitment to reform,

---

[104] Aide-Mémoire, *Kenya's Reform Agenda and Engagement with the International Criminal Court (ICC)* (dated January 28, 2011 but circulated to member states on February 8, 2011).

[105] UN Security Council, "Identical letters dated 4 March 2011 from the Permanent Representative of Kenya to the United Nations addressed to the Secretary-General and the President of the Security Council," S/2011/116 (March 8, 2011). *See also* UN Security Council, "Letter dated 23 March 2011 from the Permanent Representative of Kenya to the United Nations addressed to the President of the Security Council," S/2011/201 (March 29, 2011) (following up on the March 4 letter). Coalition government partner ODM sent a separate letter to all UN member states opposing the request to the Security Council. *See* International Crisis Group, *supra* note 99, at p. 9.

and more specifically its commitment to investigating and prosecuting those individuals currently being investigated by the ICC. There was a reasonable apprehension that an attorney general and director of public prosecutions who had close ties to the ICC suspects would be less than vigorous in their pursuit of those individuals. It was in the context of the president's failed attempt to handpick these nominees that the Security Council held an informal meeting with representatives of the Kenyan government. Following that meeting, on April 8, 2011, the president of the Security Council announced that "after full consideration" of the Kenyan request for a Security Council deferral, "the members of the Security Council did not agree on the matter."[106]

While the Kenyan government failed to draw the Security Council into the Kenya cases, it had more success with the African Union. Prior to the involvement of the ICC in Kenya, the African Union had raised concerns about the ICC's indictment of al-Bashir and Muammar Gaddafi, as both were sitting heads of state when they were indicted. After requesting, unsuccessfully, that the UN Security Council invoke its powers under the Rome Treaty to suspend for one year the case against al-Bashir, the African Union adopted a resolution at its Summit Meeting in July 2009 that "decide[d]" that "AU Member States shall not cooperate ... [f]or the arrest and surrender of President Omar El Bashir of The Sudan."[107] The Kenya government had, in fact, pointed to this resolution to justify its failure to execute the ICC's arrest warrant against al-Bashir when he visited Kenya for the promulgation of the constitution. The Kenyan government had somewhat surprisingly claimed that it was legally obligated to follow the African Union resolution (which is not at all self-evident, even by its own terms) without addressing its much clearer legal obligation to cooperate with the ICC as a party to the Rome Treaty. As the Kenyan government repeatedly failed in its attempts to have the ICC find the Kenyan cases inadmissible on the basis of complementarity and failed to convince the Security Council to intervene, the AU took up the issue in a series of resolutions that emphasized state's rights and the importance of national criminal processes over the ICC.

The African Union's predecessor, the Organization of African Unity, had embraced a definition of state sovereignty that prevented international involvement in matters perceived to be within the domestic jurisdiction of its

---

[106] *See* International Crisis Group, *supra* note 99.
[107] African Union, *Decision of the Meeting of African States Parties to the Rome Statute of the International Criminal Court (ICC)*, Doc. Assembly/AU/13(XIII), Assembly/AU/Dec.245(XIII) Rev. 1, paragraph 10, *reprinted in*, Assembly of the African Union, "Decisions and Declarations," Assembly/AU/Dec. 243–267 (XIII) Rev. 1, Assembly/AU/Decl.1–5 (XIII) (July 1–3, 2009).

member states. This emphasis on states' rights and suspicion of international intervention was in part a reaction to the legacy of colonialism, slavery, and racism. From the first sustained contact of Europeans with Africa in the seventeenth century, Europe and later North America proceeded to ignore any semblance of indigenous African autonomy or sovereignty in a quest for natural resources and slaves. European claims to African territory were organized and regulated through colonialism. The independence movement against colonialism that gained momentum in the 1950s resulted in the creation of new nation-states defined by the borders established by the European colonial powers, most notoriously at the 1878 Congress of Berlin. Given the history of exploitation and oppression, these newly independent nation-states jealously guarded their sovereignty against outside forces. One can see elements of this emphasis on state sovereignty and states' rights in the African human rights treaty, which includes provisions concerning the duties of citizens towards the state, and the importance of the stability and integrity of the state itself, provisions which are not found in any other international human rights treaties.

The replacement of the OAU with the AU signaled a shift away from a more absolutist position on state sovereignty, and was part of a general trend toward a more open approach to democracy and international justice, including human rights and international criminal law. The AU thus adopted a policy of "non-indifference" concerning the commission of international crimes within member states, which contemplates AU-sponsored military intervention to stop such atrocities. The OAU, in contrast, was largely premised on the principle of "non-interference."[108] The shift from "non-interference" to "non-indifference" may seem slight (even at the level of rhetoric), but it was meant to signal a significant shift on the part of African states. The growing openness to international processes adopted by the AU began under the OAU, which had successfully endorsed significant proposals to the Rome Statute, including the power of the prosecutor to initiate her own investigations and the obligation of states to cooperate with the ICC. This rapidly growing openness to international justice resulted in a majority of African states joining the ICC, making Africa the regional bloc with the largest participation in the ICC.

---

[108] *See* The Africa–EU Partnership, *From the Organization of African Unity (OAU) to the African Union (AU): The 50-Year Path Towards African Unity,* (May 28, 2013) www.africa-eu-partnership.org/newsroom/all-news/organisation-african-unity-oau-african-union-au-50-year-path-towards-african-unity.

Notwithstanding this more internationalist trend on the African continent, the legacy of the past continues to influence the political dynamics of the relationship between Africa and the rest of the world, including international justice initiatives like the ICC. This dynamic is clearly evident in the AU's mobilization against the ICC with respect to the Kenya cases. The African Union issued a resolution in May 2013 responding to the decisions of the Security Council not to defer the Kenyan cases and the dismissal by the ICC Pre-Trial and Appeals Chamber of the claims of inadmissibility brought by the Kenyan government. In that resolution, the AU signaled its desire to pursue mechanisms of accountability for international crimes other than that provided by the ICC.[109] The resolution also stated that the decision by the ICC to declare the Kenyan cases admissible "denie[s] the right of Kenya to prosecute and try alleged perpetrators of crimes committed on its territory in relation to the 2007 post-election violence."[110] While rhetorically this claim has some weight given the history of African exploitation, the claim is at its most basic level false, as the Kenyan government has always been able to investigate and prosecute those responsible for the post-election violence. That was always the case regardless of whether the ICC became involved in Kenya, and is contemplated and even encouraged under the ICC complementarity regime.

Notwithstanding this rhetorical claim that Kenya was being denied its right to prosecute alleged perpetrators, the AU appeared to recognize the continuing ability of Kenya to do just that when it further argued that the ICC should defer the Kenya cases not on the basis of complementarity but on the basis of *ne bis in idem*, or double jeopardy, under Article 17(1)(c) of the Rome Statute. This was, however, a curious argument to make, as it contemplated the Kenyan government actually prosecuting the ICC suspects, including by this time the current president and deputy president. The thinking was presumably that once the prosecution of the current suspects was complete, resulting in either a conviction or acquittal, the Kenyan government (as well as the individual suspects) could bring a claim under Article 17(1)(c) against any attempt by the ICC to prosecute them again. Such a prosecution would then be in violation of the well-established principle against double jeopardy. There are at least two problems with this argument. The first is that not only have no ICC suspects been convicted or acquitted by the Kenyan authorities, none (except perhaps the deputy president, William Ruto) have been the subject of a domestic investigation, much less any actual attempt to prosecute.

---

[109] African Union, *Decision on International Jurisdiction, Justice and the International Criminal Court (ICC)*, Doc. Assembly/AU/13(XXI) (May 26–27, 2013).
[110] *Id.* at p. 2.

The AU thus appeared to be arguing that the ICC should suspend its investigations and prosecutions based upon the *possibility* of a domestic investigation, prosecution, and final judgment. The AU argument based on double jeopardy thus quickly devolved into the same argument concerning existing domestic investigations or prosecutions under the complementarity provisions. Second, while both the deputy president and the former radio personality, Joshua arap Sang, *could* be prosecuted domestically in Kenya, under the newly enacted constitution, the president himself could not be, so long as he remained in office.[111] So even if the ICC were to accept the argument that it should suspend its operations in anticipation of a possible domestic prosecution that might then lead to a double jeopardy argument, such an argument would not apply to the case of the current President, Uhuru Kenyatta.

The AU also repeated the argument of the Kenyan government that recent reforms and the completion of a successful national election (in 2013) provided the framework for a national mechanism to prosecute those responsible for the post-election violence.[112] As with the numerous Kenyan government statements and submissions before the court, however, the AU was unable to point to any specific investigations or prosecutions related to the remaining four suspects.

The African Union did not limit itself to the merits of the specific cases before the ICC. In response to the Kenyan and Sudanese investigations, it developed a more long-term institutional response to limit the powers of the ICC. The African Union (with the strong support of Kenya and the Sudan) began to push for the creation of a regional criminal court. Kenya had already floated the idea of having the Kenyan cases heard before the East African Court of Justice and the African Court of Justice and Human Rights. This was a curious proposal as neither court had criminal jurisdiction and thus would require a major amendment to their powers to be able to prosecute an individual for a violation of international criminal law. The AU thus began to move to create such jurisdiction at the regional level. Africa, along with the Americas and Europe, has a regional human rights system, including an African Commission and Court on Human and People's Rights. Like its

---

[111] *The Constitution of Kenya (Rev.* 2012), Art. 143. While the constitution protects the president from domestic criminal proceedings while he is in office, it makes clear that such immunity does not apply to prosecutions "under any treaty to which Kenya is party and which prohibits such immunity." (Art. 143(4)). This exception clearly encompasses the ICC proceedings.

[112] African Union Executive Council, *Progress Report of the Commission on the Implementation of the Decision Assembly/AU/Dec.482 (XXI) on International Jurisdiction, Justice and the International Criminal Court (ICC)*, Ext/EX.CL/2(XV) (October 11, 2013), pp. 5–6.

regional counterparts, the African Commission and Court do not have criminal jurisdiction over individuals but instead address allegations of violations
committed by the state. In an attempt to bypass the jurisdiction of the ICC, the
AU proposed expanding the jurisdiction of the African Court of Human and
Peoples', Rights to include criminal jurisdiction over individuals for a range of
crimes, including the crimes within the jurisdiction of the ICC.[113] Such a
proposal has at least two problems, one concerning the court's own institutional capabilities and the other concerning the ICC's doctrine of admissibility. First, the African court is a new institution that is still struggling to
establish itself as a credible court on the African continent. Over the ten years
since its establishment in January 2004, it has only issued forty-one judgments.[114] In addition, the African Union had already moved to merge the
African Court on Human and People's Rights with the African Court of
Justice (which was meant to deal with disputes concerning all of the treaties
promulgated under the OAU and AU).[115] This "kitchen-sink" approach to
jurisdiction would be a challenge for the most seasoned and established
judicial institution.

Second, it is unclear what the legal effect of a regional criminal court would
have on the admissibility of a situation or case before the ICC. It would be
difficult to argue that an investigation or prosecution before such a regional
criminal court would make a situation or case inadmissible before the ICC,
as the Rome Statute refers to investigations or prosecutions undertaken by a
state that has jurisdiction, making no reference to other regional or international processes. The AU recognized this hurdle and thus passed a resolution
calling upon African state parties to the Rome Statute to introduce amendments to the Rome Statute that would recognize African regional judicial
mechanisms that address international crimes as meeting the requirement

---

[113] The proposed jurisdiction would, in fact, be much larger than that of the ICC, encompassing
not just the ICC crimes of war crimes, crimes against humanity, aggression, and genocide,
but also including the crime of unconstitutional change of government, piracy, terrorism,
mercenarism, corruption, money laundering, trafficking in persons, trafficking in drugs,
trafficking in hazardous wastes, and illicit exploitation of natural resources. *See* African Union,
*Protocol on Amendments to the Protocol on the Statute of the African Court of Justice and
Human Rights, Annex (Statute of the African Court of Justice and Human and People's Rights)*,
Article 28A (adopted June 27, 2014).

[114] *See* the African Court's website, http://en.african-court.org/ (last visited November 11, 2017).

[115] The protocol to merge the African Court of Justice with the African Court of Human and
Peoples' Rights was adopted by the AU in July 2008. As of this writing only five states have
ratified the protocol, falling short of the fifteen ratifications required for the protocol to come
into effect.

of complementarity.[116] Without such an amendment to the Rome Statute, a regional criminal court would have no bearing on the admissibility of a case before the ICC, a situation the AU appears to concede by pushing for the amendment. While as a legal matter such a regional criminal court would have no impact on the ICC (absent amendments to the Rome Statute), as a political matter its creation could pose a serious challenge to the legitimacy of the ICC, at least on the African continent, as it would present an African alternative to international prosecutions.

That the overall intent of the AU in creating such a regional criminal court is to decrease, rather than increase, accountability for the worst international crimes is made clear by the inclusion in the draft statute of an immunity clause for heads of state and other senior government officials.[117] In other words, the regional criminal court as currently envisioned would not have jurisdiction over heads of states or other government officials, making it the first official attempt to reverse what had been established at Nuremberg and Tokyo and taken for granted ever since, viz. that the official capacity of a perpetrator, whether as a government official or head of state, does not immunize that individual from international criminal liability before an international tribunal. Under the proposed African criminal court, heads of state responsible for genocide, crimes against humanity, or war crimes would be immune from accountability unless and until they left office. Thus Hitler, Pol Pot, Idi Amin, and the architects of the Rwandan genocide would be immune from criminal liability for the crimes they perpetrated so long as they remained in office. The inclusion of such immunity in the proposed statute should not come as a surprise, as AU resolutions have repeatedly called for such immunity before the ICC.[118]

---

[116] *See* African Union, *Decision on Africa's Relationship with the International Criminal Court (ICC)*, Ext/Assembly/AU/Dec.1 (Oct. 2013) para. 10(vi). While the final language of the Resolution calls upon member states to propose "relevant amendments to the Rome Statute," a draft of the same resolution earlier that day suggests that the intent was to propose amendments that would recognize "African regional Judicial Mechanisms dealing with international crimes in accordance with the principles of complementarity." African Union, *Decision on Africa's Relationship with the International Criminal Court (ICC) (Draft)*, Ext/Assembly/AU/Draft/Dec.1 (October 2013) Rev. 2, para. 9(viii).

[117] Article 46A *bis* reads: "No charges shall be commenced or continued before the Court against any serving AU Head of State or Government, or anybody acting or entitled to act in such capacity, or other senior state officials based on their functions, during their tenure of office." African Union, *Draft Protocol on Amendments to the Protocol on the Statute of the African Court of Justice and Human Rights*, STC/Legal/Min/7(I) Rev. 1 (May 14, 2014) p. 34.

[118] *See, e.g.*, African Union, *Decision on Africa's Relationship with the International Criminal Court (ICC)*, Ext/Assembly/AU/Dec.1 (October 2013), para. 9 ("reaffirms the principles deriving from national laws and international customary law by which sitting Heads of State and other senior state officials are granted immunities during their tenure of office").

Ironically, the inclusion of immunity for government officials in an African regional criminal court would make it impossible to argue for inadmissibility before the ICC, assuming one could get around the express language of the Rome Statute concerning investigations or prosecutions by *states* with jurisdiction. In the case against President Kenyatta, for example, there could be no conflicting investigation or prosecution to which the ICC could defer under its admissibility doctrine given that the proposed African criminal court would, by its express terms, not have jurisdiction to investigate or prosecute him as a sitting head of state. The same would presumably be true for the case against Deputy President Ruto, as under any reasonable interpretation the deputy president would qualify as a senior government official. The result is that only low-level government officials and private citizens like Joshua arap Sang might be able to avoid ICC prosecution by being prosecuted before the African regional criminal court.

THE ICC AND THE TJRC

This steady campaign by the Kenyan government against the ICC investigations and the ICC itself made it difficult for the TJRC to engage with the ICC. From the start of the potential ICC involvement in Kenya, we at the Commission had periodically discussed what relationship, if any, we should have with respect to the court and the prosecutor's office. In March 2010, our vice chair was in New York and met with members from the Office of the Prosecutor. She was informed that the then-prosecutor, Moreno-Ocampo, would be in Kenya within the next two weeks and that he would like to meet with us. No one within the Commission raised an objection to such a meeting; we were later informed that the prosecutor had cancelled his plans to meet with us. We were never told why the prosecutor changed his mind. During the entire life of the Commission, there were no formal meetings between the prosecutor's office and the Commission. This failure to engage was unfortunate for both institutions, as there was significant overlap between the focus of the Commission and the ICC investigations, raising the possibility of the operations of the one interfering with or thwarting the operations of the other.

While the Kenya situation presented for the first time an ICC investigation operating at the same time as a truth commission, a similar situation was presented in Sierra Leone where an internationalized criminal court operated alongside a truth and reconciliation commission. There are numerous potential areas of cooperation and conflict between a court and a truth commission. The success and failures of the Sierra Leone situation provides a number of lessons for truth commissions and courts operating simultaneously. Truth commissions are designed to provide a safe space for individuals to come forward and share their experiences with respect to human rights violations. Three broad categories of individuals may thus seek to take advantage of a truth commission platform: those who were harmed by a violation (sometimes referred to as victims or survivors), those who bear some responsibility for a violation (sometimes referred to as perpetrators or responsible parties), and those who do not fit into the first two categories but otherwise have some connection to the violation (these can be witnesses, investigators, bystanders, or other interested parties). While some or all of these individuals may also testify as part of a criminal prosecution (either voluntarily or under compulsion), such individuals will have far less control over the content of their testimony before a criminal court than they will before a truth commission. A criminal trial has its own narrative logic that centers on determining whether the evidence presented proves beyond a reasonable doubt the responsibility of the defendant for certain specific criminal acts. Questions concerning why an individual acted the way he did, who else might have been involved, what institutional structures allowed or compelled such action, and other similar questions are often, and quite rightly, not part of a criminal trial. By contrast, the institutional, systemic, and other attributes of gross violations of human rights are often the central focus of a truth commission. Truth commissions also explore the perspective and motives of participants, including perpetrators, which rarely, if ever, are the proper focus of a criminal trial. One could thus imagine that any number of individuals who might testify as part of a criminal trial might also want to testify before a truth commission in order to provide a more complete narrative that accurately reflects their experience.

While an individual might find it advantageous to testify before the TJRC for the aforementioned reasons, there were also risks to such individuals testifying before us. First, testimony provided before the Commission might be used to impeach the same individual's testimony before the ICC, or might even be used in evidence against that individual.[119] The act establishing the TJRC made clear that any information (including testimony) provided to us by an individual could not be used in any criminal or civil proceeding.[120] While it was clear that such testimonial immunity would bind a Kenyan court, it would not bind the ICC or any other foreign court. It was possible that, although the ICC was not bound to recognize this immunity as a matter of law, it might exercise its discretion and not take advantage of testimony or

---

[119] Impeachment could occur with respect to either a defense or prosecution witness.

[120] TJRC Act, *supra* Chapter 1, note 3, at Art. 24(3).

other information provided to the Commission. This was one of the concerns I had raised with my fellow Commissioners to support my suggestion that we should reach out and attempt to enter into an arrangement with the ICC whereby, for example, the Court might agree not to use information provided by individuals who had agreed to testify before us. It is not clear whether the ICC would have been amenable to such an agreement.

Second, the Commission might receive information related to international crimes and, more specifically, information related to the cases pending before the ICC, either through our hearings or through our independent research and investigations. Such information might be useful to the ICC with respect to its own investigations. Assuming we had not received such information through our *in camera* hearings (for which we pledged confidentiality) or some other confidential process, the question is whether we would agree to share that information with the ICC, and, if so, under what circumstances. As it turned out, we did acquire information related to some of the ICC cases, though the relevance of the information we acquired to the pending cases was not clear. Notwithstanding whether we agreed to share such information, there was a strong argument that the government of Kenya might be obligated to hand over any relevant information we might have discovered to the ICC. Under the Rome Statute, states are obligated to cooperate with the ICC concerning investigations and prosecutions, including the obligation to take and hand over relevant evidence. Therefore, it would appear that the government of Kenya might be obligated under the terms of the Rome Statute to provide the ICC prosecutor with relevant information collected by the Commission if the prosecutor asked.[121] If the government had demanded such information from us, we might have resisted, arguing that we were an independent commission and, as our oath and founding legislation indicate, we were not to take direction from individuals or organizations outside of the Commission. The dispute that would have arisen between the government and the Commission about information we had collected thus would probably have been resolved in the Kenyan courts.

While I argued a number of times that we should reach out to the ICC, if only to clarify how we would handle information related to the overlapping areas of our mandate, many of the other commissioners became increasingly reluctant to do so. This hesitancy was based on a number of concerns.

---

[121] For a useful and thorough discussion of the tension between this international obligation under the Rome Statute and domestic laws concerning the independence of a truth commission, *see* Alison Bisset, Truth Commissions and Criminal Courts (Cambridge: Cambridge University Press, 2014).

First, given the evolving relationship between the ICC and the Kenyan government, and given our dependence on the government for funding and extensions of time, some commissioners feared we would alienate our primary funding source by involving ourselves with the ICC cases. I responded to this concern in part by noting that the government had already involved us by referring to the TJRC a number of times in their filings before the court. Given that we were being used by the government in its conflict with the ICC, I argued we should at least try to influence how we were portrayed and used. Second, the political backlash against the ICC among political elites in Africa was also evident among some of the other commissioners. Many of the commissioners did not want to be seen to be supporting or assisting the ICC generally, or specifically with respect to the Kenyan cases. This critique against the ICC as a whole was based upon a complicated set of concerns, including the perception that the ICC was only involved in Africa; was controlled by, or at least heavily influenced by, western countries (many of whom had exempted themselves from ICC scrutiny); and that the ICC, and the international justice movement generally, was attempting to legalize what are and should be viewed as political issues, and thus interfering illegitimately with the domestic sovereignty of nation-states. Finally, given later events with respect to the interference of President Kenyatta's office with respect to our final report, it is possible that some of the Kenyan commissioners were reluctant to engage in activity that would, or would at least appear to, work against the interests of the ICC suspects.

While we did not engage with the ICC, and thus did not come to an agreement over the areas in which our mandates overlapped, it is likely that our activities were not affected by this lack of agreement. Officials from the UN had suggested that we reach out to the Ocampo Six to encourage them to testify before the Commission. While we did attempt to encourage public testimony by the Ocampo Six, none took us up on the offer. While it is possible that they may have been reluctant to testify because of the uncertainty over whether their testimony could be used before the ICC, my suspicion is that they would not have testified before us even if we had secured an agreement on behalf of the ICC not to use such testimony.

By June 2012, when officials from the Office of the Prosecutor reached out to me for access to our materials, the Ocampo Six had been reduced to the Ocampo Four. While we did have some relevant materials, and while I cannot definitively say whether such information would have been useful to the ICC prosecutor, it is my belief that any information we held related to the ICC cases would have had little if any impact on the ultimate outcome of those cases. I informed the ICC officials that I would be willing to approach my fellow commissioners to see if they would be willing to give them access to our materials. I told them candidly that I thought such a request would be quickly refused, as I was probably the only commissioner who would have acquiesced to such an arrangement. After further discussion, we collectively decided that I would not raise the issue with the Commission, and as far as I am aware, the ICC never reached out to us again.

POSTSCRIPT: THE CASES COLLAPSE

After requesting successive postponements for the start of the trial, the ICC prosecutor withdrew the charges against Uhuru Kenyatta in March 2015. Prior to withdrawing the case, the prosecutor had submitted a pre-trial brief summarizing the evidence that it had against Kenyatta. This summary included a list of individuals who were alleged to have been directly involved in the crimes committed by Kenyatta during the PEV who had since died, witnesses who allegedly agreed to falsify their testimony in support of Kenyatta, and prosecution witnesses who were allegedly bribed to change their testimony.[122] The changing testimony of witnesses, regardless of the reason, substantially weakened the case against Uhuru Kenyatta, leading the prosecutor to withdraw the charges.

In April 2016, the Trial Chamber "vacated without prejudice" the charges against the remaining two Kenyan suspects, Deputy President William Ruto and the radio personality Joshua arap Sang, for similar reasons.

---

[122] *See* International Criminal Court, *The Prosecutor v. Kenyatta*, Case No. ICC-01/09–02/11–796-Conf-AnxA, Trial Chamber V(B), "Public Redacted Version of "Second Updated Prosecution Pre-trial Brief," August 26, 2013, ICC-01/09–02/11–796-Conf-AnxA," January 19, 2015, paras. 87–95.

Index

The page numbers in italics indicate a more substantive treatment of the topic.